The Impact of International Trade on Wages

A National Bureau
of Economic Research
Conference Report

The Impact of International Trade on Wages

Edited by **Robert C. Feenstra**

The University of Chicago Press

Chicago and London

ROBERT C. FEENSTRA is professor of economics at the University of California, Davis, and director of the International Trade and Investment Program at the National Bureau of Economic Research.

The University of Chicago Press, Chicago 60637
The University of Chicago Press, Ltd., London
© 2000 by the National Bureau of Economic Research
All rights reserved. Published 2000
Printed in the United States of America
09 08 07 06 05 04 03 02 01 00   1 2 3 4 5
ISBN: 0-226-23963-2 (cloth)

Library of Congress Cataloging-in-Publication Data

The impact of international trade on wages / edited by Robert C. Feenstra.
    p. cm. — (A National Bureau of Economic Research conference report)
    "This volume contains revised versions of the papers and discussion presented at a National Bureau of Economic Research conference held in Monterey, California, on February 27–28, 1998"—Ackn.
    Includes bibliographical references and index.
    ISBN 0-226-23963-2 (cloth : alk. paper)
    1. Foreign trade and employment—United States—Congresses. 2. International trade—Congresses. 3. Wages—United States—Congresses. I. Feenstra, Robert C.
II. Conference report (National Bureau of Economic Research)

HD5710.75.U6 I447 2000
331.2′973—dc21
                                  99-086530

Since this volume is a record of conference proceedings, it has been exempted from the rules governing critical review of manuscripts by the Board of Directors of the National Bureau (resolution adopted 8 June 1948, as revised 21 November 1949 and 20 April 1968).

Contents

Acknowledgments

This volume contains revised versions of the papers and discussion presented at a National Bureau of Economic Research conference held in Monterey, California, on 27–28 February 1998. Financial support from the Ford Foundation is gratefully acknowledged. I thank Kirsten Foss Davis and Helena Fitz-Patrick for their dedicated assistance with the conference and the volume.

Introduction

Robert C. Feenstra

The U.S. Bureau of the Census recently reported that in 1997 the real median income of U.S. households returned to the peak achieved in 1989, which was the year before a short recession (U.S. Department of Commerce 1998a, v, xii). A number of specific subgroups have achieved or surpassed their 1989 income levels, including households maintained by persons 25–34 years or 55 years and older; households in the West, Midwest, and South; and households maintained by women. At the same time, the proportion of the population living below the poverty line has fallen to about the same level as in 1989, with the most recent decline in poverty experienced especially by African Americans and Hispanics (U.S. Department of Commerce 1998b, v–vi). Despite this good news, the *inequality* of income has continued to increase steadily. The share of income received by the lowest quintile (20 percent) of households fell from 4.4 percent in 1977 to 3.8 percent in 1987 to 3.6 percent in 1997, while the share of income received by the highest quintile of households has risen from 43.6 to 46.2 to 49.4 percent over the same period.

These recent developments are typical of the trends that have occurred since the U.S. economy recovered from the recession of the early 1980s: real incomes have been rising, but the rise has not been shared equally by all demographic groups or regions in the country. Indeed, there are reasons to believe that since the early 1980s there are new forces at work in the United States shaping the relationship between employment and earnings of different groups. Since that time, the United States has experi-

Robert C. Feenstra is professor of economics at the University of California, Davis, and director of the International Trade and Investment Program at the National Bureau of Economic Research.

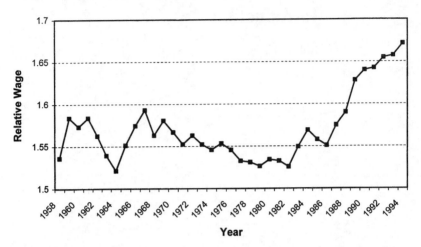

Fig. 1   Relative wage of nonproduction/production workers, U.S. manufacturing
Source: NBER Productivity Database, http://www.nber.org/nberprod.html.
Note: The wages of nonproduction and production workers are weighted by industry employment of these workers.

enced a fall in the wages of the lowest-skilled workers, measured either in real terms or relative to wages of high-skilled workers; a fall in the relative employment of less-skilled workers; and, as a result of both of these, an increase in the share of total labor income going to high-skilled workers.

To illustrate these trends, we can use data from the U.S. manufacturing sector for nonproduction and production workers. The former are often used as a proxy for higher-skilled workers, and the latter as a proxy for less-skilled workers. This treatment can certainly be questioned, since nonproduction workers include, for example, many people with little education. Nevertheless, the trends shown by the nonproduction and production workers have been shown to be similar to trends obtained when measuring skill by the education of workers, and also when looking beyond the manufacturing sector.[1] These trends are illustrated in figure 1, which graphs the relative wage of nonproduction/production workers, and figure 2, which graphs their relative employment.

Figure 2 shows a steady increase in the ratio of nonproduction to production workers used in U.S. manufacturing, with some leveling off re-

1. The breakdown of workers according to whether they are engaged in production activity or not is made in the U.S. Annual Survey of Manufactures and is used as a proxy for the occupational class or skill level of workers. While there are problems with using the production/nonproduction classification as a proxy for skill, there is evidence suggesting that in practice the classification shows trends similar to those found when skill categories are used (Berman, Bound, and Griliches 1994; Berman, Bound, and Machin 1998; Sachs and Shatz 1994). The increase in the wage of nonproduction workers relative to the wage of production workers is only a small part of the total increase in wage inequality between more- and less-skilled workers that occurred during the 1980s; see Katz and Murphy (1992) for a discussion.

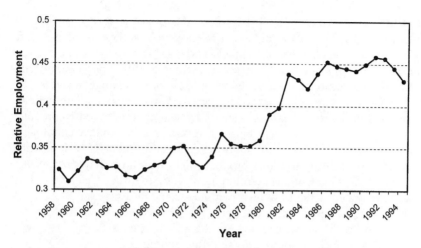

Fig. 2   Relative employment of nonproduction/production workers, U.S. manufacturing
Source: NBER Productivity Database, http://www.nber.org/nberprod.html.

cently. This increase in the supply of workers can account for the reduction in the relative wage of nonproduction workers from about 1970 to the early 1980s, as shown in figure 1, but is at odds with the increase in the relative wage after that. The rising relative wage should have led to a shift in employment away from higher-skilled workers, along a demand curve, but it has not. Thus, the only explanation consistent with the facts is that there has been an *outward shift* in the demand for skilled workers since the mid-1980s, leading to rising relative wages and employment for skilled workers.

What factors account for these changes? Most widely cited are international competition from low-wage countries and skill-biased technological change due to the increased use of computers. A large amount of research during the past decade has sought to evaluate both explanations, with the result that the latter (skill-biased technological change) is often thought to be the more important.[2] The reasons for this are twofold. First, from the Stolper-Samuelson theorem, international competition will lead to an increase in the relative wage of high-skilled workers if and only if there is an increase in the relative price of goods using these workers intensively. Since the work of Lawrence and Slaughter (1993), it has been recognized that the relative price of skill-intensive goods *did not* rise in the United States during the 1980s (although it did during the 1970s). This is the first strike against international trade as an explanation. The second comes from reasoning that even if price changes did somehow cause the increase

2. See the surveys by Freeman (1995), Richardson (1995), Wood (1995), and Feenstra (1998); and the volume by Collins (1998).

in the relative wage of skilled workers, this ought to lead firms in both tradable and nontradable industries to *economize* on these workers—shifting toward the cheaper, low-skilled workers. From figure 2, we see that exactly the opposite has occurred. According to this logic, then, international competition cannot be the main cause of the change in wages.

What is the possible response to these two strikes against international competition? From our discussion, it is clear that a response can come from several directions: (1) considering forces other than technological change that can differentially shift the demand for labor of various skills; (2) reexamining the role that product prices may have played, especially during the 1980s; and (3) questioning whether the wage trends described accurately depict the movement within specific industries and regions of the United States. These topics form the various sections of this volume, beginning with several provocative chapters that consider how and why the demand for labor of various skills has shifted.

As pointed out by Paul Krugman in the first chapter, much of the research documenting the importance of skilled-technological change has been indirect, implying that it must be present because relative wages and employment of skilled workers have moved in the same direction.[3] Krugman presents an alternative model of "quality sorting" in the labor market, in which workers' education is a signal of their skills. Higher education is required to work in a managerial position, but not all skilled workers necessarily get this education. This leads to a situation where the economy has two (stable) equilibria—a pooling equilibrium, where some skilled workers do not have higher education and do not work as managers, which has the effect of raising wages for all nonmanagerial workers; and a separating equilibrium, where all skilled workers acquire higher education and work as managers. Comparing these equilibria, the first has a more equal income distribution because the skilled workers that do not receive higher education raise the average wage for all nonmanagerial workers. In the separating equilibrium, education is acting as a signal about quality, leading to higher demand for educated workers. This means that there is greater segmentation of the workforce (high-skilled and low-skilled workers are in distinct educational and occupational groups), leading to greater wage inequality.

Krugman includes a suggestive empirical application to the economywide change in the purchasing power of factors, or in total factor productivity, within the United States. Shifts from one equilibrium to the other can lead to perverse movements in these measures, which appear to apply to the United States. In their comment, James Rauch and Magnus

---

3. Examples of papers taking this indirect approach are Berman, Bound, and Griliches (1994) and Berman, Bound, and Machin (1998). In contrast, Autor, Katz, and Krueger (1998) directly test for the impact of computers on labor demand.

Lofstrom investigate the earnings differentials between wage/salary workers and self-employed individuals. Since the self-employed know their own quality, education does not provide a signal (except to their customers), so the return to education should be greater for wage/salary earners than for the self-employed. This prediction is confirmed in Rauch and Lofstrom's data, and they also find that the earnings differentials between workers with high school and those with college educations has been increasing more for the wage/salary workers. These findings are supportive of Krugman's quality-sorting model.

In the second chapter, Edward Leamer and Christopher Thornberg examine another new model of wage determination. They treat the wages paid by industries as jointly determined with the effort level of individuals. Effort is not directly observable, but since it equals the product of hours per week and "intensity" of effort, they simply use hours as a proxy, which turns out to work quite well. Their theory suggests that capital-intensive industries should offer high-wage and high-effort jobs, while labor-intensive industries should offer low-wage and low-effort jobs. Graphing industry wages against effort (i.e., hours), we therefore expect to find an upward-sloping relationship, with the capital-intensive industries at the upper end of the curve. This is exactly what Leamer and Thornberg find, although there is also a backward-bending portion consisting of the most capital-intensive industries in some years, which they attribute to union pressures.

Comparing the wage-effort curve over different decades, they find that it twisted in the 1970s, offering lower pay for the low-paid jobs in the labor-intensive sectors, and higher pay for the high-paid jobs in the capital-intensive sectors. They attribute this shift to the fall in relative prices of labor-intensive goods during the 1970s due to globalization. In the 1980s they find that the entire curve shifted to the right, requiring more effort (i.e., hours) for the same weekly wage. They suggest that this shift is due to the increasing cost to firms of nonwage benefits, such as health care, or to the introduction of new equipment, such as computers. Thus, their analysis identifies a role for both international forces (during the 1970s) and technological change (during the 1980s) in changing the wage-effort jobs offered in different industries.

In the third chapter, Gordon Hanson, Deborah Swenson, and I consider the impact of international trade on the demand for labor by focusing on the offshore assembly provision (OAP) of U.S. trade law (formerly called the 806/807 provision and now called the 9802 provision of the Harmonized System). This provision allows U.S. firms to export component parts, have them assembled overseas, and then import the finished products, while only paying duty on the foreign value added. The program is used extensively by the *maquiladora* plants in Mexico, as well as in Asia, and principally in the apparel, footwear, nonelectrical and electrical machinery, and transportation equipment industries. Since the assembly that is done abroad makes the greatest use of low-skilled workers, we expect that it would have the effect of increasing the relative demand for high-skilled workers in the United States. Thus, outsourcing would have the same impact on the demand for labor in the United States as skill-biased technological change, and in this sense the two are observationally equivalent.

Gordon Hanson, Deborah Swenson, and I empirically investigate whether U.S. production under the OAP program uses more skilled (nonproduction) labor than the production done overseas, and how the magnitude of OAP trade responds to real exchange rates. The first issue amounts to a reality check for the theory. We find that the apparel and machinery industries give results closest to the theoretical expectations. The U.S. content of OAP imports shows up as relatively intensive in the use of nonproduction labor and increases in OAP imports shift demand away from production labor in the United States. For other industries, results that do not accord so well with the theory are obtained. The footwear industry generally has imprecise estimates, while in electrical machinery and transportation equipment some of the estimated coefficients are the opposite of their expected sign. In sum, the evidence from this program provides some support for the idea that outsourcing has shifted demand away from low-skilled workers in the United States, at least for the apparel and machinery industries.

The second section of the volume reexamines the role of product prices in determining wages. The chapter by Matthew Slaughter sets the stage by reviewing a number of past papers dealing with the link between industry prices and wages. This link is theoretically described by the Stolper-Samuelson theorem, and the papers that Slaughter reviews are empirical applications of this theorem. They ask whether the changes in wages across manufacturing are consistent with the changes in industry prices, or with the changes in industry productivity. Changes in prices are interpreted as international forces, whereas changes in productivity are interpreted as sector-specific technological change. Thus, this framework generally fits the "trade versus technology" paradigm. Slaughter identifies a number of weaknesses with this framework, not the least of which are that both prices and productivity are really endogenous and ought to be explained by underlying structural variables. The reader will find that this paper is a good entry into a large and growing literature.

James Harrigan also considers the role of prices, including those of nontraded goods. He treats imports into the United States as an intermediate input into a GNP function for the United States, distinguishing final outputs produced with high skills or low skills, three types of imports, three types of labor, and capital. The prices of the outputs and imports enter the GNP function, as do the supplies (or endowments) of labor and capital; the implied factor prices are obtained by differentiation of the GNP function. The functional form chosen—translog—allows for quite general substitution between the various outputs and inputs. Of particular interest is the impact of the output and import prices on the wages of workers, distinguished by their educational level. Harrigan finds the expected Stolper-Samuelson effect, whereby a 10 percent increase in the relative prices of skill-intensive goods raises the college–high school premium by between 2.8 and 3.8 percent. This relative price of skill-intensive goods has an upward trend in his sample during the period 1980–95, which can therefore partially explain the increase in the college–high school premium. Surprisingly, however, the upward trend in this price is driven primarily by an increase in the price of nontraded services, such as finance, insurance, real estate, and various other miscellaneous services. The direct impact of import prices on wages is negligible in his estimates.

Robert Lawrence questions whether the convention of viewing product prices as being determined by international forces, and productivity as being determined by domestic technological change, is really valid. For example, Wood (1995, 67) has suggested that imports from developing countries lead firms in the industrial countries to develop unskilled-labor-saving technologies, thereby linking trade and technological change. Lawrence examines the extent to which changes in productivity in U.S. industries are correlated with measures of trade, using either import and export prices, or quantities.[4] Both of these measures should be treated as endogenous, so he performs both ordinary least squares and two-stage least squares estimation. The results show a modest impact of import competition on productivity, although the statistical significance depends on the estimation method. Lawrence also considers the impact of these variables on the employment share of workers with just high school education. Industries with higher initial imports (especially from developing countries) show greater declines in the high school–educated share of employment, although again the statistical significance is weak.

The third section of the volume presents remarkable new evidence on regional variation in wages and employment, a theme that has begun to be studied in recent research.[5] Andrew Bernard and Bradford Jensen analyze how the wage premium (the part of wages that is not explained by worker characteristics) varies across states over time, using data on individuals at 10-year intervals. They find that state wages are much more responsive to regional employment shocks (in any industry) than to na-

4. Wood and Lawrence both recognize that a firm theoretical basis for the link between trade and productivity is lacking. The interested reader can consult work by Horn, Lang, and Lundgren (1995), which establishes a link of this type using a model where managerial effort is not directly observed by the owner of a firm.

5. For example, Lee (1999) uses regional variation in the effective minimum wage to argue that reductions in the real minimum wage during the 1980s account for much of the rise in dispersion in the lower tail of the wage distribution.

tional shocks in the same industry. In other words, labor markets are not well integrated across states in the short or medium run, so that state variation in wages can be expected to persist. Inequality of wages at the state level is measured by the difference in the 90th and 10th percentile wage premia. Bernard and Jensen find a surprising pattern of changes in inequality during the 1970s and 1980s, whereby states located around the Great Lakes have experienced rising inequality (like the national trend), but states in the Southeast have experienced falling wage inequality. Many of these state-level changes are larger than the national changes that have occurred, suggesting that the focus on national changes taken by most researchers may be missing an important part of the story.

Bernard and Jensen also correlate these wage changes with other state variables such as real exchange rates, inflows of immigrants, labor market characteristics, and so forth. After controlling for state- and time-fixed effects, the only variable that is consistently important in explaining the cross-state change in wage inequality is the share of employment in durable manufacturing. Declines in this variable are strongly associated with increases in inequality. Left open for further research, then, is the question of what factors led to the decline in durable manufacturing employment.

Some progress on this question is made by Linda Goldberg and Joseph Tracy, who analyze the effect of industry-specific real exchange rates on industry wages and employment at the state level. Like Bernard and Jensen, they find that effects at the state level are often more pronounced than at the national level, but, in contrast to them, Goldberg and Tracy find that changes in real exchange rates have an impact on wages. Dollar appreciations (depreciations) are associated with employment declines (increases) for high- and low-profit-margin industry groups. When industries are more export oriented, the adverse consequences of appreciations for employment increase, although these adverse consequences are offset when industries increase their reliance on imported inputs. Their analysis confirms the type of dynamic patterns of adjustment in local labor markets previously reported by labor economists, whereby wages increase in response to current relative demand shocks, and decrease in response to expected future relative demand shocks (presumably because the supply of labor rises).

Mary Lovely and David Richardson investigate the wage differentials offered across industries, while correcting for differences in the skill level (education) of workers. The theory that they draw on allows for trade in horizontally differentiated producer goods between northern countries, and vertically differentiated producer goods (or outsourcing) between northern and southern countries. They point out that there is no unique relationship between increases in outsourcing and inequality of wages (across different skill groups) in this model: It all depends on which exogenous change leads to the increased outsourcing. An increase in the southern human capital endowment is associated with greater inequality of wages in the northern countries, but an increase in the northern human capital endowment is associated with reduced inequality, even though both of these lead to increased outsourcing.

In their empirical work, Lovely and Richardson therefore distinguish whether changes in trade flows for the United States come from industrialized countries, newly industrialized countries, or primary-product exporters. Using data on individuals, they first estimate the industry wage premiums for workers of various education levels. An intriguing finding is that the industry differentials are usually highest for the least-educated workers, vanishing for those with college degrees. They suggest that the industry differentials may therefore reflect local labor markets for less-skilled workers. Lovely and Richardson correlate the industry wage premiums to various measures of international trade and other control variables. Some evidence that trade affects the wage differentials is found, particularly when the type of trade partner is distinguished. Trade with newly industrialized countries has the greatest effect on industry wages: Imports reduce wages and exports increase wages. Also, distinguishing workers by their level of education suggests that these impacts of trade apply most strongly to skilled workers, while the effects on less-skilled workers are sometimes insignificant or of surprising sign. In sum, the impact of international trade on industry wage differentials is quite nuanced when types of workers and trading partners are distinguished, as suggested by the theory.

In the final chapter, Lori Kletzer investigates the impact of trade and outsourcing on labor displacement with U.S. manufacturing industries. Workers laid off from an industry (but not those who quit or are fired) are called displaced, and the annual number of these relative to total industry employment is the displacement rate. This is a measure of the gross employment change in an industry and is much larger than the net change (layoffs minus new hires). Kletzer investigates whether job displacement across U.S. manufacturing industries can be explained by imports, exports, and other variables. She finds a modest role for imports in leading to greater displacement, whether it is measured as imported intermediates (outsourcing) or not, but this effect is not always statistically significant. Increases in exports have a stronger effect on reducing job displacement.

Kletzer also investigates the pattern of wage losses faced by workers displaced from various industries and rehired in others. Among the largest wage reduction is that for workers displaced from durable manufacturing and rehired in nontraded services. Some of the industries in durable manufacturing are also import competing, and so this result suggests that import competition leads to earning losses. However, other import-competing industries (such as office and accounting machines, computers, and photographic equipment) experience less job displacement, and below-average earnings losses. So the connections among import competition, job displacement, and earnings losses are complex. Nevertheless, a sizable number of workers displaced from import-competing industries experience above-average earnings losses that can be attributed at least in part to the pressures of international competition.

In sum, the papers in this volume find some role for international trade in affecting the wages earned by American workers—notably through outsourcing, as considered by Hanson, Swenson, and me, and by Lovely and Richardson—although there are certainly other powerful forces at work. It is notable that Harrigan finds so little influence from import prices in his estimation of a GNP function for the United States, and such a strong influence from nontraded goods prices. Two especially intriguing empirical findings are the shifting of the wage-effort curve analyzed by Leamer and Thornberg, and the remarkable variation in wage inequality across U.S. states measured by Bernard and Jensen. In both cases, it is possible that international competition has been among the underlying causes of these phenomena, but not in a manner that allows it to be easily separated from other causes. The results of Kletzer support those of Bernard and Jensen in that it is the decline of durable goods industries, with the resulting displacement of workers, that is associated with the largest wage losses and resulting inequality. We do not know what has caused the decline in durable goods manufacturing in the states around the Great Lakes, but international competition remains a likely candidate and worthy of further exploration.

References

Autor, David, Lawrence F. Katz, and Alan B. Krueger. 1998. Computing inequality: Have computers changed the labor market? *Quarterly Journal of Economics* 113 (4): 1169–1214.
Berman, Eli, John Bound, and Zvi Griliches. 1994. Changes in the demand for skilled labor within U.S. manufacturing: Evidence from the Annual Survey of Manufactures. *Quarterly Journal of Economics* 109:367–98.
Berman, Eli, John Bound, and Stephen Machin. 1998. Implications of skill-biased technological change: International evidence. *Quarterly Journal of Economics* 113 (4): 1245–80.
Collins, Susan M., ed. 1998. *Imports, exports, and the American worker.* Washington, D.C.: Brookings Institution.
Feenstra, Robert C. 1998. Integration of trade and disintegration of production in the global economy. *Journal of Economic Perspectives* 12 (4): 31–50.
Freeman, Richard B. 1995. Are your wages set in Beijing? *Journal of Economic Perspectives* 9 (summer): 15–32.
Horn, Henrik, Harald Lang, and Stefan Lundgren. 1995. Managerial effort incentives, X-inefficiency and international trade. *European Economic Review* 39: 117–38.

Katz, Lawrence F., and Kevin M. Murphy. 1992. Changes in relative wages, 1963–1987: Supply and demand factors. *Quarterly Journal of Economics* 107:35–78.

Lawrence, Robert Z., and Matthew J. Slaughter. 1993. Trade and U.S. wages: Great sucking sound or small hiccup? *Brookings Papers on Economic Activity,* no. 2: 161–227.

Lee, David. 1999. Wage inequality in the United States during the 1980s: Rising dispersion or falling minimum wage? *Quarterly Journal of Economics* 114 (3): 977–1023.

Richardson, J. David. 1995. Income inequality and trade: How to think, what to conclude. *Journal of Economic Perspectives* 9:33–56.

Sachs, Jeffrey D., and Howard J. Shatz. 1994. Trade and jobs in U.S. manufacturing. *Brookings Papers on Economic Activity,* no. 1: 1–84.

U.S. Department of Commerce. Bureau of the Census. 1998a. Money income in the United States: 1997. Current Population Reports, Consumer Income, P60-200, September. Available from http://www.census.gov/hhes/www/income97.html.

———. 1998b. Poverty in the United States: 1997. Current Population Reports, Consumer Income, P60-201, September. Available from http://www.census.gov/hhes/www/povty97.html.

Wood, Adrian. 1995. How trade hurt unskilled workers. *Journal of Economic Perspectives* 9:57–80.

I

Shifts in Labor Demand

1

And Now for Something Completely Different
An Alternative Model of Trade, Education, and Inequality

Paul Krugman

The dramatic growth of U.S. wage inequality since the early 1970s has been the subject of intense controversy both among economists and between economists and the broader public. To many people—including a few economists (e.g., Leamer 1998)—the explanation of that increased dispersion seems obvious: It is the result of globalization, and specifically of the growing imports of labor-intensive manufactures from developing countries. However, there are serious difficulties with an explanation of growing inequality that places the main weight on trade. For one thing, despite recent growth the value of north-south trade is still fairly small compared with the GDP of advanced economies; this means that even a complete elimination of that trade would, given reasonable estimates of factor shares and elasticities of substitution, reverse only a fraction of the observed change in wage differentials (Krugman 1995). Moreover, while trade can raise the relative demand for skilled labor by shifting the production mix toward skill-intensive sectors, in reality most of the rise in the relative employment of highly educated workers has taken place not via a change in the sectoral mix, but via a shift toward such workers within sectors—a shift that has taken place despite a sharp rise in education premia, which should have induced firms to substitute workers who were not college educated (Lawrence and Slaughter 1993).

But if globalization didn't do it, what did? An explanation that is consistent with the data is skill-biased technological change, taking place simultaneously in many sectors (and also presumably in many countries). And

Paul Krugman is the Ford International Professor of Economics at the Massachusetts Institute of Technology and a research associate of the National Bureau of Economic Research.

this is in fact the explanation that has been advanced by a number of economists, myself included, as the best available answer.

Yet even among those economists who believe that skill-biased technological change is the best explanation we have for the growing wage gap—certainly a better explanation than globalization—there is widespread uneasiness. This uneasiness stems both from the indirect nature of the evidence for such change—it is essentially inferred from the fact that the relative wages and the relative employment of the highly educated have moved in the same direction—and from the sense that technology is too much of a deus ex machina, something invoked to tie up the loose ends in our story rather than something we believe in on its own merits. I know that I am not alone in wondering whether all of us—both those who insist that globalization must be the explanation and those of us who regard the evidence against a simple Stolper-Samuelson account as overwhelming—are missing something, whether we may not all be on the wrong track.

The purpose of this paper is to offer a suggestive example of how a process quite distinct from either the simple trade or the simple technology story might be central to understanding growing inequality. The basic idea is that the labor market might, over some range of conditions, be characterized by multiple, locally stable equilibria, some more egalitarian than others. If that is the case, unequalizing shocks of modest size—shocks that could originate either in changing trade opportunities or in changing technology, or for that matter in both—could push the economy out of an egalitarian equilibrium and thus set in motion a cumulative process of growing inequality. In the specific model presented here, that process, which essentially feeds on itself, could easily be misinterpreted as exogenous skill-biased technical change.

The particular mechanism generating multiple equilibria in this model is a version of the screening/signaling hypothesis (Spence 1971; Stiglitz 1975). This approach was taken because it is the simplest labor market model with the required characteristics. It may, however, be only one of a number of possible mechanisms. For example, recent work by Acemoglu (1996), which is in somewhat the same spirit, offers a quite different mechanism involving technology choice in a frictional search model of the labor market. As we will see, there are some empirical difficulties with the specific model presented here; thus it should be considered only as a first exploration of a class of "exotic" income distribution models that might turn out to recast the nature of the debate.

The remainder of this paper is in five parts. Section 1.1 lays out the assumptions of the model. Section 1.2 develops the crucial idea of a distinction between two labor market regimes. Section 1.3 then shows how small shocks can precipitate a shift from one regime to the other, and thereby produce a cumulative process of growing inequality; it also shows how such a process might confuse someone trying to interpret the data.

Section 1.4 discusses some empirical predictions of the model, contrasting them with the predictions of alternative approaches and testing them loosely against the data. Finally, section 1.5 suggests some qualifications, extensions, and implications of the type of analysis this model represents.

1.1 Assumptions of the Model

We consider an economy endowed with two kinds of labor, "good" (G) and "bad" (B). The difference between these two kinds of workers is assumed to be inherent and unalterable. A worker's type is known to the worker himself but is unobservable to employers.

Good workers do, however, have a way to demonstrate their goodness: They can acquire a college degree. It is assumed that only good workers are capable of acquiring such a degree, so the possession of a degree proves that a worker is of type G. However, acquiring a degree is costly. Rather than explicitly model this cost, I will simply assume that G workers will choose to become educated if and only if the ratio of the wage of those with degrees to those without, w_H / w_L, exceeds some value $r > 1$.

There are also two kinds of jobs: managerial (M) and nonmanagerial (N). M jobs actually require a college degree—that is, such a job can only be filled by a good worker with an education. In N jobs, there is no advantage in being educated per se. However, good workers are known to be $\pi > 1$ times as productive in N jobs as bad workers, so that even in N employment a worker with a college degree—who is therefore certified as type G—will command a higher wage than one without a degree.

Aside from this asymmetric-information feature of the labor market, the economy may be described by the standard two-by-two model of trade theory. There are two sectors, manager-intensive X and nonmanager-intensive Y. All individuals are assumed to share the same homothetic preferences over the two goods:

$$(1) \qquad U = U(C_X, C_Y).$$

Production in each is described by a constant-returns function of managers and nonmanagers with all the usual properties:

$$(2) \qquad Q_X = X(M_X, N_X),$$

$$(3) \qquad Q_Y = Y(M_Y, N_Y).$$

In these production functions, M is simply the number of college-educated good workers employed as managers. N, however, must be measured in efficiency units because each good worker employed in a non-managerial role contributes π times as much as each bad worker. Thus the resource constraints for the economy are

(4) $$M = M_X + M_Y = G_M,$$

(5) $$N = N_X + N_Y = \pi G_N + B,$$

where G_M is the number of good workers employed as managers, and G_N is the number employed in nonmanagerial positions.

Finally, this is an open economy. It is not, however, a small open economy facing given world prices. Instead, it faces a less-than-perfectly-elastic rest-of-world offer curve. There are two reasons for using this large-open-economy setup. One is that it is arguably considerably more realistic than the price-taking assumption—for the United States alone, and certainly if we think of ourselves as modeling the Organization for Economic Cooperation and Development as a whole. More to the point for this paper, however, the large-economy setup is, for reasons that will soon become apparent, more convenient as a modeling device.

We will represent the rest-of-world offer curve by assuming that the relative price of X is decreasing in net exports of X:

(6) $$\frac{P_X}{P_Y} = D(Q_X - C_X).$$

This completes the statement of the model. Next we turn to analysis.

1.2   Labor Market Regimes

In order to analyze this model, we need to determine the relationship between the number of good workers who acquire a college education—which we will denote by H—and the payoff of such an education, which we measure by the ratio of college to noncollege wages, w_H/w_L.

The nature of that relationship depends on the regime in the labor market, which can take one of two forms. First, it may be the case that college-educated workers are employed only in managerial positions—that is, in jobs for which such an education is actually necessary, in which education is actually socially productive. I will refer to this as the *human capital regime.* Alternatively, it may be the case that some college-educated workers are employed in nonmanagerial jobs. By assumption, the education does not enhance their productivity in these jobs; its only function is to demonstrate to employers that they are good as opposed to bad workers. I will refer to this as the *quality signaling regime*—although we must bear in mind that even under this regime there will be workers whose education actually is socially productive.

Before we determine the conditions under which each regime prevails, let us examine the behavior of the economy under each. Under the human capital regime, the number of college-educated workers is the same as the number of managers, and the remaining workers form the supply of N in efficiency units:

$$(7) \qquad\qquad M = H,$$

$$(8) \qquad\qquad N = \pi(G - H) + B.$$

In terms of production and prices, then, the human capital regime constitutes an ordinary two-by-two economy, in which increases in the number of college-educated workers amount to an increase in M and a decline in N.

The properties of such an economy are very familiar. In particular, imagine either increasing M or decreasing N at constant relative goods prices. In either case, the economy would experience a Rybczynski effect: The output of M-intensive X would rise and the output of N-intensive Y fall. This would lead, at unchanged relative prices, to an increase in the excess supply of X. But given the rest-of-world offer curve (6), this means a decline in the relative price of X. So we may think in terms of a reduced-form relationship between the number of college-educated workers and relative prices:

$$(9) \qquad\qquad \frac{P_X}{P_Y} = F(H).$$

But in such a two-by-two economy there is also a direct Stolper-Samuelson relationship between relative goods prices and relative factor prices. Thus we can write a reduced-form relationship between H and relative wages of the form

$$(10) \qquad\qquad \frac{w_M}{w_N} = \phi(H), \qquad \phi' < 0.$$

We are not, however, quite there yet. Equation (10) gives the ratio of the wage per manager (which is also the wage of any college graduate) to the wage per efficiency unit of nonmanagerial labor. However, because some of the workers in nonmanagerial jobs are (unidentified) type G, the average number of efficiency units per N worker is more than one; so the wage paid per actual worker in N jobs is

$$(11) \qquad\qquad w_L = w_N \frac{\pi(G - H) + B}{G - H + B}.$$

Notice that the ratio of w_L to w_N is decreasing in H. The reason is that the more G workers who acquire college educations, the lower the expected productivity of the average worker without a degree. This complicates matters in the human capital regime, but is central to the story in the quality signaling regime.

The education premium as a function of H is therefore

(12)
$$\frac{w_H}{w_L} = \phi(H)\frac{G - H + B}{\pi(G - H) + B}.$$

This relationship can, in principle, be either downward- or upward-sloping. It will be downward-sloping if the effect of factor supplies on relative prices is strong (this effect would be nonexistent, of course, in a price-taking economy—which is why the large-economy assumption is useful) and if the screening effect is weak. I will assume that this is in fact the case, so that the curve relating w_H/w_L to H in the human capital regime looks like curve HC in figure 1.1.

It may be useful at this stage to give a specific example. Suppose that we consider a closed economy—the limiting case of a large open economy—in which both tastes and technology are Cobb-Douglas. Let μ be the share of X in expenditure, and let α and β be the share of M in the X and Y sectors, respectively. It follows immediately that a share $\mu\alpha + (1 - \mu)\beta$ of total income accrues to M and a share $\mu(1 - \alpha) + (1 - \mu)(1 - \beta)$ to N, so that

(13)
$$\frac{w_M M}{w_N N} = \frac{\mu\alpha + (1 - \mu)\beta}{\mu(1 - \alpha) + (1 - \mu)(1 - \beta)},$$

and thus

(14)
$$\frac{w_M}{w_N} = \frac{\mu\alpha + (1 - \mu)\beta}{\mu(1 - \alpha) + (1 - \mu)(1 - \beta)}\frac{N}{M} = \kappa\frac{\pi(G - H) + B}{H}.$$

Now substituting in equation (11), we find that

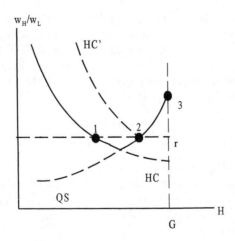

Fig. 1.1   Determining skills and wages

(15)
$$\frac{w_H}{w_L} = \kappa \frac{G - H + B}{H},$$

which is unambiguously a downward-sloping curve.

Next let us turn to the quality signaling regime. This is more straightforward. Since (some) college-educated workers are competing directly with non-college-educated workers, each college-educated worker will receive a wage equal to π times the wage per efficiency unit in N, while each noncollege worker will receive a wage proportional to the average number of efficiency units among such workers. But the total number of efficiency units among noncollege workers is

(16)
$$E = \pi(G - H) + B,$$

so the average efficiency is

(17)
$$\frac{E}{L} = \frac{\pi(G - H) + B}{G - H + B},$$

implying the relative wage equation,

(18)
$$\frac{w_H}{w_L} = \pi \frac{G - H + B}{\pi(G - H) + B},$$

which is unambiguously upward-sloping, yielding a curve like QS in figure 1.1.

Which regime prevails? The answer, of course, is whichever provides the higher relative wage. If the HC curve lies above the QS curve for some given H, college graduates can command higher wages in managerial than in nonmanagerial jobs, even if all graduates are so employed; so no college-educated workers will use their education purely to demonstrate their type. If HC lies below QS, then if all graduates worked as managers they would earn less than a certified good worker could get in a nonmanagerial job, and so some H workers will shift away from the managerial role. The overall relationship between H and w_H/w_L, then, is V-shaped; it is defined by the upper envelope of the curves HC and QS.

1.3 Equilibria and Transitions

Let us now endogenize the supply of college-educated workers. We have assumed that good workers will find it worthwhile to acquire a college education if and only if w_H/w_L exceeds some value $r > 1$. Thus in figure 1.1, which represents the most interesting case, the solid line (the upper envelope of the HC and QS curves) represents the demand for college graduates, while the broken horizontal line at $w_H/w_L = r$ represents the supply.

Clearly, there are three equilibria: one at point 1, where only some good workers get degrees and the labor market is in a human capital regime; one at point 3, where all those who can get degrees do and the quality signaling regime prevails; and an intermediate equilibrium at point 2. Which equilibrium does the economy select? For some purposes it would be essential to model the full-fledged dynamics of educational investment, including the formation of expectations about future returns. However, in recent years the interest in evolutionary game theory suddenly has made ad hoc dynamics, in which the mix of strategies followed by a population gradually changes depending on the current returns to each strategy, respectable again. Such evolutionary dynamics are particularly useful when, as in this model, there are multiple equilibria and we are looking for a selection criterion. Or to make a long story short, it is acceptable as a first cut to assume that the number of college-educated good workers rises if $w_H/w_L > r$, and falls if $w_H/w_L < r$. The equilibrium at point 2 is, then, unstable, while the other equilibria are locally stable. Alternatively, if one thinks of the strategy of good workers as probabilistic (e.g., with what probability will I go to college?), then points 1 and 3 are evolutionarily stable strategies in the sense of Maynard Smith (1982), while point 2 is not.

Where the economy ends up, then, depends on history. In particular, if it manages to get into the relatively egalitarian equilibrium at point 1, it will tend to stay there in the face of small shocks.

But now suppose that there is a progressive rise in the demand for managerial workers. This rise could be due either to growing opportunities to export the manager-intensive good X, or to manager-biased technical change. In either case, the effect under the human capital regime will be to increase the relative wage of H workers for any given level of H, an upward shift in the HC curve.

As long as this shift is not too large, the labor market will remain in the human capital regime, and the wage differential will not change. At a critical point, however, illustrated in figure 1.1 by the curve HC', the human capital equilibrium will cease to exist. At this point, even if there is no further increase in the demand for managerial workers, the economy will continue evolving toward increasing inequality. As a growing fraction of good workers become educated, the expected productivity and thus the wages of non-college-educated workers will fall, further increasing the incentive to acquire a degree, continuing until the unequal equilibrium at point 3 has been reached.

Two observations need to be made about this transition to higher inequality. The first is that if anything like this story is right, the whole attempt to apportion the causes of growing wage differentials between technology and trade may be missing the point. Either trade or technology— or more likely both—may push the economy to the critical point, but thereafter the unequalizing process simply feeds on itself, and the proximate cause may therefore be irrelevant.

The second observation is how easily such a transition might be misinterpreted by an observer—me, for example—who works with the wrong model. Suppose that exogenous forces in fact were to push HC just to the critical point and that the economy were then to evolve spontaneously from point 2 to point 3. What would we see? Because of the strong structure of this model, we can immediately determine that there will be no change at all in the wages of managers relative to the cost of one efficiency unit of nonmanagerial work. We know this because all college graduates under the quality signaling regime receive a wage equivalent to π units of N. But if these true relative factor prices are unchanged, relative goods prices must also remain unchanged, and so therefore must production, consumption, and trade. *Nothing real changes as the economy moves from point 2 to point 3, except the distribution of wages.*

But an observer who classifies labor not by unobservable quality but by education level will see two things happening: a fall in both the relative and the absolute wages of non-college-educated workers, and a fall in their relative employment. This seemingly perverse outcome will not appear to be explained by trade—neither the volume of trade nor the prices at which trade takes place will change, nor will the industry mix of employment; all of the increased demand for H and reduced demand for non-H will therefore come from within-sector shifts. The only hypothesis that will appear to be consistent with the data will therefore be skill-biased technical change—even though no technical change has in fact taken place!

1.4 Empirical Implications

At the beginning of this paper, I described some reasons why even those of us who have provisionally adopted a technology story for growing wage inequality nonetheless feel uneasy. But beyond gut feelings, is there some way to distinguish among the alternative explanations of inequality?

Suppose for a moment that we try to explain rising wage differentials with one of three pure stories: Stolper-Samuelson effects with no change in technology, skill-biased technological change with no change in factor supplies, and a pure story about transition from a human capital to a quality signaling regime (that is, the movement from point 2 to point 3 in figure 1.1). In reality, of course, there is no reason why the data should be generated by a pure story; but this comparison is nonetheless illuminating. Let us, therefore, compare the implications for three observable variables.

Skill Intensity within Industries. The original exposition of Stolper and Samuelson relied on the device of a contract curve within an Edgeworth box to make the now familiar, although sometimes still misunderstood, point that trade affects the demand for factors via its effect on the industry mix; in their analysis, a rise in the relative price of the labor-intensive good causes employment to shift toward that good. Full employment of factors is preserved via a compensating shift toward capital-intensive techniques within each sector. Thus in a pure Stolper-Samuelson account of rising wage differentials, we would expect to see the skill intensity of production falling within each industry.

Skill-biased technological change, in contrast, would tend to raise the relative demand for skilled labor within each industry. If we take factor supplies as given, however, the skill premium would have to rise enough to choke off this shift in relative demand in the aggregate; while the precise effects on each industry would depend on both the distribution of technological change and the elasticity of substitution, on average there would be no change in skill intensity within industries. (Of course, if we imagine that relative supplies of skilled labor are increasing at the same time, changes in factor prices would be less and we would therefore see increases in skill intensity within industries.)

Finally, in the transition from a human capital to a quality signaling regime, nothing real would change, but firms in both sectors would begin to employ college-educated workers for previously unskilled jobs; thus the observed skill intensity would rise in all sectors.

Factor Prices. It is a fundamental proposition in trade theory that following a change in relative prices, the bundle of factors initially employed must be at least able to afford the goods they were previously producing. (This proposition is the basis for the demonstration of gains from trade in terms of the dual; see Helpman and Krugman 1985, chap. 1.) Thus, a Stolper-Samuelson explanation of changing factor prices implies that the purchasing power of the original employment of factors in terms of output (or, given the absence of strong terms of trade effects, in terms of consumption) must rise or at least not fall.

The same is a fortiori true of an explanation in terms of technological change: Technological progress must increase the purchasing power of the initial bundle of factors for any given goods prices, and any change in goods prices can only further increase that purchasing power.

A pure transition from a human capital to a quality signaling regime, however, actually reduces the purchasing power of the initial bundle of factors, if workers are classified by education. In the transition from point 2 to point 3 in figure 1.1, neither the average wage rate nor the wage rate of skilled workers changes; but the wage rate of workers without a college education falls. Thus an index with fixed weights on the college-educated and non-college-educated wage will unambiguously decline.

Total Factor Productivity. Roughly speaking, this is dual to the measurement of factor purchasing power. If total factor productivity (TFP) is properly measured, it should not change at all in a pure Stolper-Samuelson story. It should, of course, rise if there is technological progress, so it must increase in a technology-driven account. Again, a transition from a human capital to a quality signaling regime should have a perverse implication if labor types are measured by education: There will be an increase in human capital but no increase in output, so TFP will (as measured) actually fall.

We may therefore summarize the predictions of the two standard approaches to inequality and of the exotic alternative offered here in table 1.1.

What do we observe in practice? It is a familiar point since the work of Lawrence and Slaughter (1993) that in the United States there has been a pervasive shift toward higher skill intensity within industries, with relatively little shift of the industry mix of employment toward skill-intensive products. Thus on this first criterion, the two conventional approaches seem to fail (although the technology-driven story can be rescued by supposing that factor supplies have exogenously shifted, albeit not as rapidly as factor demands).

When we come to the purchasing power of factors, what we observe for the United States over the period of rising inequality is a slow rise in average real wages (returns on capital are more problematic to measure). However, this rise in real wages has been accompanied by a rising average educational level, so that it is unclear whether the real income of the initial basket of factors has increased. Table 1.2 presents a calculation using data from Mishel (1996). The first column shows the 1979 share of workers by educational category; since the total does not add up to 100, the second column prorates the difference to derive an adjusted share. The third column shows the real hourly wage rate (in 1996 dollars) of each worker type in 1979; the fourth the real wage in 1989. As the last line of the table indicates, according to these numbers the average real wage weighted by

Table 1.1   **Predictions of Alternative Approaches Based on Change**

	Skill Intensity within Industries	Purchasing Power of Initial Factors	Total Factor Productivity
Stolper-Samuelson	Negative	Non-negative	Zero
Skill-biased technology	None	Positive	Positive
Transition to screening	Positive	Negative	Negative

Table 1.2   **Real Wages of a Constant-Skill Basket**

	1979 Share of Workforce	Adjusted Share	Real Wage, 1979	Real Wage, 1989
Non–high school	28.5	29.2	10.59	8.91
High school	41.7	42.7	11.86	10.79
Some college	15.1	15.5	12.92	12.53
College	8.8	9.0	16.55	16.98
Advanced degree	3.6	3.7	20.34	22.07
Weighted average			12.39	11.48

Table 1.3   Factors Accounting for U.S. Growth

	Output per Worker	Capital per Worker	Human Capital per Worker	Total Factor Productivity
1960–94	1.1	0.4	0.4	0.3
1960–73	1.9	0.5	0.6	0.8
1973–94	0.6	0.3	0.2	0.1
1973–84	0.2	0.3	0.5	−0.5
1984–94	0.9	0.3	0.0	0.7

1979 labor force composition actually declined approximately 7 percent during the decade of the 1980s. While this rough calculation might not stand up in the face of a careful cleaning up of the data, it is remarkable that such a fixed-weight wage index falls despite technological progress, a roughly constant labor share in GDP, and stable or improving terms of trade. The result is, at least on the face of it, inconsistent either with Stolper-Samuelson or technology-driven stories; it is consistent with the transition to a screening equilibrium.

As one might expect given its rough conceptual equivalence, calculations of total factor productivity yield similarly puzzling results. Table 1.3 shows a typical recent calculation from Collins and Bosworth (1996); it suggests that during the post-1973 period, despite what looks like continuing technological advance, growth in total factor productivity ground to a near halt. Again, a possible, although not necessarily correct, explanation is that the accumulation of human capital over that period represented a socially unproductive investment in screening.

To me, at least, this rough evidence clearly indicates not only the well-established point that Stolper-Samuelson effects cannot have been the main driving force behind changes in the wage distribution, but also that something funny is going on that is not easily mapped into a simple technology-driven story either. In particular, the aggregative implications of the transition to screening seem to fit the actual data quite well.

However, we should note that there is one important implication of the particular type of model developed here that appears to be contradicted by the data. If the multiple equilibria arise only because workers are better sorted by quality than they used to be, one ought to observe a difference in the growth of inequality by cohort: The skill premium for workers from older cohorts, who made educational decisions at a time when screening motives were not as important, should not have increased at the same rate as that for more recent cohorts (i.e., a worker who chose not to go to college in 1960 revealed less about himself than a worker making the same choice in 1975). In fact, however, cohort studies (e.g., Juhn, Murphy, and Pierce 1993) suggest comparable increases in inequality across cohorts.

1.5 Qualifications, Extensions, and Implications

It should go without saying that the model proposed here is very special, and that there are good reasons to be skeptical about the mechanism proposed. In general, signaling/screening models of the labor market have been questioned by many labor economists who wonder why employers would not attempt to create cheaper sorting mechanisms and spare good workers the huge expense of pointless college attendance. More generally, this model suggests that what looks like skill-biased technological change might actually be something else; but then again it might be skill-biased change after all.

On the other hand, the mechanism described here is only one of a class of possible positive-feedback stories about growing inequality. As mentioned in section 1.1, Acemoglu (1996) offers an alternative story roughly along the following lines. In a search economy, in which neither firms nor workers can expect to find an immediate match, firms must choose whether to implement a technology that is highly productive only if a skilled worker uses it, or a more robust technology that any worker can use. Firms will have an incentive to implement the skill-sensitive technology if they can quickly find skilled workers, so the demand curve for such workers will be upward- rather than downward-sloping. (This story does not suffer from the objection that it should apply only to younger cohorts of workers.) Other economists have suggested that since the power of an individual union depends in part on the strength of a national union movement, the dramatic decline in union membership in the United States in recent decades may represent a self-reinforcing process contributing to inequality. One might even invoke linkages that run through the political economy of policy; for example, Benabou (1996) has proposed that, over some range, increased inequality tends to lead to policies that reinforce that inequality. And no doubt there are other possible mechanisms to be considered—nor need such stories be mutually exclusive.

If anything like the mechanism proposed in this paper is indeed at work, the policy implications cut sharply across all current orthodoxies. Consider, for example, the implications for trade policy. It is possible in this kind of model that globalization could be the proximate cause of a process that then gives the false appearance of being driven by exogenous skill-biased technical change. This does not mean, however, that the process could be reversed by reversing the globalization: Even if trade tipped the balance and undermined the human capital equilibrium, once the economy is in a quality signaling equilibrium, a small downward shift in the HC curve will not push it out again. So one could blame trade for increased inequality, yet at the same time conclude that protectionism cannot do much to reduce wage differentials.

Or consider the popular proposals of Reich (1991) and others to combat inequality by promoting the acquisition of human capital—in effect, by subsidizing education. In this model, such policies would be completely ineffective once the economy is in the quality signaling regime. Indeed, they could actually be counterproductive if an economy is still in a human capital regime, but close to the critical point: Anything that encourages good workers to get educated can set in motion a cumulative process of growing inequality!

In short, while the specific model presented in this paper is implausible in its details, it may be very important as a practical matter to contemplate the possibility that the real causes of growing inequality are very different from any of the explanations that have dominated recent debate.

References

Acemoglu, D. 1996. Changes in unemployment and wage inequality: An alternative theory and some evidence. Cambridge, Mass.: Massachusetts Institute of Technology. Mimeograph.

Benabou, R. 1996. Inequality and growth. In *NBER macroeconomics annual 1996,* ed. B. Bernanke and J. Rotemberg. Cambridge, Mass.: MIT Press.

Collins, S., and B. Bosworth. 1996. Economic growth in East Asia. *Brookings Papers on Economic Activity,* no. 2: 135–91.

Helpman, E., and P. Krugman. 1985. *Market structure and foreign trade.* Cambridge, Mass.: MIT Press.

Juhn, C., K. M. Murphy, and B. Pierce. 1993. Wage inequality and the rise in returns to skills. *Journal of Political Economy* 101:410–42.

Krugman, P. 1995. Growing world trade: Causes and consequences. *Brookings Papers on Economic Activity,* no. 1: 327–62.

Lawrence, R., and M. Slaughter. 1993. International trade and U.S. wages in the 1980s: Giant sucking sound or small hiccup? *Brookings Papers on Economic Activity, Microeconomics,* no. 2: 161–210.

Leamer, E. 1998. In search of Stolper-Samuelson linkages between international trade and lower wages. In *Imports, exports, and the American worker,* ed. Susan Collins, 141–214. Washington, D.C.: Brookings Institution.

Maynard Smith, J. 1982. *Evolution and the theory of games.* Cambridge: Cambridge University Press.

Mishel, L. 1996. The state of working America. Washington, D.C.: Economic Policy Institute.

Reich, R. 1991. *The work of nations.* New York: Basic Books.

Spence, A. M. 1971. *Market signalling.* Cambridge, Mass.: Harvard University Press.

Stiglitz, J. 1975. The theory of "screening," education, and the distribution of income. *American Economic Review* 65:282–300.

Comment   James E. Rauch and Magnus Lofstrom

We begin with the empirical part of our discussion. We take the basic empirical message of Krugman's paper to be that the rise in the education wage premium is due to the choice by an increasing number of good workers to get a college education, which allows them to be distinguished from "bad" workers and therefore earn a higher wage. This lowers the average quality of noncollege-educated workers and, thus, raises the difference between the wage of the educated and the noneducated. We examine the implications of Krugman's hypothesis for the contrast between wage/salary earners and the self-employed. The latter presumably earn their true productivity rather than being pooled by their employers.

If education is only a signal and markets are perfect, there will be no education-earnings differential for self-employed of equal ability. This might be true for individuals running small retail/wholesale trade or manufacturing establishments. On the other hand, the self-employed who provide professional services benefit from having credentials. A self-employed accountant or stockbroker may only need innate ability and high school math, but has to get some formal education to obtain credentials (e.g., a CPA degree). The earnings of these individuals are likely to be set by competition from large accountant and stockbroker firms. Suppose these individuals have exactly 16 years of schooling (we discuss postgraduate education later). In this case, when we look at the earnings differential between self-employed workers with 16 years of schooling and 12 years of schooling, we see a mix of a group for which the good agents have no incentive to sort themselves by obtaining an education[1] and a group where good agents are able to earn a credential (equivalent to a signal); hence, we should see a smaller wage differential than for wage/salary earners, according to Krugman's model. Over time, as more of the good individuals choose to get a credential (signal), the education-wage differential increases for the self-employed as a whole, but not as much as for wage/salary earners. Moreover, the earnings of the self-employed with 12 years of education increase relative to wage/salary earners with 12 years of education because the overall quality of the former group declines less.[2]

We will perform crude tests of these hypotheses by examining log weekly earnings for wage/salary earners and the self-employed in 1980 and 1990. Our sample consists of males ages 18 to 64 and is drawn from the

James E. Rauch is professor of economics at the University of California, San Diego, and a research associate of the National Bureau of Economic Research. Magnus Lofstrom is a research associate of the Institute for the Study of Labor (IZA) in Bonn, Germany.

1. Some may have obtained an education anyway, for its consumption value or perhaps because they anticipated wage/salary employment and switched to self-employment later in their working lives.
2. We are indebted to Alan Krueger for this last observation.

Table 1C.1   College–High School Earnings Differentials, Wage/Salary Earners
              versus Self-Employed

	Difference, 16 and 12 Years Education Mean Log Wage
1. Wage/salary	
1980	0.3211227
1990	0.4696073
Self-employed	
1980	0.3590479
1990	0.4299948
2. Wage/salary	
1980	0.3183041
1990	0.4653192
Self-employed	
1980	0.2719227
1990	0.3574143

Note: For row 1, earnings = wage/salary income plus self-employment income for both groups. For row 2, earnings = wage/salary income for wage/salary workers and self-employment income for the self-employed.

U.S. census. Additional details are given in the appendix. Individuals are self-identified as wage/salary earners or self-employed. In tables 1C.1–1C.4, we will first use total earnings (wage/salary earnings plus self-employment earnings) for both groups and then use wage/salary earnings only for wage/salary earners and self-employment earnings only for the self-employed. We feel the latter earnings measures are more appropriate for testing the hypotheses.

In table 1C.1 we see that the earnings differential between males with 16 versus 12 years of education is indeed higher for wage/salary earners than for the self-employed in all cases except for total earnings in 1980. More importantly for Krugman's main point, the education earnings differential increased more between 1980 and 1990 for wage/salary earners than for the self-employed regardless of which earnings measure is used. In table 1C.2 we see that the earnings of the self-employed with 12 years of education improved compared to their wage/salary-earner counterparts between 1980 and 1990. All of these observations are consistent with Krugman's signaling model of increased earnings inequality.

Often the rising wage inequality in the United States is cast as a rising return to ability. Thus, within demographic groups inequality has risen steadily since the late 1960s, as Katz and Murphy (1992) show. Table 1C.3 shows no such rise among the self-employed during the 1980s when we control for a quartic in experience and years of education interacting with four education-level dummies, as in Katz and Murphy (1992, 44). As we

Table 1C.2   Earnings Differentials between Wage/Salary and Self-Employed Workers with 12 Years of Education

Earnings	Difference in Mean Log Wage between Self-Employed and Wage/Salary Earners
Wage/salary income + self-employment income	
1980	0.0647802
1990	0.1164628
Wage/salary income for wage/salary workers and self-employment income for the self-employed	
1980	−0.1210538
1990	−0.0534281

Table 1C.3   Earnings Inequality for Wage/Salary Earners versus Self-Employed

	Difference, 90th and 10th Percentiles		Variance	
	Actual	Residual	Actual	Residual
1. Wage/salary				
1980	1.346599	1.17467	0.329445	0.25176
1990	1.579453	1.30136	0.394088	0.28254
Self-employed				
1980	2.239694	1.94543	0.693338	0.59222
1990	2.415007	2.02122	0.725025	0.59407
2. Wage/salary				
1980	1.35460	1.17005	0.3263	0.24984
1990	1.57168	1.29971	0.3892	0.28031
Self-employed				
1980	2.25039	2.02838	0.6832	0.60456
1990	2.10476	1.90466	0.6399	0.54119

Note: For row 1, earnings = wage/salary income plus self-employment income for both groups. For row 2, earnings = wage/salary income for wage/salary workers and self-employment income for the self-employed.

expect, the level of inequality among the self-employed is much greater than for wage/salary earners, reflecting greater scope for ability in self-employment. Our interpretation of table 1C.3 is that it supports Krugman's claim that nothing "real" happened to change the return to ability during the 1980s and that, instead, the increase in ability differentials among wage/salary earners probably reflects the breakdown of internal labor market rigidities, as suggested by Reich (1991).

Finally, we return to the education-wage differential, but include males

Table 1C.4   College and Postgraduate–High School Earnings Differentials, Wage/
                    Salary Earners versus Self-Employed

	Difference in Mean Log Wage between 16+ and 12 Years Education
1. Wage/salary	
1980	0.3819170
1990	0.5549449
Self-employed	
1980	0.5212091
1990	0.6658614
2. Wage/salary	
1980	0.3767991
1990	0.5477357
Self-employed	
1980	0.4705068
1990	0.5957573

Note: For row 1, earnings = wage/salary income plus self-employment income for both groups. For row 2, earnings = wage/salary income for wage/salary workers and self-employment income for the self-employed.

with postgraduate education. This group includes, for example, dentists and doctors who really could not perform their jobs without formal training. We see from table 1C.4 that the relationship between the earnings differential for wage/salary earners and the self-employed is essentially reversed compared to table 1C.1. This suggests that postgraduate education is truly productive and that there is greater scope for realizing returns to this productive education in self-employment. The increase in the education earnings premium for the self-employed is still smaller than for wage/salary earners, however.

We now turn to the theoretical part of our discussion. We find the weakest element of Krugman's model to be the human capital regime, in which the increased relative supply of educated workers drives down their relative wages. Krugman gets around the factor-price insensitivity theorem (Leamer 1995) by allowing relative prices to change as a result of the United States being a large country. But this implies that a glut of college-educated workers in the United States, such as occurred in the 1970s, should lower returns to education everywhere else in the world to the same extent as in the United States. The real problem with traditional models is not the insensitivity of relative factor prices to changes in relative supplies of different kinds of factors, but rather insensitivity of relative factor prices for the same factor across countries to changes in relative country supplies. In other words, the relative country labor-demand curve is infinitely elastic for any given type of labor—the relative country wage is fixed by price competition at the margin.

One can solve this problem with traditional models by using different cones of specialization or moving beyond the two-by-two case. In keeping with the spirit of Krugman's paper, however, let us consider a model with incomplete information, specifically that of Rauch and Casella (1998). In this model, information is incomplete in product markets rather than labor markets. Incomplete information is modeled as a matching problem: It is more difficult in international than in domestic markets for producers to find the right distributors for their consumer goods, assemblers to find the right suppliers for their components, investors to find the right partners for their joint ventures, and so on. Production takes place as follows: Producers match pairwise, and, if the match is acceptable, labor is employed to realize the productive opportunity. Domestic matching takes place subject to complete information—every producer knows the type of every other producer—while international matching is effectively random. However, each producer has access only to the labor in his own country, so domestic matches must employ domestic labor, while international matches can employ labor in whichever country it is cheapest. International matches can thus serve to transfer labor demand from the country where labor is scarce to where it is abundant—the price system at work.

Although an informational barrier, such as a conventional trade barrier, is uniform across producers ex ante in this model, some producers may effectively evade it ex post if they are lucky in their international matching. If enough producers match successfully abroad, sufficient labor demand is transferred to equalize wages in the two countries. If the two countries' producer-labor endowment ratios are far enough apart, however, lucky or good matches cannot transfer sufficient labor demand to equalize wages. Rather than being constant, as with a traditional trade barrier, the proportional wage gap will increase as the producer-labor endowment ratios move further apart: The relative labor-demand curve becomes downward-sloping. However, a country's labor force is not fully insulated from changes in the labor endowment of its trading partner. As we move down the relative labor-demand curve, some bad matches become acceptable because of the gains from trade provided by the increased wage differential, generating an additional transfer of labor demand. Thus an increase in one country's endowment of labor decreases wages in both countries, but decreases its own wage more.[3]

This model offers a resolution to the "margins versus volumes" debate in the trade and wages controversy: Are choices made at the margin sufficient to equalize factor prices across various national markets, or is a certain volume of trade across the markets necessary to drive prices to equal-

---

3. In traditional models, a trade barrier that acts like a quota permits the equalization of wages when the quota is not binding, but when it is binding changes in countries' endowments can only affect their own wages.

ity? In a perfectly competitive world with no barriers to trade of any kind, this question is not well posed; if prices did not equalize, the volume of trade required to equalize them would automatically occur. In the real world, the debate has been elegantly summarized by Freeman (1995, 21–22):[4]

> If the West can import children's toys produced by low-paid Chinese workers at bargain basement prices, surely low-skilled westerners, who produce those toys at wages 10 times those of the Chinese, will face a difficult time in the job market. It isn't even necessary that the West import the toys. The threat to import them or to move plants to less-developed countries to produce the toys may suffice to force low-skilled westerners to take a cut in pay to maintain employment. In this situation, the open economy can cause lower pay for low-skilled workers even without trade: to save my job, I accept Chinese-level pay, and that prevents imports. The invisible hand would have done its job, with proper invisibility. . . . These predictions [of factor-price equalization] run counter to a wide body of evidence that domestic developments do affect wages: for instance, that the baby boom affected the pay of young workers; that the relative number of college graduates altered the premium paid for education. . . .

Having recognized the theoretical point that competition from labor in low-wage countries could affect wages of comparably skilled labor in high-wage countries even in the absence of any actual trade, the empirical method for quantifying such competition that is preferred by Freeman and many others (see, e.g., Sachs and Shatz 1994) remains factor content analysis: "if the United States imported 10 additional children's toys, which could be produced by five American workers, the effective supply of unskilled workers would increase by five. . . . This five-worker shift in the supply-demand balance would put pressure on unskilled wages to fall, causing those wages to fall in accord with the relevant elasticity" (Freeman 1995, 23). Here the impact of low-wage competition depends entirely on the volume of net trade and not at all on the comparison of prices at the margin.

In the model of Rauch and Casella under discussion, if the volume of international matches that are acceptable without wage differentials (the good matches) is sufficiently large, margins operate perfectly: Any incipient rise in the labor-scarce country's wage compared to the labor-abundant country's wage can be eliminated by a shift in the labor demanded by these internationally matched producers from the former to

---

4. We might take the liberty of clarifying Freeman's statement to state that the baby boom affected the pay of young workers *more in the United States than in China* and the relative number of college graduates *in the United States* altered the premium paid for education *more in the United States than in China.*

the latter country. But if the volume of these good international matches is insufficient, margins operate imperfectly: The elimination of an incipient increase in the labor-scarce country's wage effectively requires that this country's producers shift from matching in a complete-information environment domestically to an incomplete-information environment abroad. When margins operate imperfectly, relative wages become a downward-sloping function of relative labor supplies in the two countries. In short, the efficient operation of margins is dependent on the adequate volume of good international matches, where the volume of these matches that is adequate is determined by the ratio of the factor endowments of the two countries. The actual volume of good matches is in turn determined by some combination of what could loosely be described as the model's information or matching technology and familiarity between the trading partners.

Appendix

Sample Selection Criteria and Computation of Weekly Earnings

Data are drawn from the 1980 5 percent A sample and the 1990 5 percent sample of the U.S. Census of Population. All immigrants and a 20 percent random subsample of natives who satisfy the following criteria are included: males between the ages of 18 and 64; not residing in group quarters; not in military service; not enrolled in school; reported working at least 40 weeks; earned at least $100 per week in 1989 dollars. Weights are used and adjusted accordingly (i.e., weights for natives are multiplied by 5). Earnings reported in tables 1C.1–1C.4 are weekly wages. These are calculated by dividing annual earnings by the number of weeks worked in the year prior to the census. The number of observations range from 4,498 for self-employed males with 16 years of education in 1980 to 538,029 for wage/salary workers in 1990.

References

Freeman, Richard B. 1995. Are your wages set in Beijing? *Journal of Economic Perspectives* 9 (summer): 15–32.

Katz, Lawrence F., and Kevin M. Murphy. 1992. Changes in relative wages, 1963–1987: Supply and demand factors. *Quarterly Journal of Economics* 107 (February): 35–78.

Leamer, Edward E. 1995. The Heckscher-Ohlin model in theory and practice. Princeton Studies in International Finance no. 77. Princeton, N.J.: Princeton University, Department of Economics, International Finance Section, February.

Rauch, James E., and Alessandra Casella. 1998. Overcoming informational barriers to international resource allocation: Prices and group ties. NBER Working Paper no. 6628. Cambridge, Mass.: National Bureau of Economic Research, June.

Reich, Robert. 1991. *The work of nations.* New York: Basic Books.

Sachs, Jeffrey D., and Howard J. Shatz. 1994. Trade and jobs in U.S. manufacturing. *Brookings Papers on Economic Activity,* no. 1: 1–84.

Effort and Wages
A New Look at the Interindustry
Wage Differentials

Edward E. Leamer and Christopher F. Thornberg

2.1 Introduction

The purpose of this paper is to provide empirical support for the theory of effort in a multisector model developed in Leamer (1999). That theory is built on the familiar idea that a firm can contract with workers regarding both the wage level and the working conditions. Those features of the labor contract that enhance productivity but are disliked by workers are called "effort" and the labor market thus offers a set of wage-effort contracts with higher wages offsetting higher effort. If effort does not affect capital depreciation, the high-effort high-wage jobs occur in the capital-intensive sectors where the capital cost savings from high effort are greatest.

Among the implications of this theory are that communities inhabited by industrious workers who are willing to exert high effort for high wages have high returns to capital, and that minimum wage does not cause unemployment—it forces effort in the low-effort low-wage contracts up enough to support the higher wage. These and many other aspects of the model of endogenous effort are discussed in Leamer (1999). In this paper we focus on two implications: (1) The capital savings from effort are greatest in the capital-intensive sector, which is where the high-wage high-effort contracts occur; and (2) price declines in labor-intensive goods twist the wage-effort offer curve, lowering the compensation for low-effort work,

Edward E. Leamer is the Chauncey J. Medberry Professor of Management in the Anderson School of Management at the University of California, Los Angeles, and a research associate of the National Bureau of Economic Research. Christopher F. Thornberg is assistant professor at Clemson University.

Comments from discussant Alan Deardorff and other conference participants are gratefully acknowledged.

but increasing the marginal return for hard work. Thus, increased competition with the developing economies adversely affects the low-effort workers who find themselves having to work harder to maintain their standard of living; high-effort workers may be made better off by the increased marginal compensation for effort in high-wage high-effort jobs in the capital-intensive sectors.

We find empirical support for both of these hypotheses. We show that there is a surprisingly clear relationship among effort, wages, and capital intensity, with the higher capital intensity of the sector associated with both higher wages and higher effort. We find a twisting of the wage-effort offer curve in the 1970s, which we (somewhat casually) associate with increased globalization.

The obvious and possibly insurmountable problem that we face is how to measure effort, the hours of operation multiplied by the intensity of use. We have no measurement of job intensity, which is not merely the speed of operations, but also the attentiveness and willingness of the worker to take risks, and any other intangibles that raise productivity without increasing capital costs. Lacking any obvious measure of job intensity, we take a first step in the direction of least resistance and use production workers' annual hours as our indicator of effort. We are thereby acting as if intensity is not so negatively correlated with hours that there is no relationship between hours and effort.

Given the measurement difficulties, we should not expect much. The big surprise is that there is a remarkably clear relationship among hours, wages, and capital intensity. The capital-intensive sectors have longer annual hours and higher hourly wage rates, exactly what the theory would suggest if hours were a perfect indicator of effort. Not only do we find a wage-effort offer curve; we also find it shifting just as the theory suggests. In the 1960s, with stable relative prices but improving technologies, the curve shifts upward with higher real wages offered at every level of effort. Starting in the mid-1970s, when the relative prices of apparel and footwear and textiles and other labor-intensive goods fell substantially, the offer curve twists, with wages falling for low-effort contracts, but rising for high-effort contracts. In the 1980s, the curve began shifting to the right, with more hours required to attain any given level of earnings. The theory allows this last shift to be due either to the introduction of new machinery (computers) or to a rise in fixed costs other than capital, namely benefits.

The relationship between wages and capital intensity has been discussed in the efficiency wage literature, including papers by Dickens and Katz (1987), Katz and Summers (1989), and Krueger and Summers (1987). We view the correlation between wages and capital intensity through an entirely different theoretical lens. Empirically, the innovation of this paper is the discovery of a strong correlation between weekly hours and capital intensity.

One surprising feature of the U.S. wage-effort offer curve is that it bends backward in the early years of the sample, with the highest wages offered in sectors with relatively low effort (as measured by hours). The two-digit-level names of these unusual sectors are transportation, primary metals, and printing and publishing. These names indicate to us union effects. A union effect on wages can come from market power in the product market, since it allows producers to pass on higher costs to consumers who have nowhere else to go. Beginning in the 1970s, consumers did have somewhere else to go: auto imports from Japan and steel imports from a variety of countries. The erosion of union power seems evident in the wage-effort offer curve as the transportation and primary metal sectors increase their hours to conform more closely to the wage-hour contracts offered in other sectors. But our measure of unionization is not able to account completely for this backward-bending portion of the wage-effort offer curve. This may be due to the poor quality of the unionization data.

The most likely alternative explanation for the correlation between wages and capital intensity is the complementarity of human and physical capital. We include measures of human capital as well as rate of unioniza-tion in our equations that explain wages and hours. Unionization and education both have positive simple correlations with weekly wages and weekly hours. Controlling for capital intensity of the sector, both educa-tion and union membership have a positive and statistically significant effect on wages, but do not have a measurable effect on hours. Even after controlling for education and unionization, there remains strong evidence of the positive relationship between wages and effort that we are looking for.

Another possible explanation for the apparent wage-effort offer curve is rent sharing, with rents especially high in capital-intensive sectors. We explore this possibility by using an imperfect measure of industry rents and do not find that rents can explain away our findings.

Our analysis could be contaminated by business-cycle effects. The first response to a slowdown in sales is a reduction in hours, and only when the slowdown is judged to be long-lived is there a reduction in employ-ment. Then when sales begin to grow again, the first response is to increase hours, followed later by an increase in employment. The variation in em-ployment causes opposite variation in capital per worker because capital is a very slow moving series. This cycle in hours and capital per worker causes us concern about our choice of years for estimating the wage-effort offer curve, since the movements in the curve over time may be mostly due to the cycle. We control for the cycle by estimating the wage-effort offer curve at business-cycle peaks and business-cycle troughs and then com-paring peak with peak and trough with trough.

The theory that drives the data analysis concerns the demand for labor, but the market, of course, has to have a supply side as well. We briefly explore one labor-supply variable, gender. We find what is already rather well known: Females are more likely to be employed in low-effort low-wage sectors.

In section 2.2, we review pertinent aspects of the theory offered in Leamer (1999). Also in section 2.2, we summarize the related literature. We argue that we offer a unique theoretical viewpoint that is distinct from the efficiency-wage literature and that leads us to derive an entirely new equation that explains hours as a function of the capital intensity of the sector. In section 2.3 we discuss graphical displays of the two-digit Standard Industrial Classification (SIC) data on hours and wages. These displays conform remarkably well with the theory. The capital-intensive sectors have long hours and high hourly wage rates. We also present a formal analysis at the four-digit level that backs up what is evident in the two-digit displays. Finally, we offer some summary and concluding remarks in section 2.4.

2.2   Theoretical Two-Sector Model

This section reviews Leamer's (1999) two-sector model with endogenous effort. The key building block is a production function defined as

$$(1) \qquad Q = s \cdot h \cdot f(K,L) \equiv e \cdot f(K,L),$$

where Q is the rate of output per unit of time, K and L are the (timeless) stocks of capital and labor inputs respectively, $f(\cdot,\cdot)$ is a function homogeneous to degree one, s is the intensity of operation, h is the hours of operation, and $e = s \cdot h$ is the overall effort exerted by each worker. Intensity is influenced by speed of operations, but also includes the level of care or attentiveness a worker must exert to reduce the likelihood of breakdowns and other costly delays in the production process.

We make two additional assumptions about effort. First, we assume that labor cares about effort, but capital does not. In other words, long hours at high speed will not wear out equipment any faster than short hours at slow speed. Second, we assume that effort is continuous and completely variable, which is an assumption that affects the details but not the basic message of the model.[1] For generating most of the diagrams, we assume that each sector has fixed input technologies and the production function takes the form

---

1. There is a substantial literature built on the assumption that capital does care—that increased use causes increased depreciation. A recent working paper by Auernheimer and Rumbos (1996) includes many references, among them Calvo (1975) and Bischoff and Kokkelenberg (1987). This literature typically uses a one-sector model and focuses on intertemporal capital use questions. This paper, instead, emphasizes sectoral differences. Deardorff and Stafford (1976) provide another framework that allows both capital and labor to care about the pace and hours of operation. They write output proportional to the hours of operation and explore the coordination problem between two inputs that have different preferences regarding hours of work.

(2)
$$Q_i = e_i \cdot \min\left(\frac{L}{A_{Li}}, \frac{K}{A_{Ki}}\right),$$

where e_i is the effort level in sector i, and K and L are the capital and labor inputs. With the assumption that depreciation does not depend on worker effort, a competitive labor market will award any marginal increase in output from greater effort to the workers. Expressed differently, it is as if the workers rented the capital equipment and received the excess earnings as compensation for the effort they decide to exert. The (net) wage rate $w_i(e_i)$ applicable to effort e can be found from the zero-profit condition $p_i \cdot e_i \cdot f(K,L) = w_i(e_i) \cdot L = r \cdot K$, where r is the rental rate of capital and p_i is the price of the product.[2] Inserting the labor and capital inputs and output levels into the zero-profit condition and dividing by total output determines the set of zero-profit wage-effort contracts in sector i,

(3)
$$\frac{w_i}{P} = \frac{p_i \cdot e_i}{P \cdot A_{Li}} - \frac{r \cdot A_{Ki}}{P \cdot A_{Li}},$$

where P is an overall price index. The wage-effort zero-profit lines for two sectors are illustrated in figure 2.1.

Both zero-profit lines in figure 2.1 have negative intercepts, since at very low levels of effort the value of the output is not large enough to cover capital rental costs. Since the capital costs in the capital-intensive sector are higher, the intercept is more negative. As the effort increases, workers can be awarded higher wages in both sectors.[3] The observed labor contracts will lie along the upper envelope of these wage-effort offer curves, highlighted as the heavy curve depicted in figure 2.1. The marginal return to effort has to be lower in the labor-intensive sector, since otherwise there would be no attractive contracts in the capital-intensive sector. These intercepts and slopes dictate that the low-effort low-wage contracts are offered in the labor-intensive sector while high-wage high-effort contracts are offered in the capital-intensive sector. Also depicted in figure 2.1 is an indifference curve tangent to the wage-effort offer curve at two points. This represents an equilibrium with identical workers who are indifferent between the two prevailing contracts, high-effort high-wage and low-effort low-wage.

High effort saves capital costs. These savings are offset by the wage premiums necessary to compensate workers for high levels of effort. Multiple

---

2. Note that the rental rate of capital could also be considered to include depreciation expenses.

3. Average capital cost is $AC_K = (r \cdot K)/(q \cdot e)$, where q is the level of output when $e = 1$. The capital cost savings of effort is $\partial AC_K/\partial e = -(r \cdot K)/(q \cdot e^2)$, clearly larger at any one specific level of effort e for industries with a greater overall capital cost per worker. These cost savings are offset by the marginal increase in wages necessary to compensate workers' for their additional efforts.

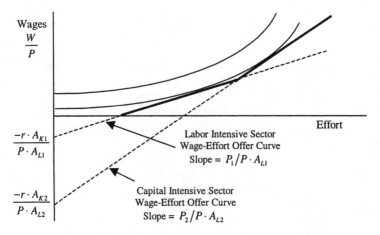

Fig. 2.1   Equilibrium in a two-sector model with fixed input technologies

shifts and other forms of capital sharing can also save capital costs. When two workers share the same capital, the intercept of the zero-profit line for each worker shifts upward toward the origin by a factor of two. This allows firms to offer better wage-effort contracts. But capital sharing does not come without costs. Among the costs of capital sharing are wage premia for the second and graveyard shifts, transitional downtimes, and increased noncapital fixed costs, such as training and benefits, as well as moral hazard problems and coordination costs. Competition among firms will lead to efficient work practices that optimally trade off the gains from capital sharing with the costs.

2.2.1   Endogenous Effort with Cobb-Douglas Technologies

If the capital/labor ratio in a sector is not fixed technologically, the wage-effort offer curve loses its flat segments, but otherwise there is no material change in the model. For example, a Cobb-Douglas production function is

$$(4) \qquad\qquad q = e \cdot k^\beta,$$

where q is output per worker, k is the capital used by each worker, and β is the capital intensity. The optimal level of capital is determined by setting the marginal revenue product of capital equal to the capital rental rate r.

$$(5) \qquad \beta \cdot p \cdot e \cdot k^{\beta-1} = r \Rightarrow k = \left(\frac{r}{p \cdot e \cdot \beta}\right)^{1/(\beta-1)}.$$

Since capital's marginal rate of productivity changes with the level of effort, the optimal level of capital inputs varies with the level of effort.

Substituting equation (4) for q and (5) for k in the zero-profit condition, $w = p \cdot q - r \cdot k$, we find that the sector wage-effort offer curve becomes

(6) $$w = p^{1/(1-\beta)} \cdot e^{1/(1-\beta)} \cdot r^{-\beta/(1-\beta)} \cdot (\beta^{\beta/(1-\beta)} - \beta^{1/(1-\beta)}).$$

This sets wage offers proportional to effort raised to a power that exceeds one and that increases with the capital intensity of the sector. A two-sector equilibrium with Cobb-Douglas production functions is displayed in figure 2.2. It is very similar to the equilibrium in figure 2.1. In fact, it is easy to demonstrate that if the line tangent to the offer curves was traced back to the y-axis, the intercept would be the negative cost of capital, $r \cdot k$.

2.2.2 Changes in Product Prices

A change in the relative price in the two sectors twists the wage-effort offer curve. Figure 2.3 depicts the initial effect of a simultaneous rise in p_2 and fall in p_1 that leaves the overall price level P constant. What this does is rotate upward the wage-effort offer line in the capital-intensive sector and rotate downward the wage-effort offer line in the labor-intensive sector. These changes render the low-effort low-wage contract in the labor-intensive sector less attractive and cause income and substitution effects in opposite directions for the two contracts. The high-wage workers experience a favorable income effect and a substitution effect in favor of higher effort (steeper wage-effort offer line). The low-wage workers experience an unfavorable income effect and a substitution effect in favor of lower effort.

With identical workers, this cannot be an equilibrium because capital constraints do not allow all workers to operate in the preferred capital-intensive sector. An increase in the capital-rental rate would be needed to ration the consequent excess demand for capital. This rise in the rental rate of capital shifts both wage-effort offer lines downward. Both the initial

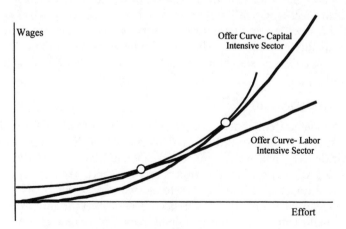

Fig. 2.2   Wage-effort offer curve with Cobb-Douglas production function

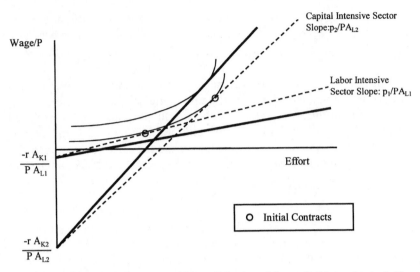

Fig. 2.3   Initial effect of a rise in the relative price of the capital-intensive tradable

rotation and the shift downward worsen the terms of the low-wage low-effort contract, and it follows that the final equilibrium selects a lower worker-indifference curve for the representative worker. The negative income effect that shifts the contracts to a lower indifference curve will also cause lower wages and higher effort in both sectors, provided that both leisure and consumption goods are normal. There is also a substitution effect that tends to drive the contracts in opposite directions; the low-effort low-wage contract shifts in favor of lower effort and lower wages, and the high-effort high-wage contract shifts in favor of higher wages and higher effort. Thus a rise in the relative price of the capital-intensive good makes workers worse off and increases income inequality. Keep in mind that the workers are indifferent between the two contracts and there is no real inequality in the model. The principal message is that the wage-effort offer curve twists, as shown in figure 2.4. We find this kind of twisting in the 1970s.

2.2.3   Heterogeneous Workers

The model presented here can easily be amended to allow for variation in workers' attitudes toward effort. This change has little impact on our empirical work, since we are studying the demand side of the labor market wage-effort offer curve, not the choices that workers make from among the offered contracts. In a model with heterogeneous preferences, materialistic workers who have a relative preference for goods over leisure would take the high-effort high-wage jobs, while humanistic workers who prefer leisure would take the low-effort low-wage work. Heterogeneity in labor

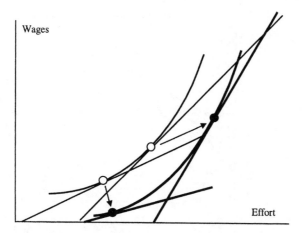

Fig. 2.4   Twisting of the market wage-effort offer curve (market response to relative price change)

supply does not affect how we study the demand side of the market very much, but this form of heterogeneity is important from a policy standpoint. The twisting of the offer curve caused by declines in the relative price of labor-intensive goods may have an adverse affect on the utility level of the humanists, but a favorable effect on the materialists. In other words, the welfare effects of changes in economic fundamentals such as relative prices may vary across groups of workers.

However, heterogeneity in ability is a serious problem for our empirical analysis. If the ability to operate expensive machinery varies across individuals, it is possible to have the more-able workers receiving high wages for low effort in the capital-intensive sectors, while the less-able workers work hard for low pay in the labor-intensive sectors. This would seriously affect our attempts to uncover the offer curve from observed contracts. We partially allow for this by including in the empirical analysis measures of education.

2.2.4   Technological Change

This subsection discusses the effect of technological change on the wage-effort offer curve. The debate regarding the increase in inequality in the United States has focused on two culprits, globalization and technological change. We have shown that globalization, taking the form of price declines for labor-intensive goods, twists the wage-effort offer curve. It is an unfortunate but familiar outcome that technological change can have almost the same effect. We would have liked in this paper to have made a substantial effort to disentangle technological effects from globalization effects, but that task requires direct indicators of both technological

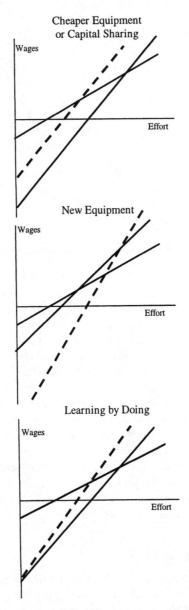

Fig. 2.5   Effect of technological change on wage-effort offer curve

change and globalization. When we occasionally slip into interpreting a certain twist of the wage-effort offer curve as a globalization effect or a technological effect, we do so loosely and based on information not contained in this paper.

Figure 2.5 depicts an initial wage-effort offer curve and the first changes that are induced by three distinct kinds of technological change in the capital-intensive sector: a reduction in the rental cost of existing equipment, the introduction of new, more costly equipment, and learning by doing. A reduction in the rental cost of the existing equipment simply shifts the intercept upward of the wage-effort offer line applicable to the capital-intensive sector, as indicated by the positioning of the new wage-effort offer line (the dashed black line). New more costly equipment creates a new wage-effort offer line that has a lower intercept but a steeper slope—meaning that the rental cost of the equipment is greater, but the productivity is higher. Learning by doing does not affect the rental cost, but it increases the productivity. Thus the intercept stays the same, but the slope increases.

These first effects of new technology create better jobs in the capital-intensive sector, and the economy in each case would have to experience an increase in the capital-rental rates (interest rate) to ration the capital and encourage workers to stick with jobs in the labor-intensive sector. This is the usual general equilibrium story. Capital is helped or hurt depending on whether the technological change is in the capital or labor-intensive sector. Unlike the usual case, labor here has a mixed experience. Before the rental rate of capital is bid up, each of the figures shows an improvement in the high-wage high-effort contracts. When the rental rate of capital is bid up to equilibrate the capital market, the wage-effort offer curve shifts downward across the board. This means that the low-effort low-wage contracts are definitely hurt by whatever kind of technological change may occur in the capital-intensive sector; but it is possible, depending on labor-supply elasticities, to have net improvement in the highest-wage highest-effort jobs remaining in the final equilibrium.

Unfortunately, the twisting of the wage-effort offer curve associated with technological change is essentially the same as the twisting associated with globalization. Thus we will not get very far trying to sort trade from technology by studying only the offer curve.

2.2.5   Previous Literature

There is a substantial previous literature on hours and wages. Unlike this paper, which explores the demand side, much of the discussion of hours in labor economics is concerned with the supply side—the worker's choice of hours. The budget constraint that is often assumed to face workers has earnings proportional to hours worked. An exception is Oi (1962), who assumes that firms experience a fixed training cost for each employee hired. The fixed costs that we emphasize are not training costs, but capital-rental charges. Another fixed cost that has recently increased in importance is worker benefits paid on a per-worker basis instead of a per-hour basis. Of course, nothing theoretically hinges on what the fixed costs are—the message of the model is that both hours and hourly wage rates should be greater the greater the fixed costs.

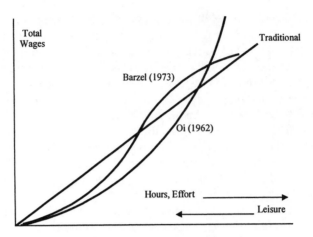

Fig. 2.6   Labor-demand functions in previous literature

Barzel (1973) adds another curved portion to the budget constraint, based on the assumption that labor productivity falls as the number of working hours increases within a fixed period of time, leading to the reversed S-shaped budget constraint cited in such empirical work as Moffit (1984). Barzel's and Oi's budget curves are displayed in figure 2.6.

There has been a substantial amount of empirical work in this field, although again most of this work has been more concerned with labor supply than labor demand. Rosen (1969) was one of the first to investigate the interindustry relationship between wages and hours. His reasoning of the apparent wage-hour trade-off was neatly summarized in his introduction: "Hours of work are an important non-pecuniary aspect of employment, even though 'industry' per se is not. On the other hand, wage and hour differences can persist because firms find certain attributes of their employees more productive and desirable than others and are willing to incur extra costs to obtain them" (250). He divides his analysis into supply and demand sides. On the demand side he, like Oi, correlates hours with the fixed costs of employing labor, including hiring costs, specific training, and unemployment-insurance premiums above the minimum levels. The demand for hours per employee is a decreasing function of the wage rate and an increasing function of these fixed costs. While he has no direct measure of these fixed costs across the industries in his sample, he derives what he believes to be suitable industry proxies from a number of demographic variables including age, education, and race. No mention of capital intensity is included in his work. He also considers short-run adjustments by including a variable to measure the sectoral growth rate and also other external effects, including unions. In general, he has more success measuring the demand side of the equation than the supply side.

On the labor-supply side are papers by Moffit (1984), Lundberg (1985), and Biddle and Zarkin (1989). These are primarily concerned with identifying the factors that influence the hours worked by individual workers, and the relationship between hours and wages as measured from the worker's perspective. They all point out that traditional ordinary least squares (OLS) wage regressions, which include hours worked as a right-hand-side variable, will not adequately measure the wage-hour relationship because of the endogeneity of hours. Biddle and Zarkin specifically control for this endogeneity and find the bias to be significant. After controlling for this bias, they find that male wages increase as a function of hours, first at an increasing and then at a decreasing rate. Less in line with our work are papers on the intertemporal behavior of hours and earnings, such as Bernanke (1986) and Abowd and Card (1987, 1989). These papers are concerned again with the supply side. Abowd and Card consider how individuals alter their hours of work over time. Bernanke is interested in how earnings and hours varied in eight industries during the Great Depression.

The efficiency-wage literature has some elements of similarity with our approach, but the differences are substantial and important. Our key variable is the capital intensity of the task—the greater the capital intensity, the greater the effort exerted by the worker. Most of the efficiency-wage theory initiated by Shapiro and Stiglitz (1984) and collected in Akerlof and Yellen (1986) makes no reference at all to the capital intensity of the operation. These efficiency-wage models are all based on the idea that firms can increase profits by raising wages above the market clearing price. These above-market wages reduce monitoring costs, since workers are induced to provide high effort by the threat of termination and thus a wage reduction.

The efficiency-wage conceptual framework is very different from ours. After controlling for ability, our framework has workers either preferring their own job or indifferent between their wage-effort contract and those contracts available to them in other jobs. The efficiency-wage theory, on the other hand, suggests that high wages reflect worker rents needed to coerce workers in the good jobs not to shirk. According to the efficiency-wage theory, workers in low-wage jobs prefer and are able to do the high-wage work, but are prevented from bidding for the better jobs in order to make the threat of firing have force in the high-wage contracts. Another important difference is that our framework has high-effort jobs in capital-intensive sectors and low-effort jobs in labor-intensive sectors. In the efficiency-wage literature, worker effort need not vary across sectors. There can be a high-effort low-wage perfectly monitored job and a high-effort high-wage imperfectly monitored job.

Empirically, the efficiency-wage literature includes one of our two fundamental equations, but not the other. Our framework explains both wages and hours as a function of capital intensity. The first equation is part of the efficiency-wage tradition; the second is not. Indeed, the efficiency-wage literature was partly instigated by the observation of the substantial differences in wages across industries. The correlation of the industry premiums with capital intensity was noted at least as far back as Slichter (1950). This has been empirically investigated in recent years in papers by Dickens and Katz (1987), Katz and Summers (1989), and Krueger and Summers (1987). The interindustry wage pattern has been shown to be steady over time and remarkably consistent across different countries. The wage premiums in the capital-intensive sectors have been attributed to variety of potential causes, including higher costs of monitoring, more inelastic labor demand, and higher cost of worker shirking (close in spirit to our own work). It has been noted that disentangling these various effects can be difficult because of the simultaneity problem, since wages and capital intensity are considered to be jointly determined.

The new empirical finding in this paper is not the well-known correlation between wages and capital intensity, but rather the correlation between weekly hours and capital intensity. This correlation may either contradict, be explained by, or complement the efficiency-wage findings, depending on other assumptions. First, consider the contradiction. The efficiency-wage literature generally assumes that weekly hours are fixed and that intensity of effort is variable and costly to observe. But if hours of work are variable and if workers prefer fewer hours, then an efficiency contract can stipulate both a higher hourly wage rate and also fewer weekly hours than the prevailing market contract. This would make us expect a negative correlation between hours and wage rates.

If, instead, employers are indifferent to the number of hours worked by each individual employee per week (monitoring problems, but no fixed costs), then the relationship between hours and capital intensity could merely be a secondary labor-supply effect caused by the high hourly wages offered in capital-intensive sectors. Workers rationally choose to work more weekly hours because of the higher opportunity cost of leisure. This view, of course, requires the additional assumption that substitution effects outweigh income effects.

Our findings could also complement the efficiency-wage literature. Some monitoring costs are like capital costs in that they are paid per worker rather than per hour. Others may be subject to learning curves and other economies of scale. Then our theory suggests that industries that incur high monitoring costs would also require their workers to exert additional effort. Thus, the interindustry wage differential would be part wage premium, part compensation for higher effort.

Distinguishing between these possibilities is not necessary for our purposes and is clearly outside the scope of this paper. Our whole approach of tracing out the wage-effort offer curve at different times and connecting its movements to changes in product prices, technology, and worker benefits represents a substantial departure from the efficiency-wage literature.

This comes from the very different conceptual frameworks that underlie wages that are determined to solve monitoring problems as opposed to wages that are instead payment for observable effort.

2.3 Empirical Evidence from the Census of Manufactures

The theory of effort can explain a large number of empirical facts, including wage differences across industries, productivity differences across countries, and the limited capital flow from high-wage to low-wage regions. The purpose of this paper is to breathe more life into this theory by showing that the U.S. labor market does seem to have a wage-effort offer curve. Two data sets are employed to this purpose, industry-level data from the Bartelsman-Becker-Gray Manufacturing Productivity database (hereafter NBER)[4] and worker-level data from the March Current Population Surveys (CPS).[5] We will assume initially that all workers are identically productive and that there is a single wage-effort offer curve with higher wages compensating for higher effort levels. This wage-effort offer curve is indexed by the capital intensity of the sector, with the high-effort high-wage contracts occurring in the capital-intensive sectors. Workers may have the same tastes and therefore be indifferent among the wage-effort contracts that are formed, or workers may have different attitudes toward effort, with the industrious (or materialistic) choosing high-effort high-wage contracts and with the slothful (or humanistic) workers choosing low-effort low-wage jobs. Later we will allow ability differences proxied by education levels.

The measurement of intensity of effort is the biggest problem we face. Effort is the product of unobservable intensity times observable hours. Fortunately, since effort is our dependent variable, measurement errors cause noise but not bias. Although we suspect that hours and intensity of work are positively correlated, it is enough that they are not so negatively correlated as to destroy any positive association between effort and hours.

Capital sharing from shift or temp work might cause us serious difficulties, but it does not. If the same capital K is used by two different work-

4. The NBER Manufacturing Productivity database, constructed by Eric Bartelsman and Wayne Gray, contains annual information on 450 manufacturing industries from 1958 to 1991. The industries are those defined in the 1972 Standard Industrial Classification and cover the entire manufacturing sector. The data themselves come from various government data sources, with many of the variables taken directly from the Census Bureau's Annual Survey of Manufactures and Census of Manufactures. The advantages of using the NBER database are that it gathers together many years of data, adjusts for changes in industry definitions over time, and links in a few additional key variables (e.g., price deflators and capital stock). For more information, see the NBER website: www.nber.org.

5. The sample represented in the Current Population Survey March demographic data was further reduced to those workers who worked between 20 and 80 hours in the previous week, who made at least $2.50 per hour in 1987 dollars, who were between the ages of 17 and 75, and who were not self-employed.

ers over the course of a day, then our measure of the capital intensity of the job correctly is equal to $K/2$, since 2 is the number of employees. Likewise, if one worker uses the equipment K for half the year, and another uses it for the other half, then the annual rental cost is also proportional to $K/2$, which we appropriately measure because the number of employees is doubled. Thus both shift work and temp work are compatible with our theory and with our empirical work. What we do not allow for are setup times associated with the handing of the capital from one worker to the next. Nor do we allow for unused capacity that is not charged against labor. But we think both of these are relatively minor concerns.

2.3.1   Evidence of the Wage-Effort Trade-off from Two-Digit Manufacturing Data

Given the potential problems with the use of hours as a measure of effort, it is perhaps remarkable that we are able to find a clear relationship across manufacturing industries between the average number of hours worked per week and hourly wages. Figure 2.7 depicts two-digit SIC data on industry average weekly hours and industry average weekly wages for production workers at six periods of time between 1950 and 1995. All six scatter diagrams have a remarkably clear association between hours and wages, exactly what we are looking for, with printing and publishing being the one outlier, offering a low-hour high-wage contract. Of course it is not surprising that people who work more hours earn more, but figure 2.7 has the increase in wages more than proportional to the average weekly hours, which we take as a reward for saving capital costs. These first data displays leave us excited about the accuracy of the theory. Low-wage low-effort contracts are being offered in the labor-intensive industries such as apparel and leather, while high-wage high-effort contracts are being offered in the capital-intensive sectors such as transport and chemicals.

Another interesting feature of the data displayed in figure 2.7 is the backward bend in the early periods, which is ironed out by 1980. The bend is associated with transportation and primary metals, which offer high wages but lower hours than some of the other sectors. Printing and publishing is on the backward-bending part of the curve in 1950, but separates entirely from the rest of the curve thereafter. We are inclined to think that the backward-bending part of the curve is due to unionization effects. Production workers in transport and primary metals have unionization rates of over 55 percent, compared to a 30 percent overall unionization rate for production workers in manufacturing industries.[6] But printing has

---

6. These numbers were calculated from the Current Population Surveys and refer to unionization rates in the 1990s. There is every reason to believe that the patterns of unionization, if not the overall numbers, have been roughly constant over time.

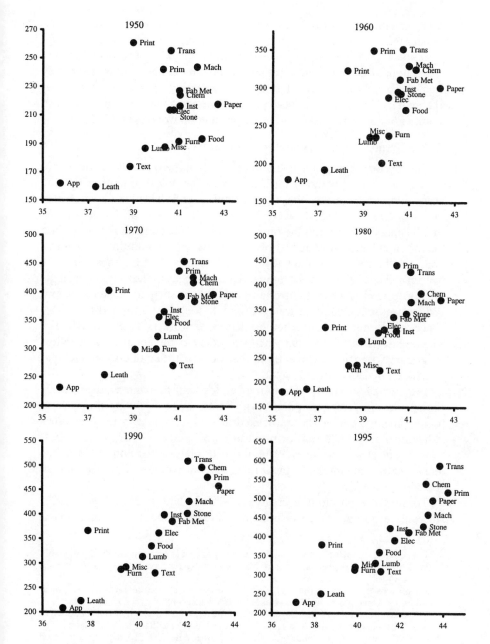

Fig. 2.7   Real weekly wages and weekly hours, 1950–95, by two-digit SIC manufacturing industries

Source: Citibase database.

Note: Wages are on vertical axis.

a unionization rate of only 14 percent.[7] It may be that printing of newspapers requires intense worker effort during relatively few hours in a day.

Textiles is another unusual sector. Textiles in 1970 and earlier had many more hours but about the same wages as apparel and leather. Relatively high-wage growth in textiles has moved the textile point closer to the rest of the scatter. This change has been accompanied by an increase in the average number of hours worked per week by production workers in this sector.

2.3.2 Trends and Cycles in Hours and Employment

We are concerned that some of these shifts in the wage-effort offer curve may be associated with the business cycle. The unit of time to which the wage-effort offer curve applies is the implicit contract period, which may be a worker's lifetime and which almost certainly covers the business cycle. If a business cycle defines the time unit, then the capital/labor ratio should be the capital stock divided by peak employment. In addition, both earnings and hours should refer to the whole cycle, not to a subset of time within a cycle. When we use annual data, the measured capital intensity is inappropriately high at the trough of the cycle when employment is low. When we use annual data we overestimate the effort level and the wages since we do not account for the idleness of workers at the trough. For these reasons, we worry that when we trace out the apparent wage-effort offer curve over time we may think that we see shifting offers when all that is happening is a business cycle.

Figure 2.8 shows how closely the employment rate and average weekly hours move together over time, with hours worked leading the cycle in employment.[8] Average hours peaked at over 41 hours in the late 1960s when unemployment was down to less than 4 percent. Average hours bottomed out at slightly over 39 hours in the late 1950s and again in the early 1980s when unemployment rates were measured at 7 percent and 10 percent, respectively.[9]

We note the run-up in average hours in the late 1980s and early 1990s to peak levels and the corresponding increase in the rate of employment

---

7. The most unionized sector inside the printing sector is newspaper publishing, with a unionization rate of 30 percent. It is unlikely that disaggregation is going to resolve this puzzle.

8. Data collected from the Bureau of Labor Statistics (BLS). The employment rate is measured as 1 − Unemployment Rate. Weekly hours are measured for production workers.

9. It is worth noting the distinct difference between average weekly hours as collected in the NBER Productivity database and the data presented here, with the BLS calculating average weekly hours at about 1 hour more than the NBER data. The BLS data were collected from the Current Population Surveys, while the NBER data were collected from the Census of Manufactures. The primary difference between these two data sets is their ultimate source, firms for the Census of Manufacturers and individual respondents for the Current Population Surveys. In the CPS, the data on hours employed per week include those employed at all jobs. Thus the average is dragged up by the set of individuals who take employment at more than one firm as well as by recollection error.

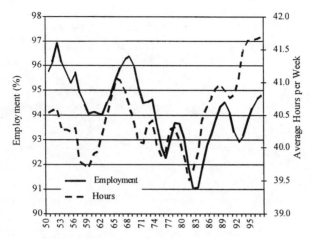

Fig. 2.8   Average employment rates and hours, production workers
Source: Bureau of Labor Statistics.

to high levels, but not to the historically high levels seen in the mid-1960s. This seems to imply that there has been some distinct break between these two series occurring in the early 1980s. We find this increase to be endemic across all industries in the NBER data. We are inclined to attribute this to a reaction to an increase in benefits, which are paid on a per-worker basis, not on a per-hour basis. Firms thus save on the costs of benefits by increasing hours. But the introduction of new, very expensive equipment can have a similar effect.

Cycles and trends are eliminated by subtracting the overall average from the sectoral hours data displayed in figure 2.9. The high-hours sectors in 1993 are displayed in panel *A* and the low-hours sectors in panel *B*. For example, a worker in apparel (in fig. 2.9*B*) worked about 4 hours less than the average production worker. This value has remained steady over the 45 years mapped out in the figure. On the top is the paper industry, where a worker works about 2.5 more hours per week than the average production worker. Notable exceptions to the stability of these results are indicated by thick black lines. They include, especially, transport and primary metals, each of which experienced an increase in average hours of about 3 hours per week. These two industries were the same two that formed the backward-bending portion of the wage-effort offer curve in the 1970s. The increase in the number of hours in these two industries is clearly due to the same reason the backward-bending portion of the wage-effort curve disappeared from the data, that is, the decline of unionization. Those changing in the opposite direction, albeit on a smaller scale, include furniture and food, which both experienced a 2-hour decline. The food sector and the furniture sector experienced a small decline in their relative capital

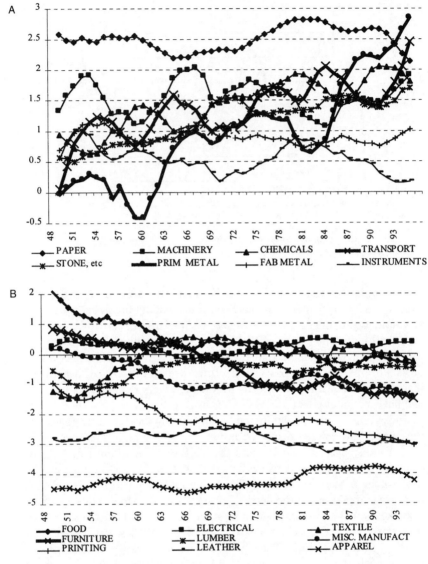

Fig. 2.9 Smoothed variation in two-digit industry hours from manufacturing mean: (*A*) high-hours sectors, (*B*) low-hours sectors

Source: Citibase database.

intensity compared to other manufacturing industries, perhaps explaining the decline in the average number of weekly hours worked in this industry.

2.3.3   Displays of the 1990 Four-Digit Industry Data

The four-digit industry data in the NBER Productivity database are considerably more noisy than the two-digit data, but the same pattern emerges. Capital-intensive sectors pay high wages and have long hours. Figure 2.10 shows the distinctly positive relationship between average weekly hours and average real weekly wages for production workers across the industries included in the NBER data in 1990.[10] Also striking is the strong positive relationship between the capital intensity of the sector, with both average hours worked per week by production workers and weekly wages. Of these two, the relationship between capital and hours is noisier. This is probably due to short-term fluctuations in industry demand that are absorbed more by hours than by wages, as well as due to the existence of greater noise in reported hours than in reported weekly earnings.

We expect a positive relationship to exist between weekly hours and weekly wages in the short run due to the inelasticity of the industry-specific labor supply and normal fluctuations in relative industry demand. This could explain the upward-sloping relationship seen in any one year. Yet as seen in the two-digit data, the pattern of wages and hours across sectors is very stable over time. For example, the correlation of weekly wages across sectors between 1990 and 1960 is 0.83, as can be seen in table 2.1. The table reports the cross-industry correlations of wages and hours at the various sample years, and both remarkably stable even over a 30-year time period. The correlation of weekly hours across sectors in 1960 and 1990 is 0.56.

Some of the association between hourly wages and weekly hours may come from the institutionalized 40-hour workweek and the legal requirement for overtime pay rates for weekly hours beyond 40. But legally mandated overtime need not have any effect even when overtime is observed. If a firm is willing to pay $430 for 42 hours of work, the contract can stipulate 42 hours at $430/42 per hour, or, to comply with the law, the contract can stipulate an hourly rate of $10 with time and a half for over-

---

10. The data have been smoothed using a three-period weighted average over the time series provided in the NBER data, where the weight is the percentage variation from the 3-year median. The reason we use this particular method is because the hours data in the NBER data are subject to what would appear to be unreasonable fluctuations in hours per production worker and hourly wages. Often hourly wages will increase by 50 percent or more, while hours worked per worker drop by 50 percent. This almost certainly is due to basic errors in the recording of the data. Using the deviation from the median as a weight eliminates the effect of large outliers in the data. It represents between 12 and 14 million production workers separated into 448 distinct manufacturing industries. Only production workers are discussed here because unfortunately data on the average hours per week for nonproduction workers are not provided in the NBER data.

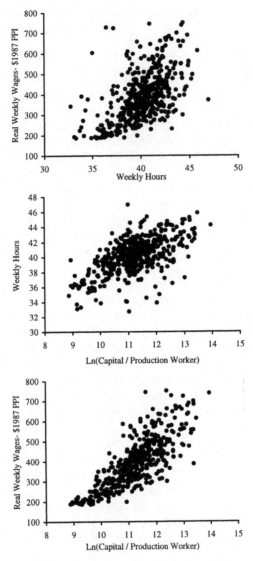

Fig. 2.10   Capital intensity, wages, and hours across four-digit manufacturing industries, 1990
Source: NBER Productivity database.

time. This would not affect the observed wage-effort offer curve. What the mandated overtime law really does is limit the flexibility of contracts over time, and it affects firms that experience variability in the demand for labor. Our focus on the longer-run aspects of the contract that are evident in the cross-sectional comparison of various industries means that man-

Table 2.1   Correlations of Weekly Wages and Hours by Four-Digit Industry across Sample Years

	1960	1965	1970	1975	1980	1985	1990	1994
Wages Correlation								
1960	1.00							
1965	0.97	1.00						
1970	0.95	0.98	1.00					
1975	0.90	0.93	0.95	1.00				
1980	0.86	0.89	0.91	0.97	1.00			
1985	0.84	0.86	0.89	0.94	0.97	1.00		
1990	0.83	0.86	0.88	0.93	0.95	0.97	1.00	
1994	0.82	0.85	0.87	0.91	0.94	0.96	0.98	1.00
Hours Correlation								
1960	1.00							
1965	0.78	1.00						
1970	0.74	0.85	1.00					
1975	0.64	0.74	0.78	1.00				
1980	0.61	0.64	0.68	0.66	1.00			
1985	0.58	0.59	0.61	0.63	0.57	1.00		
1990	0.56	0.61	0.66	0.62	0.60	0.60	1.00	
1994	0.52	0.62	0.66	0.63	0.61	0.59	0.80	1.00

dated overtime is not a substantial concern. The fact that some industries appear consistently to require that their workers work more than 40-hour workweeks despite mandated overtime pay premiums lends support to this idea.

Our model links weekly hours and weekly wages to capital intensity. Table 2.2 reports the average and standard deviation of real log capital per production worker and the average of the percentage of employees who are production workers for the 448 manufacturing sectors included in the sample. The capital intensity for each production worker is measured as total industry capital stock divided by the number of production workers.[11] The numbers in table 2.2 indicate that the average level of capital per production worker has been increasing steadily through the sample period, while the standard error of the log has been decreasing. This growth in capital intensity may be due partly to errors in measurement. For example, it is possible that there has been a shift of capital from pro-

---

11. This seems to allocate all capital to production workers, but a weaker assumption works. A formula for the total capital is $K = k_n N + k_p P$, where N and P are nonproduction and production workers and k indicates the capital intensity of the job. From this equation we can solve for the capital intensity of the production job as $(K/P) = k_n(N/P) + k_p$. The weaker assumption is that the product of nonproduction capital intensity times the nonproduction share of the workforce $k_n(N/P)$ is adequately constant across sectors. In addition to this problem, no attempt is made to allow for differences in depreciation rates across sectors and real interest rates over time.

Table 2.2   **Capital per Production Worker**

	Average Log Capital	Standard Deviation Log Capital	Production Workers (%)
1960	10.23	1.01	64.3
1965	10.35	0.98	64.4
1970	10.56	0.92	64.1
1975	10.78	0.85	64.9
1980	10.89	0.85	65.2
1985	11.08	0.85	61.3
1990	11.13	0.84	63.5
1993	11.17	0.85	62.2

Source: NBER database—weight averages for 448 manufacturing sectors.

duction to nonproduction workers, and it is also possible that the depreciation rates do not adequately account for obsolescence in this period of supposed rapid technological advance.

2.3.4 Estimation of the Wage-Effort Offer Curve with Four-Digit Data

To infer the wage-effort offer curve we estimate regressions explaining weekly hours and weekly wages as quadratic and cubic functions of the ratio of capital (K) to production employees (PE).

$$(7) \qquad \log(\textit{Weekly hours})_i = \alpha_{i,t} + \beta_{1,i} \cdot \log\left(\frac{K}{PE}\right)_i$$

$$+ \beta_{2,i,t} \cdot \log\left(\frac{K}{PE}\right)_i^2 + \mu_i,$$

$$(8) \quad \log(\textit{Weekly wages})_i = \alpha_i + \beta_{1,i} \cdot \log\left(\frac{K}{PE}\right)_i + \beta_{2,i,t} \cdot \log\left(\frac{K}{PE}\right)_i^2$$

$$+ \beta_{2,i,t} \cdot \log\left(\frac{K}{PE}\right)_i^3 + \mu_i.$$

We exclude the cubic of capital intensity from the hours equation because it is generally statistically insignificant. Data to estimate these equations are 3-year averages centered on the years 1960, 1965, 1970, 1975, 1980, 1985, 1990, and 1993. Observations are weighted by the number of production workers employed in the sector year in order to prevent the small sectors from dragging the coefficients around.

The results of these regressions are presented in table 2.3. The basic patterns of the results are as predicted and are fairly constant over the sample period. Capital intensity explains close to 40 percent of the variation in weekly hours across sectors, but somewhat more of the variation

Table 2.3   **Wage and Hour Regression Results**

Year Variance	Hours Coefficient	Wages Coefficient
1960		
R^2	0.369	0.5031
Int	2.1184 (0.0783)*	8.3832 (2.4432)*
(K/L)	0.2840 (0.0156)*	−1.3892 (0.7386)*
$(K/L)^2$	−0.0128 (0.0008)*	0.1722 (0.0737)*
$(K/L)^3$		−0.0061 (0.0024)*
1965		
R^2	0.4466	0.5626
Int	2.0819 (0.0760)*	12.6155 (2.7216)*
(K/L)	0.2890 (0.0150)*	−2.7023 (0.8125)*
$(K/L)^2$	−0.0127 (0.0007)*	0.3081 (0.0801)*
$(K/L)^3$		−0.0107 (0.0026)*
1970		
R^2	0.433	0.6083
Int	2.2968 (0.0817)*	16.6675 (3.1310)*
(K/L)	0.2337 (0.0157)*	−3.8122 (0.9069)*
$(K/L)^2$	−0.0097 (0.0008)*	0.4073 (0.0868)*
$(K/L)^3$		−0.0135 (0.0028)*
1975		
R^2	0.3821	0.6422
Int	2.2975 (0.1007)*	17.9309 (4.0029)*
(K/L)	0.2213 (0.0189)*	−4.2620 (1.1285)*
$(K/L)^2$	−0.0088 (0.0009)*	0.4512 (0.1053)*
$(K/L)^3$		−0.0148 (0.0033)*
1980		
R^2	0.3835	0.6731
Int	2.1802 (0.0994)*	15.2499 (4.2042)*
(K/L)	0.2406 (0.0184)*	−3.5119 (1.1691)*
$(K/L)^2$	−0.0096 (0.0008)*	0.3770 (0.1077)*
$(K/L)^3$		−0.0122 (0.0033)*
1985		
R^2	0.3884	0.6923
Int	1.9133 (0.1163)*	9.7820 (4.3422)*
(K/L)	0.2821 (0.0210)*	−2.0616 (1.1779)*
$(K/L)^2$	−0.0111 (0.0009)*	0.2481 (0.1059)*
$(K/L)^3$		−0.0084 (0.0032)*
1990		
R^2	0.3212	0.6751
Int	2.2617 (0.1266)*	5.2251 (4.4977)
(K/L)	0.2237 (0.0227)*	−0.7699 (1.2132)
$(K/L)^2$	−0.0085 (0.0010)*	0.1275 (0.1085)
$(K/L)^3$		−0.0047 (0.0032)
1993		
R^2	0.2647	0.6534
Int	2.2208 (0.1367)*	3.2645 (4.3934)
(K/L)	0.2351 (0.0244)*	−0.1503 (1.1794)
$(K/L)^2$	−0.0091 (0.0011)*	0.0651 (0.1050)
$(K/L)^3$		−0.0027 (0.0031)

Note: Standard errors are in parentheses.
*Significant at the 5 percent level.

in weekly wages, 50 percent in 1960 and nearly 70 percent in the 1980s. From the pair of estimated equations (7) and (8), we solve for the wage-effort offer curve by eliminating the capital intensity variable. Segments of these curves corresponding to observed capital intensities are plotted in figures 2.11, 2.12, and 2.13. The capital intensity data have a large right tail, so the capital range was determined as the minimum capital intensity observed in the data up to 2.5 standard deviations above the mean, roughly encompassing all but two outlying sectors of the sample, petroleum refining and blast furnaces. The lower-left portions of the curves represent the wage-effort contracts in the relatively labor intensive sectors, while the upper-right portions represent the contracts in capital-intensive sectors. The eight regressions are divided into three subperiods in which the shift of the curve takes a distinct form: 1960 to 1970, 1970 to 1980, and 1980 to 1993.

The wage-effort offer curves in figure 2.11 for 1960 and 1965 show the distinct backward-bending form of the wage-effort offer curve that was evident in the two-digit data in figure 2.7. The lowest curve in figure 2.11 is the wage-effort offer curve in 1960. Between 1960 and 1970, two changes appear to be happening. First, the backward-bending portion of the wage-effort offer curve has been diminishing, possibly due to the decline in the power that unions had to negotiate favorable contracts in the early 1960s. In addition, the entire curve has been shifting up and to the right.

The rightward shift is most evident in the labor-intensive sectors at the lower-left portion of the curve. This appears to be due to a relative in-

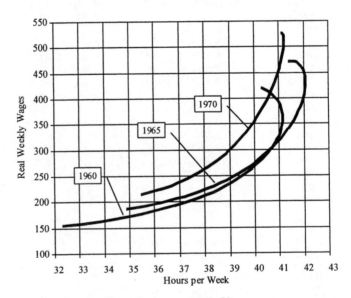

Fig. 2.11   Derived wage-effort offer curves, 1960–70

Table 2.4   **Changes in Capital Intensity**

Capital/Production Worker, 1960 (1987 dollars)	Change 1960–70 (%)
$0–9,999	56.8
$10,000–19,999	45.8
$20,000–29,999	32.5
$30,000–49,999	30.5
$50,000+	20.6

Source: NBER database, 1960–70.

Table 2.5   **Pattern of Capital Deepening from Levels Regressions**

Model	Intercept	Slope
(K/L) 1970 on (K/L) 1960	1.705	0.867
	(0.165)	(0.016)
(K/L) 1980 on (K/L) 1970	0.718	0.964
	(0.160)	(0.015)
(K/L) 1990 on (K/L) 1980	0.560	0.976
	(0.187)	(0.017)

Note: Standard errors are in parentheses.

crease in the capital intensity of these sectors. The average increase in capital intensity between 1960 and 1970 was 34 percent according to the NBER data. Yet the largest increases occurred among the labor-intensive industries, as can be seen in table 2.4, which breaks capital growth down by capital intensity in the 1960s. The most capital-intensive industries increased their capital intensity on average only 20 percent compared to over 55 percent in labor-intensive industries. This pattern of change in capital intensities is exclusive to the 1960s. Table 2.5 shows the results from three cross-sectional models regressing log capital intensity across industries on their values from the previous decade. The pattern of capital deepening can be seen in the slope coefficient. If the slope is less than 1, deepening is occurring primarily in the labor-intensive sectors, a slope greater than 1 implies deepening in the capital-intensive sectors. The slope is significantly below 1 in the 1960s, but very nearly 1 in the following 2 decades. These changes may be indicative of technological change. They may also be indicative of the movement of the most labor-intensive subsectors offshore.

The 1970s were very different from the 1960s. Figure 2.12 compares the wage-effort offer curves for 1970, 1975, and 1980. The backward-bending portion of the wage-effort offer curve completely disappeared in the 1970s. In addition, the wage-effort offer curve twisted, with the low-wage low-effort contracts experiencing a 15 percent reduction in wages and the high-

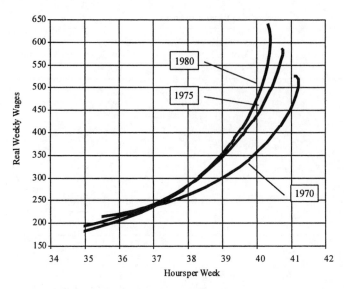

Fig. 2.12   Derived wage-effort offer curves, 1970–80

wage high-effort contracts enjoying a 20 percent increase. The ratio of real hourly wages between the two end points of the curve increased from 2.3 in 1970 to over 3.3 in 1980 and peaked at 3.5 in 1985 before it stabilized at about 3.45. We are inclined to associate this twisting of the curve with the 1970s decline in the relative price of labor-intensive manufactures that is documented in Leamer (1998).

This twisting of the observed wage-effort offer curves is not compatible with a representative worker model with a stable utility function, since the contracts in the capital-intensive sectors have unambiguously improved while those in the labor-intensive sectors have unambiguously deteriorated. This twisting of the curve could be an equilibrium if workers have heterogeneous preferences. Differences in adversity to effort may also explain a portion of the apparent rigidity of the labor market to changes in relative wages across sectors: despite the shift in the wage-effort offer curve, the distribution of production workers across sectors has remained fairly stable. This is illustrated in table 2.6, which reports employment by quintile of capital intensity. The sectors with the lowest capital/labor ratios experienced an 8.5 percent reduction in employment between 1970 and 1980. The third and fourth quintiles experienced the greatest gains, while there was actually a decline in employment in the most capital-intensive sectors.

In the 1980s the wage-effort offer curve began to shift to the right, a movement that is depicted in figure 2.13. In words, for the same wage levels, workers were required to work more hours. The increase in weekly hours was between 2 and 3 hours during this 13-year period, more at the upper end of the wage-effort offer curve than at the lower end. One pos-

Table 2.6   **Changes in Employment of Production Workers by Quintiles of Capital Intensity, 1970–80**

Capital Intensity	Employment 1970 ($\times$ 10³)	Employment 1980 ($\times$ 10³)	Change (%)
First quintile	2,589.9	2,379.4	−8.5
Second quintile	3,172.6	3,281.6	3.4
Third quintile	2,619.2	2,771.7	5.7
Fourth quintile	2,712.9	3,050.4	11.7
Fifth quintile	2,545.1	2,406.5	−5.6

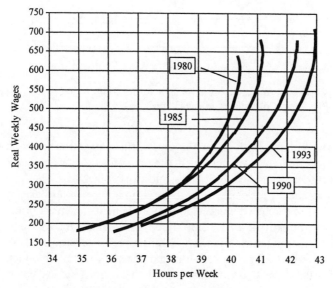

Fig. 2.13   Derived wage-effort offer curves, 1980–93

sible explanation for this shift is the increasing real capital rental costs coming from the rise in the demand for capital induced by the economic liberalizations in Asia and Latin America. Another possible explanation is the introduction of new more expensive equipment (computers and robots), which shifts the curve as illustrated in the middle panel of figure 2.5. A third possibility is the business cycle. There was a four-point decline in unemployment after the peak during the recession in 1983. The strong correlation between employment and weekly hours was highlighted in figure 2.8. Yet there are a number of reasons to doubt the business-cycle role in the sharp increase in weekly hours. One reason is the magnitude of the change. The larger change in unemployment between 1969 and 1983 (a reduction of 5.5 points) only led to a 1.25-hour decrease in average weekly hours, much smaller than the 2-hour increase seen after 1983.

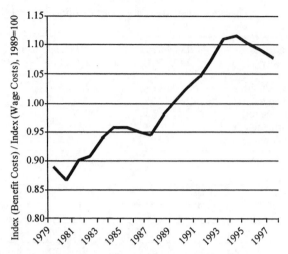

Fig. 2.14   Benefit to wage costs in manufacturing, 1989 = 100
Source: BLS Labor Cost Indexes, Manufacturing.

We think that a likely cause for part of the shift in the wage-effort offer curve since 1980 was an increase in the quasi-fixed labor costs emphasized by Oi (1962): training, payroll taxes, and worker benefits. Whether it is capital or benefits, firms can save costs paid on a per-worker basis by getting more work out of each worker; thus more benefits for more hours. Figure 2.14 plots the ratio of a BLS employee-benefits index relative to wages per worker in manufacturing in the 1980s. Between 1980 and 1996, this index increased about 25 percent. Note that the majority of this increase occurred after 1986. Unfortunately, the data do not go back beyond 1979, so there is no way to compare this trend to earlier periods.

2.3.5   Controlling for Business Cycles

According to our estimates, the wage-effort offer curve has varied systematically over time, shifting up, then twisting, and finally shifting right. The 1970 and 1980 dates at which we estimate the wage-effort offer curve were selected to conform with Leamer's (1998) claim that the 1970s were the Stolper-Samuelson decade in which there was a significant decline in the relative prices of labor-intensive tradables. But these years and the other 5-year intervals at which we estimate the wage-effort offer curve select different points in the business cycle, and some of the observed shifting may be due to the cycle rather than the fundamentals. In this section we show that in fact the timing is not essential. Comparisons, peak-to-peak and trough-to-trough, show the same shifting of the wage-effort offer curve.

We use the employment rate to define the cycle. As is evident in figure 2.8, weekly hours lead the employment rate, a feature we attribute to a delay between an increase or reduction in product demand and the actual hiring or firing of workers. To capture the cycle in demand, we use the smoothed forward rate of employment as the indicator of the business cycle, and we compare peak-to-peak and trough-to-trough changes in the wage-effort offer curve. Using smoother year-ahead rate of employment again as our guide, we set our trough years as 1961–62, 1970–71, 1975–76, 1981–82, and 1991–92. The peak years were set at 1958–59, 1967–68, 1972–73, 1977–78, 1988–89, and 1993–94. The results of these peak and trough regressions are displayed in table 2.7.

These regressions can be used to solve for the wage-effort offer curves such as those displayed in figures 2.11–2.13. When we do so, the peak-to-peak and the trough-to-trough comparisons are completely in line with our first results, which ignored the business cycle. In the 1960s, the wage-effort offer curve moved up and to the right, in the 1970s it twisted, and in the 1980s it shifted sharply to the right. In addition, when we put consecutive peak and trough years next to each other, such as 1970, 1971–72, 1973 and 1977, 1978–81, 1982, we find very little difference between the shapes of these curves. The trends we see in the wage-effort offer curves tend to be long term and appear to occur exogenous to cyclical effects.

2.3.6   Evaluation of Alternative Explanations of the Wage-Effort Offer Curve

We are excited by how well these results conform with the theory, but we need to be alert to the possibility that these findings are driven by some third factor that has nothing to do with effort. Our primary concern is that human capital is correlated with physical capital and with hours, and that what we are observing is not compensation for effort, but compensation for skill and skilled workers choosing longer hours. Unionization is also a concern. Unions might be able to bargain for a wage-effort contract above the competitive market curve. A strong union effect might account for the outlying sectors observed in the two-digit-level data. Even without unions, profit sharing may help to explain the pattern of wages. The realized returns to capital vary widely across sectors and also across time. Firms in the less competitive sectors may collect positive rents and may share those rents with workers.

The NBER data set does not include information on unionization or education. We have formed industry estimates of production worker education from the Current Population Surveys. To do this, we had to match the 71 three-digit CPS manufacturing industries with the 448 industries in the NBER productivity database.[12] Data from Kokkelenberg and Sockell (1985) on union status were used for the 1973–81 period while data from

---

12. CPS industry data at the three-digit level are available between 1971 and 1994, so the 1971 data were matched with the earlier NBER data for the regressions.

Table 2.7   Wage and Hour Regressions at the Cyclical Peaks and Troughs

	Trough					Peak					
	1961–62	1970–71	1975–76	1981–82	1991–92	1958–59	1967–68	1972–73	1977–78	1988–89	1993–94
Hours Regressions											
R^2	.394	.445	.370	.332	.293	.359	.422	.450	.474	.365	.255
Int	2.038*	2.284*	2.356*	2.427*	2.299*	2.257*	2.193*	2.092*	2.096*	2.061*	2.190*
(K/L)	.298*	.235*	.210*	.196*	.219*	.259*	.261*	.264*	.253*	.258*	.241*
$(K/L)^2$	−.0133*	−.0097*	−.0082*	−.0077*	−.0084*	−.0117*	−.0112*	−.0108*	−.0099*	−.0100*	−.0094*
Wage Regressions											
R^2	.518	.626	.649	.692	.674	.484	.540	.635	.661	.668	.646
Int	9.031*	17.448*	17.406*	12.350*	4.197	7.263*	11.239*	21.654*	18.875*	7.299	2.975
(K/L)	−1.599*	−4.045*	−4.117*	−2.667*	−.448	−1.032	−2.243*	−5.296*	−4.565*	−1.353	−.056
$(K/L)^2$	.195*	.430*	.437*	.295*	.095	.135	.260*	.550*	.480*	.182	.056
$(K/L)^3$	−.0069*	−.0142*	−.0143*	−.0096*	−.0036	−.0049*	−.0090*	−.0180*	−.0156*	−.0064	−.0024

*Significant at the 5 percent level.

Hirsch and Macpherson (1993) were used for the later years. These measures are also created from the CPS data, so they match with the NBER data in the same way that the education measures do.

Industry rents are particularly difficult to measure. The NBER data provide a measure of value added. Theoretically this variable represents employee wages; other employee benefits such as social security, which are not directly included in the wage bill;[13] ex ante capital-rental costs; industry rents, if any; and firm-specific rents that accrue to the owners of the capital:

$$(9) \quad VA_i = w \cdot Emp_i + w_B \cdot Emp_i + r \cdot Capital_i + Rent_i + \mu_{it}.$$

With the admittedly suspicious assumption that capital-rental rates and worker benefit rates are constant across industries, we can extract from value added that which is due to capital intensity and treat the residual as rent:

$$(10) \quad \frac{VA_i - w \cdot Emp_i}{Emp_i} = \alpha + \beta \cdot \frac{Capital}{Emp} + \varepsilon_i.$$

The coefficient α represents the per-worker cost of nonwage benefits plus average rents, β represents the capital-rental costs, and ε is the rent residual. Since it is impossible to separate from the constant that part which represents average rents, we use only the estimated rent residuals smoothed over seven periods to form estimates of sectoral long-run rents.[14]

Table 2.8 reports a number of basic statistics for the additional data. The average education level for production workers was slightly less than 12 years in 1993, up from only 10 years in 1960. There are distinct differences in the educational attainment of workers across sectors. In 1990 the average years of schooling varied across sectors from 9 years to 13.5 years. Around 20 percent of production workers were actively enrolled in unions or covered by a union contract in 1993, a significant decrease from the 42 percent enrollment in 1960. Again there appears to be a fairly large variation in union participation across sectors, with a maximum of 60 percent to a minimum of 2 percent in 1993. In 1960 this range stretched between 12 percent and 82 percent. The bottom of table 2.8 provides basic statistics on the computed industry rents. Note that these data have been converted to real values by dividing by the producer price index (PPI) deflator. The average rent is close to zero in each period, a function of the regression technique employed to construct this measure. Interestingly, there has been a sharp increase in the variance of rents since 1980.

Except for the percentages of unionization rate and females, all these

13. The wage data in the NBER data do not include some worker benefits.
14. For the purpose of the regression analysis, rents were also put into log form by taking the log of 100 times the absolute value and multiplying by the sign of the initial value. Values between 0.01 and −0.01 were set to 0.

Table 2.8   Additional Explanatory Variables for Wage and Hour Regressions Computed per Production Worker

	1960	1965	1970	1975	1980	1985	1990	1993
Education								
Mean	10.2	10.2	10.2	10.6	11.0	11.3	11.5	11.6
Standard deviation	0.8	0.8	0.8	0.7	0.7	0.6	0.7	0.7
Minimum	7.5	7.5	7.5	8.7	8.3	9.4	8.9	9.5
Maximum	11.8	11.8	11.8	12.4	12.6	13.0	13.5	13.7
Union Status (%)								
Mean	42.0	42.5	41.9	39.7	36.8	27.5	22.6	20.4
Minimum	12.3	12.3	12.3	5.6	4.1	4.5	2.4	2.1
Maximum	81.8	81.8	81.8	76.6	75.4	62.5	58.6	59.4
Rents								
Mean	−0.3	−0.3	−0.4	−0.5	−0.8	−0.9	−1.0	−1.0
Standard deviation	4.6	5.6	6.6	7.3	8.7	11.9	16.7	18.0
Minimum	−9.4	−13.7	−22.8	−27.6	−37.3	−44.2	−39.0	−53.8
Maximum	37.4	58.8	73.0	74.5	87.1	139.5	256.7	286.1

variables will be entered into our equation in logarithmic form. Table 2.9 reports the correlations between different variables within a data set and also between the same variables from the CPS data and the NBER data. The correlation between average weekly hours and average weekly wages across the two data sets are respectively 0.55 and 0.75, implying that the patterns seen in the NBER data are in part replicated in the CPS data despite the large differences in the collection techniques employed by the two sources.

Of the other variables, education appears to be significantly correlated with both wages and hours. Not surprisingly, educated workers are also overrepresented in capital-intensive sectors. Unionization is highly correlated with wages and positively correlated, albeit weakly, with weekly hours. This surprising result may be linked to the high positive correlation between union activity and the capital intensity of the industry. Rents are also positively correlated with capital intensity. These correlations make it possible that what we are seeing in the initial set of wage and hour regressions is only omitted variable bias and not a wage-effort offer curve. These new variables will now be included in another set of regressions.

Although the percentage of females is reported in table 2.9, we exclude this from our equations because we think it represents, at least partly, the supply side. Proper econometric estimation of the joint (supply and demand) determination of the wage-effort offer curve with heterogeneous workers is beyond the scope of this paper. The data do indicate that females tend to be employed in labor-intensive (i.e., low-wage low-effort) sectors.

Proper treatment of the human capital variable is another delicate task, which has been discussed more fully in Leamer (1999). Here we note that the model depicted in figure 2.1 is based on the assumptions that workers are fully charged for the capital they use and that the wage we observe is total earnings net of all capital charges. To put it another way, we assume that workers do not bring their own tools to the workplace, and we assume also that workers have no other sources of wealth that can be used to finance consumption. Both of these assumptions are violated by human capital, first because the wage that we observe is not net of the implicit human capital rental costs[15] and second because human capital acquired in formal education is partly financed by the government and by the worker's parents. Without these two problems, we could simply combine human and physical capital into a single capital aggregate.

This is illustrated in figure 2.15, which depicts three different jobs with differing fixed levels of human capital inputs and the same fixed level of physical capital inputs. One job uses physical capital only, the second job

---

15. An exception is firm-specific training, financed by the firm. The education variable we use merely counts the years of formal schooling, those that create human capital owned by the worker, not the firm.

Table 2.9   CPS and NBER Data Correlation Statistics (1990 data)

	Hhr	WW	KE	Chrs	CWW	Edu	Uni	Rent	Fem
NBER Data									
Hhr	1.00								
WW	0.57	1.00							
KE	0.54	0.81	1.00						
CPS Data									
Chrs	0.55	0.55	0.38	1.00					
CWW	0.45	0.75	0.55	0.66	1.00				
Edu	0.35	0.67	0.49	0.62	0.83	1.00			
Uni	0.23	0.51	0.33	0.40	0.67	0.19	1.00		
Rent	-0.01	0.26	0.34	-0.05	0.19	0.22	-0.02	1.00	
Fem	-0.39	-0.47	-0.38	-0.80	-0.75	-0.40	-0.39	0.07	1.00

Note: Correlations computed with all variables in log form.

Abbreviations: Chrs, CPS hours per week; CWW, CPS wage per week; Edu, education; Fem, female; Hhrs, NBER hours per week; KE, capital; Rent, rents; Uni, Union; WW, NBER wage per week.

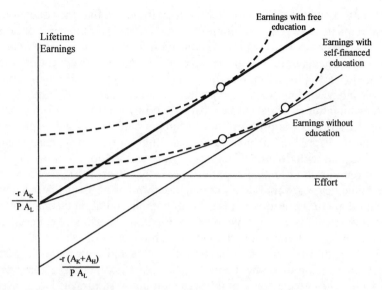

Fig. 2.15   Wage-effort offer curves by level of education

uses the same physical capital but also self-financed human capital, and the third job is the same as the second except that the human capital is provided without cost to the worker. The envelope of preferred contracts without free education is the heavy wage-effort offer curve in figure 2.15, which has the same character as the wage-effort offer curves that we have been discussing—namely, the high-effort high-(net) wage contracts are intensive in human capital. If the human capital is provided free of charge, then the offer line facing the educated worker has the slope of the original educated worker line but the intercept of the no-education line. This line of contracts with free education completely dominates the contracts if education is charged to the workers.[16]

Empirically, there are a number of directions in which this discussion of education could lead. One is nowhere. If education is free and everyone has the same ability, then the regressions of wages and hours on capital

---

16. As a side note, this resulting equilibrium suffers from two kinds of inefficiencies, too much education and too little effort. It is efficient to have some workers operating without human capital investments, but, once it is free, everyone opts for the education. It is efficient to have educated workers supplying a high level of effort, but the wealth transfer to them in the form of free human capital affords them the opportunity to take it easy and still earn high wages. The economic inefficiency here is not caused simply by some workers opting to take it easy. The inefficiency is caused by workers taking it easy while they use expensive capital. This inefficiency would not occur if human capital were transferable among workers. For example, if the wealth transfer to workers were financial or physical capital, then these wealthy workers could efficiently opt to supply low levels of effort, but they would then take jobs that did not require much capital.

intensity define the wage-effort offer curve. It may be that the educational requirements vary along the curve, but that is entirely immaterial because workers do not incur a cost for the education. If education is free, but ability is heterogeneous (and unobservable) and interacts with education, then we are in a lot of trouble and do not want to talk about it. If human capital is self-financed, then ideally we would amend equations (7) and (8) by aggregating human with physical capital and by subtracting from weekly wages a term that is proportional to human capital and that represents the human capital rental charges. We do not know how to aggregate years of education with dollars of physical capital and we do not know the implicit rental rate of human capital to net from wages. What we do is add the human capital variable to our equations and hope for the best, recognizing that our wage equation is gross of human capital rental charges but net of physical capital rent. We plan on revisiting the issues of educational financing and heterogeneity in ability in subsequent work.

Keeping all these concerns in mind, the wage and hour regressions are reestimated using the same functional forms as before, but with three new variables: the percentage of employees with union status, the log of average education, and the measure of industry rents. The variable for percentage of females was not included in these regressions, as we believe that this is a supply-side rather than a demand-side variable. Also included were two interactive variables, between union status and capital intensity and between industry rents and capital intensity. These interaction terms allow for the greater market power that employees may have in capital-intensive industries. The inclusion of the interactive term between education and capital made the results highly unstable and increased the standard errors significantly; thus it was dropped from the regressions.

We draw your attention to the set of supplemental regressions presented in table 2.10. The adjusted R^2 for each of the regressions has increased, although more so for the wage regressions than the hours regressions. The signs on the additional variables in the wage regression are mostly as would be expected, and mostly significant. The capital-intensity variable has retained a significant positive impact on both hours and wages despite the inclusion of the other variables, including education. When we include the interactive coefficients, the magnitudes are quite similar to those of the initial regressions, although additional formal analysis will be performed to verify this.

The average education of production workers has a significant effect on average weekly wages that increases over time. There was a particularly sharp rise between 1980 and 1985, a result that conforms to the literature on changes in the returns to education over this period. Holding all else equal, the average relative wage difference between a worker with 2 years of college and a high school dropout with 10 years of education increased from 31 percent in 1970 to 39 percent in 1980 to 55 percent in 1985, and

Table 2.10   Supplementary Log Wage and Log Hour Regressions

	1960	1965	1970	1975	1980	1985	1990	1993
Hours								
R^2	.401	.467	.463	.392	.390	.429	.368	.327
Int	1.774*	1.890*	2.263*	2.186*	1.994*	1.493*	2.014*	1.963*
(K/L)	.323*	.342*	.280*	.263*	.268*	.327*	.266*	.238*
(K/L)^2	-.0142*	-.0151*	-.0115*	-.0106*	-.0103*	-.0132*	-.0105*	-.0091*
Edu	.0369*	-.0486*	-.1097*	-.0573*	-.0106	.0659*	.0055	.0837*
Union	.1895*	-.0199	.0483	.0079	.2364*	-.0329	-.3577*	.0766
Union×(K/L)	-.0169*	.0039	-.0037	.0010	-.0217*	.0080	.0328*	-.0021
Rent	-.0194*	-.0192*	-.0104*	-.0092*	-.0095*	-.0126*	-.0071*	-.0091*
Rent×(K/L)	.0019*	.0018*	.0009*	.0009*	.0008*	.0010*	.0004	.0006
Wages								
R^2	.655	.667	.690	.748	.768	.803	.787	.783
Int	-.235	-.387	.257	-.785	-.385	-4.237*	-3.324*	-1.843*
(K/L)	.439*	.594*	.552*	.641*	.546*	.909*	.810*	.542*
(K/L)^2	-.0186*	-.0245*	-.0218*	-.0261*	-.0220*	-.0330*	-.0275*	-.0149*
Education	1.417*	1.111*	.932*	1.138*	1.176*	1.655*	1.440*	1.416*
Union	-2.300*	-1.827*	-2.225*	-3.151*	-4.161*	-1.310*	-.925	.493
Union×(K/L)	.2331*	.1945*	.2256*	.3218*	.4135*	.1724*	.1464*	.0277
Rent	-.0220*	-.0217	-.0175	.0036	.0421*	-.0306*	-.0549*	-.0339*
Rent×(K/L)	.0020*	.0021*	.0018	.0000	-.0034*	.0029*	.0049*	.0031*

Note: All variables in log form except union status.

*Significant at the 5 percent level.

then dropped back slightly to 48 percent in 1993. Interestingly, at the same time there was also a substantial change in the impact of education on effort. In 1970 the worker with 14 years of education worked on average 1.5 hours less than the high school dropout. By 1993 this had reversed, so that the college educated worked 1 hour more per week on average than the high school dropout. This empirical fact sets us to thinking about possible explanations. One explanation we like is that new very productive jobs emerged in the 1980s that required both high amounts of human capital and high inputs of physical capital (computers). But maybe it is the decline in the marginal tax rates, or the increasing cost of higher education, or something else entirely. Work is under way to answer this important question: Why are the educated working so much harder today than they did 30 years ago?

The interactive terms make it difficult to clearly see the impact of rents and union status on wages and hours. To facilitate the discussion of these interaction terms, table 2.11 displays the estimated impact of a 1 percent increase in union participation and in industry rents separately for a labor-intensive industry and a capital-intensive industry.[17] The impact of union status on weekly hours is very small in magnitude, but its impact on wages is significant. Not surprisingly, the presence of unions tends to raise wages in the capital-intensive sectors more than in the labor-intensive sectors. But up until 1985, unions seemed to have a negative effect on wages in labor-intensive industries. This result is possibly caused by another potential endogeneity problem, this time between capital intensity and unions. When unions successfully raise wages, firms naturally become more capital intensive. The overall decline of union presence from 39 percent in 1975 to 20 percent in 1993 may explain why this odd result has dissipated. Another interpretation is that unions seek preferred contracts in terms of both wages and effort level. In the capital-intensive sectors, where the cost of cutting effort is very high, unions opt for higher wages and perhaps not much change in effort. In the labor-intensive sectors, unions pursue the effort dimension of the contract more aggressively and end up opting for a contract that has greatly reduced effort and also somewhat reduced wages. (Here we are speaking about effort in the form of pace rather than in the total number of hours.)

We are uncomfortable with both the theory of rent sharing and also our measurement of rents, and we consequently do not place a great deal of faith in the rent results in table 2.11. According to these estimates, industry rents seem to reduce hours in labor-intensive sectors, but raise hours in capital-intensive sectors. Rents have a mixed effect over time on wages in the labor-intensive sectors, but consistently raise wages in the capital-

---

17. These industries are defined at the minimum and maximum levels of capital intensity for each time period, respectively.

Table 2.11   Variation in Union and Rents Effects (%)

	Hours			Wages			
	Low (K/L)	Average (K/L)	High (K/L)	Low (K/L)	Average (K/L)	High (K/L)	Variable Average
Unions							
1960	.07	.02	−.02	−.72	.09	.65	42.0
1965	.01	.02	.03	−.36	.19	.65	42.5
1970	.02	.01	.00	−.39	.16	.66	41.9
1975	.02	.02	.02	−.43	.32	.98	39.7
1980	.05	.00	−.04	−.59	.34	1.19	36.8
1985	.04	.06	.07	.22	.60	.95	27.5
1990	−.07	.01	.07	.37	.71	1.00	22.6
1993	.06	.05	.05	.74	.80	.86	20.4
Rents							
1960	−.63	.03	.50	−.87	−.20	.27	−1.82
1965	−.56	−.05	.37	−.60	−.02	.47	−1.72
1970	−.28	−.06	.15	−.30	.14	.53	−1.81
1975	−.19	.02	.20	.36	.37	.37	−1.94
1980	−.23	−.04	.13	1.32	.56	−.13	−1.94
1985	−.39	−.18	.02	−.50	.14	.73	−2.48
1990	−.32	−.22	−.13	−1.17	−.05	.94	−3.11
1993	−.39	−.26	−.14	−.67	.02	.64	−3.23

Note: Impact of a 1 percent increase in rents and union status on weekly hours and wages by capital intensity.

intensive sectors, reflecting the potential for profit sharing within an industry that is not fully competitive.

The point of this lengthy discussion of additional variables is primarily to determine if our initial estimate of the wage-effort offer curve is substantially contaminated by the omission of all these effects. Since we are now treating human capital as self-financed, in principle we want to trace out the wage-effort offer curve after aggregating human and physical capital and after removing from wages the implicit rental cost of human capital. This is not easily done, and what we do instead is to trace out the curve in the same way as before, using the new coefficients on the capital-intensity variables and holding fixed all the other variables at their sample averages. The results are displayed in figure 2.16. Although the shape of the wage-effort offer curves is altered slightly, the same basic patterns of change can be seen in the three periods.

2.4   Conclusion

We have provided in this paper substantial evidence that the U.S. labor market offers a set of wage-effort contracts, with effort measured by annual hours. This curve is uncovered by estimating two equations using

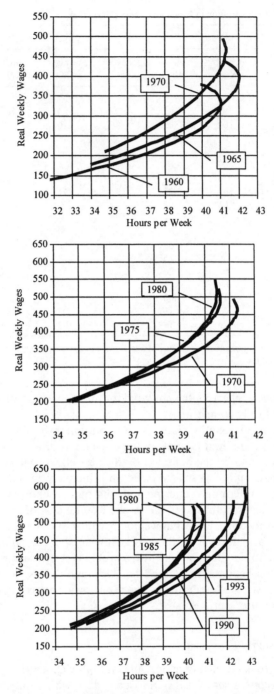

Fig. 2.16 Derived wage-effort offer curves, 1960–93, controlling for education, unions, and industry rents

industry-level data. One equation explains wages as a function of capital intensity and the other equation explains hours also as a function of capital intensity. By eliminating capital intensity from these two equations, we form a wage-hour offer curve.

We have found that this offer curve shifts in three distinctly different ways. Between 1960 and 1970, the wage-effort offer curve shifted up, with higher wages offered at every level of effort. Between 1970 and 1980, the wage-effort offer curve twisted, with the best contracts getting better and the worst contracts getting worse. Since the 1980s, the wage-effort offer curve has shifted to the right, requiring more effort for the same wage level. The upward shift in the 1960s is consistent with capital deepening, the twisting in the 1970s with price declines of labor-intensive tradables, and the rightward shift after 1980 either with the introduction of new equipment or with increases in government-mandated benefits.

The weakest link in our empirical analysis is probably the use of hours as a measure of effort. Despite problems with hours as a measure of effort, we find a consistent and significant relationship among wages, effort as measured by hours, and capital intensity. This relationship stands up even when we control for the business cycle, education, unionization, and estimated industry rents.

This is, of course, not the end of the story by any means. We should be studying tasks, not industries. We should be looking at individual-level data and data outside of manufacturing. We should be allowing more completely for heterogeneity in ability and tastes. We should have a better measure of unionization. We should explicitly link changes in the wage-effort offer curve to the fundamental drivers such as globalization, technological change, and worker benefits. Most of all, we need a better measure of effort.

Although this is not the end of the story, it is a very good beginning.

References

Abowd, John M., and David Card. 1987. Intertemporal labor supply and long-term employment. *American Economic Review* 77 (1): 50–68.

———. 1989. On the covariance structure of earnings and hours changes. *Econometrica* 57 (2): 411–46.

Akerlof, George A., and Janet L. Yellen. 1986. *Efficiency wage models of the labor market.* Cambridge: Cambridge University Press.

Auernheimer, Leonardo, and Beatriz Rumbos. 1996. Variable capital utilization in a general equilibrium, "supply side" model. College Station: Texas A&M. Working paper.

Barzel, Yoram. 1973. The determination of daily hours and wages. *Quarterly Journal of Economics* 87 (May): 220–38.

Bernanke, Ben. 1986. Employment, hours, and earnings in the depression: An analysis of eight manufacturing industries. *American Economic Review* 76 (1): 82–109.

Biddle, Jeff E., and Gary A. Zarkin. 1989. Choice among wage-hour packages: An empirical investigation of male labor supply. *Journal of Labor Economics* 7 (4): 415–37.

Bischoff, Charles W., and Edward C. Kokkelenberg. 1987. Capacity utilization and depreciation in use. *Applied Economics* 19 (August): 995–1007.

Calvo, Guillermo A. 1975. Efficient and optimal utilization of capital services. *American Economic Review* 65 (March): 181–86.

Deardorff, Alan V., and Frank P. Stafford. 1976. Compensation of cooperating factors. *Econometrica* 44 (July): 671–84.

Dickens, William T., and Lawrence F. Katz. 1987. Inter-industry wage differences and industry characteristics. In *Unemployment and the structure of labor markets,* ed. K. Lang and J. Leonard, 48–89. Oxford: Basil Blackwell.

Gros, Daniel, and Alfred Steinherr. 1993. Redesigning economic geography after the fall of the Soviet empire. Working Document no. 75. Brussels: Centre for European Policy Studies, March.

Hirsch, Barry T., and David A. Macpherson. 1993. Union membership and coverage files from the Current Population Surveys: Note. *Industrial and Labor Relations Review* 46 (3): 574–78.

Katz, Lawrence F., and Lawrence H. Summers. 1989. Industry rents: Evidence and implications. *Brookings Papers on Economic Activity, Microeconomics,* 209–90.

Kokkelenberg, Edward C., and Donna R. Sockell. 1985. Union membership in the United States 1973–1981. *Industrial and Labor Relations Review* 38 (4): 497–543.

Krueger, Alan B., and Lawrence H. Summers. 1987. Reflections on the inter-industry wage structure. In *Unemployment and the structure of labor markets,* ed. K. Lang and J. Leonard, 17–47. Oxford: Basil Blackwell.

Leamer, Edward E. 1998. In search of Stolper-Samuelson linkages between international trade and lower wages. In *Imports, exports, and the American worker,* ed. Susan Collins, 141–214. Washington, D.C.: Brookings Institution.

———. 1999. Effort, wages and the international division of labor. *Journal of Political Economy* 107 (6): 1127–63.

Lindsay, C. M. 1971. Measuring human capital returns. *Journal of Political Economy* 79 (6): 1195–215.

Lundberg, Shelly. 1985. Tied wage-hours offers and the endogeneity of wages. *Review of Economics and Statistics* 67 (3): 405–10.

———. 1988. Labor supply of husbands and wives: A simultaneous equations approach. *Review of Economics and Statistics* 70 (2): 224–35.

Moffit, Robert. 1984. The estimation of a joint wage-hours labor supply model. *Journal of Labor Economics* 2 (October): 550–66.

Oi, Walter Y. 1962. Labor as a quasi-fixed factor. *Journal of Political Economy* 70 (December): 538–55.

Rosen, Sherwin. 1969. On the interindustry wage and hours structure. *Journal of Political Economy* 77 (March): 249–73.

Shapiro, Carl, and Joseph E. Stiglitz. 1984. Equilibrium unemployment as a worker discipline device. *American Economic Review* 74 (3): 433–44.

Slichter, Sumner H. 1950. Notes on the structure of wages. *Review of Economics and Statistics* 32 (1): 80–91.

Comment   Alan V. Deardorff

This paper follows up another paper of Leamer's alone (Leamer 1999) that I have had the pleasure of discussing twice on other occasions. I've said before, and I will repeat here, that I very much like the theoretical model. It adds a dimension—effort—to the two-sector production model that yields a surprising list of interesting and plausible implications. These implications are at least consistent with a number of stylized facts, including the relationship across industries between wages and capital intensity that Leamer documents empirically in his earlier paper.

This paper goes a few steps further toward estimating ("estimate, don't test") the model empirically, primarily by measuring effort by observable hours of work and asking whether the combined relationships among hours, wages, and capital intensity are consistent with the model. To a considerable (and, to me, surprising) extent, they are. Furthermore, by repeating the empirical analysis eight times at 5-year intervals since 1960, Leamer and Thornberg are able to observe how this relationship has changed over time in ways that are at least in some cases consistent with what one would have expected from the model in response to, first, capital accumulation and, then, globalization. The findings are striking and they do, as intended, lend even greater credibility to the model. I can see nothing particularly wrong with what they do, and on the contrary I am impressed with the way they anticipated many of my concerns with additional regressions controlling for variables that they initially left out.

My comments, then, will be mostly requests for amplification and extension, as is customary for a discussant who does not actually have to do the work. I have five of these to mention, after which I will ask whether there may not be some other explanation for the patterns that they have found in the data.

This paper, like Leamer (1999), assumes fixed-coefficient technologies. That was fine for making the theoretical points in the earlier paper, but as the basis for an empirical analysis it raises the question of whether factor substitution could alter the story in ways that matter. I suspect the answer is no, but I'd like to see it addressed. I presume that factor substitution would cause what are now linear zero-profit constraints to become nonlinear. But in my own thinking, I have been unable to visualize how they would curve, and I wonder whether they could curve in such a way as to cross one another more than once. I presume that, if one had factor-intensity reversals in the more usual isoquant diagram, that would happen. For a given set of prices, it would probably not matter if they did cross more than once. An industry's zero-profit curve would be part of the enve-

Alan V. Deardorff is the John W. Sweetland Professor of International Economics and professor of economics and public policy at the University of Michigan.

lope for all industries only in one place, most likely. But as things change over time, where the curve hits the envelope might change and we could see the ordering of industries by capital intensity change. The remarkable charts in figure 2.7 suggest that this did not happen, but if one does allow for factor-intensity reversals as I've suggested, this becomes that much more surprising.

A related issue is that the theoretical model never allows for more than two goods, yet the empirical work, of course, includes many. I do not think that having multiple goods would change the story here at all, but it would somewhat change the emphasis. As told here, the story of a change in, say, relative prices seems to be mostly about how the zero-profit curves of the two industries shift and rotate, leading to shifts and, as they put it, twisting of the offer curve. But with many goods, it becomes clear that what matters most is not really the shape of the industry curves at all. In market equilibrium these must all be tangent to a single worker's indifference curve. Thus it is the indifference curves that ultimately constitute the offer curve, and that is where one should look to understand changes in its shape.

This makes it easier, I think, to understand the twisting of the offer curve that Leamer and Thornberg attribute to relative price changes. As they explain with figure 2.4, twisting is a rather mysterious phenomenon that includes changes in the curve's slope in opposite directions in different places. But what has really happened is that changes in relative prices have moved workers to a lower indifference curve, and the new offer curve reflects its shape entirely. With Leamer's assumed form for the utility function, which includes a maximum level of effort, lower indifference curves are squeezed down toward the corner formed by the horizontal axis and this maximum, and they do indeed become flatter along their bottom portions and steeper further up.

The one place where the data do not seem to conform to the model is in the backward-bending shape of this offer curve. If it really were an indifference curve, as it should be from the model, then it could not look like this, since presumably workers are unambiguously better off working fewer hours for more (total) pay. Leamer and Thornberg attribute the backward bend to the presence of unions, although as far as I can see, accounting for unions in their regressions does not remove this feature. And while I do understand the intuition that unions in some sectors might both raise wages and reduce hours, I am uncomfortable with the disconnection between this suggestion and the treatment of unions in Leamer's earlier paper. One of the nice features of that model was its treatment of collective bargaining, and I cannot see that it looked anything like this. I would prefer to see unions handled in a way that we know to be at least consistent with the model.

Another concern that I have is the employment of workers in shifts.

This issue is mentioned repeatedly in the paper, mainly to acknowledge its importance and the difficulty of addressing it. I agree with both, as well as with the suggestion that their findings are all that much more impressive given that they did not deal with it. That is, the true capital intensity of an industry is probably the ratio of capital to labor that needs to be employed simultaneously, not the ratio that may in fact be employed over a week. If a machine requires one worker to operate it, then the correct ratio is one machine per worker, even if shift operation permits it to run continuously over a week with three or four workers in staggered shifts. Thus the measured capital/labor ratios in these industries may not correctly reflect differences in these true capital/labor ratios if shift operations are feasible in some and not feasible in others. Leamer and Thornberg's response to this is to say, Yes, that's right, so isn't it impressive that we get the results that we do, even with such noisy data on capital/labor ratios. I agree.

But I also wonder if shifts could not also account for one of their findings that they find difficult to explain, namely the backward-bending offer curve. As Frank Stafford and I (Deardorff and Stafford 1976) argued years ago, as industries become more capital intensive, they first reconcile the conflicting desires of labor to get some sleep and of capital to work 24 hours a day by gradually lengthening the workday, exactly as Leamer and Thornberg find. But at some point the costs of this compromise become too great, and it becomes cheaper to add shifts and reduce hours, even though the less-popular shifts require greater pay. Is it not possible that Leamer and Thornberg's backward-bending offer curve just reflects that the most capital-intensive industries are doing exactly that—reducing hours but adding shifts? Shifts, then, together with the story that Frank and I told years ago about balancing the interests of labor and capital, may provide another alternative explanation for Leamer and Thornberg's findings that they have not addressed.

Which brings me to my final point. As I thought about their findings and wondered where they might have come from, I did not at first think of the shift explanation that I have just mentioned. Rather, as I looked at figure 2.7 and heard it described as showing backward-bending offer curves, I could not help but think I was seeing backward-bending labor-supply curves. The trouble with that, however, is that you do not expect to see all the points on a labor-supply curve at once. With only one wage paid, you will only observe one point, and if more than one wage were paid, workers would all take the highest. But if workers are not the same in all industries in terms of their productivities, but are the same in terms of their willingness to trade off labor and leisure, then one might observe exactly this pattern of low-wage workers working short hours, medium-wage workers working a bit more, and high-wage workers working a bit less.

How do we get the workers to be different? Leamer and Thornberg already allow for the possibility of differences in education, and the backward bend does not go away when they control for that. But suppose that workers differ in other ways that are not fully captured by education? Suppose that they are differently endowed with innate abilities, and that these abilities are complementary with physical capital. Then capital-intensive industries will attract these workers by paying them more, and they in turn will select their hours worked in accord with their preferences. This, it seems to me, would account for the backward-bending pattern of the data, but with a much different interpretation of what it represents. Most importantly, it would not then be the case that all those dots in a panel of figure 2.7 represent workers at the same level of utility, or that workers are indifferent between employment in transport or apparel. Instead, we would have some workers who are meaningfully better off than others, and changes in the economy such as globalization would have real, not just apparent, implications for true inequality.

I suppose that if these differences in innate ability were sufficiently correlated with education, then Leamer and Thornberg's inclusion of education in their later regressions would capture it. But if the correlation is less than perfect, would this do the trick? Leamer is the econometrician, not I, and I'm sure he can answer this. But even if the answer is yes, I suspect that there are many differences in innate ability that are not correlated with education, but that do matter for a worker's productivity in, say, fabricating metals versus stitching apparel.

So my bottom line here is that I love the model, and I am very impressed and intrigued with the empirical results of this paper. But I am not yet ready to believe that this is the main story that we should be telling about recent changes in the world economy. In particular, the notion that apparent increases in inequality are illusory—that the workers who are earning more are not really any better off, but just working harder—strikes me as both doubtful and dangerous.

References

Deardorff, Alan V., and Frank P. Stafford. 1976. Compensation of cooperating factors. *Econometrica* 44 (July): 671–84.
Leamer, Edward E. 1999. Effort, wages and the international division of labor. *Journal of Political Economy* 107 (6): 1127–63.

3

Offshore Assembly from the United States
Production Characteristics of the 9802 Program

Robert C. Feenstra, Gordon H. Hanson,
and Deborah L. Swenson

3.1 Introduction

Foreign outsourcing is a prominent feature of many recent formal models of international trade.[1] By outsourcing we mean the practice in which firms divide production into stages and then locate each stage in the country where it can be performed at least cost. Anecdotal evidence suggests that outsourcing is a key aspect of the ongoing process of globalization. An important question for public policy is whether outsourcing has contributed to the rise in inequality between the wages of skilled and unskilled workers in the United States.

Recent work by Feenstra and Hanson (1996a) suggests that outsourcing can raise the skilled-unskilled wage gap. They show that if skilled and unskilled labor are used in different intensities along a product's value chain, outsourcing from a host to a recipient country reduces the relative de-

Robert C. Feenstra is professor of economics at the University of California, Davis, and director of the International Trade and Investment Program at the National Bureau of Economic Research. Gordon H. Hanson is associate professor of economics and business administration at the University of Michigan and a faculty research fellow of the National Bureau of Economic Research. Deborah L. Swenson is assistant professor of economics at the University of California, Davis, and a faculty research fellow of the National Bureau of Economic Research.

The authors thank Shelagh Matthews Mackay of the Institute of Governmental Affairs, University of California, Davis, for locating and acquiring the data on the 9802 program. Zeeshan Ali, Patrick Carleton, Lance Tomikawa, and Shu-Yi Tsai provided dedicated work in scanning the data. Financial support from the National Science Foundation is gratefully acknowledged, as are comments from Jim Levinsohn.

1. The outsourcing phenomenon is referred to by a number of names; examples of such work include Antweiler and Trefler (1997), Arndt (1997, 1998a, 1998b), Feenstra and Hanson (1996a, 1996b), Hummels, Ishii, and Yi (1999), Jones and Keirzkowski (1997), Krugman (1995), and Leamer (1998).

mand for unskilled labor in both locations. Markusen and Venables (1995, 1996a, 1996b) focus on multinational firm activity and arrive at a similar conclusion. As long as multinational firms can choose their production location, they find that the presence of multinational activity implies a higher relative wage for skilled workers in the high-income country, and possibly in the low-income country as well. In a related vein, Krugman and Venables (1995) examine how agglomeration economies will affect cross-country wage patterns. They analyze a model with trade in intermediate goods subject to transport costs. At medium levels of transport costs, a core-periphery pattern emerges: Manufacturing agglomerates in core countries, while those in the periphery have little industry and low wages. At lower levels of transport costs, the agglomeration of manufacturing in the core disappears, leading to a fall in wage inequality across regions.[2]

Despite the theoretical interest, there are relatively few attempts to measure outsourcing empirically. Feenstra and Hanson (1996b) rely on estimates of imported manufactured inputs, as do Campa and Goldberg (1997) and Hummels, Ishii, and Yi (1999). These suffer from assuming that the import share for each input is the same across all manufacturing industries and also from excluding nonmanufactured inputs. Furthermore, these estimates do not provide any direct information on the production characteristics of the imported inputs. A common presumption of the theoretical work is that the activities being outsourced are more unskilled-labor intensive than those remaining in the industrial countries. This feature is essential to the derived result that outsourcing reduces the relative demand for unskilled labor. While this presumption is theoretically justified based on factor-price differences and common technology across countries, it should be subjected to empirical verification. In addition, the underlying causes of outsourcing—such as factor endowments, transport costs, or multinational activity—deserve further investigation.

In this paper, we study outsourcing by U.S. industry conducted through the offshore assembly program (OAP). The OAP program is the only data source, to our knowledge, that provides direct observations on foreign outsourcing. Formerly called the 806/807 provision of the U.S. tariff code and later renamed the 9802 provision of the Harmonized System code, the OAP program allows U.S. firms to export component parts and have them assembled overseas. When the finished product is imported back into the United States, duties are paid only on the foreign value added. While accounting for a relatively small fraction of total U.S. imports (8.5 percent in 1995), this program is still substantial in its effects on economic activity.

2. Matsuyama (1996) demonstrates a similar pattern of agglomeration and uneven incomes across countries. Gao (1999) has extended this type of model to allow for multinational firms and found that agglomeration breaks down more quickly (at higher levels of transport costs) due to these firms, leading to more-equal incomes across countries.

For example, virtually all of the *maquiladora* plants in Mexico are engaged in the assembly of parts under the 9802 program (Feenstra and Hanson 1997). The program leads to production in many other countries as well. Because duties are paid on foreign value added only, the administration of the program requires a separate accounting of the value of imports resulting from assembly abroad. In particular, a key distinction is made between dutiable OAP imports, which represent the value added associated with foreign production, and nondutiable OAP imports, which represent the value embodied in U.S.-made goods originally exported from the U.S. for further processing abroad. This administrative distinction allows us to estimate the production characteristics of the OAP activity.

In the next section, we provide background information on the 9802 program and summarize features of these imports for the period 1980–93. We focus on five industries: apparel, leather and footwear, machinery, electrical machinery, and transportation equipment. Together these industries account for 90–93 percent of all OAP imports and 94–95 percent of the dutiable value of OAP imports during the sample period. For apparel, leather and footwear, and electrical machinery nearly all OAP imports are from developing countries, while for transportation equipment most OAP imports come from industrial countries. OAP imports in machinery come from both sources. Overall, the share of dutiable OAP imports coming from developing countries has increased from 25 to 30 percent during 1981–93.

Our primary hypothesis is that the goods U.S. industries export abroad for further processing are more skilled-labor intensive than other goods U.S. industries produce. In section 3.3, we describe a revenue-function approach that we use to test this idea. For the five industries of study, we treat the U.S. content of OAP imports (i.e., goods exported for further processing) and all other shipments from the industry as separate outputs. Inputs include production and nonproduction labor, capital, energy, dutiable OAP imports (i.e., value added by foreign production), and remaining intermediate inputs. For several industries, the empirical evidence supports the idea that outsourcing makes U.S. industries more intensive in skilled labor. We also use the OAP import data to search for evidence of substitution between foreign labor and domestic production and nonproduction labor.

In section 3.5, we turn to the question of which factors account for the variation in the level of OAP imports across industries and over time. A higher level of dutiable OAP imports implies a higher level of foreign outsourcing in terms of value added by foreign producers. We focus on international differences in production costs as measured by the real exchange rate between the United States and the principal source countries for OAP imports. To control for variation in outsourcing patterns across industries, we construct a trade-weighted real exchange rate for each two-digit industry. We expect that an appreciation of the U.S. real exchange rate, which implies an increase in U.S. production costs relative to production costs in source countries, will be associated with higher levels of outsourcing as measured by dutiable OAP imports. Empirical results for the apparel and machinery industries are consistent with this hypothesis, while the evidence for the electrical machinery industry is mixed.

3.2 The Offshore Assembly Program

The U.S. OAP was created through a provision of the Tariff Act of 1930. The original intent of the program was to facilitate the manufacturing practices of U.S. steel firms, many of which maintained production plants in Canada and engaged in extensive cross-border shipments of intermediate inputs. Over time, the program was expanded to include other industries and all other countries (Hanson 1997). OAP imports have become an important part of U.S. trade. Between 1980 and 1990, the share of OAP imports in total U.S. imports rose from 4.7 percent to 12.2 percent and then fell somewhat to 8.5 percent in 1995 (USITC 1997).

There are two broad categories of goods that qualify for the U.S. OAP. Item 9802.00.60 of the Harmonized Tariff Schedule (HTS) of the United States (formerly item 806.30 of the Tariff Schedule of the United States, TSUSA) permits the duty-free import of metal products that are manufactured in the United States and sent abroad for further processing. Item 9802.00.80 of the HTS (formerly item 807.00 of the TSUSA) permits the duty-free entry of inputs that are manufactured in the United States and assembled abroad. To qualify for the 9802.00.80 exemption, the stated requirements are that domestic components may only be subject to assembly and assembly-related activities abroad. Since 1980, goods imported under item 9802.00.80 have accounted for over 98 percent of total OAP imports.

The data available to us consist of the value of OAP imports (i.e., imports under the 806/807 program and the 9802 program) by the disaggregate Tariff Schedule categories for 1980–88, and by Harmonized System categories for 1989–93. The latter years were available in electronic form, but the earlier years were available in hard copy, which were electronically scanned and then extensively checked for errors. This proved to be impossible for 1982 and 1988, due to the inadequate quality of the hard copy.[3] In all remaining years, both the U.S. (i.e., nondutiable) value and the foreign (i.e., dutiable) value of the OAP imports are provided. We aggregated

---

3. For 1982, the scanned data had too many errors to make correction feasible. For 1988, the hard copy was available only by month, making scanning and correction prohibitively expensive.

these data to the four-digit Standard Industrial Classification (SIC) system, so that it matches the production data available for U.S. industries.[4]

Data on the OAP imports for the five two-digit SIC industries studied here are given in table 3.1, for selected years. Shown there are the value of OAP imports in each two-digit industry relative to total shipments in that industry and relative to total OAP imports, separately for the developing (LDC) and industrial (OECD) countries. For apparel and leather and footwear, nearly all OAP imports are from developing countries, principally Mexico and the Caribbean basin countries. Electrical machinery, including electronic components such as semiconductors, also comes primarily from developing countries, principally those in Southeast Asia. In transportation equipment, most OAP imports come from industrial countries, especially Canada but also Japan and Germany, while a smaller (but increasing) share of imports comes from Mexico. Finally, in machinery the imports come from both sources. It is evident that the OAP imports are small relative to industry shipments in all cases, although they have grown substantially in apparel—from 1 to 6 percent of shipments—and also in footwear and leather—from 1 to 8.5 percent of shipments.

Additional summary statistics are provided in table 3.2, where we separate the OAP imports into those attributable to U.S.-made components and those attributable to foreign value added, the latter being subject to U.S. duties. The value of these imports are shown relative to total industry shipments. It is evident that the U.S. imports versus the dutiable share of OAP imports varies substantially across industries, where the U.S. share is highest in apparel (nearly twice the dutiable share) and lowest in transportation equipment (about one-tenth the dutiable share). A higher U.S. share suggests that a larger fraction of components parts for a given good are produced in the United States. In transportation equipment, the U.S. versus foreign dutiable share of OAP imports also varies substantially across source countries. For example, U.S.-made components account for over one-half of the value of automotive products and other transportation imported from Mexico; about one-quarter to one-third of the value imported from Canada; and less than 5 percent of the value imported from Japan, Korea, and Germany (USITC 1997, 3–7). Overall in the five industries we investigate, the share of dutiable OAP imports originating from developing countries has increased from 25 to 30 percent during 1981–93.

The cross-sectional variation in the U.S. shares of OAP imports (across four-digit industries within each two-digit group), as well as its time-series

---

4. U.S. imports by four-digit SIC categories are available from the National Bureau of Economic Research, at http://www.nber.org/data_index.html, as constructed by Robert Feenstra. The same programs used to construct the four-digit SIC import data from disaggregate sources were adapted to aggregate the OAP imports to that level.

Table 3.1   **OAP Imports by Two-Digit SIC Industry (percent)**

	Developing Countries (LDCs)		Industrial Countries (OECD)	
	Share of Industry Shipments	Share of OAP Shipments	Share of Industry Shipments	Share of OAP Shipments
	Apparel (SIC 23)			
1981	1.1	3.2		
1983	1.1	2.7		
1985	1.6	2.9		
1987	2.1	2.0	less than 0.1	
1989	3.2	4.3		
1991	4.8	9.6		
1993	6.4	9.6		
	Footwear and Leather (SIC 31)			
1981	1.0	0.5		
1983	1.0	0.3		
1985	1.9	0.4		
1987	2.8	0.4	less than 0.1	
1989	5.7	0.9		
1991	8.0	2.3		
1993	8.5	1.7		
	Machinery (SIC 35)			
1981	0.3	3.1	0.7	7.8
1983	0.6	4.5	0.5	4.2
1985	0.7	4.8	0.7	5.0
1987	1.0	3.2	1.1	3.4
1989	0.7	4.1	0.7	3.6
1991	0.6	4.6	0.7	5.5
1993	0.7	4.2	0.5	2.9
	Electrical Machinery (SIC 36)			
1981	3.7	30.2	0.3	2.8
1983	3.9	28.1	0.3	2.5
1985	2.4	14.9	0.4	2.7
1987	3.7	11.4	0.5	1.7
1989	2.4	12.1	0.4	1.9
1991	4.0	29.7	0.2	1.8
1993	3.9	22.1	0.2	1.4
	Transportation Equipment (SIC 37)			
1981	0.1	1.0	4.0	44.0
1983	0.3	3.2	4.7	47.6
1985	0.6	5.3	6.5	58.0
1987	1.6	7.3	14.1	66.4
1989	0.7	5.3	8.4	60.7
1991	0.6	5.7	2.9	29.5
1993	0.5	3.7	5.7	45.0

Table 3.2   **Summary Statistics**

	Average (%)	Annual Change
Apparel (SIC 23)		
U.S. share of OAP	1.8	0.27
Dutiable share of OAP	1.0	0.14
Production labor share	16.1	−0.21
Nonproduction labor share	6.2	−0.002
Footwear and Leather (SIC 31)		
U.S. share of OAP	1.1	0.17
Dutiable share of OAP	2.3	0.69
Production labor share	15.5	−0.28
Nonproduction labor share	6.2	0.02
Machinery (SIC 35)		
U.S. share of OAP	0.3	0.02
Dutiable share of OAP	1.0	0.03
Production labor share	12.2	−0.20
Nonproduction labor share	10.7	−0.12
Electrical Machinery (SIC 36)		
U.S. share of OAP	1.8	−0.03
Dutiable share of OAP	2.0	−0.01
Production labor share	11.4	−0.39
Nonproduction labor share	12.7	−0.13
Transportation Equipment (SIC 37)		
U.S. share of OAP	0.4	−0.003
Dutiable share of OAP	4.3	0.28
Production labor share	10.1	−0.30
Nonproduction labor share	5.2	−0.16

Notes: Averages are computed over the years 1980–93, excluding 1982 and 1988 (due to missing data in those years), and over the four-digit industries within each two-digit group. Changes are measured as average annual changes, using data for the odd-numbered years. Both averages and changes are weighted by the industry share of total manufacturing shipments.

Variable definitions are as follows:

U.S. share of OAP = 100 × (U.S. content of OAP imports)/(Value of industry shipments).

Dutiable share of OAP = 100 × (Foreign content of OAP imports)/(Value of industry shipments).

Production labor share = 100 × (Wage bill of production labor)/(Value of industry shipments).

Nonproduction labor share = 100 × (Wage bill of nonproduction labor)/(Value of industry shipments).

variation, will be a focus of our empirical investigation. The U.S. share of OAP imports in total industry shipments—as shown in table 3.2—will serve as one dependent variable. We interpret this share, quite reasonably, to be the fraction of shipments that are exported abroad for further processing. Also shown in table 3.2 are the wage bills of production and nonproduction labor, measured relative to total industry shipments. These data are taken from the NBER Manufacturing Database, with nonproduction labor used as a proxy for skilled labor and production labor used as a proxy for unskilled labor.[5] In all industries, there has been a marked decline in the share of production labor, by between two-tenths and four-tenths of a percentage point per year. In some industries, the share of nonproduction labor has also declined, but by a smaller amount. The shares of production and nonproduction labor in total industry shipments will be other dependent variables in our empirical analysis.

3.3   U.S. Revenue Function

We shall specify production in each industry in the United States as a multiple-input, multiple-output technology.[6] The outputs consist of the U.S. content of OAP imports measured relative to total industry shipments (as summarized in table 3.2), and all other shipments from the industry.[7] In some industries, we will distinguish the U.S. content of OAP imports from developing versus industrialized countries. The inputs are production and nonproduction labor, the dutiable (i.e., foreign) component of OAP imports, remaining intermediate inputs, capital, and energy.[8] In some industries, we will also distinguish the dutiable component of OAP imports coming from developing versus industrialized countries. The revenue function of the industry will be specified as depending on the prices p_i or p_j of the outputs, and the quantities x_k or x_ℓ of the inputs. The revenue function is specified as the translog form

$$(1) \qquad \ln R = \sum_i \alpha_i \ln p_i + \frac{1}{2} \sum_i \sum_j \gamma_{ij} \ln p_i \ln p_j + \sum_k \beta_k \ln x_k$$

$$+ \frac{1}{2} \sum_k \sum_\ell \delta_{ij} \ln x_k \ln x_\ell + \sum_i \sum_k \eta_{ij} \ln p_i \ln x_k,$$

where R denotes total industry revenue (assumed equal to costs), and the time subscript is omitted from all variables for brevity.

5. The NBER Manufacturing Database at the four-digit SIC level is available from the National Bureau of Economic Research, at http://www.nber.org/data_index.html.

6. Rather than specifying only U.S. production, it would be desirable to jointly model the domestic and offshore production. This would include, for example, the production and nonproduction labor used in the U.S. and abroad. Unfortunately, this integrated approach was not possible due to data limitations. In particular, the production and nonproduction labor used in the Mexican *maquiladoras* are not reported on an industry basis, but are available only for total manufacturing. This means that the foreign content of OAP imports, which we are using as an input into the U.S. revenue function, is essentially serving as a proxy for the foreign labor and capital inputs.

7. That is, "all other shipments" is measured as (Total shipments − U.S. content of OAP imports)/(Total shipments).

8. The quantity of dutiable OAP imports is constructed by taking the value of dutiable OAP imports for each four-digit SIC industry and deflating it by the price index for total industry shipments.

The shares of each of the outputs are obtained by differentiating equation (1) with respect to the log of output prices, obtaining

$$(2) \qquad s_i = \alpha_i + \sum_j \gamma_{ij} \ln p_j + \sum_k \eta_{ik} \ln x_k.$$

Similarly, if the inputs x_k are chosen optimally given their factor prices w_k then the share of industry costs devoted to each input are obtained by differentiating equation (1) with respect to the log of input quantities:

$$(3) \qquad s_k = \beta_k + \sum_\ell \delta_{k\ell} \ln x_\ell + \sum_i \eta_{ik} \ln p_i.$$

In practice, we have no information at all on the price of the U.S. content of OAP imports versus the price of all other industry shipments. So in the estimation we will ignore the output prices that appear in equations (2) and (3), and focus on the input quantities.

The coefficients η_{ik} in equation (2) measure the response of each output share to changes in the input quantities and will be referred to as *output elasticities*. These are similar to Rybzcynski derivatives for an entire economy, except that we are dealing with individual industries. Rybzcynski derivatives or output elasticities are normally defined as the impact of a change in inputs on the level of output, rather than its share. To make this conversion, write the quantity of each output as $\ln y_i = \ln(s_i R/p_i)$. Differentiating this with respect to an input quantity $\ln x_k$, using equations (1) and (2), we obtain the output elasticity:

$$(4) \qquad \frac{\partial \ln y_i}{\partial \ln x_k} = \frac{\eta_{ik}}{s_i} + s_k.$$

Thus, the coefficient η_{ik} together with the input and output shares can be used to calculate the output elasticity. As is conventional, we will define factor k to be used intensively in output i if and only if equation (4) is positive. In this way, the output elasticities provide us with indirect evidence on the factor intensities used in production.[9]

Our hypothesis is that the U.S.-content OAP imports should be more skilled-labor intensive than the rest of U.S. production. The reason for this is that the OAP program allows the less-skill-intensive activities to be shifted overseas, so that the production remaining in the United States becomes more skill intensive as a result. In the particular industry structure we model, industries produce two types of goods, final goods and goods to be exported abroad for further processing. For the latter type,

9. Note that if the U.S. content of OAP imports versus other industry shipments are likely to be produced in the same plants, it is impossible to directly measure the factor intensities of these two outputs. In other words, we are dealing with a situation of joint production, so that even with two outputs, there is no a priori presumption about the signs of the output elasticities.

non-skill-intensive production activities have been separated off and out-sourced abroad; for the former type, all production activities are still conducted in the United States. Thus, an increase in the share of dutiable OAP imports in industry shipments implies a shift toward more-skill-intensive production activities.

Turning to the factor-share equation (3), the coefficient $\delta_{k\ell}$ measures the responsiveness of each factor share to changes in the quantity of other inputs. Of particular interest is the response of production and nonproduction labor to changes in the amount of outsourcing, as measured by the quantity of dutiable OAP imports $\ln x_m$. As this input increases, our hypothesis is that the U.S. production would shift toward more skilled, or nonproduction, labor. Thus, letting $\ln x_k = \ln(s_k R/w_k)$ and $\ln x_\ell = \ln(s_\ell R/w_\ell)$ denote the log quantities of production and nonproduction labor, respectively, we are interested in the sign of

$$(5) \qquad \frac{\partial \ln(x_k/x_\ell)}{\partial \ln x_m} = \frac{\delta_{km}}{s_k} - \frac{\delta_{\ell m}}{s_\ell}.$$

The null hypothesis that equation (5) equals 0 is a test for the weak separability of production and nonproduction labor from dutiable OAP imports in the U.S. revenue function.

We shall estimate equations (2) and (3) while pooling across all four-digit industries within each two-digit group, and pooling across years. Since the output shares sum to unity, we can drop one of these share equations, and we omit the equation for the remaining value of U.S. shipments (after the U.S. content of OAP imports has been deducted). For the inputs, we estimate only the factor shares for production and nonproduction labor, where the latter is used as a proxy for skilled labor. Estimation is performed over the years 1980–93 (omitting 1982 and 1988 due to missing data), with all variables entered in levels, and not including any fixed effects for the individual four-digit industries (or for the various years). We have also experimented with using first differences of the data, thereby implicitly including industry fixed effects. Because of the missing observations (in 1982 and 1988), these differences were taken across odd-numbered years. The estimation in first differences changes a number of coefficient estimates, and also leads to substantially higher standard errors, indicating that much of the variation in the data is cross-sectional. For this reason, we focus on the estimates without fixed effects in the next section, but report the results from estimation in first differences in the appendix. In order to control for some of the most important heterogeneity across industries, we also report in the appendix estimates for the largest three-digit industries within each two-digit group.

Table 3.3   **U.S. Revenue Functions**

Independent Variables (log)	Dependent Variables (share of industry shipments)		
	U.S. Content of OAP Imports	Production Labor Share	Nonproduction Labor Share
Apparel (SIC 23), N = 385			
Production labor	−4.87 (0.52)	6.52 (0.40)	−2.14 (0.17)
Nonproduction labor	2.05 (0.58)	−0.47 (0.45)	4.98 (0.19)
Dutiable OAP imports	1.04 (0.07)	−0.52 (0.05)	−0.02 (0.02)
Other intermediate inputs	−1.70 (0.53)	−8.78 (0.41)	−2.84 (0.17)
Capital	3.22 (0.49)	1.62 (0.37)	−0.46 (0.16)
Energy	−0.20 (0.40)	1.54 (0.31)	0.27 (0.13)
R^2	0.45	0.68	0.72
Footwear and Leather (SIC 31), N = 129			
Production labor	−0.50 (0.74)	7.43 (0.56)	−3.88 (0.31)
Nonproduction labor	−1.78 (0.82)	−2.50 (0.62)	5.65 (0.35)
Dutiable OAP imports	0.35 (0.09)	−0.20 (0.07)	0.01 (0.04)
Other intermediate inputs	0.35 (0.42)	−2.71 (0.32)	−0.73 (0.18)
Capital	−0.87 (0.80)	−0.55 (0.61)	−0.23 (0.34)
Energy	0.88 (0.71)	−1.33 (0.54)	−1.13 (0.30)
R^2	0.29	0.78	0.81

Note: Standard errors are in parentheses. Estimation is in levels for 1980–93, excluding 1982 and 1988. All regressions are weighted by the industry share of total manufacturing shipments.

3.4   Estimation Results

In table 3.3, we report the results for the apparel and footwear industries, for which OAP imports come almost entirely from developing countries. The results most strongly supportive of our hypotheses are obtained for the apparel industry. In table 3.3, we find a negative impact of production labor on the U.S. content of OAP imports, measured as the share of total shipments, and a positive impact of nonproduction labor. These coefficient estimates are converted into output elasticities using equation (4), and the results are shown in table 3.5, below.[10] We see that an increase in production (nonproduction) labor has a negative (positive) impact on the U.S. content of OAP imports, measured as a level, and these results are highly significant. Thus, by our definition of factor intensities, we conclude that the U.S. content of OAP imports for apparel is intensive in the use of nonproduction (skilled) labor. Also in table 3.3, an increase in the dutiable

10. The output elasticities in table 3.5 can be computed directly from the coefficient estimates in tables 3.3 and 3.4, together with the means of the shares in table 3.2. Because the shares were expressed as percentages, they should first be converted into fractions by dividing by 100. This means that the coefficient estimates in tables 3.3 and 3.4 should also be divided by 100, before making the calculation in equation (4).

content of OAP imports decreases the share of production labor in total costs and has no impact on the share of nonproduction labor. Making the calculation in equation (5), it is clear that greater dutiable OAP imports for apparel decreases the relative demand for production labor, as reported in table 3.5.

Less interesting results are obtained for footwear and leather. In that case, both production and nonproduction labor have a negative impact on the U.S. content of OAP imports in table 3.3, and a negative output elasticity in table 3.5 (the elasticity for nonproduction labor is significant). In addition, an increase in the dutiable portion of OAP imports leads to a relative shift away from production labor in table 3.3, although this estimate is not significant. These disappointing results may be due to the fact that a very large portion of OAP imports in footwear enters into a single four-digit industry—footwear, except rubber, not elsewhere classified (SIC 3149). The use of this "not elsewhere classified" category suggests that the imports are not being attributed to the industry segment responsible for their production, so that we should not expect to obtain reliable production characteristics.

In table 3.4, we report the estimates for machinery, electrical machinery, and transportation equipment. For these industries we separate the OAP imports from developing (LDC) and industrial (OECD) countries. The strongest results are obtained for machinery, which has roughly equal imports from both sources. From table 3.5, we find that the U.S. content of OAP imports—from either LDC or OECD countries—has a negative output elasticity for production labor and a positive elasticity for nonproduction labor. Thus, the production of U.S. components is intensive in nonproduction labor. Also from table 3.5, an increase in the dutiable OAP imports from LDCs has a weakly negative effect on the relative demand for production labor, while imports from OECD countries has a weakly positive effect on relative demand for production labor, although neither of these elasticities is significant.

Turning to electrical machinery in table 3.5, about 90 percent of these imports come from developing countries, particularly Southeast Asia. Unfortunately, neither of the output elasticities reported in table 3.5 for the LDCs are significant, so we are not able to measure this production characteristic.[11] Just one of the output elasticities for the OECD countries is significant, although it has a surprising positive sign. The only result for this industry that is supportive of our hypotheses is that an increase in the dutiable content of OAP imports from LDCs leads to a negative and significant shift away from production labor.

---

11. Stronger results are obtained for electronic components (SIC 367), in appendix table 3A.4, where the U.S. content of OAP imports from LDCs leads to a positive and significant shift toward nonproduction labor, indicating that the U.S. activities use nonproduction labor intensively.

Table 3.4   U.S. Revenue Functions

Independent Variables (log)	Dependent Variables (share of industry shipments)			
	U.S. Content OAP Imports from LDCs	U.S. Content OAP Imports from OECD	Production Labor Share	Nonproduction Labor Share
Machinery (SIC 35), N = 452				
Production labor	-0.11 (0.06)	-0.19 (0.05)	8.94 (0.35)	-2.85 (0.16)
Nonproduction labor	0.15 (0.05)	0.17 (0.04)	-3.32 (0.26)	7.38 (0.12)
Dutiable OAP imports from LDCs	0.07 (0.01)	0.014 (0.006)	-0.10 (0.04)	-0.04 (0.02)
Dutiable OAP imports from OECD	0.04 (0.01)	0.11 (0.01)	0.18 (0.07)	0.01 (0.03)
Other intermediate inputs	-0.27 (0.05)	-0.31 (0.53)	-7.33 (0.29)	-4.72 (0.13)
Capital	0.03 (0.08)	0.10 (0.06)	3.80 (0.46)	-0.26 (0.21)
Energy	-0.04 (0.11)	0.04 (0.09)	-1.20 (0.65)	0.45 (0.29)
R^2	0.33	0.40	0.90	0.91
Electrical Machinery (SIC 36), N = 450				
Production labor	0.24 (0.40)	-0.05 (0.07)	8.38 (0.29)	-3.30 (0.24)
Nonproduction labor	-0.47 (0.27)	-0.04 (0.05)	-2.14 (0.19)	8.24 (0.16)
Dutiable OAP imports from LDCs	0.78 (0.06)	0.01 (0.01)	-0.33 (0.05)	-0.10 (0.04)
Dutiable OAP imports from OECD	0.10 (0.08)	0.09 (0.01)	-0.04 (0.06)	-0.06 (0.05)
Other intermediate inputs	-3.32 (0.27)	-0.22 (0.05)	-4.63 (0.20)	-3.31 (0.17)
Capital	2.06 (0.33)	-0.05 (0.06)	-0.45 (0.24)	-0.75 (0.21)
Energy	0.06 (0.32)	0.28 (0.06)	-0.19 (0.23)	0.23 (0.20)
R^2	0.52	0.19	0.77	0.95

(*continued*)

Table 3.4 (continued)

Independent Variables (log)	Dependent Variables (share of industry shipments)			
	U.S. Content OAP Imports from LDCs	U.S. Content OAP Imports from OECD	Production Labor Share	Nonproduction Labor Share
	Transportation Equipment (SIC 37), N = 135			
Production labor	0.47 (0.12)	−0.42 (0.20)	7.84 (0.34)	−5.49 (0.51)
Nonproduction labor	−0.04 (0.07)	0.24 (0.10)	−0.40 (0.18)	6.49 (0.27)
Dutiable OAP imports from LDCs	0.05 (0.01)	0.01 (0.02)	0.04 (0.03)	−0.13 (0.05)
Dutiable OAP imports from OECD	−0.01 (0.02)	0.15 (0.03)	−0.06 (0.05)	0.36 (0.07)
Other intermediate inputs	−0.22 (0.06)	−0.31 (0.09)	−6.16 (0.16)	−2.51 (0.24)
Capital	0.03 (0.08)	0.17 (0.12)	0.08 (0.20)	0.18 (0.31)
Energy	0.06 (0.11)	−0.01 (0.17)	0.05 (0.30)	0.77 (0.43)
R^2	0.41	0.30	0.97	0.96

Note: Standard errors are in parentheses. Estimation is in levels for 1980–93, excluding 1982 and 1988. All regressions are weighted by the industry share of total manufacturing shipments.

Table 3.5   **Production Characteristics**

	Apparel (SIC 23)	Footwear and Leather (SIC 31)
Impact of production labor on the U.S. content of OAP imports	−2.53 (0.29)	−0.32 (0.69)
Impact of nonproduction labor on the U.S. content of OAP imports	1.19 (0.32)	−1.61 (0.77)
Impact of dutiable OAP imports on the relative demand for production labor	−0.030 (0.007)	−0.015 (0.011)

	Machinery (SIC 35)	Electrical Machinery (SIC 36)	Transportation Equipment (SIC 37)
Impact of production labor on the U.S. content of OAP imports from LDCs	−0.19 (0.18)	0.25 (0.21)	1.36 (0.33)
Impact of nonproduction labor on the U.S. content of OAP imports from LDCs	0.53 (0.13)	−0.13 (0.14)	−0.05 (0.17)
Impact of production labor on the U.S. content of OAP imports from OECD	−0.42 (0.14)	0.087 (0.036)	−1.01 (0.52)
Impact of nonproduction labor on the U.S. content of OAP imports from OECD	0.61 (0.10)	0.11 (0.024)	0.70 (0.28)
Impact of dutiable OAP imports from LDCs on the relative demand for production labor	−0.004 (0.005)	−0.021 (0.007)	0.029 (0.013)
Impact of dutiable OAP imports from OECD on the relative demand for production labor	0.014 (0.009)	0.001 (0.009)	−0.074 (0.018)

Note: Standard errors are in parentheses.

Finally, in transportation equipment, the bulk of OAP imports come from industrial countries, especially Canada, with a small but growing portion coming from Mexico. In table 3.5 we find that the U.S. content of OAP imports from OECD countries has a negative output elasticity for production labor and a positive elasticity for nonproduction labor. Thus, production of the U.S. components is intensive in nonproduction labor. In addition, an increase in dutiable OAP imports from OECD countries leads to a relative decline in the demand for production labor in the U.S. These results are all consistent with our hypotheses. But opposite results are obtained for the U.S. content of OAP imports from LDCs. In particular, there is a positive impact of production labor on the U.S. content of OAP imports from LDCs, suggesting that these U.S. components are intensive in production rather than nonproduction labor. This result is statistically significant, but its economic meaning is unclear.

As noted in the section 3.3, the U.S. versus dutiable share of OAP imports varies substantially across source countries. The U.S.-made components account for over one-half of the value of automotive products and other transportation imported from Mexico, about one-quarter to one-third of the value imported from Canada, and less than 5 percent of the value imported from Japan, Korea, and Germany (USITC 1997, 3–7). This variation may help explain our results. Because the components sent to Mexico also require substantial U.S. manufacturing, it is quite possible that these components use more production labor in the U.S. than do other components that are sent to Canada or Japan. In this case, the U.S. content of OAP imports from LDCs could be intensive in production labor as compared to the U.S. content of OAP imports from OECD countries. Essentially, we are dealing with a "higher dimensional" case of more than two inputs, outputs, and countries, so it is perhaps not surprising to find a complex pattern of implied factor intensities.

In summary, of the five industries we have analyzed, we obtain results quite supportive of our hypotheses in apparel and machinery. For footwear and leather and for electrical machinery, the estimates have higher standard errors so that the production characteristics are not reliably measured. In transportation equipment, the results for OAP imports from industrial countries (which account for 90 percent of the imports) correspond to our hypotheses, but this is not the case for OAP imports from developing countries, for reasons we have suggested.

3.5   U.S. OAP Imports

Our results so far suggest that for a number of industries an increase in outsourcing, as measured by OAP imports, implies an increase in the skill intensity of production. The location to which products are outsourced, developing versus industrialized countries, also appears to influence the relative demand for production and nonproduction labor. To understand how outsourcing contributes to changes in the structure of labor demand, we must identify the forces that determine the extent of outsourcing within an industry. In the remainder of the paper, we consider the factors that contribute to outsourcing. We examine the extent to which the variation in dutiable OAP imports in an industry over time is associated with changes in relative cost differences between the United States and countries that are a source of OAP imports.

Trade theory attributes outsourcing to cross-country differences in relative factor endowments (Feenstra and Hanson 1996a). The existence of international factor-price differences, which result from international factor-supply differences, gives firms an incentive to spread production activities across different countries. Since we lack reliable annual data on factor endowments or factor prices for the set of countries that supply OAP imports to the United States, we use the real exchange rate to capture international differences in production costs. When the real exchange rate appreciates, the relative cost of foreign inputs declines, which we expect will

Table 3.6   **Summary Statistics for OAP Import Regressions**

	Dutiable OAP Imports	Real Exchange Rate	Real Output	Capital Intensity
Apparel (SIC 23)	2.14	1.94	7.93	−1.69
	(3.17)	(0.16)	(0.76)	(0.28)
Footwear and leather	6.84	2.68	7.01	−1.42
(SIC 31)	(3.27)	(1.14)	(0.76)	(0.25)
Machinery (SIC 35)				
OECD	1.19	1.38		
	(2.58)	(0.14)	9.17	−0.69
Non-OECD	0.89	1.55	(1.19)	(0.37)
	(1.83)	(0.16)		
Electrical machinery (SIC 36)				
OECD	0.59	1.62		
	(0.77)	(0.22)	9.29	−0.90
Non-OECD	4.52	1.58	(1.24)	(0.43)
	(6.58)	(0.22)		
Transport equipment (SIC 37)				
OECD	5.16	2.90		
	(6.89)	(0.17)	10.79	−1.21
Non-OECD	0.78	2.25	(1.13)	(0.43)
	(1.48)	(0.13)		

Notes: Averages are over the years 1980–93, excluding 1982 and 1988, and over the four-digit industries within each two-digit sector. They are weighted by the industry share of total manufacturing shipments. Standard errors are in parentheses.

Variable definitions are as follows:

Dutiable OAP imports = $100 \times$ (Dutiable OAP imports)/(Non-energy material purchases).

Real exchange rate = log(Average real exchange rate), where the real exchange rate is defined as U.S. CPI/(Country j CPI $\times$ Country j nominal exchange rate), and we use country average share of dutiable OAP imports for 1980–93 as weights.

Real output = log(Industry shipments/Industry output price index).

Capital intensity = log(Industry real shipments/Industry real capital stock).

lead to an increase the level of foreign inputs purchased by U.S. firms (as measured by the dutiable value of OAP imports).

Changes in the extent of outsourcing represent an increase in the demand for foreign-produced intermediate inputs relative to the demand for domestically produced intermediate inputs. To capture this aspect of outsourcing, the dependent variable we use is dutiable OAP imports as a share of nonenergy material purchases.[12] This variable thus captures U.S. industry demand for value added abroad. Table 3.6 reports sample means for the variables used in the analysis. Over the sample period, the mean value of dutiable OAP imports as a percentage of material purchases is 2.1 in

12. We compute nonenergy domestic inputs as (Material cost − Energy). These data are available at the four-digit industry level in the NBER Database.

apparel and 6.8 in footwear. In the remaining sectors, a sizable fraction of OAP imports originate from both developing and developed countries. In machinery, the percentages are 1.2 from the OECD and an additional 0.9 from developing countries. Transportation equipment is similar in that it draws a greater portion of imports from developed countries than from developing countries, with the percentages 5.2 and 0.8, respectively.[13] In contrast, electrical machinery receives 0.6 percent from OECD sources and a much larger 5.2 percent from developing countries. The outsourcing share rises over time in apparel and in footwear and leather, fluctuates widely in transportation equipment, and is relatively stable over time in machinery and in electrical machinery.

There is considerable variation across industries in the countries that supply OAP imports to the United States. In apparel and footwear, for instance, Mexico is a major source of OAP imports, but in transportation equipment the country's role is still minor. To control for such differences in outsourcing patterns, we create trade-weighted real exchange rates for each two-digit SIC industry. For each year, we use the IMF International Financial Statistics to compute the real exchange rate for each country responsible for OAP imports to the United States.[14] We then calculate an average real exchange rate for each of the five two-digit industries, using each country's share of total industry dutiable OAP imports as weights. We calculate the weights by taking each country's average share of dutiable OAP imports in an industry over the sample period. We choose average shares, rather than shares by year, since we want to avoid bias that would be introduced by changes in valuation. In our construction, an increase in the real exchange rate variable represents a dollar appreciation.

The trade-weighted exchange rates replicate the familiar pattern of U.S. exchange rate movements. Figure 3.1 shows the real exchange rate series for each industry. The real value of the dollar peaked in the mid-1980s, declined sharply for a few years, and then recovered somewhat in the early 1990s. While our constructed industry-specific real exchange rates follow a broadly similar pattern, there are notable cross-industry differences in the timing of exchange rate innovations. The real exchange rate peaks for autos in 1984, while it peaks for machinery in 1986 and for apparel in 1989. Cross-industry variation in outsourcing patterns thus creates cross-industry differences in exposure to movements in international relative prices.

13. The reported means are weighted by industry shares of total manufacturing shipments. Transportation equipment has six outsourcing observations that are large outliers. If they are included, the mean of the outsourcing variable is 9.1. These observations have been dropped from the sample. While their inclusion does not affect the qualitative outcome of the outsourcing regressions in table 3.8, their presence increases the size of the estimated regression coefficients markedly.

14. We measure the real exchange between the United States and country j as U.S. CPI/ (country j CPI $\times$ country j nominal exchange rate).

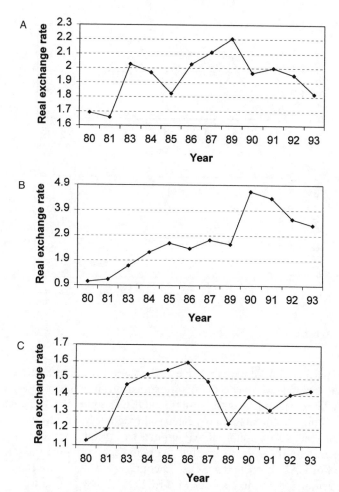

Fig. 3.1   Real exchange rate series, by industry: (*A*) **Apparel, SIC 23;** (*B*)
Footwear, SIC 31; (*C*) **Machinery, SIC 35;** (*D*) **Electrical machinery, SIC 36;**
(*E*) **Transport equipment, SIC 37**

The machinery, electrical machinery, and transportation equipment sectors are noticeably different from apparel and footwear in that they have nontrivial dutiable OAP imports from both the industrialized OECD and developing countries.[15] U.S. offshore-assembly activities in Europe or Japan may differ substantially from those in Mexico or Indonesia. In the transportation sector, for instance, U.S. and OECD labor tends to perform high-skill tasks, such as the production of auto parts, while LDC labor

15. South Korea and Mexico joined the OECD during the sample period. We classify them with the developing countries in our analysis.

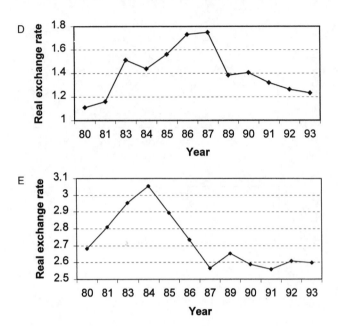

Fig. 3.1   (cont.)

tends to perform low-skill tasks, such as the assembly of automotive accessories. As a result, we may see different substitution patterns toward dutiable OAP imports in LDCs than we do in OECD countries. To control for this possibility, in the machinery, electrical machinery, and transportation equipment sectors we analyze OAP imports from LDCs and OECD countries separately. In order to do this, we refine the exchange rate variable further. For OAP imports from OECD countries, we measure the real exchange rate using country shares of OECD OAP imports as weights; for OAP imports from LDCs, we calculate the real exchange rate in an analogous manner.

The trade-weighted real exchange rates we construct vary across time, but not across four-digit industries within a two-digit sector. To control for industry-specific factors that affect outsourcing, we include real output, measured as shipments deflated by the industry output price index, and the capital/output ratio, measured as the ratio of the real capital stock to real shipments, as additional explanatory variables. Both variables are based on the NBER Database for U.S. manufacturing industries. The capital intensity of production may condition the degree of substitutability between domestic and foreign-produced inputs or may capture the ease with which production may be moved offshore. Real output controls for the overall level of industry demand, which may influence the availability of domestically produced intermediate inputs. As with the exchange rate, we take the log values of these variables.

Table 3.7   **Regression Results for Dutiable OAP Imports**

Independent Variables (log)	Dependent Variable: Dutiable OAP Imports (share of nonenergy material purchases)
Apparel (SIC 23), N = 386	
Real exchange rate	0.073 (0.013)
Capital intensity	0.004 (0.006)
Real output	−0.005 (0.002)
Constant	−0.089 (0.031)
R^2	0.082
Footwear and Leather (SIC 31), N = 121	
Real exchange rate	−0.009 (0.108)
Capital intensity	0.616 (0.106)
Real output	−0.102 (0.034)
Constant	1.692 (0.498)
R^2	0.259

Notes: The sample is all four-digit industries within each two-digit sector for the years 1980–93, excluding 1982 and 1988. Regressions are weighted by the industry share of total manufacturing shipments. Standard errors are in parentheses. See table 3.6 for variable definitions.

We estimate dutiable OAP imports separately for each of the five two-digit SIC industries during the years 1980–93. The results for the apparel and footwear industries are presented in table 3.7. For apparel, there is a positive and statistically significant correlation between dutiable OAP imports and the real exchange rate, which is consistent with the hypothesis that firms increase foreign outsourcing when U.S. production costs rise relative to foreign production costs. Dutiable OAP imports are negatively correlated with real output and have a positive, but statistically insignificant, correlation with the capital/output ratio. Thus, it appears that smaller industries or industries experiencing lower levels of demand are more likely to source production activities to offshore sites.

Similar to the estimation results for the input and output shares presented in section 3.4, the results for the footwear industry are disappointing. There is essentially a zero correlation between dutiable OAP imports and the real exchange rate. Again, we suspect that this may be attributable to the concentration of OAP footwear imports in a single four-digit industry (SIC 3149—footwear, except rubber, not elsewhere classified), which may indicate classification errors in the data for the footwear industry as a whole.

As with the production analysis, we consider dutiable OAP imports from developing (LDC) and developed (OECD) countries separately in the machinery, electrical machinery, and transportation equipment industries. The results for these industry segments are presented in table 3.8. In both machinery regressions, the coefficient on the real exchange rate is positive, which implies that firms in the United States increase their use of

Table 3.8   **Regression Results for Dutiable OAP Imports**

Independent Variables (log)	Dependent Variables (shares of nonenergy material purchases)	
	Dutiable OAP Imports from OECD	Dutiable OAP Imports from LDCs
Machinery (SIC 35), N = 518, 455		
Real exchange rate	.0082 (.0077)	.0126 (.0053)
Capital intensity	.0041 (.0032)	−.0028 (.0025)
Real output	−.0028 (.0010)	.0023 (.0008)
Constant	.0297 (.0135)	−.0344 (.0103)
R^2	.029	.046
Electrical Machinery (SIC 36), N = 463, 453		
Real exchange rate	.0041 (.0016)	−.0301 (.0129)
Capital intensity	.0020 (.0011)	.0831 (.0085)
Real output	−.0008 (.0003)	.0096 (.0023)
Constant	.0084 (.0038)	.0780 (.0301)
R^2	.041	.19
Transportation Equipment (SIC 37), N = 172, 136		
Real exchange rate	−.0077 (.0311)	−.0101 (.0056)
Capital intensity	−.0514 (.0130)	.0013 (.0017)
Real output	.0079 (.0046)	.0005 (.0006)
Constant	−.0737 (.1036)	.0259 (.0139)
R^2	.15	.025

Notes: The sample is all four-digit industries within each two-digit sector for the years 1980–93, excluding 1982 and 1988. Regressions are weighted by the industry share of total manufacturing shipments. Standard errors are in parentheses. See table 3.6 for variable definitions.

dutiable OAP imports when a stronger dollar reduces the relative cost of overseas activities. In electrical machinery, the exchange rate results are mixed; we find the expected positive correlation for imports from industrial countries, while the relationship for developing countries is negative.

In contrast, the exchange rate effects for transportation equipment are negative, although the results for OAP imports from industrialized countries are not statistically different from 0. This evidence contrasts with Swenson's (1997) finding that U.S. and Japanese auto producers located in U.S. foreign trade zones purchase more foreign inputs when their relative price is reduced by dollar appreciation. Our data do not exclude the possibility that outsourcing in the transportation sector responds to changes in relative costs. However, it is clear that the OAP component of outsourcing in this industry segment does not correspond with our predictions.

There is no common pattern of correlation between industry factors and outsourcing in the machinery, electrical machinery, and transportation equipment sectors. However, it still appears that outsourcing is generally more prevalent in the capital-intensive sectors; the coefficient for capital intensity is positive in four of the six equations. The relationship between real shipments and outsourcing is also mixed, confirming that outsourcing propensities in different industries are differentially affected by industry characteristics.

Our reported regression specification relates OAP outsourcing to current values of trade-weighted exchange rates. A maintained assumption of this specification is that firms do not face prohibitive switching costs, and that firms can quickly identify and use cheaper sources of supply. If industries are slow to respond to exchange rate changes, it is preferable to use lagged values of the exchange rate variables. When we replace the current exchange rate measure with its value in the previous period, almost all the signs on the exchange rate coefficients remain the same, although the coefficient magnitudes are generally smaller. In the new specification, the coefficients on real output and capital intensity were almost identical to our previous results. However, the overall fit of these regressions is less good than our reported results.

As a second check on our exchange rate specification, we also worked with a regression specification that includes both current and lagged exchange rate variables. With the exception of OAP imports of transportation equipment from developing countries, a small OAP sector, the new specification did not improve the explanatory power of our regressions. The sign of the current exchange rate coefficients remained the same as our previously reported results, and there was no systematic pattern on the lagged exchange rate coefficients, although almost all lagged exchange rate coefficients were indistinguishable from 0.

To test the robustness of our regression specification, in unreported results we examined how the estimated effects change if we add dummy variables for each four-digit SIC industry. For the apparel industry, there remains a strong positive correlation between dutiable OAP imports and the real exchange rate; the coefficient value is very similar to that in table 3.7. There is again a negative correlation between dutiable OAP imports and real output. One change in the results is that with industry dummy variables there is a strong negative correlation between OAP imports and the capital/output ratio. For the footwear industry, the inclusion of four-digit industry dummy variables has very little impact on the results. The exchange rate results for machinery and electrical machinery are also little changed by the alternative specification, although the inclusion of the four-digit industry dummies causes the puzzling negative exchange rate coefficient for OAP imports of electrical machinery from LDCs to shrink to insignificance. The correlation between outsourcing and both industry factors is also reversed in this segment when the four-digit industry controls are added. The remaining results for transportation equipment are little changed by the inclusion of industry controls, although here, too, the puzzling negative exchange rate coefficient for imports from developing countries shrinks further in significance.

Table 3.9   OAP Imports and Changes in Exchange Rates

	Dutiable OAP Imports	Maximum Dutiable OAP Imports	Change in OAP Imports (from 10% dollar appreciation)
Apparel (SIC 23)	2.14	40.68	0.70
Footwear and leather (SIC 31)	6.84	333.67	NA
Machinery (SIC 35)			
OECD	1.19	39.2	0.08
Non-OECD	0.89	18.1	0.12
Electrical machinery (SIC 36)			
OECD	0.59	16.2	0.04
Non-OECD	4.52	58.9	−0.29
Transportation equipment (SIC 37)			
OECD	5.16	1.08	NA
Non-OECD	0.78	13.7	−0.10

Note: NA, not applicable.
Variable definitions are as follows:
Dutiable OAP imports = 100 × (Dutiable OAP imports)/(Non-energy material purchases).
Maximum dutiable OAP imports = Maximum value of share in two-digit industry for sample period.
Change in OAP imports = 100(Real exchange rate coefficient × log(1.1)).

While there is a positive and statistically significant relationship between outsourcing and the real exchange rate in several industries, we still need to determine whether these effects are economically significant. As a policy experiment, we examine how dutiable OAP imports would change if the U.S. dollar were to appreciate by 10 percent. We calculate the implied effects and display the results in table 3.9. Given that the coefficient for the real exchange rate is statistically insignificant for footwear (SIC 31) and transportation equipment (SIC 37) imports from the OECD, we exclude these segments from the exercise.

Our results show that the predicted change in OAP imports, relative to nonenergy domestic inputs, is small in all industries. For example, a 10 percent appreciation of the dollar is predicted to raise OAP imports of machinery from the industrial OECD by a mere 0.08 percent. Nonetheless, this change is equivalent to a 6.72 percent change in OAP outsourcing if one compares the change to the average level of OAP activity in this sector. Relative to their baseline averages, it appears that the predicted responsiveness of OAP activity to changes in the relative cost of production is more pronounced for OAP activities conducted in developing countries. In these terms, the largest predicted change is found for apparel.

We repeated our analysis at the three-digit industry level for five industry sectors: office and computing machines (SIC 357), TV and radio receiving equipment (SIC 365), electronic components (SIC 367), motor vehicles (SIC 371), and aircraft and aircraft parts (SIC 372). We had two reasons for considering these sectors at the finer industry level. First, these five industries were responsible for the greatest level of OAP outsourcing in our sample, as measured by their volume of dutiable OAP imports. As a result, we expect outsourcing changes to be most visible in these large OAP activities. The next reason for selecting these industries relates to the counterintuitive nature of some of our results in tables 3.8 and 3.9. Our greatest surprise, perhaps, is our earlier finding that electronic machinery outsourcing from developing countries appears to fall when the dollar appreciates. However, electronic machinery is an industry in which the country composition of outsourcing varies widely. While the sector for electronic components and accessories, which includes semiconductors, was dominated by Southeast Asian outsourcing, other sectors such as TV and radio receiving equipment had outsourcing activities that were more internationally dispersed. A maintained assumption of our previous specification is that exchange rate effects are common to all firms within a two-digit industry. While this assumption may be innocuous in many industries, it may misrepresent the true cost changes experienced in the more heterogeneous sectors such as electronics. To explore this possibility, we created a new set of exchange rate variables that corresponded to the three-digit-industry sourcing patterns for these highly active industries. As before, these exchange rate variables are tailored to reflect the country composition of OAP outsourcing activities in each of these industries.

Table 3.10 contains the regression estimates for our more disaggregated sectors. We again consider OAP imports from developed and developing countries separately. A few changes are notable. For machinery overall, we found a fairly low responsiveness of OAP outsourcing in developing countries. When we treat office and computing machinery separately, however, we find that the measured sensitivity of OAP outsourcing in developing countries rises markedly. As the calculations in table 3.11 indicate, these effects are economically large. A 10 percent appreciation of the dollar would cause outsourcing in the office and computing machinery industry to rise by 0.752 percent. Relative to baseline levels of outsourcing in this industry, this represents a 30 percent increase.

The move to more detailed exchange rate variables also resolves some of the paradoxical findings of our previous analysis. In both TV and radio receiving equipment (SIC 365) and electronic components and accessories (SIC 376), all of our exchange rate cost measures now have the expected positive sign, which implies that outsourcing increases when the dollar appreciates. The new coefficients are not statistically significant for the first sector, but the findings are especially strong in the electronic components segment, which includes semiconductors. Economically, this effect is somewhat less powerful. While significant statistically, the implied effect

Table 3.10   Regression Results for Dutiable OAP Imports

Independent Variables (log)	Dependent Variables (shares of nonenergy material purchases)	
	Dutiable OAP Imports from OECD	Dutiable OAP Imports from LDCs
Office and Computing Machines (SIC 357), N = 48, 47		
Real exchange rate	−0.0005 (0.0089)	0.0789 (0.0343)
Capital intensity	−0.0484 (0.0186)	−0.0112 (0.0144)
Real output	−0.0292 (0.0068)	−0.0161 (0.0048)
Constant	0.2803 (0.0634)	0.1195 (0.0480)
R^2	0.251	0.230
TV and Radio Receiving Equipment (SIC 365), N = 22, 21		
Real exchange rate	0.00057 (0.00047)	0.0025 (0.0133)
Capital intensity	0.0307 (0.0102)	0.0241 (0.0826)
Real output	0.0103 (0.0028)	0.0737 (0.0246)
Constant	−0.0525 (0.0237)	−0.5464 (0.2119)
R^2	0.411	0.24
Electronic Components (SIC 367), N = 107, 108		
Real exchange rate	0.00048 (0.00008)	0.0535 (0.0113)
Capital intensity	−0.0039 (0.0025)	0.0124 (0.0286)
Real output	−0.0027 (0.0008)	−0.0059 (0.0104)
Constant	0.0257 (0.0059)	0.1231 (0.0775)
R^2	0.388	0.431
Motor Vehicles (SIC 371), N = 48, 48		
Real exchange rate	0.2936 (0.2634)	−0.0004 (0.0003)
Capital intensity	−0.3827 (0.1913)	0.0020 (0.0058)
Real output	−0.2723 (0.1017)	−0.0067 (0.0031)
Constant	2.065 (1.315)	0.1031 (0.0373)
R^2	0.119	0.075
Aircraft and Aircraft Parts (SIC 372), N = 35		
Real exchange rate	−0.0263 (0.0119)	
Capital intensity	0.0043 (0.0186)	
Real output	−0.0063 (0.0093)	
Constant	0.1050 (0.0807)	
R^2	0.077	

Notes: The sample is all four-digit industries within each two-digit sector for the years 1980–93, excluding 1982 and 1988. Regressions are weighted by the industry share of total manufacturing shipments. Standard errors are in parentheses. See table 3.6 for variable definitions.

of a 10 percent dollar appreciation on the outsourcing of electronic components from developing countries is a 4.8 percent increase in outsourcing relative to the sector's average level of outsourcing.

The move to a more detailed industry analysis does not remove all puzzles. We continue to find perverse negative coefficients on the cost variables for motor vehicle outsourcing in developing countries and aircraft and aircraft parts outsourcing from developed countries. At the same

Table 3.11   **OAP Imports and Changes in Exchange Rates**

	Dutiable OAP Imports	Change in OAP Imports (from 10% dollar appreciation)
Office and computing machines (SIC 357)		
OECD	1.61	NA
Non-OECD	2.50	0.752
TV and radio receiving equipment (SIC 365)		
OECD	1.18	NA
Non-OECD	7.93	NA
Electrical components and accessories (SIC 367)		
OECD	0.69	0.0047
Non-OECD	10.6	0.510
Motor vehicles (SIC 371)		
OECD	11.6	2.79
Non-OECD	0.93	−0.038
Aircraft and parts (SIC 372)		
OECD	1.79	−0.251

Note: NA, not applicable.
Variable definitions are as follows:
Dutiable OAP imports = 100 × (Dutiable OAP imports)/(Non-energy material purchases).
Change in OAP imports = 100(Real exchange rate coefficient × log(1.1)).

time, motor vehicle outsourcing in developed countries responds strongly in the hypothesized direction. Table 3.11 shows that developed country outsourcing in the motor vehicle industry is predicted to rise 2.79 percent if the dollar appreciates by 10 percent.

Overall, our examination of outsourcing is similar to our earlier findings for U.S. production. The best results are concentrated in apparel and machinery, where we find that increases in the cost of U.S. production, as proxied by exchange rate movements, are associated with higher levels of foreign OAP sourcing. In footwear and leather, our findings are imprecisely estimated, and the import of non-OECD electrical machinery appears to exhibit cross-industry differences that relate to the country composition of industry imports.

3.6 Conclusion

In recent years the United States and other countries have observed a growing gap between the wages paid to skilled versus unskilled workers. Although there are many possible explanations for this rising wage inequality, Feenstra and Hanson (1996a) suggest that changes in the U.S. wage structure can be attributed at least partly to foreign outsourcing. We examine trade conducted through the United States offshore assembly program to gain insight into recent outsourcing trends and their potential consequences.

As U.S. firms disperse production across countries through the OAP program, we expect the activities that they keep at home to use more skilled labor and less unskilled labor. This implies that the U.S. content of OAP imports (i.e., goods exported abroad for further processing) should be characterized by a relatively intensive use of skilled labor. We find support for this hypothesis in apparel and machinery imports through the OAP, as well as in OAP imports of transportation equipment from industrial countries.

We also examine how OAP outsourcing activities respond to changes in the relative cost of U.S. production as measured by industry-specific trade-weighted exchange rates. Here, we find that elevated U.S. costs of production in a number of industries are associated with substitution toward foreign production. While cost-induced movements toward the purchase of OAP inputs are small compared to the size of U.S. industry, the predicted response to cost changes implies a significant change in the magnitude of OAP activities.

Appendix

The estimates shown in tables 3.3 and 3.4 are obtained for the years 1980–93 (omitting 1982 and 1988 due to missing data), with all variables entered in levels, and not including any fixed effects for the individual four-digit industries. The estimation results for first differences are reported in tables 3A.1 and 3A.2. Because of missing data (in 1982 and 1988), these differences were taken across odd-numbered years.

In order to control for some of the most important heterogeneity across industries, in tables 3A.3, 3A.4, and 3A.5 we show additional estimates for machinery, electrical machinery, and transportation equipment that separate the most important three-digit industries within these two-digit groups. Fixed effects are not used in these regressions.

Table 3A.1 **U.S. Revenue Functions**

Independent Variables (log)	Dependent Variables (share of industry shipments)		
	U.S. Content of OAP Imports	Production Labor Share	Nonproduction Labor Share
Apparel (SIC 23), N = 191			
Production labor	1.37 (1.22)	9.48 (0.90)	−0.98 (0.48)
Nonproduction labor	0.57 (0.73)	−0.99 (0.54)	3.21 (0.29)
Dutiable OAP imports	0.22 (0.09)	−0.01 (0.06)	−0.04 (0.04)
Other intermediate inputs	−1.81 (1.02)	−7.30 (0.75)	−2.45 (0.41)
Capital	−3.09 (2.42)	0.84 (1.78)	1.13 (0.96)
Energy	−0.07 (0.42)	0.28 (0.31)	−0.15 (0.17)
R^2	0.07	0.45	0.43
Footwear and Leather (SIC 31), N = 62			
Production labor	−3.93 (2.84)	7.73 (1.46)	−1.13 (1.13)
Nonproduction labor	2.28 (1.98)	−3.47 (1.02)	2.16 (0.79)
Dutiable OAP imports	0.55 (0.29)	0.17 (0.15)	−0.19 (0.12)
Other intermediate inputs	−0.09 (0.69)	−0.30 (0.36)	−0.33 (0.27)
Capital	−10.68 (9.15)	−0.77 (4.74)	−2.27 (3.66)
Energy	−1.00 (1.52)	−1.24 (0.79)	−0.40 (0.61)
R^2	0.14	0.39	0.17

Note: Standard errors are in parentheses. Estimation is in first differences, taken across odd-numbered years. All regressions are weighted by the industry share of total manufacturing shipments.

Table 3A.2   U.S. Revenue Functions

Independent Variables (log)	Dependent Variables (share of industry shipments)			
	U.S. Content OAP Imports from LCDs	U.S. Content OAP Imports from OECD	Production Labor Share	Nonproduction Labor Share
Machinery (SIC 35), N = 214				
Production labor	0.09 (0.24)	0.73 (0.24)	4.36 (0.46)	−2.45 (0.59)
Nonproduction labor	−0.52 (0.30)	−0.66 (0.29)	−2.12 (0.57)	5.18 (0.74)
Dutiable OAP imports from LDCs	0.04 (0.01)	−0.01 (0.01)	0.04 (0.03)	0.002 (0.03)
Dutiable OAP imports from OECD	−0.02 (0.02)	0.08 (0.02)	0.01 (0.04)	−0.14 (0.05)
Other intermediate inputs	0.08 (0.15)	−0.57 (0.14)	−3.09 (0.28)	−3.45 (0.36)
Capital	0.21 (0.39)	0.91 (0.38)	3.26 (0.73)	0.27 (0.95)
Energy	−0.04 (0.20)	−0.06 (0.20)	−0.15 (0.37)	0.46 (0.49)
R^2	0.07	0.18	0.43	0.62
Electrical Machinery (SIC 36), N = 223				
Production labor	2.44 (1.61)	−0.05 (0.18)	6.29 (0.76)	−1.68 (0.82)
Nonproduction labor	2.67 (1.45)	0.09 (0.16)	−1.37 (0.69)	5.42 (0.74)

Dutiable OAP imports from LDCs	0.79 (0.12)	0.03 (0.01)	−0.19 (0.06)	−0.11 (0.06)
Dutiable OAP imports from OECD	0.19 (0.10)	0.09 (0.01)	−0.02 (0.05)	−0.12 (0.05)
Other intermediate inputs	−6.62 (0.99)	−0.43 (0.11)	−2.72 (0.47)	−4.62 (0.51)
Capital	−4.12 (1.51)	0.00 (0.17)	0.56 (0.72)	1.05 (0.78)
Energy	0.26 (1.24)	0.33 (0.14)	−0.16 (0.59)	1.47 (0.64)
R^2	0.42	0.36	0.29	0.43
Transportation Equipment (SIC 37), N = 62				
Production labor	−0.39 (0.19)	0.72 (0.75)	7.71 (1.61)	0.96 (2.08)
Nonproduction labor	0.20 (0.11)	0.29 (0.44)	−0.59 (0.93)	1.82 (1.21)
Dutiable OAP imports from LDCs	0.03 (0.01)	0.01 (0.03)	0.08 (0.07)	0.10 (0.09)
Dutiable OAP imports from OECD	0.03 (0.01)	0.06 (0.04)	−0.22 (0.09)	−0.06 (0.11)
Other intermediate inputs	0.23 (0.11)	−0.98 (0.44)	−5.64 (0.94)	−2.88 (1.22)
Capital	0.09 (0.10)	−0.06 (0.39)	−0.12 (0.20)	−0.63 (0.31)
Energy	0.01 (0.12)	−0.18 (0.47)	−2.15 (0.99)	−0.64 (1.28)
R^2	0.34	0.29	0.36	0.47

Note: Standard errors are in parentheses. Estimation is in first differences, taken across odd-numbered years. All regressions are weighted by the industry share of total manufacturing shipments.

Table 3A.3   U.S. Revenue Functions: Machinery

Independent Variables (log)	Dependent Variables (share of industry shipments)			
	U.S. Content OAP Imports from LDCs	U.S. Content OAP Imports from OECD	Production Labor Share	Nonproduction Labor Share
Machinery (SIC 35), N = 452				
Production labor	−0.11 (0.06)	−0.19 (0.05)	8.94 (0.35)	−2.85 (0.16)
Nonproduction labor	0.15 (0.05)	0.17 (0.04)	−3.32 (0.26)	7.38 (0.12)
Dutiable OAP imports from LDCs	0.07 (0.01)	0.014 (0.006)	−0.10 (0.04)	−0.04 (0.02)
Dutiable OAP imports from OECD	0.04 (0.01)	0.11 (0.01)	0.18 (0.07)	0.01 (0.03)
Other intermediate inputs	−0.27 (0.05)	−0.31 (0.53)	−7.33 (0.29)	−4.72 (0.13)
Capital	0.03 (0.08)	0.10 (0.06)	3.80 (0.46)	−0.26 (0.21)
Energy	−0.04 (0.11)	0.04 (0.09)	−1.20 (0.65)	0.45 (0.29)
R^2	0.33	0.40	0.90	0.91
Office and Computing Machines (SIC 357), N = 47				
Production labor	−0.21 (0.71)	0.007 (0.61)	2.97 (0.57)	−4.18 (1.51)
Nonproduction labor	0.12 (0.95)	0.13 (0.82)	−1.71 (0.77)	7.12 (2.04)
Dutiable OAP imports from LDCs	0.37 (0.08)	0.17 (0.07)	−0.06 (0.06)	−0.04 (0.17)
Dutiable OAP imports from OECD	0.07 (0.07)	0.20 (0.06)	0.19 (0.05)	−0.21 (0.14)
Other intermediate inputs	−1.06 (0.32)	−0.86 (0.28)	−1.00 (0.26)	−3.26 (0.69)
Capital	−0.06 (0.77)	−0.34 (0.66)	−1.83 (0.63)	−0.78 (1.66)
Energy	0.52 (0.66)	0.61 (0.56)	0.99 (0.53)	0.76 (1.41)
R^2	0.71	0.71	0.96	0.82

Note: Standard errors are in parentheses. Estimation is in levels for 1980–93, excluding 1982 and 1988. All regressions are weighted by the industry share of total manufacturing shipments.

Table 3A.4   U.S. Revenue Functions: Electrical Machinery

Independent Variables (log)	Dependent Variables (share of industry shipments)			
	U.S. Content OAP Imports from LDCs	U.S. Content OAP Imports from OECD	Production Labor Share	Nonproduction Labor Share
Electrical Machinery (SIC 36), N = 450				
Production labor	0.24 (0.40)	−0.05 (0.07)	8.38 (0.29)	−3.30 (0.24)
Nonproduction labor	−0.47 (0.27)	−0.04 (0.05)	−2.14 (0.19)	8.24 (0.16)
Dutiable OAP imports from LDCs	0.78 (0.06)	0.01 (0.01)	−0.33 (0.05)	−0.10 (0.04)
Dutiable OAP imports from OECD	0.10 (0.08)	0.09 (0.01)	−0.04 (0.06)	−0.06 (0.05)
Other intermediate inputs	−3.32 (0.27)	−0.22 (0.05)	−4.63 (0.20)	−3.31 (0.17)
Capital	2.06 (0.33)	−0.05 (0.06)	−0.45 (0.24)	−0.75 (0.21)
Energy	0.06 (0.32)	0.28 (0.06)	−0.19 (0.23)	0.23 (0.20)
R^2	0.52	0.19	0.77	0.95
TV and Radio Receiving Equipment (SIC 365), N = 21				
Production labor	−1.70 (4.18)	0.50 (0.32)	10.18 (2.38)	0.16 (0.94)
Nonproduction labor	0.03 (4.26)	−0.39 (0.32)	−5.07 (2.42)	1.61 (0.96)
Dutiable OAP imports from LDCs	0.17 (0.26)	0.006 (0.02)	−0.10 (0.15)	0.07 (0.06)
Dutiable OAP imports from OECD	−1.18 (0.47)	0.02 (0.04)	−0.25 (0.27)	0.01 (0.11)
Other intermediate inputs	−1.64 (2.15)	0.23 (0.16)	−4.36 (1.22)	−2.24 (0.48)
Capital	12.96 (3.68)	−0.48 (0.28)	1.94 (2.10)	−0.48 (0.83)
Energy	−3.33 (2.94)	0.02 (0.22)	3.68 (1.67)	1.81 (0.66)
R^2	0.77	0.60	0.90	0.93

(continued)

Table 3A.5 (continued)

Independent Variables (log)	Dependent Variables (share of industry shipments)			
	U.S. Content OAP Imports from LDCs	U.S. Content OAP Imports from OECD	Production Labor Share	Nonproduction Labor Share
Electronic Components (SIC 367), N = 107				
Production labor	−1.34 (1.94)	0.47 (0.50)	7.25 (0.74)	−3.36 (0.89)
Nonproduction labor	6.08 (2.08)	−0.32 (0.54)	−3.58 (0.79)	9.05 (0.94)
Dutiable OAP imports from LDCs	1.33 (0.24)	−0.05 (0.06)	−0.72 (0.09)	−0.57 (0.11)
Dutiable OAP imports from OECD	0.41 (0.22)	0.29 (0.06)	0.07 (0.09)	0.13 (0.10)
Other intermediate inputs	−7.66 (1.15)	−1.08 (0.30)	−3.78 (0.44)	−4.42 (0.52)
Capital	−4.38 (1.22)	−1.00 (0.31)	−0.91 (0.46)	−1.73 (0.55)
Energy	4.00 (1.67)	1.83 (0.43)	1.20 (0.63)	1.21 (0.76)
R^2	0.76	0.39	0.94	0.90

Note: Standard errors are in parentheses. Estimation is in levels for 1980–93, excluding 1982 and 1988. All regressions are weighted by the industry share of total manufacturing shipments.

Table 3A.5   U.S. Revenue Functions: Transportation Equipment

Independent Variables (log)	Dependent Variables (share of industry shipments)			
	U.S. Content OAP Imports from LDCs	U.S. Content OAP Imports from OECD	Production Labor Share	Nonproduction Labor Share
Transportation Equipment (SIC 37), N = 135				
Production labor	0.47 (0.12)	−0.42 (0.20)	7.84 (0.34)	−5.49 (0.51)
Nonproduction labor	−0.04 (0.07)	0.24 (0.10)	−0.40 (0.18)	6.49 (0.27)
Dutiable OAP imports from LDCs	0.05 (0.01)	0.01 (0.02)	0.04 (0.03)	−0.13 (0.05)
Dutiable OAP imports from OECD	−0.01 (0.02)	0.15 (0.03)	−0.06 (0.05)	0.36 (0.07)
Other intermediate inputs	−0.22 (0.06)	−0.31 (0.09)	−6.16 (0.16)	−2.51 (0.24)
Capital	0.03 (0.08)	0.17 (0.12)	0.08 (0.20)	0.18 (0.31)
Energy	0.06 (0.11)	−0.01 (0.17)	0.05 (0.30)	0.77 (0.43)
R^2	0.41	0.30	0.97	0.9
Motor Vehicles (SIC 371), N = 43				
Production labor	0.56 (0.94)	0.19 (0.17)	5.29 (1.71)	0.44 (0.67)
Nonproduction labor	0.42 (0.65)	−0.13 (0.12)	−0.510 (1.18)	1.57 (0.46)
Dutiable OAP imports from LDCs	0.11 (0.05)	0.0003 (0.01)	−0.09 (0.10)	−0.03 (0.04)
Dutiable OAP imports from OECD	0.03 (0.05)	0.06 (0.01)	−0.35 (0.09)	−0.12 (0.04)
Other intermediate inputs	−0.20 (0.21)	−0.15 (0.04)	−5.88 (0.38)	−1.85 (0.15)
Capital	−0.22 (0.20)	−0.01 (0.04)	0.35 (0.36)	−0.38 (0.14)
Energy	−0.43 (0.42)	0.02 (0.08)	1.90 (0.76)	0.38 (0.30)
R^2	0.49	0.63	0.99	0.99

(continued)

Table 3A.5   (continued)

Independent Variables (log)	Dependent Variables (share of industry shipments)			
	U.S. Content OAP Imports from LDCs	U.S. Content OAP Imports from OECD	Production Labor Share	Nonproduction Labor Share
Aircraft and Aircraft Parts (SIC 372), N = 24				
Production labor	−0.06 (0.09)	0.94 (0.85)	11.36 (2.48)	1.20 (3.36)
Nonproduction labor	0.05 (0.06)	−0.61 (0.57)	−0.32 (1.65)	8.05 (2.24)
Dutiable OAP imports from LDCs	0.006 (0.002)	0.02 (0.02)	0.09 (0.05)	0.13 (0.07)
Dutiable OAP imports from OECD	0.0004 (0.005)	0.11 (0.05)	−0.06 (0.14)	−0.12 (0.19)
Other intermediate inputs	−0.0006 (0.02)	−0.15 (0.19)	−6.34 (0.55)	−5.05 (0.75)
Capital	−0.06 (0.05)	0.73 (0.50)	0.16 (1.44)	−3.05 (1.95)
Energy	0.08 (0.07)	−0.45 (0.64)	−3.63 (1.85)	0.73 (2.50)
R^2	0.53	0.78	0.98	0.92

Note: Standard errors are in parentheses. Estimation is in levels for 1980–93, excluding 1982 and 1988. All regressions are weighted by the industry share of total manufacturing shipments.

References

Antweiler, Werner, and Daniel Trefler. 1997. Increasing returns and all that: A view from trade. University of British Columbia and University of Toronto. Photocopy.

Arndt, Sven. 1997. Globalization and the open economy. *North American Journal of Economics and Finance* 8 (1): 71–79.

———. 1998a. Globalization and the gains from trade. In *Trade, growth and economic policy in open economies,* ed. K. Jaeger and K.-J. Koch, 3–12. New York: Springer-Verlag.

———. 1998b. Super-specialization and the gains from trade. *Contemporary Economic Policy* 16 (4): 480–85.

Campa, José, and Linda S. Goldberg. 1997. The evolving external orientation of manufacturing industries: Evidence from four countries. NBER Working Paper no. 5919. Cambridge, Mass.: National Bureau of Economic Research.

Feenstra, Robert C., and Gordon H. Hanson. 1996a. Foreign investment, outsourcing and relative wages. In *Political economy of trade policy: Essays in honor of Jagdish Bhagwati,* ed. R. C. Feenstra, G. M. Grossman, and D. A. Irwin, 89–127. Cambridge: MIT Press.

———. 1996b. Globalization, outsourcing, and wage inequality. *American Economic Review* 86 (2): 240–45.

———. 1997. Foreign direct investment and relative wages: Evidence from Mexico's maquiladoras. *Journal of International Economics* 42 (3–4): 371–93.

Gao, Ting. 1999. Economic geography and the development of vertical multinational production. *Journal of International Economics* 48 (2): 301–20.

Hanson, Gordon. 1997. The effects of off-shore assembly on industry location: Evidence from U.S. border cities. In *Effects of U.S. trade protection and promotion policies,* ed. Robert C. Feenstra, 297–322. Chicago: University of Chicago Press.

Hummels, David, Jun Ishii, and Kei-Mu Yi. 1999. The nature and growth of vertical specialization in world trade. Chicago: University of Chicago; Stanford, CA: Stanford University; New York: Federal Reserve Bank of New York. Photocopy.

Jones, Ronald, and Henry Keirzkowski. 1997. Globalization and the consequences of international fragmentation. Rochester, N.Y.: University of Rochester; Geneva: Graduate Institute of International Studies. Photocopy.

Krugman, Paul. 1995. Growing world trade: Causes and consequences. *Brookings Papers on Economic Activity,* no. 1: 327–62.

Krugman, Paul, and Anthony Venables. 1995. Globalization and the inequality of nations. *Quarterly Journal of Economics* 90 (4): 857–80.

Leamer, Edward E. 1998. In search of Stolper-Samuelson linkages between international trade and lower wages. In *Imports, exports, and the American worker,* ed. Susan M. Collins, 141–203. Washington, D.C.: Brookings Institution.

Markusen, James R., and Anthony J. Venables. 1995. Multinational firms and the new trade theory. NBER Working Paper no. 5036. Cambridge, Mass.: National Bureau of Economic Research.

———. 1996a. Multinational production, skilled labor and real wages. NBER Working Paper no. 5483. Cambridge, Mass.: National Bureau of Economic Research.

———. 1996b. The theory of endowment, intra-industry, and multinational trade. NBER Working Paper no. 5529. Cambridge, Mass.: National Bureau of Economic Research.

Matsuyama, Kiminori. 1996. Why are there rich and poor countries? Symmetry-breaking in the world economy. *Journal of the Japanese and International Economies* 10:419–39.

Swenson, Deborah L. 1997. Explaining domestic content: Evidence from Japanese and U.S. automobile production in the United States. In *Effects of U.S. trade protection and promotion policies,* ed. Robert C. Feenstra, 33–53. Chicago: University of Chicago Press.

U.S. International Trade Commission (USITC). 1997. Production sharing: Use of U.S. components and materials in foreign assembly operations, 1992–1995. USITC Publication 3032. Washington, D.C.: USITC.

Comment   James A. Levinsohn

In international trade, economists often speak of goods as embodying factors. In that vein, this paper embodies a huge amount of labor—skilled labor I might add, for the work involved in using the data the authors collected was tremendous. This was not an example of coming up with a clever use of data pulled off of the StatCan CDs or OECD diskettes. Rather, the authors tracked down a novel and hitherto unexploited source of data, and they use this data to investigate an old problem in a new and very creative way. It is a very nice paper and a super example of what we can learn when we take time to step back from the abstract notion of international trade and look closely at the actual institutions and programs by which trade is conducted.

The problem the authors address is a long-standing one, and it will be helpful to keep the goal of the paper in mind. There is a significant amount of outsourcing going on today. It is natural to suspect that outsourcing might decrease the demand for unskilled labor relative to skilled labor. The question that the authors ask is key to addressing this suspicion. They ask: Is outsourcing relatively unskilled-labor intensive (compared to the same activity when it is not outsourced)?

There is a natural way to answer this question. Why not just get the data on input use for plants that produce a good offshore and compare that with input use for plants that produce the good domestically? If the plant that is offshore uses twice as much unskilled labor per unit of output and one-third less skilled labor compared to a plant located in the United States, then we have our answer (for that plant, anyway). Do this exercise for thousands of plants and we are there.

The problem is that the authors do not have the data necessary to conduct this exercise. Actually, for myriad reasons, it is unclear whether any-

James A. Levinsohn is professor of economics and public policy at the University of Michigan and a research associate of the National Bureau of Economic Research.

one has this data. So the authors are forced to be more creative and their solution is really very clever and very original.

The authors use the OAP (offshore assembly program) as the "experiment" with which to answer the question of whether outsourcing reduces the demand for skilled labor. The OAP lets firms outsource production and then only pay duties on the foreign value added. The idea is that through this program, firms have to report the value of the goods as they cross the Rio Grande into Mexico and the value when those same, but now finished, goods recross into Texas. What we would really like to know is whether the extra steps of production that take place abroad use relatively more unskilled labor than the production that takes place entirely in the United States. In other words, we would like to know whether the stuff that goes into the OAP program is "finished" with more unskilled labor than is the case for the same product that doesn't go into the OAP program.

The problem is that, even with this program, the authors do not have any data on the actual input use divided into production in the United States and production abroad. Again, the authors have to be creative.

They assume the industry produces two outputs. One of these outputs is OAP production, while the other is the rest of output. That is, apparel produces stuff that gets reimported and stuff that never leaves the country. In their framework, these are different products. Their hypothesis is that the stuff that is going to be reimported is more skilled-labor intensive (when it leaves the United States) than the stuff that never leaves the United States. The key idea is that if the unskilled-intensive work takes place abroad, the stuff is relatively skilled-labor intensive when it first leaves the United States.

Their methodology is to estimate what they called production functions. This was one place that I found the paper a little confusing, and it is an issue of semantics. I do not think they estimate production functions at all, but rather they estimate something very akin to a Rybczynski derivative. Clarifying the difference is important. A production function is a relationship between the output of a plant, firm, or industry, and the inputs it actually uses. The Rybczynski derivative is a relationship between the output of a plant, firm, or industry, and the total endowments it has at its disposal. The authors do not have separate data on inputs used by local plants and on inputs used by the outsourcing plants. I found this a little confusing in the paper since the section where this material is presented is called "U.S. production functions." What the authors want to do, then, is regress output shares (where the shares are the share going into the OAP program and the share produced entirely domestically) on inputs and prices. The Rybczynski derivative they want to estimate addresses the following question: Holding output prices constant, as an industry gets more of a factor, does the share of output going to offshore production increase or decrease? The Rybczynski theorem tells us that holding prices constant, as you get more of a factor, the output of the good that uses that factor intensively goes up, and the output of the other factor goes down. The authors use this insight to back out implied intensities of outsourcing relative to purely domestic production. It is actually pretty straightforward, but I have to admit that the constant references to production functions confused me. It took a while for me to figure out what was going on. Once I figured it out, I realized that this is a very clever way of using trade theory to infer factor intensities without ever having any data on the actual factors used in outsourcing and domestic production.

There is one potential problem with how this all gets pulled off. The Rybczynski approach is one in which output prices are held constant while factor endowments shift. Fine. The problem is that the authors don't actually have any price data, so they estimate their equation, in which they acknowledge that price should be a regressor, without actually including price in the regression. I'd like to stress that the authors are entirely upfront about this, but it might lead some to question just what is being estimated. In many cases, this omission would be quite serious, since in the background, prices are also moving around and we might wonder just what we are measuring when we infer factor intensities. I think this is one problem that could use a little more discussion in the paper.

Two econometric issues might warrant further discussion. The dependent variable in these regressions is a share (varying between 0 and 1), so ordinary least squares (OLS) is appropriate. A simple logistic transformation of the dependent variable will solve this and this hardly ever makes a difference in the results. The second issue is less easily addressed, but perhaps deserves acknowledgment. In the typical estimation of Rybczynski derivatives, the independent variables are country endowments. It is, in this context, quite reasonable to consider these country endowments to be exogenous variables. In this paper, "endowments" are the factors used as inputs in a particular industry, and in this case the exogeneity assumption is less obviously correct. Inputs are quite possibly choice variables suggesting that OLS is inappropriate.

The authors then look at five key industries: apparel, leather and footwear, machinery, electrical machinery, and transportation equipment. Their results are mixed. If they had stopped with apparel, the results would accord with most of our priors. Since this conference was in Monterey, I'll use a fishing analogy. If you go fishing and come back and say that you didn't catch anything, that doesn't make you a bad fisherman. Maybe there was nothing to catch. It does, however, make you an honest fisherman. These authors are honest fisherman.

Rather than having detailed factor use data for plants in the United States that produce finished products as well as factor use data for plants in the United States that outsource and the same data for the plants that do the outsource work, the authors essentially have no factor use data broken down by whether the output is outsourced and no price data. They had to put a lot of structure on the problem in order to get their data to talk. It is a creative attempt, using an original data source, but in some cases, the data just would not talk.

The authors then switch gears and address a very different question that has little to do (on the surface, anyway) with the trade and labor issue, but which is well suited to their data. They ask whether firms do more outsourcing when costs are relatively higher at home. They manage to do this without ever using any firm-level data and without observing costs. This part of the paper is perhaps a little less convincing just because, all else being equal, I think we know firms do not do less production abroad when offshore assembly gets cheaper. The empirical question is one of magnitudes, but so much is changing that might impact costs, that their exchange rate approach has some trouble extracting the signal from the noise. Many cost shifters other than exchange rates are probably moving over their sample, so it is a little hard to interpret the results from an empirical framework that does not control for any cost shifters other than the real exchange rate. If the exchange rate is highly correlated with these other excluded cost shifters, the authors are in good shape. One interpretation of the results in this section of the paper is that the empirical approach is asking whether the exchange rate is a good proxy for otherwise unobserved cost shifters, and the answer is sometimes.

II

The Role of Product Prices

4

What Are the Results
of Product-Price Studies
and What Can We Learn
from Their Differences?

Matthew J. Slaughter

4.1 Introduction

In recent years many economists have analyzed whether international trade has contributed to rising U.S. wage inequality by changing relative product prices. In this paper I survey and synthesize the findings of these product-price studies.

The theoretical framework guiding this research is the Stolper-Samuelson (SS) theorem linking product-price changes to factor-price changes. The research discussed in this paper constitutes the first large body of empirical work applying the SS theorem to the data. Before these studies there was relatively little empirical research on the SS theorem. Deardorff's (1984) chapter in the *Handbook of International Economics,* entitled "Testing Trade Theories and Predicting Trade Flows," does not cite a single empirical study of it. And in a famous book commemorating the 50th anniversary of the landmark paper by Stolper and Samuelson (Deardorff and Stern 1994), of the 10 essays reprinted as "seminal contributions to the Stolper-Samuelson literature" (5), only one is empirical (Magee 1980).

My survey and synthesis of the product-price studies has three parts. First, borrowing language from Deardorff (1994) I lay out several theoretical statements of the SS theorem to preview some of the empirical issues involved in applying it to data.

Second, I survey the product-price studies on rising U.S. wage inequal-

Matthew J. Slaughter is assistant professor of economics at Dartmouth College and a faculty research fellow of the National Bureau of Economic Research.

For helpful comments the author thanks Robert Baldwin and conference and preconference participants. The author thanks the Russell Sage Foundation for financial support through grants no. 85-96-18 and no. 85-97-18.

ity. In the following order I cover Bhagwati (1991), Lawrence and Slaughter (1993), Sachs and Shatz (1994), Feenstra and Hanson (1995), Leamer (1998), Baldwin and Cain (1997), Krueger (1997), Feenstra and Hanson (1999), and Harrigan and Balaban (1997). Together these nine studies demonstrate how the methodology has evolved. By surveying these papers in this order I can relate each study to those preceding it.

Finally, I synthesize the findings of these nine studies and draw two main conclusions. The first conclusion is that this literature has refined a set empirical strategies for applying the SS theorem to the data from which important methodological lessons can be learned. To preview some of the main results, the "facts" about product prices are relatively sensitive to the selection and weighting of industries sampled and to the decade considered. In contrast, the "facts" are relatively insensitive to the extent of data aggregation and the measurement of skills.

The second main conclusion is that despite the methodological progress that has been made, research to date still has fundamental limitations regarding the key question of how much international trade has contributed to rising wage inequality. Most importantly, more work needs to link the various exogenous forces attributable to international trade to actual product-price changes. Stated alternatively, the literature to date has made substantial progress understanding how to relate a given change in relative product prices to changes in relative factor prices. But it has made less progress understanding whether these product-price changes have anything to do with international trade. Two other important areas needing further work are the need to explore how slowly the Heckscher-Ohlin clock ticks and the need to complement product-price data with other data that might overcome potential limits of the product-price data.

The rest of the paper is organized as follows. Section 4.2 presents the theoretical framework for understanding the product-price studies. Section 4.3 surveys each of the nine studies. Section 4.4 synthesizes the studies and highlights the overall methodological progress. Section 4.5 discusses the limitations of these studies. The conclusions are stated in section 4.6.

4.2 Theory Guiding the Data: Alternative Statements of the Stolper-Samuelson Theorem

Deardorff (1994) surveys alternative statements of the SS theorem that have appeared during the past 50-plus years. Each articulation requires a different set of assumptions and thus applies to different contexts. Below I quote (verbatim) Deardorff's six versions. This list serves two purposes. First, it provides some theoretical context for judging how well researchers have related theory to data. Second, it previews some of the major empirical issues that researchers have had to address.

General Version: An increase in protection raises the real wage of the scarce factor of production and lowers the real wage of the abundant factor of production.

Restrictive Version: Free trade lowers the real wage of the scarce factor and raises that of the abundant factor compared to autarky.

Essential Version: An increase in the relative price of a good increases the real wage of the factor used intensively in producing that good and lowers the real wage of the other factor.

Strong Version with Even Technology: A rise in the price of any good, all other prices remaining constant, causes an increase in the real return to the factor used intensively in the producing that good and a fall in the real returns to all other factors.

Friends and Enemies Version: Every good is a friend to some factor and an enemy to some other factor.

Correlation Version: For any vector of goods-price changes, the accompanying vector of factor-price changes will be positively correlated with the factor-intensity-weighted averages of the goods-price changes.

Deardorff very clearly discusses the theoretical relationships among all six versions; the interested reader is strongly encouraged to read this discussion. To complement this, I make four points about applying these versions to the empirical issue of rising wage inequality.

First, only two of the versions mention anything about international trade. This underscores that the essence of all SS versions is the link between product prices and factor prices imposed by the zero-profit conditions equating price with average cost that must hold in all perfectly competitive industries with actual production.[1] These zero-profit conditions imply a systematic relationship between the entire set of product prices facing domestic producers and the entire set of factor prices paid by these producers. Analytically, the economy's entire set of zero-profit conditions can be written as follows:

$$(1) \qquad\qquad P = A \times W,$$

where P is an $(N \times 1)$ vector of N domestic product prices, W is an $(M \times 1)$ vector of M domestic factor prices, and A is an $(N \times M)$ technology

---

1. Actually, product markets need not be perfectly competitive for the SS theorem to apply. What is truly essential is not perfect competition, but rather the existence of a systematic link between product prices and factor prices. Perfect competition is only one way of obtaining this systematic link: It restricts price to be just equal to average cost. An alternative might be imperfect competition that fosters a positive—but unchanging—price-cost markup. Another alternative, analyzed extensively in Helpman and Krugman (1985), is monopolistic competition in which sufficient entry by new firms ensures zero profits in equilibrium.

matrix (which might also depend on W) whose a_{ij} element tells the number of units of factor i required to produce one unit of product j. Each row of equation (1) corresponds to one of the N products, and in words the equation says that for each product price equals average costs. It is important to notice that factor prices are not indexed by industry; with the assumption of perfect interindustry factor mobility, each factor has only one national price. This is a key aspect of all versions of the SS theorem.

Holding constant technology, equation (1) can be rewritten in terms of percentage changes for (sufficiently small) changes. This yields the following equation:

(2) $$P^* = \theta \times W^*,$$

where P^* is an ($N \times 1$) vector of N domestic product-price changes, W^* is an ($M \times 1$) vector of M domestic factor-price changes, and θ is an ($N \times M$) initial cost-share matrix (which depends on technology and, perhaps, W), whose θ_{ij} element tells the share of factor i in the average costs incurred producing one unit of product j.[2] Changes in product prices faced by domestic firms generate changes in domestic factor prices paid by firms as described by equation (2). This is true whether the product-price changes are caused by international trade or any other force. Indeed, many SS versions apply even to countries in autarky with all products nontraded. The empirical implication of this is the need for a way to determine what portion of observed product-price changes are attributable to international trade. Equation (2) will be an important reference point.

It is worth emphasizing that the phrase "caused by international trade" must be treated carefully. As Deardorff and Hakura (1994) discuss, this phrase can be misleading in that international trade (i.e., the flows of goods and services across countries) is the endogenous outcome of (among other things) international differences in tastes, technology, endowments, and barriers to trade. International trade and product prices are simultaneously caused by things; trade does not cause product-price changes. Thus, attributing causality from international trade to domestic product prices requires a bit more precise language. Specifically, it requires reference to some aspect of the international-trade equilibrium that can be plausibly taken as exogenous to domestic product prices.

Following Deardorff and Hakura, I propose four distinct restatements of the phrase "international trade can change domestic product prices," each of which elaborates on "international trade."

1. A change in domestic political barriers to trade can change domestic product prices.

---

2. Note that going from equation (1) to equation (2) uses the fact that cost minimization implies that $dA \times W = 0$. This says that any small changes in factor use must not change costs, given that costs were initially minimized.

2. A change in foreign political barriers to trade can change domestic product prices.

3. A change in international natural barriers to trade can change domestic product prices.

4. A change in foreign tastes, technology, and/or endowments can change domestic product prices.

Think of domestic product prices as depending both on international product prices and on any trade barriers that wedge between international and domestic prices. If the country is small, then international prices are independent of domestic trade barriers and other parameters. Otherwise, domestic trade barriers and other domestic parameters do affect international prices. Given this setup, statements 1 through 3 address how domestic prices depend on the wedge—and, if the country is large, how they depend on international prices as well. Statement 4 addresses how domestic prices depend on developments abroad communicated to the domestic economy through changes in international prices.

Overall, to meaningfully analyze whether "international trade changes product prices," one must have sufficient data to restate the issue into something like one of these four statements. Without some data on trade barriers, tastes, technology, and endowments, actual price changes cannot be empirically linked to some exogenous aspect of international trade.

A second key point about Deardorff's six SS versions is that the best guide for empirical work depends on the world's dimensionality. The first three versions hold only in worlds with two factors and two products. The Strong Version holds only for worlds with the same number of factors and products (more than two allowed) and only under certain technology restrictions. Only the last two versions hold for any arbitrary number of factors and products. If one thinks that the world cannot be reasonably approximated as two by two, then one should focus on the last three versions. If one is uncomfortable assuming the world is even, then one should focus on the last two versions.

The third key point is that only the Correlation Version directly addresses something other than real-wage changes. This matters because all nine product-price studies surveyed here focus on rising inequality, not the absolute losses of the less skilled.[3] In light of the discussion regarding dimensionality, this point suggests that the Correlation Version might be the best guide for empirical work on relative wages. The Friends and Enemies Version focuses on the price change of only a single product, and it claims only that this single price change will raise the real return to one unidentifiable factor and lower the real return of some other unidentifiable

---

3. It is also true that most less-skilled workers have suffered real-wage declines in recent decades. For many less-skilled workers the declines have been staggering; for example, the real hourly earnings of male high school dropouts fell by 20 percent from 1979 to 1993.

factor. In contrast, the Correlation Version relates any vector of relative product-price changes and allows these changes to be systematically related to relative factor-price changes to relative factor prices. Granted, one cannot predict for certain what will happen to any particular relative factor price. But one can say that, on average, factors employed intensively in rising- (falling-) price industries will experience relative price increases (declines). This result seems closest in spirit to the empirical issue of rising wage inequality.

The fourth key point is that all six SS versions do not consider intermediate inputs. In reality, intermediate inputs matter a lot; for nearly 40 years, in U.S. manufacturing input purchases have accounted for well over 50 percent of the value of final shipments. Accordingly, any empirical work must account for the fact that firms hire both primary factors and intermediate inputs. Rewriting equation (1) to account for intermediate inputs suggests alternative ways of doing this. Define matrix B as the $(N \times N)$ matrix of intermediate input requirements whose b_{ij} element tells the number of units of intermediate input i required to produce one unit of product j. Then the set of zero-profit conditions in (1) can be rewritten as follows:

$$(3) \qquad P = B \times P + A \times W.$$

Equivalently, these zero-profit conditions can be rewritten two other ways:

$$(3') \qquad P = [(I - B)^{-1} \times A] \times W,$$

$$(3'') \qquad (P - BP) = A \times W,$$

where I is an $(N \times N)$ identity matrix.

This suggests two alternative ways to account for intermediate inputs when linking product prices to factor prices. Following equation (3'), one can measure factor use not in direct terms, but rather in total terms, accounting both for direct factor use and indirect factor use through intermediate inputs. That is, one can relate factor prices to $[(I - B)^{-1} \times A]$ rather than just to A. Alternatively, following equation (3''), one can continue using just direct factor use as regressors, but construct the regressand to be gross output prices less input prices weighted by the B matrix.

To summarize this theoretical preview of the empirical work, these alternative versions of the SS theorem provide some helpful guideposts. Assume, as most researchers have, that the U.S. economy has less-than-free trade with countries abroad, more than two products and two factors, and intermediate inputs. Given these assumptions, the most appropriate version of the SS theorem for guiding empirical work is probably the Correlation Version. That is, for any given change in product prices and factor prices consistent with equation (2), in the data one should try to demonstrate the following:

(4) $\text{Cor}(P^*, \theta \times W^*) > 0.$

All this requires a substantial amount of data. In terms of the explanatory variable, one needs some systematic way to identify the effect of one or more exogenous characteristics of international trade on domestic product prices while controlling for nontrade influences on these prices. To identify how this exogenous force of international trade affects relative wages, one also needs industry-level data on domestic product prices, and on the prices and quantities of inputs and factors employed.

4.3   A Survey of Nine Product-Price Studies

In this section I cover the following product-price studies: Bhagwati (1991), Lawrence and Slaughter (1993), Sachs and Shatz (1994), Feenstra and Hanson (1995), Leamer (1998), Baldwin and Cain (1997), Krueger (1997), Feenstra and Hanson (1999), and Harrigan and Balaban (1997). Together, these papers demonstrate how the methodology of product-price studies has evolved. Where appropriate, other related papers will be mentioned. By surveying these nine papers in this order I can relate each to the relevant work preceding it. For each paper, I refer the interested reader to exact pages with the key results. Table 4.1 summarizes key aspects of each of the nine studies (with some details and terminology to be clarified in the rest of this section).

Bhagwati (1991) is the first researcher I am aware of to link rising U.S. wage inequality to international trade working through product prices. He plots (51, fig. 7) quarterly observations from 1982 through 1989 of the U.S. price indexes for exports and imports of all manufactures aggregated together. Observing that import prices rose more quickly than the export prices after 1986, Bhagwati concludes that "the trade-focused explanation [of rising wage inequality thanks to declining relative prices of imported products which presumably employ less-skilled labor relatively intensively] ... therefore carries little plausibility, at least at first blush" (51).

Lawrence and Slaughter (1993) (LS) are the first researchers to use price data disaggregated by industry and also to use direct measures of industry factor use. They use three sets of U.S. manufacturing prices: imports, exports, and domestic production. The export and import prices cover all industries at the two-digit and three-digit Standard Industrial Classification (SIC) levels for which the Bureau of Labor Statistics (BLS) assembles the data. These data do not cover all manufacturing industries; for example, the import prices cover 18 of the 20 two-digit SIC industries, but only about 50 of the 143 three-digit SIC industries. LS assume (195, n. 55) "that the price movements in these industries are reasonably representative" of all industries. The domestic prices cover all three-digit SIC industries. LS refer to the traded prices as "international prices" whose "changes . . . [are]

Table 4.1   Summary of the Nine Product-Price Studies

Study	Time Period	Methodology	Skills Measure	Key Results
Bhagwati (1991)	1980s	Description of time series of U.S. terms of trade	Assumes exports more skill-intensive than imports	No clear trend in terms of trade
Lawrence and Slaughter (1993)	1980s	Consistency-check regressions using U.S. manufacturing prices (export, import, and domestic)	Job classification	No clear trend in relative prices
Sachs and Shatz (1994)	1980s	Consistency-check regressions using U.S. manufacturing prices plus dummy for computer industry	Job classification; educational attainment	Relative-price declines in unskilled-intensive sectors
Feenstra and Hanson (1995)	1980s	Description of domestic prices vs. import prices for three countries	Assumes domestic activity skill-intensive relative to outsourced imports	Domestic prices rose by more than import prices did in all three countries

Leamer (1998)	1960s–80s	Mandated-wage regressions using U.S. domestic manufacturing prices and TFP data, too	Job classification; earnings per worker	Relative-price declines in unskilled-intensive sectors during 1970s only
Baldwin and Cain (1997)	1960s–80s	Mandated-wage regressions using U.S. manufacturing prices (export, import, and domestic)	Job classification; educational attainment	Relative-price declines in unskilled-intensive sectors during 1970s for some specifications
Krueger (1997)	1990s	Consistency-check regressions and mandated-wage regressions	Job classification; educational attainment; earnings per worker	Relative-price declines in unskilled-intensive sectors
Feenstra and Hanson (1999)	1980s	Mandated-wage regressions extended to a two-stage procedure with structural forces like outsourcing	Job classification	Outsourcing mandated rising inequality during 1980s
Harrigan and Balaban (1997)	1960s–80s	Regression analysis of cost-share equations from U.S. GDP function	Educational attainment	Relative-price declines of tradables relative to nontradables

prompted by international trade" (198–99). Thus, they model the United States as a small price-taking economy facing product prices determined exogenously abroad. For domestic prices, LS assume (202, n. 63) that "changes in these domestic price deflators tracked changes in international prices. This is a weaker assumption than the law of one price: it allows prices to differ across countries by some fixed constant," presumably due to U.S. trade barriers. Because LS assume that all product-price changes come from foreign developments, when analyzing industry differences in total factor productivity (TFP) growth, they assume that U.S. technology changes do not influence product prices (199).

For each price sample, LS test whether in the 1980s—defined as 1980–89—the prices of skilled-labor-intensive products rose relative to the prices of unskilled-labor-intensive products. Each industry's skill intensity is measured as the industry's direct employment ratio of nonproduction to production workers (NPW/PW). LS identify the pattern of price changes two ways. First, (196–97, figs. 8 and 9) they pool all industries in each price sample and regress the industries' percentage change in product prices over the 1980s against the industries' skill intensity in 1980. That is, they estimate via ordinary least squares (OLS) the following regression:

$$(LS) \qquad P^{*1980s}_j = \alpha + \beta(NPW/PW)^{1980}_j + e_j.$$

Second, to complement these regressions for each price sample they construct a weighted average of all decadal price changes using nonproduction-employment weights and then production-employment weights (199, table 3, and 203, table 4). For the domestic prices, LS construct these weighted averages for the 1970s and 1960s as well.

The basic finding by LS is that they estimate β to be 0 or negative, not positive, for their various series of traded prices: Industries with higher relative direct employment of nonproduction to production workers did not have larger price increases during the 1980s. These estimates are corroborated by the weighted averages. LS interpret these results as evidence against the hypothesis that international trade contributed to rising U.S. wage inequality by raising the relative price of skilled-labor-intensive products.

Sachs and Shatz (1994) (SSh) follow the LS methodology with two minor changes and one major change. First, they define the decade of the 1980s as 1978–89. Second, they use a slightly different dependent variable, the share of production employment in total industry employment. Their major difference from LS is the treatment of the computer industry (SIC 357 at the three-digit level, SIC 3573 at the four-digit level). They argue (37) that LS "should have separated the effects of computer prices from the other sectors." The reason is that the computer-industry price data are exceptionally mismeasured: "The relative prices of computers fell sharply during the decade, matching extraordinary productivity increases. The ex-

act measurement of these price and productivity changes is highly problematic, so that it is important that these changes do not overwhelm the
message in the rest of the data." Thus, using both import prices and the
full sample of three-digit SIC domestic prices, SSh run the following regression using OLS:

(SSh) $P^{*1980s}_j = \alpha + \beta(PW/(PW + NPW))^{1980}_j + \beta_c(D_{\text{computers}}) + e_j.$

The main results from these regressions (38, table 16) are that β is estimated to be negative (insignificantly so for import prices and significantly
[with a t-statistic of -1.98] for domestic prices) while β_c is also estimated
to be negative (very significantly so [t-statistic of -13.40] for domestic
prices). Thus, SSh find among the noncomputer sample that industries
employing a larger share of production workers had lower relative price
increases over the 1980s. SSh conclude this supports the hypothesis that
international trade contributed to rising U.S. wage inequality by raising
the relative price of skilled-labor-intensive products.

Unlike the previous three papers, Feenstra and Hanson (1995) (FH95)
analyze the data from a Ricardian perspective rather than a Heckscher-
Ohlin perspective. In their framework countries make completely different sets of products, unlike the Heckscher-Ohlin framework where all
countries are (usually) assumed to be in the same cone of diversification.
Importantly, FH95 are the first researchers to move away from the assumption that U.S. prices merely reflect international prices for the same
products. They highlight the fact that during the 1980s (defined as 1980
through 1989) in the United States, Germany, and Japan, domestic prices
rose by more than import prices did (17–18, and 105, table 1). This fact is
consistent with their model of international outsourcing, which raises
wage inequality both in the United States and abroad (16, prop. 3). As
marginal production activities relocate from the United States to countries
abroad, the relative demand for skills rises in both countries. A corollary
of this shift is that U.S. prices rise by more than foreign prices. Thus if
one interprets U.S. import prices as representative of the basket of foreign
production, the fact about domestic versus import prices is consistent with
outsourcing raising U.S. (and foreign) wage inequality.

Leamer (1998) uses a Heckscher-Ohlin perspective to analyze the wage
implications of product-price shifts during the 1960s (defined as 1961–71),
1970s (1971–81), and 1980s (1981–91). The data analysis has a descriptive
component where "the empirical facts are presented with only a 'light'
touch of the HO framework" followed by a "formal data analysis . . .
which is based explicitly on the one-cone HO model" (15).

Leamer's descriptive analysis tracks domestic product prices for two-
digit-level industries relative to the overall producer price index (PPI) (162,
fig. 10, and 169, fig. 14). The key sectors are textiles and apparel, two very

labor intensive industries. Leamer reports that the 3 decades behaved very differently. During the 1960s the prices of textiles and apparel fell relative to the overall PPI by a relatively modest 8 percent and 4 percent, respectively. During the 1970s their relative prices plunged by 30 percent. Finally, during the 1980s their relative prices were quite stable. The key message from these descriptive facts are that the 1970s, not the 1960s or 1980s, appear to be the decade where U.S. relative prices of unskilled-labor-intensive products fell markedly.

For his more structural analysis, Leamer uses the zero-profit conditions written in equation (1). In differentiating these equations to express them in terms of changes, however, Leamer does not assume away changes in technology and their possible feedback to prices—he explicitly allows these changes in his framework. Thus, along with Baldwin and Cain, Leamer is one of the first researchers to consider causes of product-price changes other than some aspect of international trade. Differentiating equation (1) for (sufficiently small) changes while allowing technological progress yields the following equation:

$$(2')\qquad\qquad P^* = \theta \times W^* - TFP^*,$$

where P^* is defined, as earlier, as an $(N \times 1)$ vector of product prices; θ and W^* now include both primary factors and intermediate inputs; and TFP^* is an $(N \times 1)$ vector of TFP growth in all industries.

As equation $(2')$ indicates, technological progress can affect equilibrium prices for products and/or factors. The key question is how much does technological progress feed into product-price declines? Consistent with their assumption that the United States is a small price-taking economy, LS assumed zero pass-through from TFP growth to product prices. Leamer explicitly relaxes this assumption by considering pass-through rates (identical across all industries) of both 0 and 1 from technological progress to value-added product prices (i.e., P less the cost-share-weighted prices of intermediate inputs). Having controlled for some effect of TFP on product prices, Leamer then assumes that the amount of actual product-price changes not accounted for by technological progress can be attributed to what he terms "globalization." He does not attribute these globalization price changes to anything more specific, such as trade barriers or foreign developments communicated to U.S. product prices through the U.S. terms of trade.

Leamer thus distinguishes two forces affecting U.S. factor prices: technological progress and globalization price changes. The relative magnitude of these forces depends on how large a pass-through coefficient from technology to product prices is assumed. Leamer uses regressions to estimate a link from these forces to factor prices. For technology changes, Leamer pools all industries to estimate the following:

(L-T) $[(1 - \lambda) \times TFP_j^*] = (\theta_{ij})\beta_{it} + e_j,$

where λ is the pass-through coefficient from technology to value-added product prices. Similarly, for globalization price changes Leamer pools all industries to estimate the following:

(L-G) $[P_j^* + (\lambda \times TFP_j^*)] = (\theta_{ij})\beta_{ig} + e_j,$

where $P_j^* + (\lambda \times TFP_j^*)$ is the vector of globalization price changes.

In both equations (L-T) and (L-G) Leamer interprets the parameter estimates as "mandated" factor-price changes. "These are the changes in factor costs that are needed to keep the zero profits condition operative in the face of changes in technology [i.e., β_{it}] and product prices [i.e., β_{ig}]" (23). Stated differently, the regressions estimate the factor-price changes mandated by changes in technology and/or product prices to maintain zero profits in all sectors. The error term in each equation allows the zero-profit conditions not to bind exactly (for whatever unspecified reasons). Because the econometric fit is not perfect, the mandated factor-price changes can be interpreted as the changes "consistent with the least change in profits in the economy" (29). These mandated factor-price estimates β_{it} and β_{ig} can then be compared with actual factor-price changes. "If the two conform adequately, we will argue that we have provided an accurate explanation of the trends in wages" (23). Thus the parameter estimates are tested by directly comparing them with actual data. Overall, these regressions can be interpreted as an accounting exercise. What changes in factor prices are mandated from the observed changes in technology and/or product prices—and what share of actual changes do these mandated changes explain?

In Leamer's regressions, intermediate inputs are measured as materials purchased. For primary factors, he uses capital and either labor or labor disaggregated between more-skilled and less-skilled workers. Leamer measures skills in two distinct ways. One is the classification between nonproduction and production workers. Concerned that this measure excessively misclassifies actual skills, Leamer constructs an alternative skill ranking of industries based on their average earnings per worker (higher average earnings are translated into a higher mix of more-skilled workers). Changes in product prices and technology are the annualized changes over the decades as he defines them and cost shares are measured for the first year of each decade. In equation (L-T) Leamer assumes that technological progress affects the prices of primary factors only. In equation (L-G) Leamer constrains the parameter estimate on intermediate inputs to equal the actual observed price change for intermediate inputs; thus, he accounts for inputs by following equation (3″). Finally, Leamer weights industries by either employment or value added.

For the various combinations of dependent variable and decade, Leamer reports three sets of results. One uses just capital and labor as factors, the second uses capital plus labor disaggregated by Leamer's skills definition, and the third uses capital plus labor disaggregated into non-production and production workers (190, table 6, 192, table 7, and 194, table 8). The results for wage inequality related to globalization changes in product prices are as follows. For each decade there are four combinations of skill measure (Leamer's or NP vs. P) and pass-through rate (0 or 1) to consider. The 1960s results are somewhat mixed; in two of the cases the estimates warrant rising inequality while the other cases warrant falling inequality. The 1970s cases are more clear; in three of the four cases (all except the NP/P measure combined with zero pass-through) the estimates warrant strongly rising inequality. And for the 1980s the results generally split across skill measures. With Leamer's measure and both pass-through assumptions, the estimates warrant essentially unchanged or falling inequality, while, with the NP/P measure and both pass-through assumptions, the estimates warrant rising inequality (although given the reported standard errors, this rise does not appear to be statistically significant). From the results of these 3 decades, Leamer concludes "that the 1970s was the Stolper-Samuelson decade with product-price changes causing increases in inequality" (31).

The methodology of Leamer closely parallels that of Baldwin and Cain (1997) (BC).[4] Their empirical analysis consists of a comprehensive set of descriptive facts (57–58, table 1) followed by a more structural approach. Like Leamer, BC also regress a set of cross-industry zero-profit conditions expressed as changes to estimate mandated factor-price changes that can be compared with actual factor-price changes. Unlike Leamer, however, because of concerns that technology data are poorly measured (15), BC do not incorporate TFP measures in their econometric analysis. Their alternative "is to infer from the general equilibrium trade model the biases in the regression coefficients" (15) that are introduced by omitting technological change. Beyond technology, BC account for the influence of national factor supplies as well. Rather than somehow incorporating these influences in the zero-profit regression analysis, BC evaluate their importance in separate analyses of industry outputs, factor/employment ratios, and net exports.

The econometric component of their product-price analysis basically follows equation (2) with the inclusion of an additive error term plus a

4. The work of Baldwin and Cain—and indeed, all the studies in this paper—is in turn related to Baldwin and Hilton (1984), who model cross-country differences in factor prices as being accounted for by cross-country differences in unit production costs. The key difference between this early study and those surveyed in this paper is that Baldwin and Hilton explored cross-country differences factor by factor whereas the other studies explore within-U.S. differences over time in more-skilled and less-skilled wages.

constant to allow for "possible trends in price variables due to 'outside' forces" (22),

(BC) $$P_j^* = \alpha + (\theta_{ij})\beta_i + e_j.$$

In estimating this equation, BC expand the scope of previous work in several ways. First, like Leamer, they cover three time periods defined as 1968–73, 1973–79, and 1979–91. Second, they include all industries in the economy, not just manufacturing industries. Altogether they have 79 two-digit SIC industries used in input-output (I-O) tables constructed by the Bureau of Economic Analysis (BEA). To ease comparability with previous research, their main results are reported two ways, for all industries together and for just manufacturing industries. Third, they obtain employment from the Current Population Surveys (CPS), which report skills by educational attainment. Educational data are probably a better measure of skills than the commonly used nonproduction-production job classification (which is only meaningful for manufacturing industries). Moreover, these data allow more flexible definitions of skill groups. BC work with three groupings: 1–12 years and 13 or more years; 1–11 years and 12 or more years; and 1–11 years, 12 years, and 13 or more years. In addition to labor, BC also include physical capital. To control for intermediate inputs BC use I-O tables to construct total factor cost shares (i.e., they construct cost shares as given by equation (3′)). These I-O tables are available only for the years covered by the Census of Manufacturing, so BC use cost shares from 1967 for their first time period, 1972 for their second period, and 1977 for their final period. In their main analysis, BC use annualized changes in domestic product prices (with the end points for each period taken as 3-year averages to prevent outlier years from influencing the results). In addition, for manufacturing BC replicate their analysis for the 1980s using export and import prices from 1982 through 1992 (total price changes, not annualized). Finally, BC use both unweighted and weighted least squares with either employment or output weights.

BC describe aggregate price movements between more-skilled and less-skilled categories in their table (57–58). For each of the Census of Manufactures years plus the year 1980, BC calculate the domestic price ratio of industries intensively using more-skilled workers to industries intensively using less-skilled workers. They construct this price ratio for two industry samples, all sectors and just manufacturing. Within each sample, each industry is placed in a skill category based on whether its total employment ratio (i.e., ratio of direct employment plus indirect calculated from I-O tables) of workers with 13 or more years of education to workers with 12 or fewer years is above or below the median industry's ratio. From 1967 to 1972 both price ratios fell. From 1972 to 1980 the price ratio for all sectors continued to fall, but the manufacturing price ratio rose. Finally, from

1980 to 1992 the price ratio for all sectors rose sharply, while the manufacturing price ratio declined. Note that these descriptive price movements
within manufacturing generally match those found by Leamer: During the
1970s the relative price of unskilled-labor-intensive products fell, but during the 1980s this relative price did not fall further.

BC report their main OLS estimation results in their tables 3–7 (60–64);
their appendix 1 (66–67) reports analogous results for the weighted regressions. Again, their overall methodology is first to estimate equation (BC)
for each time period/factor set combination and then to discuss what combinations of changes in trade, technology, and endowments most plausibly
explain the observed price patterns and implied mandated factor-price
changes indicated by β_i.

For the period 1968–73, OLS price regressions for both all industries
and just manufacturing industries and for all three factor sets mandate a
decline in wage inequality. BC argue that this implied decline in the relative
price of skilled-labor-intensive products was caused primarily by an expanding relative endowment of skilled labor, which in turn expanded the
relative output of skilled-labor-intensive products. The weighted regressions yield the same qualitative result.

For the middle period 1973–79, the OLS price regressions again mandate a decline in wage inequality for both all industries and for just manufacturing industries. Analyzing the supporting data on outputs, endowments, and net exports, BC conclude that endowment changes were not
as strong an influence in this period. The three-labor-type regressions for
manufacturing only suggest that trade might have helped lower the warranted wage of high school dropouts relative to high school graduates.
The weighted regressions for this period look qualitatively similar for all
industries together, but qualitatively different for just manufacturing. The
manufacturing weighted estimates tend to indicate a mandated rise, not
fall, in wage inequality—particularly when outputs are the weights.

Finally, for the period 1979–91 BC estimate different mandated-wage
patterns across the two industry groups. For all industries together, BC
find a mandated rise in wage inequality. For just manufacturing they find
a mandated decline in wage inequality (particularly so for the two cases
with only two labor types). These manufacturing results are matched by
the regressions using the BLS export and import prices. In light of the
fact that the manufacturing results suggest that international trade was
generating mandated declines in wage inequality rather than the actual
rises in inequality (40), BC argue that the most likely explanation for the
observed price patterns is a combination of skill-biased technological
change and demand shifts toward skilled-labor-intensive products. The
results from the weighted price regressions look qualitatively similar, although the manufacturing results are weaker when weighted for the cases
with only two labor types.

Krueger (1997) is the only study in this survey to focus on the 1990s, defined in his data as 1989–94. He follows the methodology of both LS and SSh by regressing industry product-price changes on direct factor employment. Specifically, he follows SSh by using the fraction of production workers by industry, measured as the average over the years 1989, 1990, and 1991. He also runs this regression both with and without a dummy variable for the computer industry:

(K-1) $\quad P_j^{*1990s} = \alpha + \beta(PW/(PW + NPW))_j + \beta_c(D_{computers}) + e_j.$

In addition, Krueger also follows Leamer and BC by regressing a set of cross-industry zero-profit conditions expressed as changes to estimate mandated factor-price changes that can then be compared with actual factor-price changes. Unlike Leamer and BC, Krueger does not attempt in any way to distribute observed product-price changes between trade and nontrade causes. Thus, his mandated-wage specification is

(K-2) $\qquad\qquad\qquad P_j^* = \alpha + (\theta_{ij})\beta_i + e_j.$

Krueger's data cover the 150 four-digit SIC manufacturing industries, which have at least 75 percent of their output going to final consumer demand (i.e., "finished processor" industries). The product prices are the domestic producer prices such as those used in many of the earlier studies. In his cost-share matrix Krueger includes more-skilled labor, less-skilled labor, capital, and materials. Thus, like Leamer he accounts for intermediate inputs as suggested by equation (3″). For equation (K-1), Krueger uses the nonproduction-production classification; for robustness he also incorporates average worker educational attainment by industry from the CPS. To calculate industry cost shares of less-skilled labor in equation (K-2), Krueger multiplies industry total employment by the average annual earnings of a high school dropout and then divides this product by industry value of shipments. More-skilled cost shares are calculated as total payroll less this product, all divided by the industry value of shipments. All regressions are estimated with weighted least squares using 1988 values of shipments as weights.

Krueger's results from equation (K-1) are reported in his figures 1 (22) and 2 (23), table 4 (28; col. 1 and 2), and table 5 (29; col. 2). His main finding is that β is estimated to be statistically significantly less than 0 with virtually the same point estimate either with or without the computer dummy variable. That is, the data indicate a positive correlation between product-price increases and skill intensity. Measuring skill intensity by educational attainment yields the same result.

The result from equation (K-2) is reported in his table 5 (29; col. 1). The main finding here is an estimated mandated rise in wage inequality: The difference between the estimated β_i for skilled and unskilled labor is 0.52

and is statistically significant at the .0001 level. In an unreported robustness check, Krueger obtains qualitatively similar results from OLS and median regressions, although the estimated rise in warranted inequality is smaller (17). Thus Krueger draws the same conclusion from the results of both equation (K-1) and (K-2): "fairly robust evidence that price growth was relatively lower in less-skill intensive industries between 1989 and 1995. . . . The magnitude of the price changes is roughly compatible with observed wage changes for skilled and unskilled workers" (19–20).

Feenstra and Hanson (1999) (FH99) also use the mandated-wage framework used by Leamer, BC, and Krueger. However, FH99 differ from these earlier studies in two important ways. First, they do not consider product-price changes alone to contain any direct evidence of the role of international trade on factor prices. Rather, building on their earlier model of outsourcing, FH95, they argue that outsourcing manifests itself in industry-level data as TFP growth. Because outsourcing changes the mix of activities done within industries, "this will shift the entire production function for activities done at home, and therefore show up in the industry aggregate production function as a change in total factor productivity" (10). Second, they allow for technological change to affect product prices rather than assuming some quantity for it—either 0, under the small-economy assumption, or some nonzero value as in Leamer (1998).[5]

Their empirical approach thus involves two steps. First, they regress the sum of observed value-added product-price changes and observed TFP on measures of outsourcing and investment in high-technology equipment. This first-stage regression decomposes observed price and TFP changes into components attributable to various structural forces, among them outsourcing. Second, they regress each decomposed component on factor-cost shares to estimate mandated factor-price changes attributable to each structural force. The coefficient estimates from this second regression are interpreted as the economywide wage changes mandated by that structural force that, ceteris paribus, would have appeared in the actual economy. Their crucial second-stage mandated-wage regression of FH99 is

(FH)   "Outsourcing" $(P_j^* + TFP_j^*) = (\theta_{ij})\beta_i + e_j.$

FH99 use two measures of outsourcing. One "narrow" measure tracks imports of intermediate inputs only from the same two-digit industry as the good being produced. A second "broad" measure tracks all imported intermediate inputs regardless of industry. In their analysis, FH99 actually use the narrow measure and then the difference between the broad and narrow measures. FH99 also try two stage 1 specifications: one with the

---

5. With regard to mandated-wage regressions, FH99 also point out that mandated-wage regressions like equation (2') fit the data perfectly (i.e., have $R^2 = 1$) if one includes as a regressor differences between industry-specific and economywide changes in factor prices. They account for industry-specific wage changes in their measure of TFP.

structural variables entering linearly and another with these structural variables interacting with the quantities of primary factors. Thus, for their period of analysis, 1979–90, FH99 actually estimate four total versions of the (FH) equation. For all regressions, FH99 use 447 of the 450 four-digit SIC manufacturing industries; three are excluded because of inadequate data on materials. The nonproduction-production classification is used to separate more-skilled from less-skilled workers, and capital is included as a third primary factor. Also, FH99 test the robustness of their results by using alternative measures of computerization, and they adjust their standard errors on β_i because the second-stage regressand is constructed with parameter estimates from the first-stage regression. All regressions use weighted least squares with average value of shipments during the relevant period as weights.

The key stage 1 results are reported in their tables 4 (932) and 7 (936), and stage 2 results in tables 5, 6 (933–34), and 8 (937). In the stage 1 regressions, both outsourcing and computer use are estimated to be positively correlated with price-plus-TFP changes. In the stage 2 regressions, narrow outsourcing generally mandates a significant rise in wage inequality, while broad outsourcing generally mandates smaller and insignificant rises in wage inequality. In their baseline specifications, FH99 report that narrow outsourcing accounts for about 15 percent of the observed rise in inequality. In most specifications, high-technology capital mandated somewhat larger rises in inequality than outsourcing.

Finally, Harrigan and Balaban (1997) (HB) analyze product-price changes using a methodology different from the mandated-wage regressions. Their goal is to model economywide wages as determined jointly by technology, endowments, and product prices—which can be influenced by, among other things, international trade. Thus, like Leamer and BC, HB consider wage determinants other than international trade. HB start with a national revenue function with the standard properties implied by perfect competition, profit maximization, and nonjointness of production. HB then assume that this revenue function can be written as a general translog function with parameter restrictions implied by the standard properties. From this functional form, a set of equations can be derived that relate each factor's share in total national income to technology, factor supplies, and product prices. With appropriate data these cost-share equations can be estimated, and the parameter estimates linking factor cost shares with technology, endowments, and product prices can be combined with observed changes in these regressors to decompose actual wage changes into components due to technology, endowments, and prices.

HB apply this model to U.S. data from 1963 through 1991 by decomposing the economy into four primary factors and four products. The primary factors are high school dropouts, high school graduates plus some college, college graduates, and physical capital. There are two tradable and two nontradable industries, one each intensive in more-skilled labor and the other two intensive in less-skilled labor. Total industry factor intensities are determined using both direct and indirect factor employments from 1977 I-O tables. Thus like BC, HB focus on the entire U.S. economy and not just tradables.

HB consider U.S. product prices to be endogenous and thus require instruments for consistent estimation. For domestic prices their instrument set includes a set of domestic variables such as factor supplies, TFP, and government demand. For tradables prices HB use a set of international variables meant to capture the effect of developments abroad communicated to the United States through changes in our product prices. More specifically, they construct variables aimed at measuring "the presence of each country's labor supply in the international market" (9). To do this, for each year HB separate all countries into four income quartiles and then sum across all countries in each quartile the product of each country's labor force multiplied by its ratio of gross trade to GDP. Thus, HB are the first researchers to try to model the effect on U.S. prices of international trade in terms of foreign changes in productive capacity communicated to the United States through changes in our product prices.

The main results from their wage decomposition are reported in their table 5 (23). HB find that the most important relative-price change contributing to rising wage inequality was the large increase in the price of nontraded skill-intensive products relative to tradables and to the other nontraded sector. The effects of changes in tradables' relative prices are less clear: parameter estimates for these variables are relatively imprecise. This suggests that the international instruments might be weak.

4.4   Synthesis of Existing Findings and Methodological Progress

Having surveyed each of the nine product-price studies individually, I now try to synthesize their similarities and differences. I do this in three steps. First, I discuss how research has refined a set of empirical strategies for applying the SS theorem to the data. Second, I comment on some important methodological issues regarding the robustness of results. The "facts" about product prices and their warranted wage changes are relatively sensitive to the selection and weighting of industries sampled and to the decade considered. On the other hand, the "facts" are relatively insensitive to the extent of data aggregation and the measurement of skills. Third, in light of these methodological issues I summarize what the "facts" seem to be about product-price changes and their mandated wage changes.

4.4.1   A Methodological Progression

A summary of the empirical methodologies surveyed in section 4.3 is provided here (recall these studies were also summarized, without the regression equations, in table 4.1).

1. Bhagwati (1991). Discussion of U.S. terms of trade.
2. Lawrence and Slaughter (1993). Regression analysis:

(LS) $$P^{*1980s}_j = \alpha + \beta(NPW/PW)^{1980}_j + e_j.$$

3. Sachs and Shatz (1994). Regression analysis:

(SSh) $$P^{*1980s}_j = \alpha + \beta(PW/(PW + NPW))^{1980}_j + \beta_c(D_{\text{computers}}) + e_j.$$

4. Feenstra and Hanson (1995). Descriptive comparison of domestic and import prices.
5. Leamer (1998). Discussion of industry relative prices plus regression analysis:

(L-T) $$[(1 - \lambda) \times TFP^*_j] = (\theta_{ij})\beta_{it} + e_j,$$

(L-G) $$[P^*_j + (\lambda \times TFP^*_j)] = (\theta_{ij})\beta_{ig} + e_j,$$

6. Baldwin and Cain (1997). Discussion of industry relative prices plus regression analysis:

(BC) $$P^*_j = \alpha + (\theta_{ij})\beta_i + e_j.$$

7. Krueger (1997). Regression analysis:

(K-1) $$P^{*1990s}_j = \alpha + \beta(PW/(PW + NPW))_j + \beta_c(D_{\text{computers}}) + e_j.$$

(K-2) $$P^*_j = \alpha + (\theta_{ij})\beta_i + e_j.$$

8. Feenstra and Hanson (1999). Regression analysis:

(FH) $$\text{“Outsourcing” } (P^*_j + TFP^*_j) = (\theta_{ij})\beta_i + e_j.$$

9. Harrigan and Balaban (1997). Regression analysis of cost-share equations from translog representation of U.S. revenue function.

How do these different approaches relate to each other? By listing them in this order, I think one can identify a progressive refinement in the application of the SS theorem to the data.

First, the studies of Bhagwati, LS, and SSh I call "consistency checks." That is, these studies analyze whether observed product-price changes were consistent with rising wage inequality in the sense that the relative price of skilled-labor-intensive products rose relative to those of unskilled-labor-intensive products. Bhagwati simply assumes that exports (imports) employ more-skilled (less-skilled) labor relatively intensively. LS, and SSh following LS, refine this assumption by using disaggregated data to identify the pattern of relative factor use.

These first three studies have some important limitations in terms of the distance between the SS theorem and the empirical analysis and in terms of appropriately accounting for data complexities. One important limitation is that a consistency check on product prices cannot make the important link to factor prices. It cannot answer the important question of how much product-price changes might have contributed to actual factor-price changes. Another major limitation is that these regressions of product-price changes on factor-employment levels is not a tight implication of the SS theorem's zero-profit logic as summarized in equations (1) and (2). Equation (1) relates price levels to factor-employment levels (i.e., to the A matrix), while equation (2) relates price changes to factor cost shares (i.e., to the θ matrix). Regressing price changes on employment levels seems to capture the broad intuition of the SS theorem, but it uncomfortably mixes the levels and changes versions of the zero-profit conditions central to the SS theorem.

There are some data limitations as well. One is that these studies assume that the United States does not affect world prices; changes in domestic (or export or import) prices reflect changes in world prices triggered abroad that are communicated to the price-taking U.S. economy. Another limitation is that these studies ignore capital and any other primary factors of production. Given this, their results are best interpreted as a test of the General, Restrictive, or Essential Versions of the SS theorem under the maintained assumption that other primary factors do not matter. A third limitation is that they measure only direct factor intensities; they do not account for factor use embodied in intermediate inputs.

The later studies improve on the consistency check methodology in several ways. Most importantly, they have less distance between the SS theorem and their empirical analysis. The mandated-wage regressions of Leamer, BC, Krueger, and FH99 come closer than the consistency checks to testing the Correlation Version of the SS theorem that, as discussed in section 4.2, is probably the version most applicable to the issue of rising wage inequality. And these regressions follow directly from the zero-profit conditions expressed in terms of changes in equation (2), rather than mixing changes with levels. Product-price changes (or some other trade-related exogenous force such as outsourcing working through prices and TFP for FH99) are the dependent variable, factor-cost shares are the independent variable, and factor-price changes are the parameter estimates. These estimates have a clear interpretation in light of equation (2) as the "best guess" factor-prices changes mandated by changes in the dependent variable to maintain zero-profits in all producing sectors. In terms of the SS Correlation Version in equation (4), these mandated "best guesses" estimate the correlation between changes in the dependent variable and changes in the cost-share-weighted factor prices. Comparing actual with mandated factor-price changes indicates how much of the actual factor-price changes can be accounted for by the dependent variable. The ability to do this accounting within the mandated-wage framework solves one of the major limitations of the consistency check framework. (This is not to say that descriptive consistency checks are abandoned altogether: Leamer and BC complement their regressions with stylized facts, and Krueger also estimates LS-style regressions.) And as Leamer and FH99 demonstrate, this mandated-wage framework can be used not just for product-price changes, but for technology changes as well.[6]

The mandated-wage studies also have the advantage of allowing better treatment of some data complexities. Several of them try to relax the assumption of a small price-taking U.S. economy, as will be discussed later in greater detail. In addition, these studies also account for intermediate inputs as well as primary factors.

Mandated-wage regressions might appear odd because the exogenous variable is the regressand rather than the regressor, while the dependent variable of interest (factor-price changes) is estimated rather than the regressand. The most important reason a standard regression cannot be used is that the dimensionality of the data prevents inversion of the θ matrix. For example, the NBER Productivity Database used by LS, Leamer, and FH99 contains 450 four-digit SIC manufacturing industries, but only three primary factors plus two intermediate inputs. With more products than factors, in equation (2) the θ matrix is not square and thus cannot be inverted to obtain a set of equations equating wage changes with product-price changes multiplied by an inverted θ matrix.

This lack of invertibility suggests that the warranted-wage regressions can be interpreted as an accounting exercise, rather than as identifying causation in the way regressions are usually presumed to. Warranted-wage regressions estimate what changes in factor prices are mandated from the observed changes in technology and/or product prices. With these mandated changes one can determine what share of actual wage changes is accounted for by the driving exogenous change. Note that because the exogenous change enters the regression as the dependent variable, the mandated-wage methodology cannot analyze two or more exogenous forces in the same regression—it can process only one exogenous force at a time.

Overall, the product-price methodology has advanced from consistency checks to warranted-wage regressions. I argue that this progression has moved empirical work closer to the motivating SS theorem in a number of important ways.

4.4.2   How Robust Are the "Facts"?—Methodological Issues

The variety of empirical methods used in this research area raises the issue of how robust the results are in relation to various methodological

6. Building on these examples, Haskel and Slaughter (1998) use the mandated-wage framework to document that the sector bias of skill-biased technological change appears to account for much of the fall and subsequent rise in wage inequality during the 1970s and 1980s in both the United Kingdom and United States.

choices. In this section I discuss how sensitive the results are to four robustness issues: the selection and weighting of industries sampled, the decade considered, the extent of data aggregation, and the measurement of skills.

Robustness to Industry Selection and Weighting

The SS theorem's zero-profit conditions apply to all domestic industries currently producing positive output. In the matrix equations (1) and (2), there are N rows corresponding to all N industries currently producing. Any domestic industry not currently producing is assumed to have average costs exceeding the industry's price; thus that industry has no zero-profit equality. This suggests that empirical work on the SS theorem requires data on all operating domestic industries.

This raises two separate issues. One is whether to limit the sample to just all operating domestic industries that are tradable. As discussed in section 4.2, four of the versions of the SS theorem do not explicitly involve international trade. The link between product prices and factor prices holds even in autarky. Given this, focusing on just tradable industries seems appropriate when trying to understand product-price changes attributable to international trade.[7] The other issue is conditional on a selected sample: Are all available industries included in the data analysis? Theory suggests that all data should be included. Missing industries introduces the risk of the analysis not being representative of the appropriate full sample.

How robust are empirical results to sample selection? First, results definitely depend on whether all sectors or just tradables are analyzed. Looking at all sectors together, BC and HB find an increase in the price of skill-intensive nontradables during the 1980s. In light of SS versions that do not directly involve international trade, this suggests that one cause of rising inequality was rising relative prices for skill-intensive nontraded products. For the subset of just the tradable manufactures, LS, Leamer, and BC all find no strong trend in relative prices during the 1980s. This finding suggests that trade did not contribute to rising inequality. Clearly, in comparing studies one must be careful to identify differences driven by sample selection of tradables versus nontradables.

Conditional on the selection of the overall set of industries to analyze, the empirical results also depend on whether data on all available industries is included. In some cases results have been somewhat robust to sample selection. For example, both LS and BC use import and export prices for manufacturing industries despite the fact that these data do not exist for every single manufacturing industry. Import prices exist for only

---

7. Another reason to focus on just tradable industries is that if external competitiveness conditions are sufficient to determine an economy's factor prices, then that economy's nontraded product prices are determined automatically by these factor prices and the state of nontraded production technology. In this case, with fixed nontraded technology, nontraded product prices mechanically follow national factor prices.

18 of the 20 two-digit SIC industries and only about 50 of the 143 three-digit SIC industries. Despite this, both LS and BC find no strong trend in relative prices during the 1980s for these smaller samples, matching the results of Leamer and BC using the full set of 450 four-digit manufacturing industries. But in other cases the issue of inadequate sample selection appears to be very crucial. For example, Krueger's analysis of the 1990s uses only 150 of the 450 four-digit SIC manufacturing industries. He acknowledges that his sample of finished-processor industries is incomplete and comments that in "a later draft of this paper, I hope to obtain data for non-finished goods industries" (1997, 8, n. 8). It seems reasonable to wonder whether his analysis is representative of manufacturing overall during this period.

Because the NBER Productivity Database covering all four-digit manufacturing industries now extends through 1994, this can be checked. I have used these data to replicate Krueger's findings for the sample of finished-processor industries and then to see what results obtain when the sample is expanded to include all industries. Because I do not have all of Krueger's data to replicate his construction of factor-cost shares, I follow Leamer's approach for constructing cost shares for nonproduction labor, production labor, capital, energy, and materials. These alternative measures seem reasonable in that they replicate Krueger's results. The cost-share regressors are for 1989 and the dependent variable is the annualized rate of change in industry price. For all sets of industries I regress product-price changes on the cost shares to estimate the mandated factor-price changes.

Table 4.2 reports the results. The first three rows replicate Krueger's finding that for the sample of finished-processor industries the mandated wage increase for nonproduction labor exceeds that for production labor. The next three rows expand the sample to all manufacturing industries. Qualitatively, the parameter estimates between the two labor types have flipped. Now production labor has a larger mandated wage increase than nonproduction labor—this implies a mandated decline, not increase, in wage inequality. The final three rows show that the nonfinished-processor industries are driving the different results for overall manufacturing. For this sample of industries, the annualized mandated decline in inequality is larger than that of manufacturing overall. Notice that the results are robust to alternative weighting schemes for industries.[8]

On balance, then, it seems that Krueger's results for the 1990s are particular to his sample of industries. Table 4.2 suggests that for the full sample of all manufacturing industries the product-price changes during the early 1990s were not mandating increased wage inequality.

The issue of sample selection can even hinge on the presence or absence

---

8. Results are also robust to using 1988 or 1990 cost shares and to using the total-period price change. A similar difference between the full manufacturing sample and just the finished-processor industries shows up for regressions of price changes on the share of production workers in total employment.

Table 4.2   Mandated Factor-Price Changes (1989–94)

Industry Sample	Estimation Method	Nonproduction Labor	Production Labor
Finished-	OLS	0.073	0.029
processor		(3.503)	(1.609)
industries	WLS	0.055	0.036
	(value of shipments)	(2.091)	(1.793)
	WLS	0.071	0.006
	(employment)	(3.278)	(0.308)
All industries	OLS	0.057	0.058
		(2.391)	(3.714)
	WLS	0.005	0.104
	(value of shipments)	(0.082)	(2.002)
	WLS	0.036	0.081
	(employment)	(0.818)	(1.988)
All non-finished	OLS	0.040	0.071
processor		(1.259)	(3.436)
industries	WLS	0.007	0.125
	(value of shipments)	(0.098)	(1.970)
	WLS	0.041	0.115
	(employment)	(0.837)	(1.999)

Source: NBER Productivity Database.
Notes: Mandated factor-price changes are the coefficients from a mandated-wage regression pooling all industries in the indicated sample to estimate product-price changes on input cost shares. Numbers in parentheses are *t*-statistics. OLS, ordinary least squares; WLS, weighted least squares.

of a single industry, with computers being the trickiest case. SSh do not literally drop computers from the sample, but they effectively do so with a dummy variable for this industry. As discussed earlier, SSh treat computers differently because of concerns that reported computer prices do not adequately reflect the extent of this industry's quality upgrading. They argue that accounting for computers this way improves on specifications such as LS.

How much do computers really matter for the SSh results? They do not report results for equation (SSh) excluding the computer dummy, but this can easily be done using the NBER's Productivity Database. SSh use three-digit data; I use the four-digit data assuming that more-disaggregated data are better. SSh report unweighted regressions; for robustness I also use value of shipments and employment to weight industries. Table 4.3 reports the results. The key message is that "computers matter." Without a computer-industry dummy, no strong relationship appears between product-price changes and the share of production workers in total industry employment. But, as was reported for SSh earlier, with a computer-industry

Table 4.3   **Consistency Check of Product-Price Changes against Skill Intensity (1978–89)**

Industry Sample	Estimation Method	Coefficient on Production Share	Coefficient on Computer Dummy
All industries, without computer dummy	OLS	−0.007 (−0.594)	NA
	WLS (value of shipments)	0.008 (0.813)	NA
	WLS (employment)	0.003 (0.931)	NA
All industries, with computer dummy	OLS	−0.017 (−2.449)	−0.168 (−69.658)
	WLS (value of shipments)	−0.025 (−2.518)	−1.70 (−52.504)
	WLS (employment)	−0.031 (−3.036)	−0.173 (−47.639)

Source: NBER Productivity Database.

Notes: Coefficient estimates are from the regression (SSh), $P_j^*1980s = \alpha + \beta \, (PW/(PW+NPW))_j^{1980} + \beta_c \, (D_{computers}) + e_j$, estimated both with and without a dummy variable for the computer industry (SIC 3573 revision 2 industry). Numbers in parentheses are *t*-statistics. OLS, ordinary least squares; WLS, weighted least squared; NA, not applicable.

dummy effectively removing this industry a strong negative relationship appears among the noncomputer industries.

Given that computers (and perhaps other single industries?) can play such an important role, when can industries be excluded from an analysis? Lack of data seems to be one justifiable reason. Examples include LS and BC's using all tradables' price data that exist and FH99's excluding three industries that did not have materials prices. LS explicitly state their assumption that their smaller samples are representative of overall manufacturing (Lawrence and Slaughter 1993, 195, n. 55 and 202, n. 63).

The issue of selectively excluding data that do exist seems to be a trickier issue. SSh invoke the criterion of bad data quality. They do not elaborate on this point, however, either in terms of why computer price data are so bad in absolute terms or, more importantly, relative to other industries. Presumably other industries also had quality improvements that need to be accounted for in constructing "true" price changes.

At the very least, when possible, the direction of bias introduced by "bad" data should be considered before excluding data. For example, SSh claim that reported computer prices do not adequately control for quality improvements. Stated another way, they argue that the reported price decline for computers, in absolute value, understates the true quality-adjusted price decline for computers. This suggests that the reported price decline in computers is biased upward toward 0. The solution that SS use of dummying out the computer industry actually reinforces this bias rather than mitigating it. Rather than using information about the direction of bias, the dummy variable effectively sets the price change for the computers to 0 when estimating the cross-industry relationship between price changes and relative employment. To control for the bias introduced by computers, therefore, the results without the computer dummy are arguably better than the results with the computer dummy.

Related to the issue of industry selection is the issue of industry weighting. The logic of the SS theorem suggests that empirically all industries should be weighted equally. The link from product prices to factor prices relies on the existence of industries, not their sizes. Thanks to the assumption of perfect interindustry factor mobility, as long as an industry has positive output its product price affects factor prices in every industry. That is, as long as an industry has some positive output it accounts for one of the rows in matrix equations (1) and (2), regardless of how large the industry is. A product-price change in even the smallest industry is qualitatively just as important as a product price in the largest industry. This suggests that any data analysis should weight all industries equally.

Given the theoretical preference for equally weighted industries, weighting data differently probably requires empirical justification. For example, as BC suggest (Baldwin and Cain 1997, 22, n. 29) one might weight larger industries more heavily if smaller industries had poorer quality data. Another reason to weight might be that many smaller sectors are residual categories of a wide range of products.

Does weighting industries differently matter? In finite samples, ordinary and weighted least squares yield different parameter estimates. On balance, the answer appears to be maybe. Instances where weighting does not change the qualitative results include Krueger's work on the 1990s (and the extensions thereof in table 4.2). BC offer the most insight on this issue with their very thorough reporting of both unweighted and weighted results using both employment and output as weights. For the 1960s and 1980s results look very similar across the weighted and unweighted specifications. But for manufacturing industries during the 1970s, weighting seems to matter much more. Their unweighted results suggest a mandated fall in inequality, but their weighted results—particularly with output weights—suggest a mandated rise in inequality. This difference seems particularly important when compared with Leamer's conclusion that the 1970s was the Stolper-Samuelson decade, with a large rise in mandated inequality. Leamer reports this finding only for weighted specifications, not unweighted ones. Employment and value-added weights give similar results, but "unweighted regressions are entirely different" (Leamer 1998, 29, n. 5).

Robustness to Different Decades

Different decades appear to have different product-price trends. Assuming for the moment that the evidence presented in the previous studies is correct, on balance it appears that the U.S. prices of unskilled-labor-intensive products relative to skilled-labor-intensive products held relatively constant during the 1960s and 1980s, but declined during the 1970s and 1990s. Thus it is important not to generalize about the pattern in U.S. product prices without specifying the particular time period. For example, Krueger concludes that his evidence of declining relative prices during the 1990s "is consistent with Sachs and Shatz (1994), but inconsistent with Lawrence and Slaughter (1993)" (1997, 19). Because SSh and LS analyze the 1980s, not the 1990s, it is not clear that there should be any necessary relationship among results across different decades.

Importantly, the results for each given decade appear to be fairly robust to the end points chosen. For example, LS, Leamer, and BC all find no strong trend in manufacturing relative prices during the 1980s, even though each study defines the decade slightly differently.[9]

Robustness to Data Aggregation

The SS theorem is largely silent on this point. In theory, different industries are distinguished by their different relative employment of factors as dictated by their different production technologies. Empirically, it is generally assumed that more-disaggregated data is better.

The results appear to be quite robust to data aggregation. Many studies of the manufacturing sector use four-digit SIC industries (Leamer, Krueger, and FH99). Studies using three-digit data (LS, SSh, and BC) and/or two-digit data (LS and BC) obtain qualitatively similar results to the more-disaggregated studies. For example, the finding of constant relative manufacturing prices during the 1980s is obtained at the four-digit level (Leamer), the three-digit level (LS and BC), and the two-digit level (LS and BC).

Robustness to Measurement of Skills

Trade theory is largely silent on this point of how to measure skills. It is generally accepted that the nonproduction-production classification for manufacturing workers suffers more misclassification of skills than a categorization based on education. However, this claim is a statement about noisiness of data, not necessarily bias.

In fact, the nonproduction-production classification does not appear to be a biased measure of skills. Studies using this measure tend to obtain results similar to other measures such as educational attainment. Again, for the 1980s the conclusion of relatively stable relative product prices and thus little mandated change in wage inequality is obtained from studies using the nonproduction-production classification (LS and Leamer, for

9. Obviously there were other differences among these three studies, so the role of time period alone cannot be determined with certainty. Unfortunately, none of the studies reports a robustness check of its own methodology to the way the decades are defined.

the case of zero pass-through), using educational attainment to identify two labor groups (BC with two different cut-off points between the two groups), and using skills inferred form actual wages paid (Leamer). Similarly, for the 1990s for the sample of finished-processor industries Krueger obtains the same result for equation (K-1) using both the nonproduction-production classification and average years of education. The results for equation (K-2) are qualitatively the same for the nonproduction-production classification (reported in table 4.1) as for Krueger's skill measure using minimum wages.

*A Summary of the "Facts" Regarding
Product Prices and Mandated Wages*

In light of the previous discussion about methodological robustness, here is a summary of the "facts" regarding product-price changes and the mandated-wage changes. To organize the summary I use decades. HB do not break their analysis by time period, so I report one of their important findings in the 1980s.

The 1960s have been analyzed by BC and Leamer. The consensus finding seems to be a slight decline in the relative price of skill-intensive industries, both in manufacturing and in all sectors overall. These price changes suggest a mandated decline in wage inequality during this period.

The 1970s have been analyzed by BC and Leamer. The consensus finding between BC and Leamer seems to be a moderate to substantial decline in the relative price of non-skill-intensive industries both in manufacturing and in all sectors overall. These price changes suggest a mandated rise in wage inequality during this period.

The 1980s have been analyzed by Bhagwati, LS, SSh, FH95, Leamer, BC, FH99, and HB. The consistency checks of Bhagwati and LS and the descriptive facts of Leamer and BC all find no clear pattern of price changes across tradable industries during this period. The consistency check of SSh does find evidence of a relative-price decline for non-skill-intensive industries, but only after dummying out the computer industry. The mandated-wage regressions of Leamer and BC on manufacturing industries both find no clear pattern of mandated changes in wage inequality during this period. The structural estimates of HB corroborate this. FH95 find that the greater rise in domestic prices relative to import prices is consistent with their model of outsourcing, and FH99 find that changes in their narrow measure of outsourcing working through observed TFP and product prices led to mandated rises in wage inequality. Both BC and HB find a rise in the relative price of skill-intensive nontradable industries during this period, which mandated a rise in wage inequality.

The 1990s have been analyzed by Krueger. Based on a sample of one-third of manufacturing industries, both his consistency check and his mandated-wage regressions find a mandated rise in wage inequality from

1989 through 1994. However, the evidence in table 4.2 for all manufacturing suggests, if anything, a mandated decline in wage inequality.

4.5   Limitations of Current Research and Directions for Future Research

Despite the methodological progress that has been made, research to date still has fundamental limitations regarding the key question of how much international trade has contributed to rising wage inequality. In this section, I highlight three important limitations: the need for a clearer understanding of how product-price changes are related to exogenous forces attributable to international trade, the need to explore how slowly the Heckscher-Ohlin clock ticks, and the need to complement product-price data with other data to overcome potential limits of product-price data.

4.5.1   Decomposing Product-Price Changes

Most importantly, more work needs to link exogenous forces attributable to international trade to actual product-price changes. Stated alternatively, the literature to date has made substantial progress in understanding how to relate a given change in relative product prices to changes in relative factor prices. But it has made relatively less progress in understanding whether these product-price changes have anything to do with international trade.

This criticism of product-price studies is not new. Indeed, in a comprehensive survey of rising inequality Freeman (1995, 29) made the very same point 3 years ago: "Perhaps the biggest problem with these studies is that they ignore potential determinants of changes in sectoral prices and potential reasons for the proportion of unskilled workers in a sector to be correlated with changes in prices, save for trade." But what is important is that 3 years later, despite some progress, the criticism still applies.

The studies of Bhagwati, LS, SSh, and Krueger assume (explicitly or implicitly) that U.S. product prices are determined in the rest of the world without any influence from U.S. variables. This assumption is a reasonable first pass at the data, but it is almost certainly not correct. The other studies in this survey move away from this assumption in various ways. Leamer decomposes observed product-price changes into two components, technological progress and globalization price changes. However, he does not attribute these globalization price changes to anything more specific, such as trade barriers or foreign developments communicated through the U.S. terms of trade. BC consider three forces acting on product prices, international trade, technology, and endowments. Like Leamer, however, they do not specify anything more specific regarding what trade's force consists of. FH99 use regression analysis to explain observed price-plus-TFP changes with outsourcing and computerization. In estimating the mandated wage changes driven by each of these forces they allow an endogenous response of product prices. Finally, instead of using direct measures of domestic product prices in tradable industries, HB instrument for these prices using data on foreign labor endowments and trade quantities.

These latter studies, which attempt to decompose product-price changes among various causes, are an improvement on the earlier first-pass studies. Nevertheless, it seems that much more work is needed here. As discussed in section 4.2, in theory the question of how international trade causes product-price changes can be refined with reference to at least four distinct trade-related forces that are plausibly exogenous to domestic firms at a point in time: U.S. political trade barriers, foreign trade barriers, worldwide natural trade barriers, and developments abroad in parameters such as tastes, technology, and endowments that are communicated to the United States via the international prices constituting our terms of trade. None of the nine studies in this survey uses data on political or natural trade barriers. And only HB use data on foreign parameters to help explain U.S. domestic product prices.

Granted, decomposing product-price changes requires more data. But, as HB demonstrate, at least some progress could be made here. For example, perhaps sensible use could be made of net export patterns among countries. Ideally there would be sufficient data on all forces affecting product prices—both trade-related and otherwise—to account for price movements similar to how FH99 account for price-plus-TFP movements in terms of outsourcing and computerization.

Having a clearer decomposition of product-price changes could contribute greatly to understanding both what has caused past price changes and what might cause future price changes. As an illustration, consider the relative prices of textiles and apparel, two of the most unskilled-labor-intensive industries in U.S. manufacturing. In his descriptive facts, Leamer documents that the relative producer prices of these unskilled-labor-intensive sectors declined dramatically during the 1970s, but stabilized during the 1980s. There are at least two alternative trade-related explanations for why the decline halted. One is that these sectors enjoyed more protection in the 1980s thanks to the more-binding Multi-Fiber Arrangement (MFA). Another is that the price declines of the 1970s forced domestic producers to eliminate the very unskilled-labor-intensive sectors within textiles and apparel and to focus on the relatively skilled-labor-intensive sectors. With the rest of the world continuing to produce the very unskilled-labor-intensive sectors, this second story implies the United States moved to a different cone of diversification.

These two stories carry very different implications for future U.S. product prices and thus factor prices. In the first case, the 1980s price stabilization is a temporary lull that will disappear as the MFA is phased out and/or as countries like China with comparative advantages in unskilled-labor-intensive products continue to integrate into the world economy. Thus, this first case foreshadows further trade-induced rises in U.S. inequality. The second case, however, has much rosier implications. It suggests that the United States has already incurred the pain of losing some of its unskilled-labor-intensive industries. As countries like China continue to expand production and thus lower the relative prices of these products, no downward pressure is put on U.S. unskilled wages. Instead, all U.S. factors enjoy a consumption real-wage increase. Clearly, a better understanding of the relative causes of U.S. domestic price changes would help distinguish which of these very different futures seems more likely.

4.5.2   How Slowly Does the Heckscher-Ohlin Clock Tick?

The Heckscher-Ohlin (HO) framework of the SS theorem assumes that within a country each factor of production can move costlessly from one industry to another. In this sense, HO theory is a long-run theory: It focuses on how the economy operates once factors have had sufficient time to locate in whatever industries they choose. In contrast, the Ricardo-Viner (RV) framework assumes that within a country some factors cannot move across industries—perhaps because these factors incur prohibitively high moving costs. In this sense, RV theory is a short-run theory: It focuses on the economy when some factors cannot relocate from their current industry.

When a shock hits the economy (e.g., a change in international product prices), most trade economists presume that RV theory describes how the economy reacts in the short run, while HO theory describes how the economy reacts in the long run. It is well known that the reactions usually look very different depending on the time horizon. For example, after a price rise in some industry a country's relatively scarce factor can enjoy short-run wage increases for those employed in that industry—but in the long run these increases reverse and the factor suffers wage declines.

Despite these clean theoretical results, there is very little empirical evidence on what this transition from short run to long run looks like in reality. This lack of evidence poses a potentially very serious problem for almost all the empirical work to date on the effect of international trade on wage inequality. Every study surveyed in this paper tries to explain inequality changes with contemporaneous product-price changes. Thus, for example, researchers exploring rising inequality during the 1980s analyze trends in product prices during the 1980s. The implicit assumption in all these studies is that the U.S. economy is sufficiently HO in nature that price shocks over some time period affect the economy as predicted by HO theory in that same period.

But what if that assumption is incorrect? What if the U.S. economy has sufficiently important short-run frictions—such as imperfect information, high costs of reallocating capital across sectors, and people reluctant to relocate geographically—that price shocks over some time period do not generate HO factor-price effects in that same period? A lot of research indicates that these frictions can matter for several years. For example, Blanchard and Katz (1992) find that in states hit by aggregate demand drops, people can take between 5 and 10 years before deciding to move away to recover economically. The more important these frictions are for any given shock, the longer it takes the economy to adjust in an RV manner before switching over to an HO manner.

If price shocks do not generate HO wage effects over the same time horizon, then the basic methodology of linking prices and wages contemporaneously is incorrect such that the common conclusion that trade has contributed very little to rising income inequality needs further exploration. To see this, again consider the finding in Leamer (1998) that during the 1970s the U.S. experienced a sharp decline in the relative price of unskilled-labor-intensive products. By most measures (e.g., college–high school premium) inequality did not rise until the 1980s. If price shocks and wage effects occur contemporaneously, then these two facts do not support the idea that trade mattered. But if the U.S. economy contains extensive frictions that prevent interindustry factor mobility for several years, then this 1970s price shock might not have generated wage effects until the 1980s. In this case, trade-induced price changes might have mattered a lot.

This discussion indicates that a full understanding of trade's effect on income inequality must address the issue of timing: How slowly does the HO clock tick? If it ticks decade by decade rather than year by year, the literature's current thinking might need revising.

4.5.3 Potential Limitations of Price Index Data: What About Cones?

One final issue to consider is the inability of price index data to identify the crucial issue of how relative factor prices depend on a country's product mix.

As discussed earlier, the SS theorem involves the prices of only those industries with current domestic production. Price changes for industries not domestically produced simply entail consumption-deflated real-wage changes for all domestic factors. Cheaper foreign T-shirts are a good thing for even less-skilled U.S. workers if no U.S. firms produce T-shirts. Whether or not the United States makes T-shirts depends on forces such as the national endowment mix and level of technology. Thus changes over time in product mixes can matter greatly for the economy's links between product prices and factor prices.

There is a potential problem with the domestic, export, and import price data used by the studies in this paper. All these data are price indexes designed to measure the prices of unchanging baskets of goods. All three series are produced by the BLS, and the *Handbook of Methods* (U.S. Department of Labor 1992) details the various methods for eliminating product changes from the indexes. This is done both by selecting a fixed basket of goods to price and by systematically eliminating from transaction prices any changes due to quality changes (except in instances of "drastic" introductions and/or eliminations of products).

The price index methodology suggests that the BLS price data tend not to reflect changes in product mixes either by domestic producers or foreign producers. Price increases that are due to quality upgrading get reduced, while price decreases that are due to quality reductions get increased. Thus, there is an important tension between the theory of cones of diversification and the empirical reality of price index construction.

How might this price problem be addressed? Alterman (1991) points out that the import and export unit values that can be constructed from Census Bureau trade-flow data do not adjust for quality changes. In principle, one might be able to compare BLS traded-price indexes with traded-goods unit values to look for evidence of changing product quality. For example, if domestic producers are moving toward higher-quality products, then export unit values should rise faster than export price indexes. Indeed, Alterman does a direct comparison like this and reports the "puzzling" result that during the 1970s and 1980s BLS import price indexes tend to rise faster than the Census unit values. Alterman suggests that one might expect quality-adjusted price indexes to rise more slowly if import quality is rising over time. But thinking about different countries moving into different cones suggests an alternative view. Perhaps the average quality of U.S. imports is declining, not rising as is usually presumed, as foreign producers increasingly concentrate on unskilled-labor-intensive products. In this case, quality-adjusted price indexes should rise faster than unit values, as the data actually show. Another possible solution to changing product mixes and price indexes is suggested by Feenstra (1994), who develops a methodology for adjusting import-price data to account for new product varieties.

4.6 Conclusion

This paper has attempted to provide a comprehensive survey and synthesis of research on how product-price changes have contributed to rising U.S. wage inequality. It has surveyed nine product-price studies, which together demonstrate how the methodology of product-price studies has evolved. After surveying each paper individually I synthesized the findings and drew two main conclusions. The first conclusion is that this literature has refined a set of empirical strategies for applying the SS theorem to the data from which important methodological lessons can be learned. The second main conclusion is that, despite the methodological progress that has been made, research to date still has fundamental limitations regarding the key question of how much international trade has contributed to rising wage inequality.

References

Alterman, William. 1991. Price trends in U.S. trade: New data, new insights. In *International economic transactions: Issues in measurement and empirical research,* ed. Peter Hooper and J. David Richardson, 109–43. NBER Studies in Income and Wealth vol. 55. Chicago: University of Chicago Press.

Baldwin, Robert E., and Glen G. Cain. 1997. Shifts in U.S. relative wages: The role of trade, technology, and factor endowments. NBER Working Paper no. 5934. Cambridge, Mass.: National Bureau of Economic Research.

Baldwin, Robert E., and R. Spence Hilton. 1984. A technique for indicating comparative costs and predicting changes in trade ratios. *Review of Economics and Statistics* 46:105–10.

Bhagwati, Jagdish. 1991. Free traders and free immigrationists: Strangers or friends? Russell Sage Foundation Working Paper. New York: Russell Sage Foundation.

Blanchard, Olivier, and Lawrence Katz. 1992. Regional evolutions. *Brookings Papers on Economic Activity,* no. 1: 1–61.

Deardorff, Alan V. 1984. Testing trade theories and predicting trade flows. In *Handbook of international economics,* ed. Ronald W. Jones and Peter B. Kenen, vol. 1, 467–517. Amsterdam: Elsevier Science.

———. 1994. Overview of the Stolper-Samuelson theorem. In *The Stolper-Samuelson theorem: A golden jubilee,* ed. Alan V. Deardorff and Robert M. Stern, 7–34. Ann Arbor: University of Michigan Press.

Deardorff, Alan V., and Dalia Hakura. 1994. Trade and wages: What are the questions? In *Trade and wages: Leveling wages down?* ed. Jagdish Bhagwati and Marvin Kosters, 36–75. Washington, D.C.: American Enterprise Institute.

Deardorff, Alan V., and Robert M. Stern, eds. 1994. *The Stolper-Samuelson theorem: A golden jubilee.* Ann Arbor: University of Michigan Press.

Feenstra, Robert C. 1994. New product varieties and the measurement of international prices. *American Economic Review* 84:157–77.

Feenstra, Robert C., and Gordon H. Hanson. 1995. Foreign investment, outsourcing, and relative wages. In *Political economy of trade policy: Essays in honor of Jagdish Bhagwati,* ed. Robert C. Feenstra and Gene M. Grossman, 89–127. Cambridge, Mass.: MIT Press.

———. 1999. The impact of outsourcing and high-technology capital on wages: Estimates for the United States, 1979–1990. *Quarterly Journal of Economics* 114:907–40.

Freeman, Richard B. 1995. Are your wages set in Beijing? *Journal of Economic Perspectives* 9:15–32.

Harrigan, James, and Rita A. Balaban. 1997. U.S. wages in general equilibrium: Estimating the effects of trade, technology, and factor supplies, 1963–1991. New York: Federal Reserve Bank of New York. Mimeo, September.

Haskel, Jonathan, and Matthew J. Slaughter. 1998. Does the sector bias of skill-biased technological change explain changing wage inequality? NBER Working Paper no. 6565. Cambridge, Mass.: National Bureau of Economic Research.

Helpman, Elhanan, and Paul R. Krugman. 1985. *Market structure and foreign trade.* Cambridge, Mass.: MIT Press.

Krueger, Alan B. 1997. Labor market shifts and the price puzzle revisited. NBER Working Paper no. 5924. Cambridge, Mass.: National Bureau of Economic Research.

Lawrence, Robert Z., and Matthew J. Slaughter. 1993. International trade and American wages in the 1980s: Giant sucking sound or small hiccup? *Brookings Papers on Economic Activity, Microeconomics,* no. 2: 161–211.

Leamer, Edward E. 1998. In search of Stolper-Samuelson linkages between international trade and lower wages. In *Imports, exports, and the American worker,* ed. Susan Collins, 141–214. Washington, D.C.: Brookings Institution.

Magee, Steven M. 1980. Three simple tests of the Stolper-Samuelson theorem. In *Issues in international economics,* ed. Peter Oppenheimer, 138–53. London: Oriel Press.

Sachs, Jeffrey D., and Howard Shatz. 1994. Trade and jobs in U.S. manufacturing. *Brookings Papers on Economic Activity,* no. 1: 1–84.

U.S. Department of Labor. Bureau of Labor Statistics. 1992. *Handbook of methods.* Bulletin no. 2214. Washington, D.C.: U.S. Government Printing Office.

Comment   Robert E. Baldwin

Matthew Slaughter has written an extremely valuable paper for economists interested in the impact of international trade on U.S. wages. Focusing on papers based on the product-price/factor-price relationships embedded in the Stolper-Samuelson theorem, he begins by discussing the empirical feasibility of implementing alternative theoretical versions of this theorem. He then thoroughly reviews nine such studies, carefully pointing out and synthesizing the similarities and differences among the authors in assumptions and statistical methodology that do and do not seem to matter for differences in the authors' findings. In his concluding remarks on the limitations of current research and suggestions for future research, Slaughter emphasizes the failure of the studies thus far to determine clearly the relative importance of international versus domestic factors in influencing changes in relative wages or the ranking in importance of the various international forces that operate on relative wages. He also stresses our lack of understanding of the time framework within which various domestic or international forces affect relative wages. I am in general agreement with Slaughter's appraisals of the strengths and drawbacks of the various studies, but will suggest a somewhat different ordering in importance of these, as well as providing additional examples of his general themes.

By applying the small-country assumption to the United States, four of

Robert E. Baldwin is the Hilldale Professor of Economics Emeritus at the University of Wisconsin–Madison and a research associate of the National Bureau of Economic Research.

the nine studies reviewed (Bhagwati, Lawrence and Slaughter, Sachs and Shatz, and Krueger) assume that U.S. product prices are not influenced by any U.S. real variables such as changes in relative factor endowments, changes in technology, or changes in tastes. Leamer (1996) also makes this assumption in his paper, except with regard to the effect of domestic technological progress (as measured by total factor productivity growth) on domestic prices. In his empirical analysis, Leamer regresses changes in domestic prices and total factor productivity growth on factor shares, allowing alternatively for a 0 and 100 percent pass-through effect of total factor productivity growth on domestic prices. The results yield mandated growth rates in the wages of high- and low-skilled labor, as well as in the earnings of capital that he attributes to "globalization." In view of the intense policy debate about the effects of globalization on American workers, I think this is a somewhat unfortunate use of the term. As Leamer points out himself, if domestic as well as international economic conditions affect domestic prices, he may be attributing to "globalization" relative price effects that are due to important economic changes (other than domestic technological changes) strictly internal to the United States. One such change is the increase in the endowment of more-educated labor relative to the endowment of less-educated labor that has taken place in the United States over the last few decades. For example, the proportion of U.S. workers with only 1–11 years of education fell from 36 percent to 10 percent between 1967 and 1992, while the proportion of workers with 13 years or more of education rose from 25 percent to 53 percent between these years.

We should drop the small-country assumption when applying the Stolper-Samuelson framework to large developed countries, such as the United States. Estimations of import- and export-demand elasticities, as well as studies of the pass-through effects of exchange rate changes, provide ample evidence that this assumption is not valid for the United States. Dropping the assumption makes it much more difficult to estimate the relative wage effects stemming from international factors, but avoiding a difficult decomposition problem by an unrealistic assumption may misinform the policy debate on trade issues. The 1997 paper by Feenstra and Hanson demonstrates how progress still can be made in assessing the relative importance of trade and technical change on relative wages even when industry prices are not assumed to be exogenous.

Unlike the Leamer and Feenstra and Hanson papers, my colleague Glen Cain and I do not include a measure of total factor productivity growth in our regression analysis in order to control for the effect of technology. Unfortunately, these efforts are hampered by the lack of a suitable measure of exogenous technological change for an industry. The measure used, total factor productivity (TFP) from Bartelsman and Gray (1996), includes several variables that are endogenous with respect to current-period product prices for an industry, namely, current labor and capital quantities, current wages and returns to capital, and the current price and quantity of industry output. The simultaneity problem is especially severe because TFP includes the current product price, which is the model's dependent variable. Our alternative is to infer from the general equilibrium trade model and from the standard properties of regression analysis the biases in the regression coefficients of the factor shares that would exist with varying types of technological change. However, for comparative purposes and to illustrate further some of the points Slaughter makes, I report regression results using our data set when the standard TFP measure is included.

Table 4C.1 presents estimates of what Leamer terms "total mandated annualized earnings growth" for two types of labor and a capital proxy,

Table 4C.1   **A Comparison of Leamer's "Total Mandated Annualized Earnings Growth" under Various Assumptions Using BC Data Set**

	0 Percent Pass-Through (%)			100 Percent Pass-Through (%)		
	1968–73	1973–79	1979–91	1968–73	1973–79	1979–91
Weighted Regressions (by employment); No Constant Term						
Labor (years of education)						
1–12	−0.10	−6.39	−1.38	1.15	−6.64	−1.46
(1–12 minus 13+)	(11.18)	(−14.65)	(−5.95)	(13.93)	(−14.57)	(−5.85)
13+	−11.28	8.26	3.97	−12.78	7.93	3.89
Capital	−0.82	−5.42	−2.72	0.20	−5.76	−2.80
Unweighted Regressions; No Constant Term						
Labor (years of education)						
1–12	3.10	−6.06	−0.85	4.14	−6.40	−0.92
(1–12 minus 13+)	(19.56)	(−14.90)	(3.40)	(20.21)	(−14.91)	(−5.52)
13+	−16.46	8.84	−4.25	−16.07	8.51	4.60
Capital	−1.57	−5.46	−3.00	−0.54	−5.79	−3.08
Unweighted Regressions; with Constant Term						
Labor (years of education)						
1–12	0.07	−10.61	−6.20	0.91	−10.65	−6.83
(1–12 minus 13+)	(20.06)	(−14.90)	(−3.40)	(20.06)	(−13.82)	(−3.70)
13+	−19.99	3.21	−3.18	−19.15	3.17	−3.13
Capital	−1.92	−6.35	−2.14	−1.09	−6.40	−3.87
Actual Average Annual Growth of Real Wages (%)						

Years of Education	1967–72	1972–79	1979–92
1–12	2.97	−0.37	−0.60
13+	2.40	−1.00	−0.00

assuming alternatively a 0 percent pass-through of productivity changes into price changes and a 100 percent pass-through. Results from three econometric specifications are given. The first follows Leamer in reporting a weighted regression (where the weights are industry employment) without a constant term. The second set of results is based on an unweighted regression without a constant term, while the third set of regressions is unweighted but includes a constant term.

As is apparent from the table, even with TFP data included in the regressions, the product-price approach performs badly with our data in predicting the magnitude of the actual rates of change of the real wages of less-educated and more-educated labor over the periods covered. At best, it only seems possible to use the approach to analyze the differences between the growth rates of wages for the two groups, and then not in absolute terms but in terms of whether inequality increases or decreases. For example, all three sets of regressions both with 0 and 100 percent pass-through correctly predict the trend toward greater wage equality in the period 1968–73. In contrast, none of the three variations correctly predicts the continued increase in wage equality between 1973 and 1979. However, two of the three regressions under the assumption of a 0 percent pass-through and all of the regressions under the assumption of a 100 percent pass-through correctly predict the increase in wage inequality in the 1979–91 period. In terms of a change toward greater or less wage equality, in only one case (the unweighted regression without a constant term for 1979–91) do the differences between weighting and not weighting and between including a constant term or not matter for the results.

To elaborate further on Slaughter's analysis of what differences in assumptions and statistical methodology seem to matter most for differences in results, I used our data set to investigate how the labor-share coefficients in the price regressions differ when the regressions are modified in the following manner: (1) the computer sector is excluded from the data set, (2) direct rather than direct and indirect input-output coefficients are used, (3) labor shares by industry are calculated using actual industry wages by education level rather than the nationwide wage for a particular education group, and (4) primary products and services are included in the regression analysis in addition to manufacturing industries. For the period 1968–73, our basic regression for manufacturing industries and the regressions for all four of these variations correctly predict a rise in the wages of unskilled (1–12 years of education) workers relative to skilled (13+ years of education) workers. All the regressions except the one omitting the computer sector also correctly predict the continued reduction in wage inequality during the period 1973–79. However, for the period 1979–91, only the regression omitting the computer sector and the regression including primary products and services correctly predict the increase in wage inequality during these years.

These results reinforce Slaughter's point that the extent of industry coverage seems to matter greatly. This suggests that technology shocks move across industries in a very uneven manner in terms of their impact on the relative wages of broad groups with similar levels of education. This may bring about not only the significant differences in relative wage changes among different groups of industries such as services and manufacturing, but also the large differences in the coefficients on labor shares within the manufacturing group. The forces tending to eliminate excess profits and rents and change the relative wages of a particular skill group across all industries clearly seem to be operating, but in an imperfect manner that apparently makes relative price and productivity changes a poor short-run predictor of relative wage changes.

References

Bartelsman, Eric J., and Wayne Gray. 1996. The NBER manufacturing database. NBER Technical Working Paper no. 205. Cambridge, Mass.: National Bureau of Economic Research.

Feenstra, Robert C., and Gordon H. Hanson. 1997. Productivity measurement and the impact of trade and technology on wages: Estimates for the U.S., 1972–1990. NBER Working Paper no. 6052. Cambridge, Mass.: National Bureau of Economic Research.

Leamer, Edward E. 1996. In search of Stolper-Samuelson effects on U.S. wages. NBER Working Paper no. 5427. Cambridge, Mass.: National Bureau of Economic Research.

International Trade and American Wages in General Equilibrium, 1967–1995

James Harrigan

5.1 Introduction

Wage inequality in the United States has increased since the late 1970s, a trend that coincides with an increase in imports. General equilibrium trade theory suggests that these trends may be related, and the theory suggests where to look for links. The purpose of this paper is to use general equilibrium theory and econometrics to analyze time-series data on the prices and quantities of labor, output, and imports, with a view to understanding the forces that have led to increased wage inequality. I take it for granted that an increase in wage inequality is a worrying phenomenon, with social and political as well as economic implications, and that an understanding of the causes of increased wage inequality is an important task for applied economics.

Since the Stolper-Samuelson theorem of trade theory suggests that relative wages may be related to international trade and outlines the mechanism through which trade may affect wages, it is not surprising that a number of economists have used the Stolper-Samuelson theorem in their attempts to explain the growth in wage inequality. Matthew Slaughter's contribution to this volume (see chap. 4) is a good survey of this line of research.

One of the virtues of the Stolper-Samuelson theorem is that it is a gen-

James Harrigan is a senior economist at the Federal Reserve Bank of New York and a faculty research fellow of the National Bureau of Economic Research.

The author is indebted to Rita Balaban and Susan Miller for their collaboration in analyzing much of the data used in this paper, and to Sairah Burki for indispensable research assistance. He also thanks Robert Feenstra, Jonathan Eaton, and the other conference participants for their constructive comments. The views expressed in this paper are those of the author and do not necessarily reflect the position of the Federal Reserve Bank of New York, the Federal Reserve System, or the National Bureau of Economic Research.

eral equilibrium result and is therefore well suited to analyzing economywide trends in wages that are common across sectors, age groups, and so on. In some ways, however, the Stolper-Samuelson framework is an overly restrictive way of organizing a study of the relationship between trade and wages. In particular, the Stolper-Samuelson theorem is derived from a one-cone model; that is, it applies only when there are no changes in the product mix. By ruling out changes in the product mix, the Stolper-Samuelson framework also rules out any effect of factor-supply changes on factor prices. The Stolper-Samuelson theorem also has the disadvantage that there is no direct link between trade volumes or import prices and factor prices: The chain of causation is from international prices to domestic final-goods prices to factor prices.

In this paper, I use a less restrictive general equilibrium model, in which factor-supply changes may affect factor prices and changes in the product mix are not ruled out. The model also has the feature that import prices have a direct (as well as an indirect) effect on factor prices. Using U.S. data on prices and quantities of factor supplies, final goods, and imports, I estimate general equilibrium factor-price elasticities, which allow a comparison of the relative importance of various causes of wage changes. I find that relative final-goods prices and relative factor-supply changes are both strongly related to wage changes, and that imports have had a negligible direct effect. The results do not rule out an influence of imports on wages through their effect on domestic prices, but an informal analysis of U.S. price changes suggests that they are determined primarily by domestic rather than foreign influences.

5.2   The Model

The standard neoclassical trade model takes factor supplies as given, with prices of final goods determined in international markets. Within a final-goods sector, domestic output and imports are treated as perfect substitutes, so that they have the same price in equilibrium. In such models, the vector of net exports is residual, arising from differences between domestic demand and supply.

The most cursory glance at disaggregated import statistics, however, makes it clear that imports are often intermediate goods, which are combined with domestically produced intermediates and domestic primary-factor services to produce final output. As shown by Rousslang and To (1993), even imported goods such as consumer electronics and autos have a very large share of domestic value added in the form of shipping, distribution, marketing, and service. This suggests modeling the demand for imports as arising from the production sector, so that (for example) an increase in the final demand for consumer goods leads to a demand for imported inputs.

There is a large literature on trade in intermediate goods that traces out the channels through which trade influences domestic prices and quantities, but here I follow Kohli (1991, chaps. 5 and 11) and take a reduced-form approach that is appropriate for the empirical work that follows. This model imposes no restrictions on the numbers of goods or factors, nor is joint production ruled out. I treat domestic output, which may be consumed domestically or exported, as being produced using primary factors and imports. The GNP identity is

$$(1) \qquad \pi = \mathbf{p} \cdot \mathbf{y} - \mathbf{p}_M \cdot \mathbf{m} = \mathbf{w} \cdot \mathbf{v},$$

where $\mathbf{p}$ and $\mathbf{y}$ are the prices and quantities of domestically produced goods, $\mathbf{p}_M$ and $\mathbf{m}$ are the price and quantities of imports, and $\mathbf{w}$ and $\mathbf{v}$ are the prices and quantities of primary factors.[1] The output quantity $\mathbf{p} \cdot \mathbf{y}$ might be called *gross GNP,* that is, GNP before imports have been paid for. Dividing the definition of π through by π gives $1 = s_Y - s_M$, where s_Y and s_M are the shares of final output and imports in GNP, respectively. This makes clear that the share of domestically produced goods in GNP, s_Y, exceeds 1. The share of imports in GNP, s_M, is defined as a positive number, and imports are measured as positive throughout.

Technology is assumed to be constant returns to scale, and all agents act as competitive price takers. For given prices and factor supplies, the competitive equilibrium will maximize the value of GNP, and this maximized value is given by the GNP function,

$$(2) \qquad \pi = r(\mathbf{p}, \mathbf{p}_M, \mathbf{v}, t),$$

where t is time.[2] The properties of the maximization problem ensure that this function is convex in $\mathbf{p}$ and concave in $\mathbf{p}_M$ and in $\mathbf{v}$. In addition, equation (2) is homogeneous of degree one in ($\mathbf{p}$, $\mathbf{p}_M$), and homogeneous of degree one in $\mathbf{v}$. As usual with such dual functions, differentiation of the GNP function with respect to $\mathbf{p}$, $\mathbf{p}_M$, and $\mathbf{v}$ gives the final output, gross import, and factor price vectors,

$$(3) \qquad \mathbf{y} = r_p(\mathbf{p}, \mathbf{p}_M, \mathbf{v}, t),$$

$$(4) \qquad -\mathbf{m} = r_{pM}(\mathbf{p}, \mathbf{p}_M, \mathbf{v}, t),$$

$$(5) \qquad \mathbf{w} = r_v(\mathbf{p}, \mathbf{p}_M, \mathbf{v}, t).$$

Equations (3) and (4) are homogeneous of degree zero in ($\mathbf{p}$, $\mathbf{p}_M$), and homogeneous of degree one in $\mathbf{v}$, while equation (5) is homogeneous of degree one in ($\mathbf{p}$, $\mathbf{p}_M$), and homogeneous of degree zero in $\mathbf{v}$. Closing the model requires the specification of the demand for domestically produced

---

1. Boldface variables are vectors.
2. All variables are implicitly indexed for time.

goods **y** and the supply of imports **m**, but for now I will simply take the prices of final output and imports as given.

This simple theoretical model can be used to specify an empirical model by making a functional form assumption for equation (2). The translog functional form has good approximation properties and has proven useful in many empirical studies, including Kohli (1991) and Harrigan (1997), so I adopt the assumption that $r(\mathbf{p}, \mathbf{p}_M, \mathbf{v}, t)$ can be well approximated by a translog. For notational convenience, define the vector $\mathbf{q} = (\log \mathbf{p}, \log \mathbf{p}_M)$ and redefine **v** as the log of factor supplies. Then the translog GNP function is a quadratic in **q**, **v**, and t:

$$(6) \quad \log \pi = k + \mathbf{a} \cdot \mathbf{q} + \mathbf{b} \cdot \mathbf{v} + d_1 \cdot t + \frac{1}{2} \cdot \mathbf{q}' A \mathbf{q} + \frac{1}{2} \cdot \mathbf{v}' B \mathbf{v}$$

$$+ \frac{1}{2} \cdot \mathbf{q}' C \mathbf{v} + d_2 \cdot t^2 + t \cdot (\mathbf{d}_1 \cdot \mathbf{q} + \mathbf{d}_2 \cdot \mathbf{v}).$$

The matrices A and B are symmetric. Where ι is a conformable vector of ones, homogeneity requires $\mathbf{a} \cdot \iota = 1$, $\mathbf{b} \cdot \iota = 1$, $A\iota = 0$, $B\iota = 0$, $C\iota = 0$, $C'\iota = 0$, $\mathbf{d}_1 \cdot \iota = 0$, and $\mathbf{d}_2 \cdot \iota = 0$. Differentiation of equation (6) with respect to **q** and **v** gives the output, import, and factor share equations

$$(7) \qquad \mathbf{s}_{y,-m} = \mathbf{a} + A\mathbf{q} + C\mathbf{v} + t \cdot \mathbf{d}_1,$$

$$(8) \qquad \mathbf{s}_v = \mathbf{b} + C'\mathbf{q} + B\mathbf{v} + t \cdot \mathbf{d}_2,$$

where $\mathbf{s}_{y,-m} = (\mathbf{s}_y' \ -\mathbf{s}_m')'$ is the combined vector of the vector of final output shares of GNP, $\mathbf{s}_y$, and the negative of the vector of (positive) import shares of GNP, $-\mathbf{s}_m$. The term $\mathbf{s}_v$ is the vector of factor shares of GNP. Equation (7) is the share version of equations (3) and (4), while equation (8) corresponds to equation (5). If the actual GNP shares differ from equations (7) and (8) by a stationary stochastic process, then the parameters of the equations can be estimated statistically. Homogeneity implies that the two sets of equations (7) and (8) are each linearly dependent, and the symmetry of A and B combined with the appearance of C in both sets of equations means that there are numerous cross-equation restrictions that make systems estimation efficient. With technological progress that changes the form of equation (2) over time, the time trends in equations (7) and (8) can be interpreted as the reduced-form effect of technological progress on GNP shares.[3] The elasticities of the endogenous variables (factor prices, final output, and imports) with respect to the exogenous variables (factor supplies and prices of final output and imports) are simple functions of the

3. In Harrigan and Balaban (1999), we modeled the effects of technological progress more explicitly and measured Hicks-neutral technological progress using indices of total factor productivity (TFP). The data needed for TFP calculations are not available for the longer sample used in this paper.

parameters of equations (7) and (8) combined with the levels of the various GNP shares.[4] The factor price elasticities, in particular, are of interest, since they give an answer to the question: "What determines wages?"

5.3 Measurement and Estimation

I implement the model given by equations (7) and (8) using annual U.S. data from 1967 to 1995. The length of the sample is determined by data availability; import price data are not available before 1967, and output and labor data for years later than 1995 are not yet available. In this section, I briefly discuss the measurement and aggregation issues involved, and conclude the section with an explanation of the estimation methodology.[5]

The primary data sources are the U.S. National Accounts (USNA; for import, output, and price data), the Bureau of Economic Analysis (BEA; for GNP and capital stock data), and the Current Population Survey (CPS; for labor data). All the data used in this paper are publicly available.

With only 29 time-series observations and a wealth of disaggregated raw data, it is both crucial and problematic to construct aggregates that are appropriate for a study of wage determination. I choose to analyze a model with four primary factors of production (three types of labor, and capital), two final goods (high-skill-intensive and low-skill-intensive), and three types of imports (oil imports and two nonoil import aggregates).

The three labor aggregates that I analyze are (1) high school (HS) dropouts (workers who did not complete high school), (2) HS graduates (workers who completed high school, but who did not complete a 4-year college degree), and (3) college graduates (workers who have completed a 4-year college degree). Data on wages and employment were gathered from the March CPS, 1964–96. The CPS provides, among other variables, information on age, education, industry of employment, and both earned and unearned income. Details of the construction of the wage and weeks worked variables are contained in appendix B. For capital stock I use the real net stock of private nonresidential capital equipment and structures from the BEA.

Data on GNP by two-digit Standard Industrial Classification (SIC) code are available from the BEA. I aggregate economic activity into two sectors based on whether the two-digit industry is more or less intensive in skilled workers than the economy as a whole. This classification was chosen based on two considerations. First, with a short time series it was necessary to have a small number of aggregates. Second, I wanted to group sectors with similar factor shares, since theory informs us that it is the rela-

---

4. The exact formulas for the elasticities are given in appendix A.
5. Much of the data collection and analysis described in this section was done in collaboration with my co-authors on related projects, Rita Balaban and Susan Miller. I thank both for their permission to use the fruits of their labors in this paper.

Table 5.1   Composition of Aggregates

Output	
Nontraded	Traded
Unskilled-Labor Intensive	
Public utilities, transportation, construction, communications, wholesale and retail trade	Oil refining, mining, tobacco, leather, primary metals, lumber, textiles and apparel, stone, furniture, fabricated metals, agriculture, paper, food
Skilled-Labor Intensive	
Government enterprises; finance, insurance, and real estate (FIRE); miscellaneous other services (health care, business services, entertainment and recreation, education, legal, lodging)	Transportation equipment, rubber, chemicals, industrial machinery, instruments, electronic equipment, printing and publishing, miscellaneous manufactures

Nonoil Imports
Imports 1
Food and beverages, nonoil industrial supplies, services
Imports 2
Capital goods, consumer goods, autos, other goods

Notes: Disaggregate sectors are classified as unskilled-labor intensive if the share of total (direct and indirect) cost accounted for by less than college educated labor was less than the economywide average in 1977.

tive factor intensity of sectors that influences the Stolper-Samuelson responses of factor prices to goods-price changes. I used CPS data on the educational composition of the labor force by sector and BEA data on sectoral capital stocks to calculate the direct shares of each factor in sectoral value added. These data were combined with the 1977 input-output table to calculate the total (direct plus indirect) factor intensity of each input-output sector, since the total factor intensities are what matter for the Stolper-Samuelson effects. A sector is classified as skilled-labor intensive if the share of cost accounted for by workers with at least some college (13 or more years of education) is greater than the economywide average. The composition of the aggregates is listed in table 5.1. For reference, the components of each aggregate are grouped into traded and nontraded sectors in table 5.1, but this distinction plays no role in the empirical model.

It would be ideal to classify imports in the same way that domestic output is classified, by skill intensity. Unfortunately, this is not possible. I construct three import aggregates from the more disaggregated USNA data: oil imports; and two nonoil categories, Imports 1 (food and beverages, nonoil industrial supplies, and services) and Imports 2 (capital goods, con-

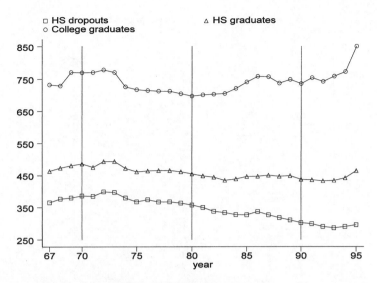

□ HS dropouts   △ HS graduates
○ College graduates

Fig. 5.1   Average real weekly wages by educational attainment, 1967–95, 1992 dollars

sumer goods, autos, and other goods).[6] These aggregates were constructed statistically, by aggregating sectors with highly correlated price and quantity changes.

In the derivation of equations (3)–(5) I took prices as fixed, which is not an appropriate statistical assumption. Consistent estimation of the translog equation system given by equations (7) and (8) requires valid instruments for the prices, which are correlated with prices, but not with contemporaneous output and import quantities or factor prices. Good instruments are those that are correlated with international supply and domestic demand conditions, and, fortunately, there is no shortage of plausible instruments in this context. To represent international supply, I use the lagged real GNP and lagged real exchange rate for three major trading partners of the United States: Canada, Japan, and Germany. Domestic demand conditions are represented by lagged values of the factor supplies and the lagged ratio of government purchases to potential GNP. Finally, I include an oil-shock dummy equal to 1 in 1974 and 1980, the years when exogenous spikes in world oil prices showed up in the U.S. import price of oil.

Figures 5.1 and 5.2 show wages and employment over the sample pe-

---

6. The binding data constraint for analyzing imports is a consistent price series, and the only broad-based and long-term price series are those reported in the USNA. The USNA classification system is based on end use rather than production, and it is not possible to construct a useful concordance from the import data to the SIC-based data that was used to construct the output aggregates.

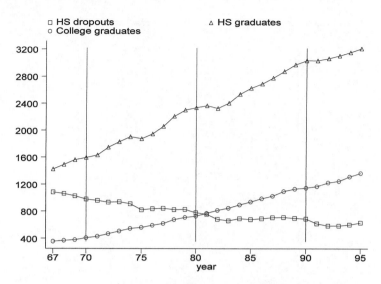

Fig. 5.2   Annual weeks worked by educational attainment, 1967–95, millions

riod. As is well known, real wages have stagnated since 1973, recovering for all three educational classes only in the past few years. At the same time, the labor force has become steadily more educated, with the number of HS dropouts decreasing, and the number of college graduates increasing steadily.

Figure 5.3 shows the wage of college graduates compared to HS graduates, which fell through most of the 1970s and has risen steadily since. Figure 5.4 shows the price of goods relatively intensive in highly skilled workers, or high-skill-intensive goods, compared to the price of goods relatively intensive in less-educated workers, or low-skill-intensive goods. In a pattern suggestive of a Stolper-Samuelson-like effect of relative prices on relative wages, this relative price is highly correlated ($\rho = 0.81$) with the relative wage plotted in figure 5.3.

The behavior of relative prices has been a key point of contention among economists who have looked for Stolper-Samuelson effects (see Slaughter, chap. 4 in this volume, for a discussion), so it is worth scrutinizing the sources of the dramatic changes in relative prices seen in figure 5.4. As noted in table 5.1, oil refining is included in the low-skill sector, which naturally leads to the suspicion that the swings in relative price of skilled and unskilled goods is driven by the well-known fluctuations in the price of oil. In fact, this is not the case: The correlation between the relative prices including and excluding oil is 0.97.

Table 5.2 analyzes the behavior of the price aggregates in greater detail. In looking at rows under the "Nontraded, skilled-labor intensive" heading, it becomes clear that changes in the price of skilled services largely

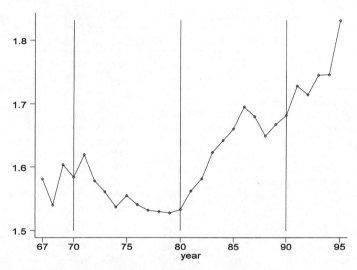

Fig. 5.3   College graduate/high school graduate relative average weekly wage, 1967–95

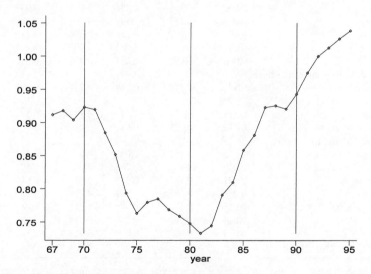

Fig. 5.4   Relative price of high-skill-intensive to low-skill-intensive goods, 1967–95, 1992 = 1

account for the price swings between 1970 and 1990 seen in figure 5.4. The two large sectors FIRE (finance, insurance, and real estate) and other services (a grab-bag sector that includes health care, business services, entertainment, education, and law) had price declines of around 15 percent during the 1970s and price increases on the order of 40 percent during

Table 5.2   **Relative Price Changes 1970–90**

	Price Change 1970–80			Price Change 1980–90		
	Share 1970	Value Added	Gross Output	Share 1980	Value Added	Gross Output
Nontraded, unskilled-labor intensive						
Wholesale and retail trade	0.173	−0.076	−0.065	0.156	−0.138	−0.058
Construction	0.076	0.099	0.063	0.067	0.063	0.007
Transportation	0.044	−0.172	−0.066	0.042	0.000	−0.029
Communications	0.028	−0.401	−0.329	0.032	0.150	0.148
Utilities	0.028	0.270	0.597	0.030	0.443	0.012
Traded, unskilled-labor intensive						
Agriculture	0.034	−0.094	−0.012	0.025	−0.339	−0.223
Food	0.023	−0.204	−0.040	0.021	−0.028	−0.109
Mining	0.047	2.680	1.211	0.021	−0.452	−0.288
Fabricated metals	0.015	−0.014	0.031	0.012	−0.023	−0.047
Paper	0.010	−0.020	0.025	0.011	0.094	0.022
Primary metals	0.014	0.031	0.099	0.010	−0.094	−0.096
Apparel	0.008	−0.433	−0.272	0.006	−0.118	−0.075
Lumber	0.007	0.056	0.058	0.006	−0.105	−0.093
Stone	0.008	0.021	0.049	0.006	−0.176	−0.089
Oil refining	0.009	7.411	1.836	0.005	−0.932	−0.417
Furniture	0.004	−0.312	−0.145	0.004	0.076	0.017
Textiles	0.005	−0.530	−0.236	0.004	−0.221	−0.107
Tobacco	0.002	0.099	0.053	0.003	3.134	1.063
Leather	0.002	0.059	0.011	0.001	0.041	0.004
Nontraded, skilled-labor intensive						
Other services	0.178	−0.140	−0.114	0.244	0.472	0.334
Finance, insurance, real estate	0.119	−0.172	−0.147	0.141	0.377	0.311
Government enterprises	0.016	−0.028	0.012	0.017	0.028	0.022
Traded, skilled-labor intensive						
Transport equipment	0.035	0.151	0.027	0.026	−0.152	−0.067
Industrial machinery	0.030	−0.162	−0.086	0.024	−0.491	−0.291
Chemicals	0.021	0.187	0.143	0.021	−0.080	−0.049
Electronics	0.021	−0.387	−0.219	0.019	−0.255	−0.139
Printing and publishing	0.015	−0.124	−0.081	0.016	0.259	0.150
Instruments	0.014	−0.373	−0.246	0.014	−0.031	−0.023
Rubber	0.012	−0.088	0.004	0.011	−0.165	−0.093
Miscellaneous manufactures	0.004	−0.046	0.025	0.004	−0.193	−0.123

Notes: This table reports sectoral proportional relative price changes, grouped by the aggregates defined in table 5.1. For each decade, the first column lists the sector's share of GDP at the start of the decade, and the next two columns give the change in the value added and gross output prices relative to overall GDP.

the 1980s. Unfortunately, the data do not permit greater disaggregation of the service sectors. Excessive aggregation combined with the well-known problems of measuring real output in services suggest that these numbers should be interpreted with caution.

Turning to the data for "Traded, unskilled-labor intensive" sectors, the

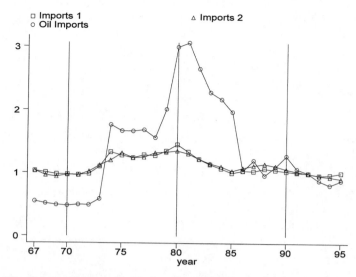

Fig. 5.5   Prices of imports relative to GDP, 1967–95, 1992 = 1
Note: Imports 1 comprises food and beverages, nonoil industrial supplies, and services; Imports 2 comprises capital goods, consumer goods, and autos.

collapse in the price of textiles and apparel during the 1970s stands out. This is the relative price that Leamer (1996) focuses on as an explanation for the rise in the skill premium during the 1980s. While small sectors may be influential, it is worth noting that even in 1970 these two sectors accounted for only 1.5 percent of GDP, a share that fell to 1 percent by 1980. Finally, note the large drops in the prices of the skilled-labor-intensive high-tech tradables, electronics and instruments, from 1970 to 1990.

Figure 5.5 plots the price of the three types of imports relative to the overall GDP deflator, with 1992 = 1. The price of imported oil has had far and away the biggest swings, while the price of nonoil imports rose slightly during the 1970s and has fallen fairly steadily since. The relative price of the two types of nonoil imports has not fluctuated much, although Imports 1 (food and beverages, nonoil industrial supplies, and services) has been flat as a share of GNP, while Imports 2 (capital goods, consumer goods, and autos) has risen steadily, as seen in figure 5.6.

5.4   Results

This section reports the results of estimating the system of equations given by (7) and (8). With two output categories and three types of imports, equation (7) amounts to five GNP-share equations, only four of which are linearly independent. The four primary factors lead to four factor-share GNP equations, three of which are linearly independent. The result is a system of seven linear equations, where each GNP share is a

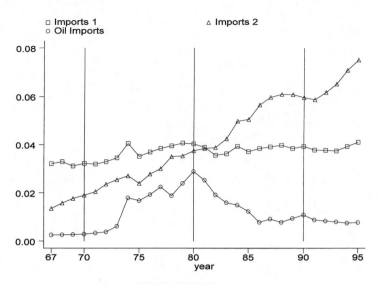

Fig. 5.6   Imports as a share of GDP, 1967–95

function of the log of two output and three import prices as well as three labor supply and one capital stock variables, a constant, and time. Theory provides homogeneity and symmetry conditions, which are implemented as within-equation and cross-equation restrictions on the system of equations. Concavity in prices and convexity in factor supplies together supply nine inequality restrictions, one for each equation, which may or may not be binding. Details on the exact form of the equations and constraints are given in appendix A.

The seven linearly independent equations are estimated jointly by generalized method of moments (GMM). Maximization of the objective function subject to the inequality constraints is a quadratic programming problem, with the constraints imposed where binding (at the optimum, six constraints bind; see appendix A for details). Misspecification tests for first-order autocorrelation fail to reject the null of no autocorrelation, and sample autocorrelation coefficients are small; details are in appendix A.

Table 5.3 reports the parameter estimates. Each column represents one of the nine equations, and the rows are the explanatory variables, all in logs except for time. Because of homogeneity, one of the first five columns is equal to the sum of the other four, and one of the last four columns is equal to the sum of the other three; the same applies to the first five and second four rows. The symmetry of cross-effects is also evident in the table—the cross-price effects on the output-import shares, the cross-quantity effects on the factor shares, and the equality of the factor quantity/output-import share and price/factor-share effects. (Standard errors are in parentheses below each slope coefficient.) Because the slopes are derivatives of shares

Table 5.3   Regression Results

| | GDP Shares | | | | | | | | |
| | Final Output | | Imports | | | Primary Factors | | | |
	High Skilled	Low Skilled	Imports 1	Imports 2	Oil Imports	HS Dropout	HS Graduates	College Graduates	Capital
Prices									
High skilled, final output	2.337	-2.582	-0.184	0.054	0.376	0.549	-1.114	0.282	0.282
	(0.51)	(0.69)	(0.13)	(0.17)	(0.08)	(0.14)	(0.37)	(0.20)	(0.45)
Low skilled, final output	-2.582	2.436	0.569	-0.092	-0.331	-0.761	0.926	-0.153	-0.012
	(0.69)	(1.01)	(0.20)	(0.25)	(0.11)	(0.20)	(0.53)	(0.28)	(0.65)
Imports 1	-0.184	0.569	-0.287	-0.100	0.002	0.328	-0.290	0.049	-0.087
	(0.13)	(0.20)	(0.08)	(0.08)	(0.02)	(0.06)	(0.14)	(0.10)	(0.18)
Imports 2	0.054	-0.092	-0.100	0.110	0.029	-0.100	0.471	-0.184	-0.187
	(0.17)	(0.25)	(0.08)	(0.13)	(0.03)	(0.07)	(0.19)	(0.13)	(0.24)
Oil imports	0.376	-0.331	0.002	0.029	-0.076	-0.017	0.007	0.006	0.004
	(0.08)	(0.11)	(0.02)	(0.03)	(0.02)	(0.02)	(0.06)	(0.03)	(0.08)
Factor supplies									
HS dropouts	0.549	-0.761	0.328	-0.100	-0.017	0.454	-0.667	-0.483	0.696
	(0.14)	(0.20)	(0.06)	(0.07)	(0.02)	(0.09)	(0.16)	(0.11)	(0.19)
HS graduates, some college	-1.114	0.926	-0.290	0.471	0.007	-0.667	2.276	-1.653	0.044
	(0.37)	(0.53)	(0.14)	(0.19)	(0.06)	(0.16)	(0.58)	(0.24)	(0.66)
College graduates	0.282	-0.153	0.049	-0.184	0.006	-0.483	-1.653	1.003	1.133
	(0.20)	(0.28)	(0.10)	(0.13)	(0.03)	(0.11)	(0.24)	(0.24)	(0.35)
Capital	0.282	-0.012	-0.087	-0.187	0.004	0.696	0.044	1.133	-1.874
	(0.45)	(0.65)	(0.18)	(0.24)	(0.08)	(0.19)	(0.66)	(0.35)	(0.89)
Other									
Constant	4.702	6.654	-1.665	0.211	-9.902	7.403	0.508	8.063	-15.973
	(2.28)	(3.32)	(0.87)	(1.18)	(0.40)	(0.99)	(3.23)	(1.53)	(4.25)
Time	0.063	-0.052	-0.015	0.024	-0.020	-0.030	0.012	0.011	0.007
	(0.01)	(0.02)	(0.00)	(0.01)	(0.01)	(0.01)	(0.01)	(0.01)	(0.01)

Notes: Dependent variables are GDP shares, listed as columns. Explanatory variables are GDP shares, listed as columns. Explanatory variables are in logs (except for time), listed as rows. Standard errors are in parentheses below the slopes, and parameters are multiplied by 10 for readability. All nine equations are estimated jointly by constrained GMM; see also appendix A for details on the instruments, cross-equation restrictions, and inequality constraints.

Table 5.4   General Equilibrium Factor Price Elasticities

	HS Dropouts	HS Graduates, Some College	College Graduates	Capital
Factor supplies				
HS dropouts	−0.425	−0.064	−0.112	0.373
	(0.10)	(0.04)	(0.05)	(0.08)
HS graduates, some	−0.284	−0.039	−0.286	0.440
college	(0.17)	(0.14)	(0.10)	(0.27)
College graduates	−0.278	−0.158	−0.337	0.687
	(0.11)	(0.06)	(0.11)	(0.14)
Capital	0.986	0.260	0.735	−1.501
	(0.20)	(0.16)	(0.15)	(0.35)
Final output prices				
High-skill-	1.279	0.433	0.818	0.810
intensive goods	(0.15)	(0.09)	(0.08)	(0.18)
Low-skill-	−0.408	0.616	0.330	0.391
intensive goods	(0.21)	(0.12)	(0.12)	(0.26)
Import prices				
Imports 1	0.312	−0.104	−0.015	−0.071
	(0.07)	(0.03)	(0.04)	(0.07)
Imports 2	−0.145	0.073	−0.117	−0.114
	(0.08)	(0.04)	(0.06)	(0.09)
Oil imports	−0.057	−0.037	−0.036	−0.037
	(0.02)	(0.02)	(0.01)	(0.03)

Notes: Each column represents a set of elasticities of a factor price with respect to exogenous changes in one of the four factor supplies and the five prices. Standard errors are in parentheses below each elasticity. These elasticities are derived from the estimated parameters reported in table 5.3, combined with GDP shares for 1982. By construction, for each factor price the factor supply elasticities sum to 0, and the price elasticities sum to 1.

with respect to log levels, the results of table 5.3 are somewhat hard to interpret, and I will focus my discussion on the elasticities reported in table 5.4.

Table 5.4 shows factor-price elasticities for 1982 that are derived from table 5.3 and the GNP shares for 1982 (1982 was chosen as a representative year in the middle of the sample). Each column is a set of elasticities of one of the four factor prices with respect to each of four factor quantities and five prices (with standard errors in parentheses below each elasticity). The factor-supply effects clearly show that the factor prices respond to factor-supply changes; except for HS graduates, the own-effects are negative and statistically significant, and there are substantial cross-effects as well. The fairly large own-elasticity for HS dropouts of −0.425 implies that the declining numbers of HS dropouts served to prop up their wages substantially. The different types of labor appear to be competitors in general equilibrium; a 10 percent increase in the supply of one type of worker reduces the wage of the other types by 1 to 3 percent.

Of particular interest is that the effect of capital accumulation is to increase the college graduate–HS graduate premium: Subtracting the capital elasticity of HS graduate wages from the capital elasticity of college graduate wages gives an elasticity of the college graduate–HS graduate premium of $0.735 - 0.260 = 0.475$, so that a 10 percent increase in the capital stock raises the college graduate–HS graduate premium by almost 5 percent. The return on capital is increased by increases in all types of labor, and the point estimate of the effect is increasing in the level of education. These results together are consistent with the view that technological progress is both skill-biased and embodied in new capital goods.

The large factor-supply effects on factor prices found here are inconsistent with the one-cone models used by most of the researchers surveyed by Slaughter (chap. 4 in this volume). Since these elasticities are calculated holding prices constant, they are not picking up the indirect effect (through induced price changes) of factor-supply changes emphasised by, for example, Krugman (1995). In short, wages appear to respond directly to factor-supply changes, and factor-price insensitivity, to use Leamer's (1995) useful phrase, does not hold empirically. There are a number of theoretical reasons for the empirical failure of factor-price insensitivity, including more factors than goods or joint production. The most economically intuitive explanation is that the factor-supply changes that have taken place have been large enough to lead to changes in the product mix. In particular, as capital and skilled labor have become more abundant, the economy may have stopped producing some low-skill-intensive goods and shifted toward a more skill- and capital-intensive product mix, in the process reducing the economywide demand for less-educated workers. This interpretation makes no reference to the skill bias of technological progress and is consistent with the pattern of elasticities seen in table 5.3.

Turning to the effect of relative price changes, the elasticities of HS-graduate and college-graduate wages with respect to the price of high-skill-intensive and low-skill-intensive goods is consistent with Stolper-Samuelson-like reasoning: By comparing the size of the elasticities, it can be seen that a 10 percent increase in the relative price of skill-intensive goods raises the college-HS premium by 2.8–3.8 percent. This result offers a partial explanation for the time path of the college premium since 1970; as shown in figure 5.4, the relative price of skill-intensive goods has had a long-term upward trend, but fell during the 1970s. The same can be said for the college-HS premium, as seen in figure 5.3. To the extent that the relative price fall was due to a decline in the relative demand for skill-intensive goods, the elasticities reported in table 5.4 show how relative wages responded. The price effects on the return to capital are similar to effects on the wage of college graduates, with no statistically significant difference in the elasticities.

Only for HS dropouts are there magnification effects, with one wage elasticity greater than 1 and one less than 0. This is surprising in light of the generality of magnification effects that was shown by Jones and Scheinkman (1977), which requires only the lack of joint production. The simplest way to rationalize the scarcity of magnification effects is to note that the empirical aggregates may be obscuring substantial heterogeneity. For example, an increase in the aggregate price index for high-skill-intensive goods might include increases in some component prices and decreases in others; the resulting aggregate effect on a particular wage would then be a weighted average of the individual price effects, and the average effect would tend to be less than 1 and greater than 0. A similar argument applies if the factor-supply aggregates encompass distinct factors whose individual elasticities with respect to a particular price change differ in sign.

The final set of elasticities show the effect of import prices on factor prices, and they are generally small. Oil import price increases have a statistically significant negative effect on all factor prices, with a doubling of the oil price reducing wages and the return to capital by 3.5 or 4 percent. An increase in the price of Imports 1 (food and beverages, industrial supplies, and services) benefits HS dropouts and hurts HS graduates, with the opposite being true for an increase in the price of Imports 2 (capital goods, consumer goods, and autos). There are no measurable nonoil import price effects on the wages of college graduates or the return to capital.

With small elasticities and small changes in relative import prices (see fig. 5.5), I conclude that import competition has had a negligible direct effect on U.S. wages in the past 3 decades. Of course, import-price changes may have contributed to the changes in the relative prices of domestic final output, which (according to table 5.4) have influenced relative wages. For example, the large drop in textile and apparel prices (see table 5.2) is surely in large part due to import competition. However, as noted previously the biggest swings in relative prices documented in table 5.2 seem to have occurred primarily in services and high-tech goods, with technological progress clearly a major force in (at least) the latter category. To my knowledge, there are no scholarly studies of relative price determination in the United States that might shed light on the causes of the changes shown in table 5.2, and until we understand the causes of these price changes we cannot rule out an important role for import competition.

It is important to keep in mind that all the results reported here are conditional on a number of bold assumptions. These assumptions come in two categories: those having to do with measurement and those having to do with theory. Among the important assumptions are that the prices of final goods and imports have been measured accurately, and that price changes do not simply reflect changes in product mix or quality. A related assumption concerns the labor aggregates, where I have not controlled for age or experience, nor have I modeled labor supply. On the theoretical front, the model here is fairly general in that imposes little beyond homogeneity and symmetry. But these assumptions are not meaningfully testable, nor is the assumption that the translog is an acceptable functional form, or that the adjustment of, for example, wages to equilibrium in response to labor-demand shocks generally takes place within 1 year.

The fundamental limitation of this exercise is that the time-series data are short, and I am asking subtle questions. I hope that the data analysis is sufficiently compelling that it will move the reader's posterior some distance from her or his prior, but I make no claim that this paper is definitive.

5.5 Conclusion

This paper has argued that understanding the causes of increased wage inequality requires an empirical general equilibrium approach. I implemented such a model for the United States using data on prices and quantities of labor, capital, final output, and imports.

The results of the model are striking. Changes in factor supplies have large effects on relative factor prices, and the pattern of effects is consistent with skill-biased technological change that is embodied in new capital goods; changes in relative final-goods prices can partially explain the time path of the college graduate–HS graduate wage differential; and nonoil import price changes appear to have had at most small direct effects on relative wages, and big oil price increases hurt all factors roughly equally. In other words, these results support the view that the causes of increased wage inequality are mainly domestic rather than foreign. An important caveat to this view is that foreign prices and quantities may have an important influence on domestic relative prices, which were shown to affect domestic relative wages, but an analysis of this possibility is beyond the scope of this paper.

Appendix A
Functional Form and Estimation

This appendix discusses the details of the functional form and estimation of the model given in section 5.2 of the paper.

Equations (7) and (8) give the shares of output, imports, and factors in national income as functions of output prices, import prices, and factor supplies. As noted in the text, there are four linearly independent output/import-share equations and three linearly independent factor-share equations, and maximum likelihood estimates are invariant to which equation is omitted. Writing these out and incorporating the symmetry of the matrices A and B give the following seven equations to be estimated:

(A1) $s_1 = a_1 + a_{11}p_1 + a_{12}p_2 + a_{13}p_{M1} + a_{14}p_{M2} + a_{15}p_{M3} + c_{11}v_1$
$$+ c_{12}v_2 + c_{13}v_3 + c_{14}v_4 + d_{11}t,$$

(A2) $s_2 = a_2 + a_{12}p_1 + a_{22}p_2 + a_{23}p_{M1} + a_{24}p_{M2} + a_{25}p_{M3} + c_{21}v_1$
$$+ c_{22}v_2 + c_{23}v_3 + c_{24}v_4 + d_{21}t,$$

(A3) $-s_{M1} = a_3 + a_{13}p_1 + a_{23}p_2 + a_{33}p_{M1} + a_{34}p_{M2} + a_{35}p_{M3} + c_{31}v_1$
$$+ c_{32}v_2 + c_{33}v_3 + c_{34}v_4 + d_{31}t,$$

(A4) $-s_{M2} = a_4 + a_{14}p_1 + a_{24}p_2 + a_{34}p_{M1} + a_{44}p_{M2} + a_{45}p_{M3} + c_{41}v_1$
$$+ c_{42}v_2 + c_{43}v_3 + c_{44}v_4 + d_{41}t,$$

(A5) $r_1 = b_1 + c_{11}p_1 + c_{21}p_2 + c_{31}p_{M1} + c_{41}p_{M2} + c_{51}p_{M3} + b_{11}v_1$
$$+ b_{12}v_2 + b_{13}v_3 + b_{14}v_4 + d_{12}t,$$

(A6) $r_2 = b_2 + c_{12}p_1 + c_{22}p_2 + c_{32}p_{M1} + c_{42}p_{M2} + c_{52}p_{M3} + b_{12}v_1$
$$+ b_{22}v_2 + b_{23}v_3 + b_{24}v_4 + d_{22}t,$$

(A7) $r_3 = b_3 + c_{13}p_1 + c_{23}p_2 + c_{33}p_{M1} + c_{43}p_{M2} + c_{53}p_{M3} + b_{13}v_1$
$$+ b_{23}v_2 + b_{33}v_3 + b_{34}v_4 + d_{32}t,$$

where p_1 and p_2 are output prices, import prices are p_{M1}, p_{M2}, and p_{M3}, and factor supplies are v_1, v_2, v_3, and v_4. National income shares are denoted s_j for output and import quantities ($j = 1, 2, M1, M2, M3$), and r_i for factors ($i = 1, 2, 3, 4$). All variables are implicitly subscripted for time, and all parameters (a, b, c, and d) are fixed, unknown constants to be estimated. Note that in equations (A3) and (A4), s_{M1} and s_{M2} are defined as positive numbers, so that $-s_{M1}$ and $-s_{M2}$ are negative numbers. The following substitutions into equations (A1)–(A7) are implied by homogeneity:

$$a_{15} = -a_{11} - a_{12} - a_{13} - a_{14} \qquad c_{14} = -c_{11} - c_{12} - c_{13}$$

$$a_{25} = -a_{12} - a_{22} - a_{23} - a_{24} \qquad c_{24} = -c_{21} - c_{22} - c_{23}$$

$$a_{35} = -a_{13} - a_{23} - a_{33} - a_{34} \qquad c_{34} = -c_{31} - c_{32} - c_{33}$$

$$a_{45} = -a_{14} - a_{24} - a_{34} - a_{44} \qquad c_{44} = -c_{41} - c_{42} - c_{43}$$

$$b_{14} = -b_{11} - b_{12} - b_{13} \qquad c_{51} = -c_{11} - c_{21} - c_{31} - c_{41}$$

$$b_{24} = -b_{12} - b_{22} - b_{23} \qquad c_{52} = -c_{12} - c_{22} - c_{32} - c_{42}$$

$$b_{34} = -b_{13} - b_{23} - b_{33} \qquad c_{53} = -c_{13} - c_{23} - c_{33} - c_{43}.$$

Elasticities are time-varying functions of the parameters of the translog and the national income shares. Using the notation that $\varepsilon(x,y)$ is the elasticity of x with respect to y, some of the elasticities of the endogenous variables are as follows:

Output quantities

(A8)
$$\varepsilon(y_j,p_j) = a_{jj}/s_j + s_j - 1 \geq 0$$

(A9)
$$\varepsilon(y_j,p_k) = a_{jk}/s_j + s_k, \quad j \neq k$$

Imports quantities

(A10)
$$\varepsilon(m_j,p_{Mj}) = -a_{jj}/s_j - s_j - 1 \leq 0$$

(A11)
$$\varepsilon(m_j,p_{Mk}) = -a_{jk}/s_j - s_k, \quad j \neq k$$

Factor prices

(A12)
$$\varepsilon(w_i,v_i) = b_{ii}/r_i + r_i - 1 \leq 0$$

(A13)
$$\varepsilon(w_i,v_k) = b_{ik}/r_i + r_k, \quad i \neq k$$

(A14)
$$\varepsilon(w_i,p_j) = c_{ji}/r_i + s_j, \quad j = 1, 2, M1, M2, M3$$

The inequality restrictions on these elasticities come from the requirement that $r(\mathbf{p}, \mathbf{p}_M, \mathbf{y}, t)$ is convex in $\mathbf{p}$ and concave in $\mathbf{p}_M$ and in $\mathbf{v}$. With five prices and four factor supplies, there are a total of nine inequality restrictions. They can be rewritten in terms of the shares in the data as

(A15)
$$a_{11} \geq (1 - s_1) \cdot s_1,$$

(A16)
$$a_{22} \geq (1 - s_2) \cdot s_2,$$

(A17)
$$a_{33} \geq -s_3 \cdot (1 + s_3),$$

(A18)
$$a_{44} \geq -s_4 \cdot (1 + s_4),$$

(A19)
$$-(a_{11} + a_{22} + a_{33} + a_{44} + 2a_{12} + 2a_{13} + 2a_{14} + 2a_{23} + 2a_{24} + 2a_{34})$$
$$\geq s_5 \cdot (1 + s_5),$$

(A20)
$$b_{11} \leq (1 - r_1) \cdot r_1,$$

(A21)
$$b_{22} \leq (1 - r_2) \cdot r_2,$$

(A22)
$$b_{33} \leq (1 - r_3) \cdot r_3,$$

(A23)
$$(-b_{11} - b_{22} - b_{33} - 2b_{12} - 2b_{13} - 2b_{23}) \leq (1 - r_4) \cdot r_4.$$

Table 5A.1   **Inequality Constraints**

Constraint	Lagrange Multiplier
(A15) Convex in skilled output price	50.1
(A15) Convex in unskilled output price	22.3
(A16) Concave in Imports 1 price	0.0
(A17) Concave in Imports 2 price	0.0
(A19) Concave in Imports 3 price	35.2
(A20) Concave in HS dropouts quantity	33.6
(A21) Concave in HS graduates quantity	42.0
(A22) Concave in college graduates quantity	0.0
(A23) Concave in capital stock	53.0

To implement these inequalities, I substitute the maximum sample values of the expressions on the right-hand side for the greater-than inequalities, and I substitute the minimum sample values for the less-than inequalities. This ensures that the inequalities hold for all observations.

Estimation of the system of equations (A1)–(A7) is by inequality-constrained GMM, which in this linear model with Gaussian errors is equivalent to constrained three-stage least squares (3SLS). The estimator minimizes the objective function subject to the nine inequality constraints (A15)–(A23), using a sequential quadratic programming algorithm implemented in the software package Gaussx. When the constraints are binding, the Lagrange multiplier on the constraint is positive, and the value of the Lagrange multipliers are reported in table 5A.1. The size of the Lagrange multipliers is related to how binding the constraints are, but tractable test statistics based on the Lagrange multipliers are not available even asymptotically (see Wolak 1989).

The errors appended to equations (A1)–(A7) are assumed to be serially uncorrelated. This assumption is tested against the alternative of AR1 errors using a Lagrange multiplier test as follows (see, for example, Davidson and MacKinnon 1993, sec. 10.10):

1. Estimate the model and collect the residuals from each estimated equation.
2. For each equation, regress the residuals on their lag as well as all the exogenous and predetermined variables in the model, including instruments.
3. The t-statistic on the lagged residual is a valid test statistic for the null of no-first-order autocorrelation.

When this procedure is carried out for each equation separately, the t-values obtained range 0.046 ($p = 0.96$) to 1.75 ($p = 0.11$). As pointed out by Berndt and Savin (1975), in a singular equation system such as the ones estimated in this paper, the autoregressive parameter must be the same in each equation. This suggests estimating all seven residual regressions together by SURE and imposing the restriction that the autoregressive parameter is the same in each equation. The result of this procedure is a t-statistic of -1.25 ($p = 0.223$) on the lagged residual. To summarize, both the single equation and pooled tests fail to reject the null of no autocorrelation. This is no doubt because the time trends in equations (A1)–(A7) soak up any potential persistence in the errors.

The estimated covariance matrix of the parameters is the usual GMM/3SLS estimate, and the standard errors reported in table 5.3 come from this estimate. With binding inequality constraints, however, the confidence intervals around the estimated parameters are not symmetric, so t-statistics should be interpreted carefully. Since the estimated elasticities in table 5.4 are linear functions of the data and the estimated parameters from table 5.3 (see equations [A8]–[A14]), the standard errors on the elasticities are simply equal to the relevant parameter standard error divided by the relevant factor share. For example, the elasticity of factor price i with respect to goods price j is given by equation (A14), and the standard error on this elasticity is the standard error of c_{ji} divided by r_i.

Appendix B
Construction of Labor Data

Data on wages were gathered from the March Annual Demographic file of the Current Population Survey (CPS), 1964–96. The CPS provides, among other variables, information on labor force participation, age, education, industry of employment, and both total income and income components. The data on income and employment refer to the preceding year; hence the series include the years 1963–95.

The sample includes the weekly wage and salary earnings of all non-self-employed workers who were between the ages of 16 and 65 and worked at least 1 hour for pay in the previous year. I omitted self-employed workers because they tend to misrepresent their true income and may also have negative earnings. Wage and salary data were chosen because they contain a good measure of earned income by industry and education. Ideally, an hourly measure would be the best measure of relative labor supply or total effort for each educational group. However, neither hourly wages nor number of hours worked is asked consistently in this data set and an imputed hourly wage would not be reliable.[7]

---

7. The survey asks how many hours were worked last week, which can be very different from the average number of hours worked per week in the previous year. The latter is more important since we must match it with the previous year's income data.

I use weekly wages as opposed to annual wages because the relative number of total workers by group (picked up by annual numbers) can vary from the relative number of total weeks worked (picked up by weekly numbers). The method used for computing weekly wages is described here.

For 1964–75, actual number of weeks worked is not recorded. However, a categorical variable is provided that indicates whether the earner worked 0, 1–13, 14–26, 27–39, 40–47, 48–49, or 50–52 weeks in the previous year. Actual weeks worked for the years 1976–88,[8] were used to fit values for the missing data by regressing each categorical variable for weeks on 755 cells that controlled for race, sex, education (as defined later), census region, and experience.[9]

Each coefficient from these equations was then regressed on a weighted time trend, where the weight was equal to the number of observations, to see if weeks worked by cell could be predicted based upon a linear trend. For those that were significant at the 10 percent level, a number-of-weeks-worked value was fit. For those that were not significant, a weighted average was used to estimate the number of weeks worked with a given weeks category. Here, each cell mean was weighted by the number of observations for a given cell in year t divided by the total number of observations for a given cell over the entire time period 1976–88.[10]

Next, a weekly wage was computed by dividing the annual wage and salary income by the number of weeks worked for each observation. Finally, a mean wage for each educational group (as defined later) was computed as a weighted average of each cell within that educational group. More explicitly, the mean wage[11] of each cell in the HS-dropout group, for example, was weighted by the number of weeks that cell worked in a given year t relative to the total number of weeks worked by all HS dropouts in year t. It is this weighted mean that is used in the analysis.

Before proceeding, it should be noted that the CPS top codes annual wage and salary incomes above a certain level. Prior to computing the average weekly wage, we corrected for this censoring by adopting the method employed by Katz and Murphy (1992). That is, we multiplied each top-coded value by 1.45.

We divided workers into three educational groups: did not complete high school (0–11 years of education), completed high school and some college (12–15 years of education); and college graduates (16+ years of education).[12] Individuals were assigned to a grade based on their comple-

---

8. The data from 1964–88 are contained in a uniform data file. The years 1989–92 were not used for this fitting procedure to omit any changes in survey method or data adjustment that might have occurred in these later survey years.

9. The procedure used to compute experience is described in Murphy and Welch (1992).

10. A more detailed description of this imputation process is available from the author.

11. It should be noted that there are many observations within each cell. The mean wage of the cell is weighted by the March supplemental weight.

12. This is the same breakdown used by Baldwin and Cain (1997).

tion of that grade, with one exception. Those individuals who did not complete the 13th grade were grouped with the 13th grade instead of the 12th because, based on Park (1996), it is better to treat these individuals as having some college education rather than associating them with those who only have a high school diploma.

Total wage and salary employment was obtained from the Bureau of Labor Statistics, from which the share of total employment for each skill was computed.

References

Baldwin, Robert E., and Glen Cain. 1997. Shifts in U.S. relative wages: The role of trade, technology, and factor endowments. NBER Working Paper no. 5934. Cambridge, Mass.: National Bureau of Economic Research.
Berndt, Ernst R., and Neil E. Savin. 1975. Estimation and hypothesis testing in singular equation systems with autoregressive disturbances. *Econometrica* 43: 937–57.
Davidson, Russell, and James G. MacKinnon. 1993. *Estimation and inference in econometrics.* Oxford: Oxford University Press.
Harrigan, James. 1997. Technology, factor supplies and international specialization: Estimating the neoclassical model. *American Economic Review* 87 (4): 475–94.
Harrigan, James, and Rita A. Balaban. 1999. U.S. wages in general equilibrium: The effects of prices, technology, and factor supplies, 1963–1991. NBER Working Paper no. 6981. Cambridge, Mass.: National Bureau of Economic Research.
Jones, Ronald, and Jose Scheinkman. 1977. The relevance of the two-sector production model in trade theory. *Journal of Political Economy* 85 (5): 909–35.
Katz, Lawrence F., and Kevin Murphy. 1992. Changes in relative wages in the United States, 1963–1987: Supply and demand factors. *Quarterly Journal of Economics* 107 (1): 35–78.
Kohli, Ulrich. 1991. *Technology, duality, and foreign trade.* Ann Arbor: University of Michigan Press.
Krugman, Paul. 1995. Technology, trade, and factor prices. NBER Working Paper no. 5355. Cambridge, Mass.: National Bureau of Economic Research.
Leamer, Edward E. 1995. The Hecksher-Ohlin model in theory and practice. Princeton Studies in International Finance no. 77. Princeton, N.J.: Princeton University, Department of Economics.
———. 1996. In search of Stolper-Samuelson effects on U.S. wages. NBER Working Paper no. 5427. Cambridge, Mass.: National Bureau of Economic Research.
Murphy, Kevin M., and Finis Welch. 1992. The structure of wages. *Quarterly Journal of Economics* 107 (1): 285–326.
Park, Jin-Heum. 1996. Measuring education over time: A comparison of old and new measures of education from the Current Population Survey. *Economic Letters* 50 (3): 425–28.
Rousslang, Donald J., and Theodore To. 1993. Domestic trade and transportation costs as barriers to international trade. *Canadian Journal of Economics* 26 (1): 208–21.
Wolak, Frank A. 1989. Testing inequality constraints in linear econometric models. *Econometrica* 41:205–435.

Comment   Jonathan Eaton

Jim Harrigan provides us with a very elegant and general framework with which to address the question at hand: Were changes in U.S. import prices responsible for growing U.S. trade inequality? While the approach is rooted in factor-endowments theory, it casts off many of the special and unrealistic assumptions that bound much previous empirical work. Here, factor endowments can affect factor prices; technologies can shift, quite generally, over time; and no cross-country similarities are invoked.

The framework delivers a set of equations relating sector shares, import shares, and factor shares to domestic goods prices, import prices, factor endowments, and, to capture the effect of technical progress, time. Harrigan estimates this set of equations, imposing the various restrictions implied by theory, on annual U.S. data for 29 years.

Harrigan finds that changes in factor supplies and in domestic prices, but not in import prices, are the culprits behind growing U.S. wage inequality. Because he has taken a more rigorous and general approach than has come before, any subsequent work on U.S. wage inequality is going to have to take Harrigan's findings seriously. But more work must be done before these results displace others at center stage. For one thing, some of the steps used to get to them are on a somewhat precarious footing. For another, the results themselves raise as many questions as they answer.

Where would one like some reassurance about the estimates themselves? Harrigan acknowledges that 29 observations provide a rather meager source of data for identifying the many parameters of the model. Still, anyone looking at figures 5.3 and 5.4 can see the comovement between the returns to skill, on one hand, and the price of skill-intensive goods, on the other. But what about the effect of factor endowments on factor rewards? The three series on factor endowments, depicted in table 5.2, appear to the naked eye pretty much as trend lines with small wobbles around them. Since the econometric specification attributes trends to technical progress, any inference about how factor endowments affect factor rewards must come from the wobbles. Given that one of the two key findings is the inverse relationship between factor endowments and factor rewards, it would be good to know more about what in the data drives the result. Some analysis of subperiods would be useful here.

What about the second key finding on the effect of domestic prices on factor rewards? Harrigan provides striking evidence of comovement between the relative wages of skilled workers and the relative price of skill-intensive goods. But it is not clear what we should make of this comove-

Jonathan Eaton is professor of economics at Boston University and a research associate of the National Bureau of Economic Research. When these comments were written, he was visiting professor at the Laboratoire d'Economie Quantitative d'Aix-Marseille.

ment. By entering domestic final-goods prices separately from import prices, he has dispensed with the trade economist's standard small-open-economy excuse for ignoring demand. But instead of modeling demand, Harrigan uses a set of kitchen-sink instruments to deal with the potential for simultaneity bias. We do not see the first-stage regressions, nor do we know what happens without instrumenting. A concern is that, with 29 annual observations, 10 (by my count) instruments are likely to fit the price series so well that instrumenting has little effect. Procedures exist to avoid first-stage overfitting, and this situation seems an appropriate place to use them.

These estimation issues aside, what are we to make of the results themselves? They present us with at least two major puzzles.

First, why did final-goods prices move? Supply-side explanations (such as technological progress) must be ruled out, since production is already modeled. So the answer has to be on the demand side. But how big a shift in demand is needed (1) under plausible assumptions about the elasticity of substitution in demand between high- and low-skill-intensive goods and (2) given the elasticity of transformation in their supply implied by the model? I would expect both elasticities to be fairly high. Yet figure 5.4 indicates swings in relative prices during the period of 25–30 percent, suggesting pretty big demand shifts.

Second, how do the results here jive with what happened to factor use within industries? Central to earlier discussion were findings, by Lawrence and Slaughter (1991) and by Berman, Bound, and Griliches (1994), for example, that the ratio of skilled to unskilled workers had risen during the period of rising wage inequality within industries. This evidence has been widely seen as bad news for trade-based explanations for growing wage inequality. But it is bad news for any demand-based explanation. Whether the demand for low-skilled workers fell because of imports from low-wage countries or because of a shift in tastes toward skill-intensive goods, within industries firms should have responded to the lower wages of unskilled workers by hiring more of them, contrary to what apparently happened. It would be useful, and should be straightforward, to extend Harrigan's framework to incorporate within-industry factor demands to see how the model goes about reconciling their evolution over this period with its explanation of what happened to output, import, and factor shares.

Harrigan suggests that within-industry heterogeneity may explain some of the paradoxes in what he finds, and such heterogeneity might help reconcile Harrigan's findings with evidence on intraindustry factor demands. But one would then like a theoretical framework that introduced intraindustry heterogeneity explicitly.

To summarize, Harrigan has not only made a very nice analytic contribution to the trade-and-wages literature, he has provided intriguing new evidence on the relationship between goods prices and factor rewards. But his explanation for it is at odds with other information we have. The next step is to put all this evidence together to see where we stand.

References

Berman, Eli, John Bound, and Zvi Griliches. 1994. Changes in the demand for skilled labor within U.S. manufacturing: Evidence from the Annual Survey of Manufactures. *Quarterly Journal of Economics* 109:367–97.

Lawrence, Robert, and Matthew Slaughter. 1991. International trade and American wages in the 1980s. *Brookings Papers on Economic Activity,* no. 2: 161–210.

6

Does a Kick in the Pants Get You Going or Does It Just Hurt? The Impact of International Competition on Technological Change in U.S. Manufacturing

Robert Z. Lawrence

International competition and technological change are frequently treated as independent sources of change. Anne Krueger (1980) pointed out, for example, that productivity growth was a far more important source of employment shifts in U.S. manufacturing than import competition. Similarly, the debate over growing wage inequality in the United States over the past 2 decades has been split between those emphasizing trade and those emphasizing technological change. There are, however, reasons to question the implicit assumption that trade and technology are independent causes. Indeed, it is likely that causation runs in both directions. Changes in technology are surely an explanation for trade flows and international competition could well affect technological change. Ignoring these interactions could be seriously misleading.[1] In particular, if international competition induces technological change, it could be a more important source of employment and wage changes than studies assuming their independence might conclude.

Moreover, the effect of international competition on technological

Robert Z. Lawrence is a member of President Clinton's Council of Economic Advisers. A research associate of the National Bureau of Economic Research, he is on leave from the John F. Kennedy School of Government where he is the Albert L. Williams Professor of International Trade and Investment.

The author is grateful to Julan Du and Yu-Chin Chen for research assistance. He is also grateful to Alan Krueger and other seminar participants for very helpful comments. The author thanks John Fernald, Jim Stock, and Mike Scherer for very useful discussions. Part of this research was funded by a grant from the U.S. Department of Labor.

1. Kapstein (1996), for example, dismisses the studies that have found a strong role for technology and a weak role for trade on the grounds that trade has induced technological change. Similarly, Wood (1994, 167) has argued that "in the North many firms have reacted to Southern competition by devising new production techniques that use less unskilled labor."

change is an important subject in its own right. It is often argued that the dynamic effects of free trade, for example, are far more important than the static benefits that come from improved resource allocation. Indeed, it is these dynamic effects that are believed to explain the evidence that more-open economies grow faster (Sachs and Warner 1995).

In this paper, therefore, after a brief conceptual review, I explore the effect of international competition on technological change empirically. Empirical work is particularly important since this effect is theoretically ambiguous. Competition could indeed spur innovation but it could also stifle it by making it less profitable. "Sometimes," as the saying goes, "a kick in the pants gets you going," but "sometimes it just hurts." However, resolving this issue in the data is no easy matter because "trade" and "technological change" are endogenous as well as interdependent variables.[2] One major challenge for this work, therefore, is dealing with issues of simultaneity. Indeed, throughout this paper I will show how results obtained using ordinary least squares (OLS) specifications may be dramatically changed when endogeneity is controlled for. A second major challenge lies in selecting appropriate measures of technology and international competition. In the paper I will proxy "international competition" with both price and quantity measures, and "technology" with measures of total factor productivity (TFP) and the skill ratio (i.e., the ratio of employment of workers with some college education to those with a high school degree or less).

In this paper I will present results in which both price and quantity measures suggest that import competition had a positive impact on U.S. TFP growth in manufacturing in the 1980s. This impact was larger in industries that are relatively less skill intensive and on average stronger in industries competing with developing countries. In the face of an elastic demand for the products of these industries, therefore, this effect would have actually raised the relative wages of less-skilled workers. I will also present evidence that import competition may have stimulated the rising skill intensity in manufacturing. This effect could have contributed to the rising skill premium.

6.1 Theory

It is not a simple matter to predict and measure the impact of increased international competition on the rate and direction of technological change at the industry level. One difficulty relates to the ambiguity of the effects in theory, another to the practical problems in distinguishing technical change from other shifts in resource allocation. There are several theoretical considerations that suggest that the impact of increased inter-

---

2. See Deardorff and Hakura (1994).

national competition on innovation (1) could be either negative or positive and (2) could well differ in export and import-competing industries.

One impact of international competition could come from "learning by doing." Productivity growth could be related to the scale of operation. To the degree that these effects are external to the firm but related to the size of the industry, we might expect to see positive effects in export industries that expand in response to increased trade and negative effects in import-competing sectors that would contract in response to trade.

A second impact could stem from "learning by watching." Trade will expose firms to new competitors and ideas. To the degree they are able to learn from foreign competitors, this could stimulate innovation in all exposed sectors. In this case, the effects should be positive for both export and import-competing sectors.

A third impact could occur through endogenous responses to the changes in market structure as a result of increased international competition. Here, as with competition in general, the arguments are varied. On the one hand, there is the view, often ascribed to Hicks, that "monopolists seek the quiet life" and will tend to rest on their laurels and avoid innovations, particularly when these might undermine the rents they enjoy from existing technologies. In this view, the increased rivalry over market share gives competitive firms a greater incentive to develop new products and processes that will help them defend their market position. On the other hand, there is the view of Schumpeter that too much competition can retard innovation, particularly if the rewards from innovation are rapidly eroded. Indeed, the rationale for patents rests precisely on the view that temporary monopolies are required to induce innovation. In addition, even monopolists may have incentives to innovate strategically to continue to exclude rivals and to reduce production costs. In fact, it is likely that neither perfect competition nor pure monopoly are conducive to innovation, and that intermediate market structures that provide a combination of rents to innovation and competitive pressures will do more to stimulate innovation, which suggests that the impact of increased international competition depends on whether the industry initially has more or less than the optimal balance of rents and competition.

A fourth impact could occur because of economies of scale. Once knowledge is obtained, marginal costs may be close to zero, but obtaining knowledge may entail large fixed costs. The implication, as Adam Smith recognized long ago, is that the extent of the market can play a crucial role in achieving cost reduction. Firms innovating for global markets, therefore, may be able to realize these scale economies far better than those confined to local markets. Indeed, Rivera-Batiz and Romer (1991) have demonstrated how increased economic integration can cause a permanent increase in the worldwide rate of growth.

Fifth, as in any economy, in an open economy changes in relative prices will affect resource allocation and the returns from particular productive activities. In a price-taking small open economy, improvements in the terms of trade will create an incentive to shift resources toward export industries and away from import-competing industries. Similar effects might occur as a result of the reduction of trade barriers. Under these circumstances, in the short run, export industries would become more profitable, while import-competing sectors would become less profitable. The volume of trade rises, but the incentives to invest, in both innovation and in physical capital in exports and import-competing industries, would be very different. If new investment embodied new technologies, we would not find it surprising that until resources had been reallocated, productivity growth was particularly rapid in export industries and sluggish in those competing with imports. Research and development (R&D) spending and other innovation activity could, similarly, follow the same patterns.

There are paradigms that are different from those of traditional profit maximization in which managers may be stimulated to innovate when international competition threatens their rents. This involves the existence of managers who satisfice rather than maximize and behave under conditions of what is sometimes termed bounded rationality. Basically, they do not innovate continuously, but do so when subjected to an unusual stimulus. In this world, increased import competition may spur competition, while the greater profitability of exports could actually do the reverse.[3]

Thus far I have considered innovation in general. But assuming that international competition does stimulate innovation, there is also an issue of the direction in which innovation is likely to occur—in particular, whether innovation will be biased toward saving particular factors of production. The rewards to improvements in production technology will relate to the benefits from cost reduction it brings about.[4] These benefits will depend on (1) the relative costs of performing the research to save on the use of particular factors, (2) the share of particular factors in costs, and (3) the scale of output—the benefits of reducing unit costs are larger, the larger the scale of operation. If there are fixed costs in discovering a way to make unskilled labor more attractive (e.g., investing in discovering the best training methods), it will be more attractive to undertake such discoveries, the greater the share of unskilled labor in the production process. This suggests that if international trade raises the incentives to innovate in a particular industry, it could also stimulate changes that save on the factor of production used relatively intensively in that industry.[5]

International trade may also increase awareness of alternative technolo-

3. See Rodrik (1992).
4. For a discussion of factor bias see Binswanger (1974).
5. Adrian Wood (1994) has suggested that competition with developing countries could induce skill-biased technological change. He argues that competitive pressures induce producers of unskilled-intensive products to automate, that is, to use factors that are relatively cheaper in developed countries (i.e., capital and skilled labor). But, as Wood realizes, this

gies in a particular direction. In the case of competition with other developed countries, the technologies may or may not have a particular factor bias. However, since developing countries are unlikely to be pioneering more skill-intensive or automated production technologies, the channel that operates through emulation is unlikely to lead to greater automation when developed countries experience competition from developing countries. We would not expect technological changes in developed countries such as the United States to use more capital- or skill-intensive production methods when experiencing competition from developing countries.

This discussion has focused on the direct impact of international competition on industry-specific innovation. It should be noted, however, that there may also be general equilibrium effects. To the degree that increased import competition with labor-intensive products operates through Stolper-Samuelson effects to raise the relative cost of skilled and educated workers, we might expect technological change to save on other factors and to use unskilled labor more intensively throughout the economy. What we have seen in the United States, for example, is that the use ratio of skilled workers has increased and the wage of skilled workers has increased. This implies necessarily that the share of skilled workers in the wage bill has increased. If an invention can save a certain quantity of more-skilled labor, therefore, it will become more attractive. So we might expect that the bias that will result from the relative price effects will tend to result in relatively more-skilled-labor-saving technical change.

In sum, therefore, expanded trade could subject domestic U.S. industries to price pressures. These pressures, in turn, could stimulate innovation and inspire emulation. But they could, by lowering profitability and the scale of operations, reduce innovation. In addition, trade could alter the costs and incentives for both neutral and factor-biased technological change.

However, undertaking empirical work is not easy. It is important to make clear what we mean by technological change. In this study, the term implies a change in the production function, that is, the set of available technologies of production, and not resource shifts among known technologies. In practice, however, it is difficult to distinguish outward shifts in the production function from the effects of changes in the composition of output. Trade may be expected to induce increased specialization—a phenomenon that could occur within as well as between industries. For example, if international competition induced a U.S. automobile firm to outsource its labor-intensive parts production to Mexico, measured productivity might rise, but this might reflect a change in activities, rather than a technological improvement.

---

requires the additional assumption that the actors were previously operating under bounded rationality because it raises the question of why they were not moved to adopt these techniques earlier.

Similarly, increased competition could lead to the elimination of the least efficient firms and the expansion of the more productive firms— again, not necessarily innovation—but this could shift recorded productivity for some period of time.

Third, in models of imperfect competition, firms with pricing power will have markups that depend on the demand elasticity that they face. The impact of increased competition will be to reduce these markups, raise output, and increase levels of capacity use. This again would induce a one-time shift that raises productivity, but need not reflect a technological improvement.

Finally, it should be noted that even if we could obtain precise estimates of the impact of trade on technological change, inferring the impact of these changes on wages is by no means straightforward. In some models, in which product demand is perfectly elastic, the sectoral incidence of the change is all that matters; in other cases, it is factor bias.[6]

6.2 Previous Studies

There is anecdotal and case-study evidence on the impact of import competition on innovation in the United States (see MacDonald 1994; McKinsey 1992; Dertouzos, Lester, and Solow 1989). In particular, there are accounts of the changes brought about by competition in U.S. industries such as automobiles, steel, and copier machines.[7] There have also been studies of the impact of trade on R&D spending—presumably a leading indicator of future productivity growth. Using detailed case studies and more general regression analysis, for example, Scherer (1992) and Scherer and Huh (1992) have studied U.S. firms' R&D-spending responses to international competition. They find a mixture of responses. Some firms aggressively innovated in the face of competition; others simply submitted. On average, however, in the short run, R&D-to-sales ratios declined. Companies were more aggressive the greater their domestic sales, the more concentrated the markets in which they competed, and the more diversified their domestic operations. Companies with only U.S. operations were more submissive than those with multinational holdings. Zietz and Fayissa (1992) have tested the impact of import competition on R&D expenditure in the United States and found an association that is positive, but only for high-tech industries.[8]

6. See Krugman (2000) and Leamer (1998, 2000).
7. There is also evidence that competition has affected price-cost margins. Domowitz, Hubbard, and Petersen (1986) found that imports affected prices, but according to MacDonald (1994, 721) these effects tend to be small, even in concentrated industries.
8. Benjamin and Ferrantino (1998) examine a sample of countries in the Organization for Economic Cooperation and Development and find a positive association between productivity growth and export performance, but no association between import growth and productivity.

These considerations suggest that responses to trade could be different, depending on the degree of competition in the market.[9] These studies suggest that sometimes the spur of competition seems to help, particularly when there are reasons to suspect the domestic industry might have become complacent or when it has some surplus that it could allocate to increased R&D. Indeed, MacDonald (1994) found that in the United States, increases in import competition led to large statistically significant increases in labor-productivity growth in highly concentrated industries, but not in other industries.[10]

In sum, therefore, the literature suggests that trade might have stimulated R&D and technological change, particularly in concentrated import-competing sectors. However, there remain many unsettled issues. First, these studies did not use measures of TFP as the measure of technology. As previously noted, if trade leads to the elimination of particularly labor-intensive activities, average industry labor productivity might rise, but this would not indicate technological change. The same would be true if trade induced increased investment.[11] Second, the studies model trade as operating through the impact on quantities. To be sure, this is one way to capture trade pressures, but price channels might also be important. Indeed, import competition could depress profit margins, thereby inducing less technological change even where actual trade volumes are small. Third, there seems to have been little work on the effects of trade on the bias of technological change. This study, therefore, will try to make progress in dealing with these deficiencies. The following section will consider the impact of trade on TFP in U.S. manufacturing during the 1980s using both price and quantity measures of import competition. The next section will explore skill-biased technological change.

6.3 Trade and Total Factor Productivity Growth

6.3.1 Regression Model

Consider a regression model in which technological change, measured by TFP growth in U.S. manufacturing industries, is driven by domestic R&D intensity (*R&D*), industry concentration (*CONC*), international

9. U.S. imports from developing countries typically occur in sectors that are highly competitive, such as apparel and leather. It is thus less likely that the technology-inducing effects of the developing countries' imports will be significant. In contrast, these effects may be more important for trade with developed countries, more of which occurs in concentrated sectors.

10. Macdonald uses a model in which labor productivity growth in measured over 4-year time spans. These are regressed on the average growth in output, concentration, the change in import penetration growth in earlier period, an interaction of import penetration growth and concentration, and time dummies and other industry characteristics.

11. Indeed, Collins and Bosworth (1996) find that increased investment rather than higher TFP explains most of the association between growth and openness.

competition (T), and the interaction between concentration and competition ($CONC*T$):

$$TFP = a_1 + a_2 R\&D + a_3 CONC + a_4 T + a_5 CONC * T.$$

The incorporation of R&D as a determinant of productivity growth is straightforward. As the previous discussion makes clear, a less competitive market structure could be associated with innovation or it might detract from technological development. This structure is best captured by a measure of concentration. Capturing the impact of trade is more difficult. Traditionally, quantitative measures of imports, exports, and the trade balance have been used in productivity regressions. In this research, however, these will be supplemented by trade price measures.

Using either import prices or quantities as an independent variable, however, is problematic because these variables are not exogenous. This means that a credible estimate should control for the impact of joint causation. This will be done using a two-stage estimation procedure with instrumental variables techniques. In particular, for instrumenting import prices, a foreign cost index has been constructed by using industry-specific source-weighted foreign wholesale price indexes expressed in U.S. dollars.[12] Similarly, the endogeneity of import quantities will be controlled for with instrumental variables using a number of measures designed to capture the factor intensity of production, such as the skill ratio (skill intensity) and the ratio of plant and equipment (capital intensity), which are suggested by the Heckscher-Ohlin trade theory as likely determinants of trade. Finally, overall productivity growth (and changes in the relative use of skilled labor) could differ depending on whether competition originated from developed or developing countries. Thus, the specification will differentiate imports by their origins.

6.3.2 Data

The data are primarily from the NBER Manufacturing Database, which contains data drawn from the annual survey of manufacturing for U.S. industries at the three-digit Standard Industrial Classification (SIC) level. These data include estimates of TFP export volumes, and import volumes. Trade price data are taken from the Bureau of Labor Statistics (BLS), estimates on employment by education from the Current Population Surveys (CPS) tapes, concentration ratios and R&D spending from Scherer (1992), imports by country from Sachs and Shatz (1994), and national wholesale prices and exchange rates from the International Financial Statistics of the International Monetary Fund.

---

12. Import shares in 1985 are used as weights. A similar methodology was used by Revenga (1992) to estimate the impact of trade on wages.

6.3.3   Results

Import Prices

Table 6.1 reports the regression analysis undertaken for 27 three-digit industries for which import price data are available.[13] The TFP variable is the annual average change over the period of estimation. In regression 1, there is a negative relationship between TFP growth and import prices, which is statistically significant at the 90 percent level. The coefficient is sizable—each 1 percent fall in import prices induces a 0.21 percent rise in TFP. This regression suggests that competitive pressures induce technological change. However, since it is run in OLS, the regression could also reflect contamination by a common global technological shock, which induces a spurious correlation, or a shock located in the United States, which induces foreigners to lower their prices. In particular, since the United States is a large market, faster productivity growth and thus lower U.S. prices could induce lower import prices.

Indeed, regression 2 casts some doubt on the confidence we can place in the result that trade induces faster productivity growth. Once simultaneity is accounted for using the weighted foreign wholesale prices as an instrument, the coefficient is no longer statistically significant (although it does become larger). In contrast to regression 1, this result suggests no independent impact operating through the impact on prices. However, it should be noted that unfortunately the wholesale price instrument is a weak one, so that this is not a result in which we can have much confidence. In addition, we find that interacting the import price variable with the concentration variables has the effect of eliminating the significance of the import price variable (regression 3). An *F*-test on the import price variable and the interaction with concentration together is not significant.

The computer industry has been dummied out of the sample, since its productivity growth is so large that it could overwhelm the results. If the computer industry is added to the sample, the coefficient on import prices in the OLS version of the regression increases to 0.51 and is again significant. In addition, the coefficient on R&D also becomes significant. However, in this case as well, the coefficient loses its significance, and it declines

---

13. Correlations of the data for the period 1978–89 confirm two key features. First, imports from developing countries are intensive in less-skilled workers and industries that are not concentrated. Imports from poor countries relative to demand in 1978 and changes in this measure over the 1980s are positively associated with the share of high school–educated workers in employment (correlation coefficients *r* of 0.26 and 0.38, respectively). In contrast, imports from developed countries in 1978 had almost no relationship to the share of high school–educated employment and changes in these imports were negatively associated with this share (*r* = −0.16). Imports from developed countries in 1978 were positively associated with concentration (*r* = 0.14), whereas the coefficient for imports from developing countries was far lower (*r* = 0.03). The correlations suggest no systematic relationships between TFP growth and skill intensity. The correlation between TFP growth and the shares of high school–educated and of production workers in industry employment is very low.

Table 6.1   TFP Change

	Dependent Variable: TFP80-89			
	OLS (1)	TSLS (2)	OLS (3)	TSLS (4)
Constant	0.011*	0.018	0.008	−0.111
	(1.857)	(0.834)	(0.999)	(−0.068)
Concentration	0.009	0.008	0.018	0.299
	(0.656)	(0.506)	(0.883)	(0.078)
R&D	−0.244	−0.162	−0.255	−0.866
	(−1.595)	(−0.546)	(−1.636)	(−0.103)
Price change	−0.213*	−0.517	−0.023	6.914
	(−1.803)	(−0.567)	(−0.066)	(0.073)
CR*Price change			−0.517	0.299
			(−0.603)	(0.078)
$D_{computer}$	0.153**	0.142**	0.153**	0.187
	(10.971)	(3.941)	(10.816)	(0.400)
R^2	0.931	0.910	0.932	
Adjusted R^2	0.918	0.894	0.916	
F-statistic	74.11	56.48	57.64	2.75
Instrumental variable		WPPI		WPPI
N	27	27	27	27
Weighted by	emp78	emp78	emp78	emp78

Note: Numbers in parentheses are t-statistics.
  Variable definitions are as follows:
  TFP80-89 = average annual growth of log total factor productivity from 1980 and 1989.
  Concentration = concentration ratio of the top four firms in 1977.
  R&D = ratio of R&D expenditures to sales in 1977.
  Price change = the average annual growth rate of log import price between 1980 and 1989.
  CR*Price change = interaction term of concentration with price changes.
  $D_{computer}$ = dummy variable indicating the computer industry.
  WPPI = import-share-weighted change in log PPI in U.S. dollars.
  The endogenous variable in TSLS is price change.
*Significant at the 90 percent confidence level.
**Significant at the 95 percent confidence level.

in magnitude in the instrumental variables estimation. Overall, therefore, these results hint at an impact of international competition on productivity growth, but it is not a relationship that is robust to specification or the use of a weak instrumental variable.

Import Quantities

In table 6.2, annual average TFP growth for 107 three-digit manufacturing industries during the period 1978–89 is explained as a function of concentration ratios, R&D-to-sales ratio, the share of exports in domestic production in the first year of the period, and import shares in domestic demand in the first year of the sample period. In table 6.3, the import-

Table 6.2   **OLS and TSLS Regressions with First-Year Import Penetration, 1978–89**

	Dependent Variable: TFP78-89			
	OLS (1)	TSLS (2)	OLS (3)	TSLS (4)
Constant	0.004*	0.005	0.004	0.009**
	(1.702)	(1.147)	(1.502)	(2.018)
Concentration	−0.007	0.006	−0.006	−0.004
	(−1.096)	(0.586)	(−0.930)	(−0.439)
R&D	0.082	0.219**	0.080	0.132
	(1.451)	(2.215)	(1.418)	(1.453)
Import78	0.044**	0.028		
	(3.837)	(0.487)		
LDC-import78			0.072**	−0.137
			(2.865)	(−1.389)
DC-import78			0.030*	0.044
			(1.838)	(0.687)
Export/shipments	−0.025**	−0.090**	−0.023**	−0.046**
	(−3.151)	(−2.495)	(−2.834)	(−2.059)
R^2	0.208		0.219	
Adjusted R^2	0.177		0.179	
F-statistic	6.68	1.97	5.54	1.40
Instrumental variables		dlhsed, ky78, py78, ey78		dlhsed, shs79, ky78, py78, ey78
N	107	107	105	105
Weighted by	emp78	emp78	emp78	emp78

Note: Numbers in parentheses are t-statistics.
Variable definitions are as follows:
TFP78-89 = annual average change in the log of total factor productivity over the period 1978–89.
Concentration = four-firm concentration ratio in 1977.
R&D = ratio of R&D to sales in 1977.
Import78 = ratio of imports to domestic demand (shipments − exports + imports) in 1978.
LDC-import78 = ratio of imports from developing countries to domestic demand in 1978.
DC-import78 = ratio of imports from developed countries to domestic demand in 1978.
Export/shipments = ratio of exports to domestic shipments in 1978.
Endogenous variables are Import78, LDC-import78, and Export/shipments.
*Significant at the 90 percent confidence level.
**Significant at the 95 percent confidence level.

demand variables are interacted with the concentration variables. All regressions are weighted by 1978 levels of employment. Regression 1 in table 6.2, which is run as OLS, yields a positive and statistically significant coefficient on the share of imports in domestic demand. This result is important and particularly powerful because in general we might expect that, ceteris paribus, the United States would tend to have low levels of imports in industries in which productivity growth was high; that is, the coefficient might well be biased downward. In the previous section, the use of price

Table 6.3   **OLS and TSLS Regressions with Import Penetration and Its Interaction with Concentration Ratio, 1978–89**

	Dependent Variable: TFP78-89			
	OLS (1)	TSLS (2)	OLS (3)	TSLS (4)
Constant	0.004	0.017	0.004	0.012
	(1.156)	(0.534)	(1.377)	(0.642)
Concentration	−0.006	−0.030	−0.007	−0.012
	(−0.677)	(−0.319)	(−0.832)	(−0.224)
R&D	0.082	0.222*	0.063	0.076
	(1.452)	(1.798)	(1.123)	(0.411)
Import78	0.051*	−0.128		
	(1.697)	(−0.312)		
LDC-import78			−0.031	−0.392
			(−0.531)	(−0.581)
DC-import78			0.071*	0.098
			(1.820)	(0.295)
CR*Import78	−0.016	0.465		
	(−0.246)	(0.386)		
CR*LDC-import78			0.300*	0.996
			(1.940)	(0.379)
CR*DC-import78			−0.110	−0.250
			(−1.309)	(−0.230)
Export/shipments	−0.026**	−0.097**	−0.024**	−0.040
	(−3.131)	(−2.004)	(−2.860)	(−1.426)
R^2	0.208		0.254	
Adjusted R^2	0.169		0.200	
F-statistic	5.31	1.04	4.72	1.20
Instrumental variables		dlhsed, ky78, py78, ey78		dlhsed, shs79, ky78, py78, ey78, pvship
N	107	107	105	105
Weighted by	emp78	emp78	emp78	emp78

Note: Numbers in parentheses are *t*-statistics.

Variable definitions are as follows:

TFP78-89 = annual average change in the log of total factor productivity over the period 1978–89.

Concentration = four-firm concentration ratio in 1977.

R&D = ratio of R&D to sales in 1977.

Import78 = ratio of imports to domestic demand (shipments − exports + imports) in 1978.

LDC-import78 = ratio of imports from developing countries to domestic demand in 1978.

DC-import78 = ratio of imports from developed countries to domestic demand in 1978.

CR*import78 = interaction of concentration and the share of imports in domestic demand.

CR*LDC-import78 = interaction of concentration and the share of imports from developing countries in domestic demand.

CR*DC-import78 = interaction of concentration and the share of imports from developed countries in domestic demand.

Export/shipments = ratio of exports to domestic shipments in 1978.

Endogenous variables are Import78, LDC-import78, DC-import78, CR*import78, CR*LDC-import78, CR*DC-import78, Export/shipments. Instruments are defined in the appendix.

*Significant at the 90 percent confidence level.

**Significant at the 95 percent confidence level.

changes as the measure of competitive pressures was biased toward finding a relationship and gave us reason for suspicion. However, taken together these results appear to confirm a positive effect of import competition on TFP growth. The negative coefficient on the export variable, which is significant, is surprising. The equation also indicates that the R&D-to-sales ratio is a predictor of productivity growth, although it is not significant, and concentration has a negative impact, but again is not significant. When imports are separated by origin in this OLS specification, it appears that the positive impact is associated both with imports from developing and developed countries, although the impact from developing countries is larger for any given increase in imports as a share of total demand and more statistically significant.

When the regression is estimated using two-stage least squares (TSLS), however, as in the case of the price specification, again the import variable loses its significance, although R&D is now significant. Likewise, in the TSLS specification the variables that separate imports by origin both lose their significance. However, the instruments have low F-statistics—an important problem which, as discussed in the appendix, gives rise to problems in interpretation. Since the import variables used in the regression reflect imports in the first year, the problem of endogeneity is likely to be less serious than in the import price specification and it is possible that given the weakness of the instruments, the TSLS estimation may do more harm than good. This suggests that it is appropriate to place more reliance on the OLS results.

In table 6.3, the interaction between the concentration ratio and imports is explored. Whereas MacDonald (1994) and others have found important interactive effects between concentration and import competition, these do not emerge strongly here. In regression 1, the significance of the import variable and the coefficient on the interaction between imports and concentration is not significant. The regression has also been estimated in a TSLS version using factor-intensity instrumental variables for the import variable. In this version of the regression, the coefficient on concentration is increased, but it is still not significant. When imports are distinguished by their origins, the influence of imports from developing countries appears to have been more important than that of imports from developed countries. However, in both the OLS and the TSLS versions of the regression, the coefficients on imports from both developed and developing countries and their interaction with concentration are not statistically significant.

It should also be reported that variables that measured changes in the share of imports over the estimation period never came in significant when entered alone or when entered in interaction with the concentration ratio. This was the case in both the OLS and TSLS specifications. Similarly, changes in imports from developed and developing countries over the estimation period were not significant in either the OLS or TSLS estimates when entered separately.

In sum, these results provide some indication that international competition with imports has raised productivity growth. It is interesting to estimate the induced impact on productivity growth that is attributable to imports and to ask whether these induced effects tended to increase or reduce the relative wages of unskilled workers. To undertake these estimates, I have used the OLS regressions in table 6.2, which produced significant effects for the impact of trade.

In the first set of calculations I derive estimates for each industry of the impact on TFP growth due to imports from all sources by multiplying the 1978 share of imports in total demand by a coefficient of 0.044. Weighted by employment, on average, TFP growth in these manufacturing industries was increased at an annual rate of 0.355 percent. When weighted by employment of the high school–educated, the impact was 0.36 percent, that is, slightly higher than the effect when weighted by employment of the college-educated, 0.34 percent. A regression of the estimated impact of imports against the share of high school–educated employment weighted by 1978 employment confirms that there was a positive relationship between the induced impact of imports and the use of unskilled labor, but it is not statistically significant.

In a second set of calculations I use the separate estimated effects of imports from developed and developing countries. For developed countries, the mean impact weighted by employment was 0.203 percent annually, larger than the weighted mean impact for imports from developed countries of 0.157 percent annually. For developing countries, the impact of trade when weighted by employment of workers with a high school education or less, 0.217 percent, was larger than the impact when weighted by employment of workers with a college education, 0.168 percent. In contrast, the impact of trade with developed countries was larger when weighted by college-educated workers, 0.163 percent, than when weighted by high school–educated workers, 0.155 percent. Added together, we obtain estimates of 0.373 percent and 0.331 percent when high school– and college-educated employment weights, respectively, are used. An employment-weighted regression of the estimated effects due to developing country imports against the share of high school–educated workers in employment yields a positive and statistically significant coefficient (t-statistic = 3), whereas a similar regression for the effects due to developed country imports has a negative coefficient that is not significant. All told, therefore, it appears as if imports had a small but positive impact on relative productivity growth in unskilled-labor-intensive sectors. The estimated impact of exports on productivity growth is negative. It also turns out that there is a statistically significant negative relationship between the share of exports in production and the share of high school–

educated employment. Thus, taking account of exports strengthens further the result that trade induced relatively faster productivity growth in low-skill industries.

In sum, therefore, these results lend support to the conjecture made by Wood (1994) that competition with developing countries has induced relatively rapid productivity growth in low-skill industries. However, if we assume that the relevant model for relating this effect to the skill premium is the traditional trade model in which world prices are given, we would have expected this effect to have lowered the skill premium (similar to an increase in the price of low-skill industries). If we abandon that model and assume an inelastic demand for U.S. products produced in low-skill sectors, we would be able to raise the estimated role played by trade in explaining the rise of the skill premium. Alternatively, if we follow Wood and assume that by the end of the period all the low-skill goods have actually become noncompeting, then this evidence would also support his view that without trade, the relative demand for unskilled workers would have been higher.

6.4   Trade and Factor Bias

There does not appear to have been a strong sectoral bias to total productivity growth. In particular, the correlations between industry TFP growth and measures of skill mix, such as the ratio of nonproduction to production workers or the ratio of high school–educated to college-educated workers, is weak. Yet it is the shift in this mix within sectors, which has been identified with skill-biased technological change, which is probably the most important source of the shift in the demand for labor. Indeed, CPS data have been used to estimated the ratio of full-time high school–educated workers (i.e., workers with a high school diploma or less) to college-educated workers (i.e., workers with some college education). These indicate that over this decade in the typical three-digit-level manufacturing industry the shift averaged about 1.15 percent annually. Weighted by employment, the shift was 1.1 percent or 12.7 percent over the decade. What accounts for this shift?

One suggested explanation relates to changes in technology—particularly to the impact of computers. A second relates more broadly to the notion that labor-management relations in manufacturing have changed as a result of production methods that demand more-skilled workers. A third possibility is that the shift has somehow been induced by international competition, that technology has shifted in manufacturing to economize on the use of production workers. In addition, however, there is a fourth possibility—that the data reflect mix effects because the international outsourcing of production worker employment has led to a concentration of production in more skill-intensive activities. A fifth notion is that firms have simply become "fat and mean." As David Gordon (1996) argued, in response to increased competitive pressures, U.S. firms have reacted by laying off their blue-collar workers, but at the same time have actually added more white-collar labor.

It is also important in thinking about this issue to distinguish between technological change and technological progress. This is particularly the case because productivity growth in the manufacturing sector has not been particularly rapid. If the "fat and mean" hypothesis is correct, for example, there might have been change, but not necessarily progress.

6.4.1 Evidence

There is evidence that some of the change is driven by new investments and R&D. Berman, Bound, and Griliches (1994) found that 40 percent of the shift toward nonproduction labor can be attributed to the introduction of computers during the 1980s. (Similarly, they found that entered alone in a regression, R&D spending accounts for just under 40 percent of the shift, and that taken together the R&D and computer variables account for about one-half of the shift away from production labor.) Krueger (1993) has found evidence linking wages and computer investment. Allen (1996) reports that returns to schooling and the wage gap between high school and college graduates increased much more in industries with a rising employment share of scientists and engineers than in other industries. He concludes that R&D activity has had an impact on relative earnings across a broad range of occupations and that the employment of college graduates increased most in industries with rising R&D.[14] Similarly Mincer (1991) found that the ratio of earnings of college graduates to earnings of high school graduates increased with R&D intensity.

There is also some empirical support for a role for trade. Feenstra and Hanson (1999) find that the rise in import penetration explains about 15 percent of the increase in the share in the wage bill of manufacturing during 1979–90 (although in some regressions they obtain higher effects). This result could be capturing changes in the ratio of production to nonproduction workers as well as their relative wages. Bernard and Jensen (1997) find that exporting explains a rise in skill intensity both because it increases growth in skill-intensive plants and because it induces a rise in skill intensity within export plants.

The literature also suggests that the distinction between technological change and technological progress could be important. In particular, while there are positive associations between the rising skill intensity and computers and capital-equipment investment, the link between these invest-

14. Allen finds that about 25 percent of the growth in the wage gap between college and high school graduates in an average industry can be explained by technological change (1996, 29).

ments and hiring decisions and productivity growth is much less apparent. Indeed, according to Berndt and Morrison (1995), increases in the share of high-tech office equipment in capital are negatively correlated with the growth in multifactor productivity, and there is only limited evidence of a positive impact on profitability. Allen (1996) reports that accelerating TFP growth is correlated with increased employment shares for high school graduates and lower employment shares for college graduates and high school dropouts.[15] These are grist for the mill of the "fat and mean" hypothesis advanced by Gordon (1996).

6.4.2 Results

The simple correlation coefficients among the variables to be used in the regression analysis are interesting. The correlation between changes in the share of high school–educated workers and the ratio of high school– to college-educated workers in 1979 is positive (0.30). Similarly, high R&D and increases in capital intensity are associated with reductions in the high school–educated share: $r = -0.4$ for R&D and $r = -0.31$ for changes in the ratio of capital to output. Variables that reflect the notion of "fat and mean" are also significant. Concentration is associated with a rise in more-educated workers ($r = 0.36$), while changes in TFP are associated with increases in the ratio of high school–educated workers rather than the reverse ($r = 0.23$). Finally, the role of imports is less significant, particularly those from developing countries. Imports may be leading to upskilling (greater skill intensity), but the effect appears to be due to trade with developed countries ($r = 0.23$) rather than developing countries ($r = 0.04$).

This correlation analysis suggests, therefore, that the increase in skill intensity has been particularly rapid in skill- and R&D-intensive sectors in which investment has been strong and in which competition, particularly in imports from developed countries, play a role. However, perhaps somewhat paradoxically, TFP has not been strong.

Table 6.4 reports the regression analysis. These use data on 107 three-digit manufacturing industries to explain changes in the ratio of high school–educated to college-educated workers (as measured by the change in the share of high school–educated workers). In this TSLS regression, variables are weighted by 1978 employment, and several variables have strong explanatory power. High initial shares of high school–educated workers are associated positively with changes in the ratio of high school– to college-educated workers (HS/COL). In other words, the declines in HS/COL tend to be large in skill-intensive industries. Increases in capital intensity are associated with statistically significant declines in the HS/COL ratio, supporting the notion of the complementarity between capital goods

---

15. For a more complete discussion of the impact of computers on productivity see Landauer (1995).

Table 6.4　　　　　**Changes in Employment Share of High School–Educated Workers, 1978–89**

	Dependent Variable: Change in HS/COL	
	Equation 1, TSLS	Equation 2, TSLS
High-school-share79	0.021**	0.003
	(2.073)	(0.120)
Change in output	−0.300	−0.245
	(−1.779)	(−1.482)
Change in capital/	−0.332**	−0.317*
output	(−2.063)	(−1.803)
Concentration	−0.013	−0.003
	(−1.534)	(−0.287)
R&D	0.187	0.075
	(1.045)	(0.385)
Import78	−0.066**	
	(−3.079)	
DC-import78		−0.124
		(−1.597)
LDC-import78		0.025
		(0.284)
Change in imports	0.023	
	(0.490)	
Change in DC-		−0.042
imports		(−0.513)
Change in LDC-		0.074
imports		(0.791)
Constant	−0.014	−0.006
	(−1.489)	(−0.399)
R^2	0.193	
F-statistics	6.74	3.74
Instrumental variables	py78, ey78, ky78, vship78, sm78	pemp78, vship78, sm78, py78, ey78, ky78
N	107	105
Weighted by	emp78	emp78

Note: Numbers in parentheses are t-statistics.

Variable definitions are as follows:

Change in HS/COL = average annual change in the share of workers with high school education or less, over the period 1979–90.

High-school-share79 = share of workers with high school education or less in 1979.

Change in output = average annual change in log output.

Change in capital/output = average annual change in log(capital/output).

Concentration = concentration ratio in 1997.

R&D = ratio of R&D spending to sales in 1977.

Import78 = share of imports in domestic demand in 1978.

Change in imports = annual average change in share of imports in domestic demand over the period 1978–89.

DC-import78 = share of imports from developed countries in domestic demand in 1989.

LDC-import78 = share of imports from developing countries in domestic demand in 1989.

Change in LDC-imports = average annual change in the share of imports from developing countries in domestic demand.

Change in DC-imports = average annual change in the share of imports from developed countries in domestic demand.

Endogenous variables are Change in output, Import78, Change in imports. Instruments are defined in the appendix.

*Significant at the 90 percent confidence level.

**Significant at the 95 percent confidence level.

investment and the demand for skilled labor. Concentration is associated with declines in the HS/COL ratio (although the variable is not quite significant). Initial R&D intensity is not significant. Rapid increases in industry output are an additional significant variable—indicating it was the industries that were expanding that increased their skill ratios most. These variables, which account for most of the explanatory power, are consistent with the hypothesis that technical progress in high-skill industries associated with investment was driving the declines in HS/COL.

What role does trade play? Again, we have treated levels and changes in the ratio of imports to domestic demand as well as output growth as endogenous variables using the same instruments as in the previous regressions. The ratio of imports to domestic demand in 1978 is significant in the regression. This indicates that increases in the skill ratio were particularly rapid in industries with high levels of imports in 1978. However, changes in imports over the period are not significant. International competition appears to have played some role in shifting demand toward college graduates, and the impact does not appear to be due simply to the mix effects induced because of imports. Indeed, this result emerges even more clearly in regression 2, which differentiates imports by origin. The coefficient on the import share from developed countries is larger than that on imports in the TSLS estimation, although the *t*-statistic drops to 1.6. The import share of imports from developing countries is not significant. Nor is growth in imports from developing or developed countries associated with a statistically significant decline in the HS/COL ratio. Apparently, again, mix effects associated with increases in imports do not appear to be significant. Overall, therefore, there is some evidence of an association between imports from developed countries and a decline in the HS/COL ratio.

The coefficients from regression 1 can be used to estimate the overall impact of import competition from developed countries. Recall that over the period, the employment-weighted annual average decline in the share of high school–educated workers in manufacturing was 1.1 percent. Using the equation to estimate the employment-weighted average change attributable to imports suggests that it averaged 0.53 percent, about one-half of the overall change in manufacturing.

However, this shift needs in turn to be related to the economywide HS/COL ratios to derive an estimate of the impact on relative wages. In 1979, for example, manufacturing accounted for about 28 percent of high school–educated employment in the economy. Thus a decline in the share by 7.4 percent, which is the estimated impact of the induced change in the skill ratio due to trade, would represent a decline in overall high school–educated employment of 2 percent and a decline in the HS/COL ratio economywide of 4 percent. In a model with unitary elasticities of substitution, therefore, this would explain a similar 4 percent rise in the skill premium—a sizable impact.

6.5 Concluding Comments

This study has explored the impact of international competition on technological change as reflected in changes in total factor productivity and the skill ratio in U.S. manufacturing during the period 1978–89. The theoretical survey suggests that the effects of such competition could be positive or negative, with the response hinging on, among other factors, the competitive structure of the industry. Indeed, other empirical studies have found market structure important in determining the response of R&D spending and labor productivity to import competition. The empirical investigation here confirmed that international competition can affect total productivity growth. It also shows the importance of differentiating between imports from developed and developing countries.

Both the price and the quantity proxies for international competition produced statistically significant effects. In particular, trade with developing countries appears to have stimulated relatively faster TFP growth in industries with a relatively large share of imports from developing countries. Since such industries also employ relatively higher shares of workers with a high school education or less, this implies that international competition has led to relatively faster productivity growth in unskilled-labor-intensive sectors. In models with perfectly elastic product demand, this lowers the skill premium, suggesting that taking account of this impact would lower the role played by trade in explaining the skill premium.

In contrast to the case of TFP, exposure to competition with developed, rather than developing countries was associated with a more rapid increase in the ratio of high school– to college-educated employment, an impact that could have reduced the demand for unskilled workers and raised the skill premium.

In many of the regressions run for this study, most of which are not reported, there was, surprisingly, no evidence that increased imports from developed or developing countries were associated with a shift in the mix of U.S. output within industries toward relatively less-labor-intensive production methods. In both OLS and TSLS specifications, changes in the share of imports were not statistically significant.

It is appropriate to emphasize the tentative nature of these conclusions. The results obtained here are clearly very sensitive to specification and estimation technique. Theory suggests that causation runs between international competition and technological change in both directions, and the dramatic differences in results using OLS and TSLS confirm the power of this interdependence. Since, in general, we were only able to find weak instruments, this is clearly an important area for future research.

Appendix

Methodological Issues Related to Two-Stage Least Squares Estimation

In the regressions in this paper, endogeneity of the variables creates a problem that casts doubt on the validity of the OLS estimation method, which we attempt to deal with by using TSLS. In selecting appropriate instrumental variables for explaining trade quantities, variables representing the factor characteristics of production have been used. The prospective instrumental variables are searched within three categories of variables, namely, the human capital intensity, physical capital intensity, and labor intensity. We have variables of *shs79* (the share of workers with high school education or less in 1979) and *dlhsed* (the log growth rate of workers with high school education or less) to represent human capital intensities of the products. We also have *ky78* (capital intensity per output in 1978), *py78* (plants per output in 1978), and *ey78* (equipment per output in 1978) to reflect the physical capital intensities of the products. Furthermore, we regard the variables of *pvship* (the proportion of wage income in the total value of shipments in 1978) and *ppem* (the proportion of production workers in total employment in 1978) as indicating the labor intensity of the products. In table 6.1, we use *WPPI* (import-share weighted change in log PPI in U.S. dollars) as an instrument for price change (log import-price change).

One critical issue associated with using instrumental variables is whether those instruments are highly correlated with the endogenous variable, that is, the relevance of instrumental variables.[16] To test the relevance of an exogenous variable as an instrumental variable to a particular endogenous variable in the regression equation, we regress that endogenous variable on the instrumental variable and the other right-hand-side variables in the regression equation. If the coefficient of the instrumental variable is statistically significant at the 95 percent confidence level and/or the first-stage F-statistic is reasonably large (e.g., greater than 10), then this instrumental variable would be regarded as relevant or strong; otherwise it is regarded as irrelevant or weak. Unfortunately, we were generally only able to obtain weak instruments.

Given that the instrumental variables are in general not strong, in all the regressions we need to be concerned with the estimator bias caused by weak instruments in TSLS regressions. Staiger and Stock (1997) develop an asymptotic distribution theory for single-equation instrumental variables regressions when the instruments are weak. They suggest that compared with TSLS estimators, the LIML (limited-information maximum-

16. For a discussion of these issues see Bound, Jaeger, and Baker (1995), Brundy and Jorgenson (1971), Chamberlain and Imbens (1996), and Staiger and Stock (1997).

likelihood) estimator shows a smaller bias since the LIML estimator rapidly becomes median unbiased. They thus reach a constructive conclusion, for the applied work with one endogenous variable in the right-hand side of the single equation, that estimator bias is less of a problem for LIML than TSLS, so that the LIML estimator may be a better choice. We have undertaken LIML estimates particularly for those regressions that include only one right-hand-side endogenous variable and find that the estimation results are qualitatively equivalent to those of TSLS. Nonetheless, the presence of weak instruments remains a problem in this study.

References

Allen, Steven G. 1996. Technology and the wage structure. NBER Working Paper no. 5534. Cambridge, Mass.: National Bureau of Economic Research, April.
Benjamin, Nancy, and Michael J. Ferrantino. 1998. Trade, trade policy and productivity growth in OECD manufacturing. Working Paper no. 98-03-A. Washington, D.C.: U.S. International Trade Commission, March.
Berman, Eli, John Bound, and Zvi Griliches. 1994. Changes in the demand for skilled labor within U.S. manufacturing: Evidence from the Annual Survey of Manufactures. *Quarterly Journal of Economics* 109 (2): 367–97.
Bernard, Andrew B., and J. Bradford Jensen. 1997. Exporters, skill upgrading, and the wage gap. *Journal of International Economics* 42 (1–2): 3–31.
Berndt, Ernst R., and Catherine J. Morrison. 1995. High-tech capital formation and economic performance in U.S. manufacturing industries: An exploratory analysis. *Journal of Econometrics* 65:9–43.
Binswanger, Hans. 1974. A microeconomic approach to induced innovation. *Economic Journal* 84:940–58.
Bound, J., D. Jaeger, and R. Baker. 1995. Problems with instrumental variables estimation when the correlation between the instruments and the endogenous explanatory variable is weak. *Journal of the American Statistical Association* 90: 443–50.
Brundy, James M., and Dale W. Jorgenson. 1971. Efficient estimation of simultaneous equations by instrumental variables. *Review of Economics and Statistics* 53 (3): 207–24.
Chamberlain, Gary, and Guido W. Imbens. 1996. Hierarchical Bayes models with many instrumental variables. NBER Technical Working Paper no. 204. Cambridge, Mass.: National Bureau of Economic Research.
Collins, Susan M., and Barry P. Bosworth. 1996. Economic growth in East Asia: Accumulation versus assimilation. *Brookings Papers on Economic Activity*, no. 2: 135–91.
Deardorff, Alan, and Dalia Hakura. 1994. Trade and wages: What are the questions? In *Trade and wages: Leveling wages down?* ed. Jagdish Bhagwati and Marvin Kosters, 76–107. Washington, D.C.: AEI Press.
Dertouzos, Michael L., Richard K. Lester, and Robert M. Solow. 1989. *Made in America: Regaining the competitive edge.* Cambridge, Mass.: MIT Press.
Domowitz, Ian, R. Glenn Hubbard, and Bruce C. Petersen. 1986. Business cycles and the relationship between concentration and price-cost margins. *RAND Journal of Economics* 17 (1): 1–17.

Feenstra, Robert, and Gordon Hanson. 1999. The impact of outsourcing and high-technology capital on wages: Estimates for the United States, 1979–1990. *Quarterly Journal of Economics* 114 (3): 907–40.

Gordon, David M. 1996. *Fat and mean: The corporate squeeze of working Americans and the myth of managerial "downsizing."* New York: Martin Kessler/Free Press.

Kapstein, Ethan. 1996. Workers and the world economy. *Foreign Affairs* 75 (3): 16–37.

Krueger, Alan B. 1993. How computers have changed the wage structure: Evidence from microdata, 1984–89. *Quarterly Journal of Economics* 108:33–60.

Krueger, Anne O. 1980. Protectionist pressures, imports and employment in the United States. NBER Working Paper no. 461. Cambridge, Mass.: National Bureau of Economic Research.

Krugman, Paul. 2000. Technology, trade and factor prices. *Journal of International Economics* 50 (1): 51–71.

Landauer, Thomas K. 1995. *The trouble with computers.* Cambridge, Mass.: MIT Press.

Leamer, Edward. 1998. In search of Stolper-Samuelson linkages between international trade and lower wages. In *Imports, exports and the American worker,* ed. Susan Collins, 141–202. Washington, DC: Brookings Institution.

———. 2000. What's the use of factor contents? *Journal of International Economics* 50 (1): 17–49.

MacDonald, James M. 1994. Does import competition force efficient production? *Review of Economics and Statistics* 76 (4): 721–27.

McKinsey Global Institute. 1992. *Service sector productivity.* Washington D.C.: McKinsey Global Institute.

Mincer, Jacob. 1991. Human capital responses to technological change in the labor market. NBER Working Paper no. 3207. Cambridge, Mass.: National Bureau of Economic Research.

Revenga, Ana L. 1992. Exporting jobs? The impact of import competition on employment and wages in U.S. manufacturing. *Quarterly Journal of Economics* 107 (1): 255–82.

Rivera-Batiz, Luis A., and Paul M. Romer. 1991. International trade with endogenous technological change. NBER Working Paper no. 3594. Cambridge, Mass.: National Bureau of Economic Research, January.

Rodrik, Dani. 1992. The limits of trade policy reform in developing countries. *Journal of Economic Perspectives* 6:87–106.

Sachs, Jeffrey, and Howard Shatz. 1994. Trade and jobs in U.S. manufacturing. *Brookings Papers on Economic Activity,* no. 1: 1–84.

Sachs, Jeffrey, and Andrew Warner. 1995. Economic reform and the process of global integration. *Brookings Papers on Economic Activity,* no. 1: 1–95.

Scherer, F. M. 1992. *International high-technology competition.* Cambridge, Mass.: Harvard University Press.

Scherer F. M., and Keun Huh. 1992. R&D reactions to high-technology import competition. *Review of Economics and Statistics* 74 (2): 202–12.

Staiger, Douglas, and James H. Stock. 1997. Instrumental variables regression with weak instruments. *Econometrica* 65 (3): 557–86.

Wood, Adrian. 1994. *North-south trade, employment and inequality.* Oxford: Clarendon Press.

Zietz, Joachim, and Bichaka Fayissa. 1992. R&D expenditure and import competition: Some evidence for the U.S. *Weltwirtschaftliches Archiv* 128 (1): 52–66.

Comment   Alan B. Krueger

Aristotle recognized that some questions are inherently more difficult to answer than others. If these difficult questions are really important, they are nonetheless worth trying to answer, although Aristotle argued the burden of proof that one applies would need to be relaxed in these cases. The topic of this paper is unquestionably important. In the long run, productivity growth is (almost) everything. Trade may influence productivity growth in a number of subtle and not so subtle ways, outlined by Robert Lawrence in his provocative paper. But the causal effect of trade on productivity is extremely difficult to determine. It is unclear whether much headway can be made.

To see the conceptual difficulty in ascertaining the effect of foreign competition on productivity, consider figure 6C.1, which displays isoquants in skilled (L_s) and unskilled (L_u) labor space. Initially, the industry can produce Q units of output with the combination of labor inputs indicated by the isoquant Q_1. Given relative wages, firms choose the factor/skill ratio L_u/L_{s1}, that is, point a. Now suppose there is an exogenous opening of trade with a country that is relatively well endowed with less-skilled workers (e.g., China). Almost everyone would expect this change in international competition to lower the wage of unskilled workers relative to skilled workers through Stolper-Samuelson effects, although there is considerable debate as to how much relative wages would change. A relative decline in unskilled wages would cause the industry to substitute unskilled for skilled workers, moving to point b in the diagram. Lawrence rightly does not consider this shift to be a change in productivity because the production function is constant. Instead, he would like to measure shifts in the isoquant. That is, suppose productivity increases as a result of the stimulus from trade, and the amount of skilled and unskilled labor required to produce the original Q units of output in the new regime is depicted by the isoquant Q_2. If the industry maintained its initial factor ratios, how much has productivity increased?

Figure 6C.1 highlights the considerable difficulties in answering this question. Changes in factor ratios must be accounted for. Lawrence sensibly uses total factor productivity (TFP) growth to abstract from changes in factor shares, but the TFP figures are only an approximation, and the approximation is worse as the elasticity of substitution between inputs strays from 1. Since several studies place the elasticity of substitution between college- and high school–educated workers at around 1.5, using the TFP measure will make it appear that trade matters even if all that has happened is that factor shares have shifted with a fixed production tech-

Alan B. Krueger is the Bendheim Professor of Economics and Public Affairs at Princeton University and a research associate of the National Bureau of Economic Research.

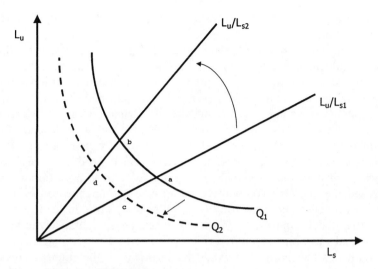

Fig. 6C.1   Hypothetical isoquants

nology.[1] Moreover, causation could run in the opposite direction. For reasons having nothing to with trade, U.S. firms could discover more efficient production techniques (shifting the isoquant from Q_1 to Q_2), driving down the price of the good and causing trade flows to shift. Causality runs from technological change to trade, not vice versa. Lawrence uses instrumental variables to address the latter problem, but as explained later, there are reasons to doubt the validity of the instruments.

A number of other conceptual and practical problems arise in the statistical analysis. Consider, for example, the problem caused by analyzing industry-level data that combine different firms and industry segments into the same three-digit manufacturing industry. It is likely that increased international competition would cause firms to close down their least productive, low-value-added plants, leaving just the high-productivity plants to be counted in the data. This selection process will make it seem as if international trade raises productivity, while in reality it might just cause low-productivity plants to go out of business—the production function is unchanged.

Also, by focusing on the intensive margin of technological change (i.e., producing existing goods better), the paper misses the effect of trade on the extensive margin (i.e., discovering new products and producing them at all). If the extensive margin is ignored, Marco Polo's importation of gunpowder to the West would be missed, for example. I suspect the extensive margin of product innovation and imitation is a major channel through

1. On the elasticity of substitution between college- and high school–educated workers, see, e.g., Katz and Murphy (1992).

which trade affects productivity. Of course, this is empirically a difficult topic to study.

Lawrence does an excellent job of cataloging the sundry ways in which trade could affect productivity. The bottom line is that theoretical reasoning provides no clear empirical prediction. I suspect the relationship between trade and technology is even more complicated than his analysis suggests. For example, there could be a "feedback loop" in which increased trade causes unskilled workers' relative wages to decline in the United States, which in turn induces companies to generate unskilled-labor-using technology, which in turn leads firms to produce more abroad because unskilled labor is really cheap abroad, and so on. Moreover, increased international competition could cause companies to devote resources to sales and marketing (e.g., more cola wars), instead of to research and development. Such advertising expenses are unlikely to have a beneficial effect on productivity.

With this background, it would be surprising if the empirical results were not open to alternative interpretations. Table 6.1 provides perhaps the most tantalizing results in the paper. These regressions relate the growth rate of TFP to changes in import prices, industrial concentration, and R&D. To address the potential simultaneity problem mentioned previously, Lawrence uses a plausible instrumental variable for import prices, foreign wholesale prices. Unfortunately, the sample consists of only 27 industries, so the results are not very precise. The OLS estimates suggest that increases in import prices lead to slower TFP growth, while the TSLS estimates yield an even larger (but statistically insignificant) negative effect of import prices on TFP growth. These coefficient estimates imply large economic magnitudes, but the imprecision of the estimates (especially the TSLS estimates) render the results almost entirely inconclusive. As I understand it, the sample size is restricted because industry price changes are only available for a small number of industries. But the reduced-form models (i.e., the relationship between TFP growth and wholesale prices) could be estimated for a much larger sample of industries. Given the magnitude of the coefficient estimates, I think these estimates would be worth calculating.[2]

Tables 6.2 and 6.3 contain the main empirical results of the paper. It seems to me, however, that the models estimated in these tables do not address the central question raised by the paper, even if the instruments were valid. In particular, the models relate TFP growth to import- and export-penetration rates. But the theoretical discussion concerns an increase in competition—a kick in the pants—not the level of competition. It is quite

---

2. I would also note that, unlike the TSLS estimates, the reduced-form models are not subject to small-sample bias from weak instruments.

possible that the import and export rates reflect steady-state levels, so they would provide a poor proxy for any additional stimulus to innovation due to new competitive pressures. In other words, there is no new "kick in the pants"; the boot is raised no higher than it was in steady state. I would think the appropriate explanatory variable would be the change in imports or exports. Lawrence reports, however, that when he included the change in imports as an explanatory variable it had a statistically insignificant effect.

For this reason, the results in tables 6.2 and 6.3 strike me as less than compelling. In addition, it is unclear to me why the growth rate of workers with a high school education or less is an appropriate instrumental variable for these equations because trade-induced technological change may cause a change in factor intensities. Also, as Lawrence notes, it is disconcerting that import- and export-penetration rates have opposite effects. In my opinion, it is premature to use these results to calculate the implied effect of trade-induced technological change on the relative demand for skilled and unskilled workers.

Lastly, Lawrence provides an analysis of changes in the employment share of high school–educated workers. These results complement a growing literature on the determinants of shifts in factor intensities across industries (see, e.g., Autor, Katz, and Krueger 1998). It is difficult to separate out the effect of imports on interindustry skill upgrading from the effects of skill-biased technological change due to other sources, however. This problem is not solved by the TSLS estimates; some of the variables that Lawrence uses to instrument for imports (e.g., the equipment share) could also be used as instruments for skill-biased technological change. This concern notwithstanding, there is the intriguing finding that, across industries, relatively more imports from advanced countries are associated with employment shifts away from workers with a high school degree or less, while imports from less-developed countries are essentially unrelated to skill upgrading.

I am skeptical that cross-industry analyses of trade and TFP growth can yield many definitive answers. In addition to the reservations already described, one might expect the creative process that leads to technological innovation to differ across industries. At a particular time, some industries have more scope for technological breakthroughs than others. Therefore, I think a sensible way for future research in this area to proceed would be to look across countries at the same industrial sector. For example, productivity growth in selected sectors could be compared between countries that opened up to trade and those that did not open up to trade. This type of analysis could be done for many industries. Perhaps there is much to be learned from the pattern of industries in which trade leads to productivity increases or decreases. I would think building up from such "case study" research is a more promising route to answering the important question of whether trade influences technological change.

References

Autor, David H., Lawrence F. Katz, and Alan B. Krueger. 1998. Computing inequality: Have computers changed the labor market? *Quarterly Journal of Economics* 113 (4): 1169–213.
Katz, Lawrence F., and Kevin Murphy. 1992. Changes in relative wages, 1963–1987: Supply and demand factors. *Quarterly Journal of Economics* 57:35–78.

III

Variation in Wages across States and Industries

7 Understanding Increasing *and* Decreasing Wage Inequality

Andrew B. Bernard and J. Bradford Jensen

7.1 Introduction

Consider two very similar economies (A and B) in 1970, sharing almost all the same markets for inputs and tradables. Economy A has a somewhat higher income per capita, an unemployment rate several points higher, and, most importantly, substantially lower wage inequality. Now move forward 20 years to 1990 and reconsider the same economies. The income gap has narrowed, but has not been eliminated, and the unemployment gap has remained, although both have higher levels. However, the paths of income inequality have been quite different. The formerly more unequal economy (B) has actually experienced a reduction of inequality over the period, while the initially low inequality economy (A) has seen such a large increase that their relative positions have been reversed.

This story does not fit the usual image of the evolution of income inequality during the 1970s and 1980s. A more common impression is that the increase has occurred throughout the U.S. economy and even throughout the industrialized world. This apparently common experience has actually frustrated empirical work into the sources of the overall increase in inequality as researchers have found few industries and few countries where the demand for less-skilled workers has increased.

Andrew B. Bernard is associate professor of business administration at the Amos Tuck School of Business at Dartmouth College and a faculty research fellow of the National Bureau of Economic Research. J. Bradford Jensen is director of the Center for Economic Studies at the U.S. Bureau of the Census and adjunct associate professor at the University of Maryland.

The authors are grateful to conference participants, especially Lee Branstetter, and seminar participants at the NBER Summer Institute and Yale University for helpful comments. The authors thank Mark Hooker for the government procurement data and Barry Hirsch for the unionization data. All errors are the authors'.

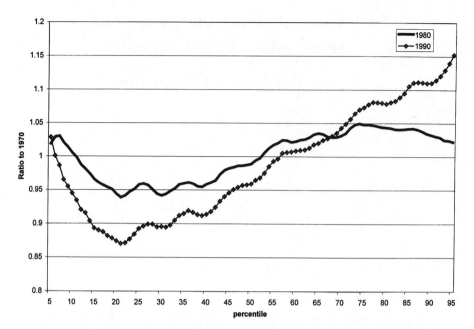

Fig. 7.1   Changes in the distributions of log wages (centered moving average over 5 percentiles)

The rise in wage inequality in the United States during the 1980s has been well documented (Levy and Murnane 1992). Figure 7.1 shows the change in log wages in 1980 and 1990 relative to 1970 for male workers from the 5th to the 95th percentiles in the distribution.[1] From 1970 to 1980, wage earners below the 53rd percentile lost ground relative to those above them. The largest relative declines occurred in the 15th to 40th percentiles, while the largest relative gains occurred in the 75th to 90th percentile range. In the 1980s, relative wages declined for the bottom two-thirds of the distribution, while rising sharply for the top wage earners. The relative wage movements remain very similar, even after controlling for observable characteristics such as education, race, location, and experience, as shown in figure 7.2.[2] The bottom half of the distribution declines, in relative terms, between 1970 and 1980, while fully 80 percent of the distribution suffered falling relative wages from 1980 to 1990.

These striking changes in relative wages have generated a large literature by way of explanation. Indeed, the search for culprits has now extended

---

1. The sample is described in section 7.2. The figure shows the relative wage change for a particular point in the wage distribution, not for an individual worker. The geometric means have been removed for all years. The change in the geometric mean was negative in the 1970s and positive in the 1980s.

2. Figure 7.2 plots the distribution of residuals from the regressions in table 7.3.

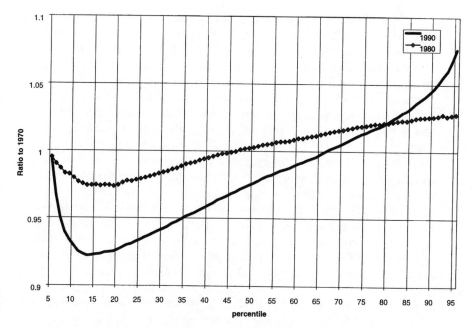

Fig. 7.2   Changes in the distribution of residual wages

worldwide and a growing body of papers has attributed rising unemploy-ment in continental Europe to the same forces that are generating rising inequality in the United States and the United Kingdom (e.g., see Berman, Bound, and Machin 1997).[3]

Is it true that wage inequality increases have occurred throughout the industrialized world? Are there actually economies that experienced de-clines in wage inequality during this period? In this paper we argue that the rise in wage inequality has been far from uniform among a set of econo-mies that are thought to have many more similarities than differences. In particular, examples of economies with declining inequality from 1970 to 1990 are close at hand: Virginia (−7.0 percent), North Dakota (−5.9 per-cent), North Carolina (−4.0 percent), Hawaii (−4.0 percent), Georgia (−3.9 percent), Mississippi (−2.8 percent), and South Carolina (−1.3 per-cent). Economies with dramatically rising inequality over the same period include Oregon (24.5 percent), Wyoming (23.2 percent), Michigan (21.9 percent), New York (20.8 percent), and Pennsylvania (20.5 percent).[4]

3. These authors point to inequality increases in some less-developed countries as further evidence of the worldwide aspect of this phenomenon.
4. The inequality measure is the 90-10 difference in log real wages after controlling for education, experience, race, and other characteristics. The numbers are the changes in the 90-10 difference from 1970 to 1990.

We argue that any theory of the rise in income inequality in the United States as a whole should also be capable of explaining the wide variety of outcomes across individual states. In this paper we revisit the debate over the sources of the increase in wage inequality in the United States by focusing on the evolution of inequality in different labor markets. Prior research on inequality has almost always assumed that workers can be pooled across regions in an attempt to identify sources of the increase in relative demand for skilled workers.[5] A key element in our analysis is the extent of integration of U.S. labor markets. If shocks to regions are transmitted quickly throughout the economy, then regional labor markets will provide little additional information in the search for the causes of increasing wage inequality. However, if shocks to regional labor demand (and supply) are only slowly transmitted to the rest of the economy, then we can use them to identify important sources of the increases in wage inequality.

The large literature on wage inequality has identified a set of potential culprits. These typically include (roughly in order of prominence in the literature) skill-biased technological change (Bound and Johnson 1992; Katz and Murphy 1992; Berman, Bound, and Griliches 1994), international trade (Borjas and Ramey 1994, 1995; Wood 1995), immigration (Topel 1993), and labor market institutions such as unions and minimum wage changes (DiNardo, Fortin, and Lemieux 1996; Fortin and Lemieux 1997). One difficulty that previous researchers have encountered is the apparently ubiquitous rise in inequality both within and between groups of workers and industries. This has led to a general consensus among researchers that changing demand across industries, with the possible exception of international trade, has not played a significant role in the rise in wage differentials.[6] Examples of these conclusions appear frequently in the literature on wage inequality:

> It is clear that not very much of the wage changes of the 1980's can be explained . . . by changes in the industrial wage structure or in the incidence of unionism. It is necessary to focus . . . on changes in relative competitive wage levels. (Bound and Johnson 1992, 380)

> Measured changes in the allocation of labor demand between sectors . . . can account for a large minority of the secular demand shifts in

5. Bound and Holzer (1996) also use the PUMS from the Decennial Census to examine the importance of regional shocks on college/high school and black/white wage differentials. They find important effects from local demand shocks as well as supply effects from migration at the top end of the wage distribution. Additional work using regional data to examine inequality include Topel (1993) and Borjas and Ramey (1995). The former uses broad regional measures to discuss the impact of immigration on wages. The latter uses wage data on metropolitan areas to assess the effect of foreign competition on the returns to education.

6. Based on anecdotal evidence (questioning economists at conferences), we have found widespread, if not universal, agreement with the proposition that cross-industry effects are not a significant source of increased inequality. However, it is hard to get individual researchers to identify the citations that are the basis for this opinion.

favor of groups with rising relative wages. . . . The majority of the required demand shifts in favor of more-educated workers and females reflect difficult to measure changes in within-sector relative labor demand. (Katz and Murphy 1992, 76)

. . . we find that less than one-third of the shift of employment from production to non-production workers can be accounted for by "between-industry" shifts. . . . (Berman, Bound, and Griliches 1994, 368)

In their survey article, Levy and Murnane conclude emphatically: "However, the plight of young, less educated males cannot be viewed primarily as a consequence of deindustrialization. Declines in the relative demand for less educated workers occurred within industries—most dramatically within manufacturing where semiskilled jobs declined at a much faster rate than overall manufacturing employment" (1992, 1372).

Subsequent research has often started from the assumption that industry-level changes in demand are at best small contributors to the overall rise in inequality. However, almost all of the previous work on the inequality rise has focused on the longitudinal aspects of any given data set and ignored variations across geographic units.

Why have economists concluded that changing industry mix, and in particular the loss of manufacturing jobs, was not a major factor in the inequality rise? Research on the rise in inequality has been quite careful about creating appropriate groups by worker characteristics (industry, occupation, education, experience, race, and sex) with the notable exception of location. Katz and Murphy (1992), in their highly influential paper on the topic, divide workers into 12 industries, three occupations, and eight gender-education groups. All these, however, make no distinction for the location of the individual—an appropriate assumption if wages and employment are determined by national integrated labor markets.

In this paper, we construct measures of inequality for each state in the United States. While the identification of individual states with separate labor markets is not ideal,[7] the extent to which individual states experience distinct shocks to the labor market will allow us to identify the importance of those shocks in the widening of the income distribution. One caveat concerns aggregate shocks that do not differ across states. Krugman (1995) and Berman, Bound, and Machin (1997) argue that skill-biased technological change has been pervasive, both within countries and across countries. In our approach, we will miss aggregate shocks that move the wage distribution homogeneously across states.

We concentrate on a set of guiding questions. Does the level of wage

---

7. Identifying Connecticut as a distinct labor market from those in New York, Massachusetts, or Rhode Island is not correct. This distinction is perhaps still preferable to assuming that the market for labor in Connecticut is integrated with Georgia, Arizona, and so on.

dispersion vary across regions? Are increases in inequality uniform across states? Are increases in inequality proportional to initial inequality? Does this heterogeneity across regions allow us to identify the sources of rising inequality?

The plan for the paper is quite simple. We start by assessing the assumption that regional labor markets are not well integrated, at least in the short or medium term. Then, we provide evidence on the large variation in inequality of both returns to observable characteristics such as education and residual wage inequality (unobservable characteristics) across states at any point in time. We then document the variation in the changes of state residual wage inequality from 1970–90 and attempt to associate these movements with common explanations for the inequality rise.

7.2   Evidence on the Integration of U.S. Labor Markets

A key assumption we will maintain in searching for causes of the rise in wage inequality is that labor markets in the United States are integrated only in the long run. There is little recent research on the extent of the integration of labor markets across regions in the United States. Blanchard and Katz (1992) consider the consequences of state-specific shocks on the paths of unemployment, wages, and migration over various time horizons. While their conclusions support the argument that labor markets are integrated in the long run (beyond 10 years), there are substantial disturbances to local labor markets in the short and medium term. Blanchard and Katz find that the effects of an employment shock on the unemployment rate peak at 2 years and are completely dissipated after 6 years. Wages show a more persistent response with the maximal decline occurring 6 years after a negative employment shock and some effects lingering for more than 10 years.

We provide two additional pieces of evidence on the integration of regional labor markets. First, we calculate the returns to different levels of education in each state. Strongly integrated state labor markets should not display large, persistent differentials in education returns. Next, we estimate the relative impact of regional and industry employment shocks to plant-level wages. If integration fails in the near term, we hypothesize that regional employment shocks should have a stronger and more immediate impact on wages than industry shocks.

7.2.1   Persistence of Education Premia

For our state-level analyses, the data on wages come from the Public Use Micro Samples (PUMS) from the Decennial Censuses of 1970, 1980, and 1990. The samples of the population available for those years are 1 percent, 5 percent, and 5 percent, respectively. We restrict our attention to the real weekly wages of nonimmigrant adult males, ages 18–65 inclusive, employed 14 weeks or more during the year and not self-employed. We use a simple wage regression, estimated separately for each state for each year.[8]

(1) $\ln WW = f(g(\text{experience}), \text{race}, \text{education}, \text{weeks worked}, \text{location})$,

where $g(\cdot)$ is a quartic in experience and there are two dummy variables for race (black and Hispanic) and four for education (no high school degree, some college, college degree, advanced degree [6+ years of tertiary education]). The location variable is a dummy for residents outside a standard metropolitan statistical area (SMSA).

The education premia are percentage differences from the wages of a male worker with a high school degree in the same state and are reported in table 7.1. The premia show substantial heterogeneity across states. In 1970, workers with a college degree, on average, earned 55 percent more than high school graduates in South Dakota, but only 28 percent more in Utah. The mean state wage premium for a college degree in 1970 was 43 percent and the standard deviation across states was 5.9 percent. Similarly, in 1970, the negative effect of not finishing high school ranged from −11 percent in Nevada to −34 percent in Tennessee.

In 1990, education premia continued to show substantial dispersion across states. The wage premium for a college degree ranged from 27 percent in Wyoming to 52 percent in Texas. The mean and standard deviation across states were 43 percent and 6.2 percent, respectively. The range of premia across states was substantial for all levels of education for all years, suggesting that, at any time, regional labor markets support very different relative returns to education.

The existence of different education premia in any year might be explained by temporary shocks to the regional labor markets. However, the premia are also quite persistent over time. Correlations across decades typically range from 0.5 to 0.8.[9] Except for the "some college" category, all the education premia show significant positive correlations over time. Figures 7.3 and 7.4 show the "advanced degree" and "no high school degree" premia. This evidence suggests that even during 10- or 20-year intervals, labor markets in different states do not adjust to equate the returns to education.[10]

---

8. Our specification of the log wage regression follows that often employed in the literature on inequality (see Juhn, Murphy, and Pierce 1993; Gottschalk 1997).

9. The single exception is "some college," where the correlation was 0.04 between 1970 and 1980. This result is driven largely by Wyoming and Alaska.

10. One objection to this interpretation is that the variation in state education premia merely reflects the quality of education provided in the state, which is itself persistent over time.

Table 7.1   Education Premia by State (%)

State	No High School Diploma			Some College			College Degree			Advanced Degree (6+ years)		
	1990	1980	1970	1970	1980	1990	1970	1980	1990	1990	1980	1970
AK	−20.5	−18.9	−27.2	9.4	17.2	10.5	39.2	37.5	35.9	51.4	47.7	50.2
AL	−27.2	−28.5	−27.7	11.7	5.9	9.0	48.9	37.6	48.7	60.4	46.6	55.1
AR	−23.5	−26.0	−28.8	12.7	9.2	10.2	48.4	38.9	46.4	58.8	39.4	56.5
AZ	−22.2	−25.4	−18.2	9.8	5.2	12.7	37.8	32.2	48.7	67.7	41.4	37.4
CA	−28.1	−23.4	−16.7	12.9	8.3	12.3	41.6	34.5	45.3	66.7	44.7	49.9
CO	−20.5	−19.7	−19.7	10.0	7.3	10.0	38.4	36.0	46.4	65.6	41.2	47.0
CT	−21.3	−20.2	−16.5	13.2	8.4	9.9	52.2	44.5	48.2	65.2	55.8	56.3
DC	−18.2	−21.5	−24.1	8.2	7.2	8.9	42.2	49.7	54.2	82.7	71.8	59.3
DE	−23.3	−21.8	−22.6	11.1	6.2	9.8	49.2	45.7	47.3	64.3	54.3	72.9
FL	−21.4	−20.6	−19.7	12.1	8.5	13.6	44.2	38.3	50.1	67.3	50.3	55.4
GA	−25.8	−29.1	−27.5	14.1	9.5	13.9	43.5	40.9	50.0	61.0	46.8	47.5
HI	−20.7	−20.8	−24.7	16.7	8.6	8.8	47.4	38.9	38.9	57.9	51.7	64.2
IA	−25.7	−18.1	−17.7	6.6	8.3	7.6	41.4	31.4	38.3	53.8	31.7	34.2
ID	−24.2	−19.1	−15.6	16.8	4.5	3.4	36.8	26.8	33.6	51.9	34.1	53.6
IL	−21.8	−20.7	−20.0	9.1	7.1	11.0	40.1	31.6	46.8	62.6	36.5	46.0
IN	−24.6	−23.7	−21.0	10.8	6.0	9.8	42.1	31.1	43.9	55.7	29.6	34.4
KS	−23.4	−19.4	−18.3	13.3	7.6	7.4	47.2	34.7	43.4	59.3	35.4	42.6
KY	−27.8	−27.5	−29.3	4.8	6.8	10.6	40.7	32.6	46.9	58.0	34.0	38.8
LA	−28.7	−27.1	−22.4	10.4	7.4	5.4	42.4	33.5	39.7	51.5	33.0	44.9
MA	−22.9	−22.6	−21.8	10.8	8.7	9.1	44.9	39.1	44.0	59.8	51.1	52.1
MD	−22.2	−23.8	−26.7	9.5	6.9	10.9	45.4	40.9	47.4	64.1	54.4	59.1
ME	−22.2	−20.2	−20.4	13.0	9.2	7.9	47.0	34.4	38.4	50.7	42.9	62.1
MI	−19.7	−18.4	−17.4	6.8	9.2	12.4	36.7	31.9	43.5	58.5	37.8	35.1

MN	−23.2	−19.5	−19.9	10.4	7.2	9.7	42.6	32.6	42.4	60.1	39.8	40.9
MO	−23.8	−22.6	−20.2	9.0	7.7	12.1	44.2	34.0	43.9	62.0	37.7	39.8
MS	−25.1	−27.0	−28.3	9.8	7.8	8.5	40.5	34.7	34.3	55.3	39.4	42.2
MT	−23.1	−17.5	−21.2	2.5	3.3	8.4	29.3	22.3	31.2	46.0	29.3	36.1
NC	−24.5	−25.2	−26.6	12.1	9.8	15.0	50.2	44.0	53.7	61.8	50.4	50.3
ND	−20.3	−12.4	−27.5	5.9	9.6	8.4	40.0	34.1	46.1	52.3	31.9	50.9
NE	−24.2	−26.8	−21.8	9.3	8.9	8.5	41.5	35.4	39.6	55.6	34.9	43.6
NH	−17.5	−23.5	−18.8	12.8	8.5	14.0	42.2	35.7	39.8	59.0	43.3	36.7
NJ	−20.2	−20.7	−21.6	13.3	8.9	12.3	48.2	41.2	44.6	66.0	54.6	55.9
NM	−24.3	−20.9	−24.7	10.9	6.0	10.0	45.6	34.8	44.5	71.0	47.4	60.8
NV	−16.5	−15.0	−10.7	7.5	8.1	13.6	35.4	29.7	49.7	58.8	41.3	52.1
NY	−24.8	−23.2	−21.9	14.4	10.3	11.5	50.0	39.2	47.9	67.8	52.9	57.0
OH	−22.8	−22.1	−18.3	9.9	5.8	11.2	46.6	31.6	41.4	61.3	35.4	43.9
OK	−23.5	−22.3	−24.3	10.3	7.3	12.7	45.5	37.2	41.9	60.9	39.1	46.3
OR	−19.5	−16.0	−18.9	7.9	3.5	6.1	33.9	24.4	33.6	52.6	25.9	32.5
PA	−20.0	−19.9	−17.9	12.3	7.1	10.3	49.2	36.1	48.8	67.1	45.4	51.9
RI	−21.7	−23.8	−22.8	9.2	4.3	8.5	42.7	35.3	36.2	58.1	47.1	53.6
SC	−25.8	−24.9	−27.7	10.9	7.7	5.2	46.8	39.7	45.0	55.7	49.4	30.5
SD	−22.8	—	−24.2	5.9	—	16.1	39.4	—	55.3	52.8	—	41.4
TN	−27.9	−30.4	−34.5	12.7	9.0	8.4	49.2	39.5	45.2	64.9	44.6	43.8
TX	−27.1	−25.0	−25.2	13.2	7.8	10.7	52.4	38.8	42.6	66.9	38.4	47.1
UT	−26.4	−13.9	−20.5	3.9	4.5	3.7	31.5	26.1	27.9	54.7	31.0	32.3
VA	−25.5	−26.2	−30.0	11.7	9.1	15.3	50.4	42.8	52.4	67.4	57.5	61.9
VT	−24.0	−30.0	−23.1	9.0	8.6	6.0	30.4	31.8	35.4	44.8	42.3	52.0
WA	−22.8	−14.3	−14.0	7.2	7.8	9.7	37.6	28.7	42.8	51.5	33.7	43.4
WI	−24.1	−18.9	−14.7	8.2	4.7	9.0	39.3	28.4	36.4	56.5	32.2	32.1
WV	−24.3	−26.1	−26.8	8.5	4.5	5.5	40.4	30.9	32.6	53.0	32.5	47.5
WY	−21.5	−13.0	−12.7	5.4	3.9	24.3	27.0	22.6	48.6	40.6	21.9	46.1

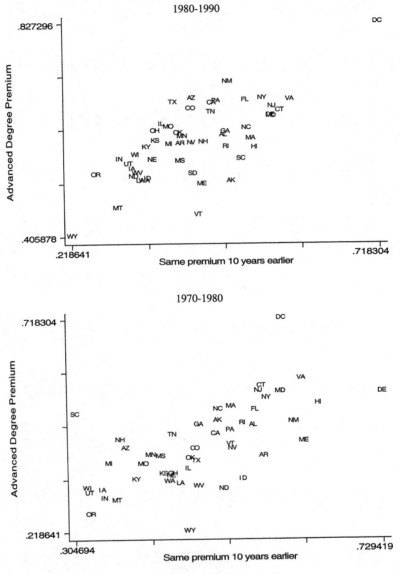

Fig. 7.3   Persistence of advanced degree premium

7.2.2   State and Industry Employment Shocks

We use plant-level data from the manufacturing sector to explore whether industry or regional employment shocks have a greater impact on wages. We make use of the plant-level data from the Annual Surveys of Manufactures (ASM) from 1972 to 1987, which cover wages and employment and include approximately 50,000 plants each year. We estimate an equation of the form

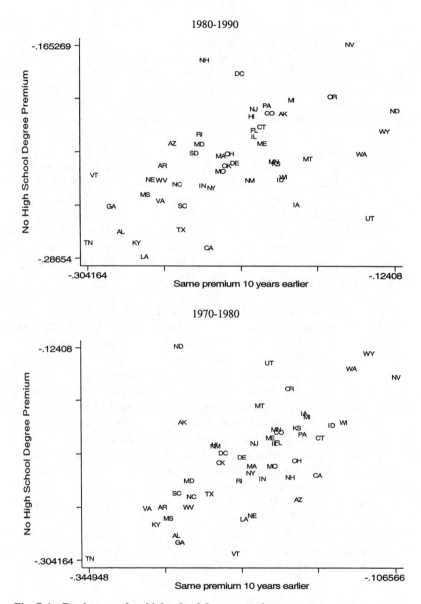

Fig. 7.4   Persistence of no high school degree premium

$$(2) \quad \Delta \ln w_{ispt} = d_t + A(L)\Delta \ln N_{i,\notin s,t} + B(L)\Delta \ln N_{\notin i,s,t} + \varepsilon_{ispt},$$

where $\Delta \ln w_{ispt}$ is the percentage change in wages at plant p in (two-digit) industry i in state s from time $(t - 1)$ to t; $\Delta \ln N_{i,\notin s,t}$ is the change in employment in the industry outside the state; $\Delta \ln N_{\notin i,s,t}$ is the change in employment in the state outside the industry; d_t is a vector of time dummies; and ε_{ispt} captures all other shocks to the plant. We include nine annual lags of the employment changes to allow for slow adjustment of wages. The dependent variable is the percentage change in the average real wage per worker at the plant less the average change across all plants. For each plant, the state employment shocks are constructed as the percentage change in employment in the state outside the two-digit-level industry of the plant. Similarly the industry shock is the percentage change in employment in the same two-digit-level industry outside the state. Both types of employment shocks are adjusted to be mean 0 in given year.

In using this specification, we are making the assumption that shocks to individual plants are small relative to the labor market as a whole. In addition, we are assuming that annual changes in the wage are driven exclusively by shocks to labor demand. If, as we suspect, labor-demand shocks to the region regardless of industry are relatively more important than nationwide industry labor-demand shocks, we should expect to see larger coefficients on recent lags of the state employment changes, and lower, delayed responses to industry employment changes.

The results for the regression are presented in table 7.2 and the cumulative effect of a 1 percent negative employment change is shown in figure 7.5. The response path for the two types of wage shocks is quite different and in accord with the prediction that regional labor markets clear much more quickly than national labor markets. Wages immediately fall more than twice as much in response to a state employment shock than an industry shock. The wage response to a 1 percent decrease in state employment peaks at 0.21 percent after 3 years before gradually diminishing. Industry shocks are fully felt only after 8 years. The response of plant wages confirms our hypothesis that labor markets clear only locally in the short run and that shocks are transmitted nationally only after long delays.[11]

In this section, we have assembled evidence that state labor markets are not well integrated in the short or medium term. The persistence of regional employment shocks on relative wages, the magnitude and persistence of the state education premia, and the relative importance of regional rather than industry shocks to employment on local wages all lead us to conclude that shocks to state labor markets will have important effects on the level and distribution of wages.

7.3   Returns to Observable Characteristics

The literature on rising wage inequality has identified several distinct trends in the data. As noted by numerous authors, the overall increase in wage dispersion consists of at least two distinct phenomena. One is the increase in returns to observable worker characteristics such as experience

11. We have also run the plant-wage regressions including shock to the own-industry state. The results do not change.

Table 7.2   Response of Plant Wages to Employment Shocks

	Dependent Variable: Change in Plant Average Wages $(t - 1$ to $t)$ (%)		
	Coefficient	t-statistic	p
State employment change			
t	0.0714	4.72	0.0001
$t - 1$	−0.0063	−0.39	0.6981
$t - 2$	0.0528	3.47	0.0005
$t - 3$	0.0926	6.82	0.0001
$t - 4$	−0.0674	−4.58	0.0001
$t - 5$	0.0101	0.67	0.5023
$t - 6$	−0.0818	−5.39	0.0001
$t - 7$	0.0483	3.25	0.0012
$t - 8$	−0.0665	−4.00	0.0001
$t - 9$	−0.0245	−1.32	0.187
Industry employment change			
t	0.0272	3.49	0.0005
$t - 1$	−0.0066	−0.80	0.4222
$t - 2$	0.0121	1.44	0.149
$t - 3$	0.0159	2.06	0.0397
$t - 4$	0.0325	3.45	0.0006
$t - 5$	0.0195	2.13	0.0329
$t - 6$	0.0250	2.43	0.0152
$t - 7$	0.0399	4.01	0.0001
$t - 8$	0.0259	2.56	0.0104
$t - 9$	−0.0232	−1.65	0.0998

Notes: State employment change is the percentage change in employment in the state excluding the industry. Industry employment change is the percentage change in employment in the industry outside the state. All changes are normalized to be mean 0 in every year.

and education. The second is the dramatic rise in within-group inequality, called returns to skill. In the rest of this paper, we concentrate almost exclusively on the increase in the returns to unobserved skill and leave aside the issue of the increasing returns to education. Since, by definition, skill is not directly observable, we follow others in the labor literature (see Juhn, Murphy, and Pierce 1993; Gottschalk 1997) and calculate the returns to skill as the residual from a standard wage regression.

We again estimate the wage regression separately for the 3 census years, pooling the data across states, but allowing for variation in state mean wages.[12] The wage regression is of the form given in equation (1) and the results are given in table 7.3.[13]

12. This might seem odd after our discussion of the magnitude of state education premia. However, none of the results on residual wage inequality are sensitive to whether we estimate individual state regressions or a pooled national regression.

13. Allowing for interaction terms between the experience function and other variables did not change the results on residual inequality.

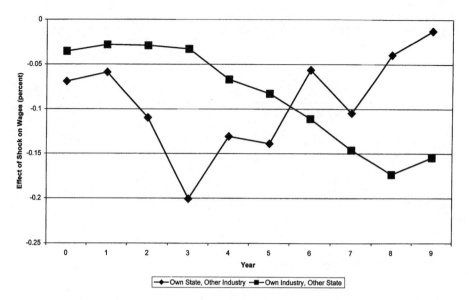

Fig. 7.5 Response of plant wages to regional and industry employment shocks (cumulative effect of a 1 percent decline in employment)

The well-known pattern of returns to observable characteristics is evident in these regressions. In 1970, relative to high school graduates, men without high school diplomas earned almost 22 percent less, while college-degree holders earned almost 44 percent more. Men with some college earned a more modest wage premium of 11 percent, while individuals who acquired additional tertiary education gained on average an extra 5 percent above college-degree holders. Observables explain 31 percent of the overall variation in log wages in 1970.[14]

In general, the 1980 results confirm prior research and show a modest decline in the premium for tertiary education relative to high school–diploma holders, as well as a slight worsening of the relative position of men without high school diplomas. By 1990, however, the returns to education had changed significantly. The wages for men without a high school diploma had decreased further, while the returns to a college degree rose over 10 percent, and the returns for further tertiary education had jumped almost 20 percent. In 1990 observable characteristics explained 40 percent of overall wage variation, a sizable increase from both 1970 and 1980.

---

14. Throughout this paper, we restrict our discussion to the education variables among observable characteristics.

Table 7.3   Wage Regressions (log real weekly wages)

Variable	1970	1980	1990
Intercept	-0.157***	-5.70e-6	-4.70e-6
	(26.00)	(0.013)	(0.012)
Black	-0.325***	-0.262***	-0.206***
	(98.55)	(167.20)	(138.81)
Hisp	-0.227***	-0.205***	-0.161***
	(33.48)	(107.66)	(118.45)
Exp	0.161***	0.142***	0.155***
	(176.70)	(348.86)	(357.82)
Exp2	-8.28e-3***	-7.39e-3***	-7.72e-3***
	(107.90)	(201.65)	(207.81)
Exp3	1.83e-4***	-1.72e-4***	-1.74e-4***
	(77.67)	(145.04)	(149.34)
Exp4	-1.49e-6***	-1.50e-6***	-1.50e-6***
	(62.98)	(119.73)	(122.52)
Nohsd	-0.218***	-0.231***	-0.248***
	(91.61)	(189.26)	(205.27)
Somecoll	0.109***	0.078***	0.112***
	(38.28)	(68.47)	(113.67)
BA	0.436***	0.359***	0.463***
	(122.51)	(253.57)	(383.99)
Advdeg	0.485***	0.438***	0.631***
	(103.75)	(249.52)	(411.41)
Weekwrk	3.27e-3***	5.95e-3***	10.09e-3***
	(26.28)	(118.27)	(223.23)
Nonmetro	-0.101***	-0.090***	-0.108***
	(43.15)	(75.07)	(101.24)
N	406,536	2,094,208	2,223,036
R^2	0.31	0.30	0.40

Note: State dummies included. Numbers in parentheses are *t*-statistics.
***Significant at the 1 percent level.

7.4   Residual Wage Inequality: The Nation

While the regressions in table 7.3 show part of the story of the increase in inequality, the bulk of the variation in wages remains unexplained by observable worker characteristics. Increasing returns to education explain only part of the overall increase in wage inequality. From the regressions, we calculate the distribution of the wage residual and consider the changes in the distribution over the period. We consider three measures of the residual distribution of log weekly wages, the 90-10 wage differential, the 90-50 wage differential, and the 50-10 wage differential.

The first half of table 7.4 reports the levels and changes in those measures for the 3 years and two intervals from the pooled national regression. Given the large literature on the increase in within-group inequality, it is not sur-

Table 7.4   **Changes in Residual Wage Inequality**

	1970		1980		1990
Pooled National Regressions					
90–10 ratio	1.164		1.209		1.282
Change		0.045		0.073	
90–50 ratio	0.512		0.535		0.582
Change		0.023		0.047	
50–10 ratio	0.652		0.675		0.701
Change		0.023		0.026	
Separate State Regressions					
90–10 ratio	1.151		1.202		1.275
Change		0.051		0.073	
90–50 ratio	0.507		0.531		0.579
Change		0.024		0.048	
50–10 ratio	0.643		0.671		0.697
Change		0.028		0.026	

prising that we also find a large increase in residual wage inequality as measured by the 90-10 differential in the 1970s (4.5 percent), and especially in the 1980s (7.3 percent).[15] Changes in the 1970s are split evenly between increases at the top and bottom, while during the 1980s increases in inequality at the top half of the distribution were twice as large as those in the bottom half.

In the second half of table 7.4, we compute our three residual inequality measures after allowing all the returns to observable characteristics to vary across states. This specification lets us see how much of the increase in inequality is due to state-specific changes in the returns to age, education, and so on. Allowing the returns to individual characteristics to vary across states does reduce residual wage inequality for the country as a whole. However, the magnitude of the reduction is quite small and the changes over time are unaffected. For the remainder of the paper, we consider only the distribution from the pooled regression.

7.5 Residual Wage Inequality: The States

Thus far we have confirmed the rise in returns to education over time as well as the increase in residual inequality at the national level during both the 1970s and the 1980s. However, in section 7.2, we argued that while regional labor markets are integrated over long horizons, they display substantial evidence of segregation in the short and medium run. To use the information on individual states, we construct measures of the 90-10 differential for every state (plus the District of Columbia) in each of

15. These increases are somewhat smaller than those reported elsewhere (e.g., Katz and Murphy 1992). This difference is most likely due to the fact that we allow the coefficients on individual characteristics to vary over time.

our 3 years (see table 7.5). While the national 90-10 differential was 1.164 in 1970, the same measure for the states ranged from 1.013 in Connecticut to 1.188 in Oklahoma (the median state) to 1.369 in Louisiana and a phenomenal 1.634 in Alaska. The average state 90-10 difference was 1.195 with a cross-state standard deviation of 11.4 percent.

The figures for 1980 and 1990 show similar heterogeneity across states. In 1980, residual inequality ranged from 1.086 in New Hampshire to 1.215 in Utah (median) to 1.603 in Alaska. The state mean had increased to 1.222 with a drop in the standard deviation to 9.1 percent. Ten years later, the average 90-10 differential had increased dramatically to 1.274 and the dispersion remained relatively unchanged (8.3 percent). As with the education premia, the returns to unobserved skill varied widely across states in every year.

7.5.1   Increasing and Decreasing Inequality

The variation in the levels of inequality across states dwarfs the changes in national inequality over time. In any of the 3 years, a large number of states have 90-10 differentials substantially above or below the national average. In addition, states follow very different paths over time both in terms of levels and rankings. Georgia starts with the 9th highest level of inequality in 1970, but by 1990 Georgia ranks 32nd and inequality has fallen almost 4 percent in the state. In contrast, New York moves 25 places from 15th lowest to 12th highest with an increase of more than 20 percent in the 90-10 differential. In fact, the changes in state wage inequality show at least as much heterogeneity as the levels themselves.

While there is no doubt that residual inequality was rising at the national level during the 1970s, 18 states actually experienced a decline in inequality during the decade (see table 7.6). At the other extreme, 6 states had inequality increases at twice the national rate. Even during the 1980s, a time of dramatically increasing inequality for the country as a whole (7.3 percent), 2 states saw inequality decrease, and 7 others had increases of less than 3 percent. In fact, 36 states had slower inequality increases than the nation. For the entire 20-year period, while the national 90-10 residual increased over 11 percent, 7 states had net declines in inequality. The locations of states with the highest and lowest inequality changes can be seen clearly in figure 7.6. In both decades, states with larger black circles, representing those with the largest rises in inequality, are geographically clustered around the Great Lakes. On the other hand, the states with the lowest inequality rises, or decreases, are more likely to be in the Southeast.

Increases in inequality are correlated in the 1970s and 1980s. States with higher-than-average inequality increases in the first decade were more likely to also have above-average increases in the 1980s (see fig. 7.7), but they explain only 27 percent of the overall variation in state inequality growth in the 1980s.

Table 7.5 **Wage Inequality 90-10 Differentials**

State	1970	State	1980	State	1990
CT	1.01310	NH	1.08611	NH	1.12899
PA	1.02655	RI	1.11204	RI	1.15529
WI	1.04326	CT	1.11629	VT	1.15984
ME	1.04486	PA	1.12144	CT	1.16751
OH	1.05025	OH	1.12743	MD	1.16879
IN	1.05591	WI	1.13308	DE	1.17011
NJ	1.06629	ME	1.13324	VA	1.18657
MA	1.06794	VT	1.13559	NC	1.18868
MI	1.07588	NJ	1.13705	ME	1.19048
OR	1.08399	MA	1.13778	MA	1.19698
IL	1.09182	NC	1.14656	WI	1.212
MN	1.09303	MN	1.15227	SC	1.21238
NH	1.10414	MD	1.15645	IA	1.22263
RI	1.12168	IA	1.16078	NE	1.22336
NY	1.12348	SC	1.162	NJ	1.22705
MD	1.12970	IL	1.16625	PA	1.2311
VT	1.13820	NE	1.16896	OH	1.23172
WY	1.14331	IN	1.17185	SD	1.23475
UT	1.14368	VA	1.17399	KS	1.23572
WA	1.14643	KS	1.17642	GA	1.2473
ID	1.15516	DE	1.18211	WA	1.24785
KS	1.16597	MI	1.19022	IN	1.25021
IA	1.16600	NY	1.20196	AR	1.25295
DE	1.16842	ID	1.20926	MN	1.25504
AR	1.18471	WA	1.21082	ID	1.25917
OK	1.18845	UT	1.21519	TN	1.26158
CO	1.21090	AR	1.22184	AL	1.26277
NE	1.21220	TN	1.22387	HI	1.26464
MO	1.21952	MO	1.2261	ND	1.28276
SC	1.22551	GA	1.23226	IL	1.28486
NC	1.22848	HI	1.2403	MI	1.29513
WV	1.22918	OR	1.24477	CO	1.2965
SD	1.23490	OK	1.24943	UT	1.29686
CA	1.23703	CO	1.25027	MO	1.31029
TN	1.25293	ND	1.25173	OK	1.31197
VA	1.25664	AL	1.2536	MS	1.32043
AL	1.26142	FL	1.27309	KY	1.32224
AZ	1.26375	TX	1.28065	FL	1.32839
MT	1.26999	WV	1.28073	OR	1.32906
TX	1.27554	CA	1.28309	NY	1.33142
FL	1.28121	KY	1.2869	DC	1.33349
DC	1.28421	MT	1.29133	TX	1.34339
GA	1.28618	NV	1.29379	NM	1.35397
NM	1.30236	AZ	1.31669	CA	1.35524
HI	1.30438	NM	1.31818	AZ	1.35716
KY	1.30978	WY	1.32922	NV	1.36228
NV	1.33925	MS	1.32971	WY	1.37519
ND	1.34187	LA	1.37362	WV	1.38325
MS	1.34829	DC	1.37483	MT	1.38571
LA	1.36953	AK	1.60314	LA	1.39944
AK	1.63356	SD	—	AK	1.60416

Note: Residuals from national-level regressions.

Table 7.6   **Changes in Wage Inequality 90-10 Differentials**

State	1970–80	State	1980–90	State	1970–90
ND	−0.09014	DE	−0.012	VA	−0.07007
VA	−0.08265	MS	−0.00928	ND	−0.05911
NC	−0.08192	AL	0.00917	NC	−0.0398
HI	−0.06409	MD	0.01234	HI	−0.03974
SC	−0.06351	VA	0.01258	GA	−0.03888
GA	−0.05391	GA	0.01504	MS	−0.02785
NV	−0.04547	VT	0.02425	SC	−0.01313
NE	−0.04324	HI	0.02435	AL	0.00136
TN	−0.02906	LA	0.02582	DE	0.0017
KY	−0.02288	ND	0.03103	TN	0.00865
MS	−0.01857	AR	0.03111	NE	0.01116
NH	−0.01803	KY	0.03534	KY	0.01246
RI	−0.00963	NM	0.03579	VT	0.02164
FL	−0.00812	WA	0.03704	NV	0.02303
AL	−0.00781	TN	0.03771	NH	0.02484
IA	−0.00522	AZ	0.04047	LA	0.02991
VT	−0.00261	NC	0.04212	RI	0.03361
LA	0.00409	NH	0.04288	MD	0.03908
TX	0.00512	RI	0.04325	FL	0.04718
MO	0.00657	WY	0.04596	NM	0.05161
KS	0.01045	CO	0.04623	IA	0.05663
DE	0.0137	ID	0.04992	TX	0.06786
NM	0.01582	SC	0.05038	AR	0.06824
MT	0.02134	CT	0.05122	KS	0.06975
MD	0.02674	NE	0.0544	CO	0.0856
AR	0.03713	FL	0.0553	MO	0.09076
CO	0.03937	ME	0.05724	AZ	0.09342
CA	0.04607	MA	0.0592	WA	0.10143
WV	0.05156	KS	0.0593	ID	0.10402
AZ	0.05295	IA	0.06185	MT	0.11572
ID	0.0541	OK	0.06254	CA	0.11822
MN	0.05924	TX	0.06274	OK	0.12351
OK	0.06098	NV	0.06849	MA	0.12903
WA	0.06439	CA	0.07215	ME	0.14562
MA	0.06984	IN	0.07837	UT	0.15318
NJ	0.07076	WI	0.07892	WV	0.15407
UT	0.07151	UT	0.08167	CT	0.1544
IL	0.07443	MO	0.08419	NJ	0.16076
OH	0.07718	OR	0.08429	MN	0.16202
NY	0.07848	NJ	0.09	WI	0.16874
ME	0.08838	MT	0.09438	OH	0.18147
WI	0.08982	WV	0.10251	IL	0.19304
PA	**0.09489**	**MN**	**0.10278**	**IN**	**0.1943**
CT	**0.10318**	**OH**	**0.10429**	**PA**	**0.20455**
MI	**0.11434**	**MI**	**0.10491**	**NY**	**0.20794**
IN	**0.11593**	**PA**	**0.10966**	**MI**	**0.21925**
OR	**0.16078**	**IL**	**0.11861**	**WY**	**0.23188**
WY	**0.18592**	**NY**	**0.12946**	**OR**	**0.24507**

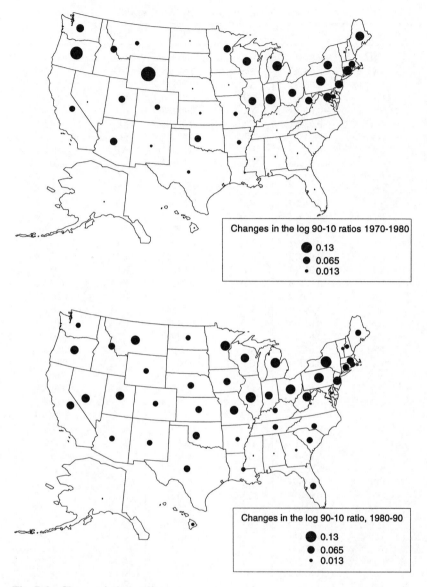

Fig. 7.6   Changes in inequality
Note: Actual dot sizes vary continuously. The legend provides three reference points.

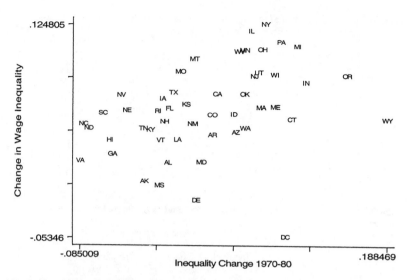

Fig. 7.7   Persistence in inequality changes

7.5.2   The Extreme States and Their Importance

Table 7.6 reports the state changes in wage inequality sorted by performance during each decade. The 12 extreme states, 6 with big increases and 6 with declines or small increases, are in boldface. The differences between the two groups are striking. The six with the biggest increases in the 1980s (New York, Illinois, Pennsylvania, Michigan, Ohio, and Minnesota) are all large industrialized states that suffered disproportionately from the recession in the beginning of the decade and lost a large number of manufacturing jobs. The six best performers (Delaware, Mississippi, Alabama, Maryland, Virginia, and Georgia) are mostly southern states that expanded manufacturing employment during the decade.

While there is little doubt that states experienced very different changes in residual inequality, it does not immediately follow that this heterogeneity was important for the national increase. To quantify the importance of the individual states, we calculate the 90-10 differential with and without the groups of states that had the biggest and smallest changes. Table 7.7 reports the 90-10 differentials for all states together and two groups of 44 (one without the top 6 and one without the bottom 6).

Excluding the 6 states with the lowest growth in wage inequality, the overall increase for the United States would have been 19.6 percent higher during the 1970s and 9.6 percent higher in the 1980s. The states that had the largest increases in wage inequality during the 1980s had an even larger effect on the aggregate measure. Inequality increases would have been 36 percent lower in the 1970s and 23 percent lower in the 1980s without the

Table 7.7   Impact of States with Largest and Smallest Inequality Increases

	1970	1980	1990
90-10 Difference (levels)			
All states	1.164	1.210	1.282
Excluding six smallest	1.154	1.209	1.289
Excluding six largest	1.204	1.228	1.285
90-10 Difference (changes)			
All states		0.046	0.073
Excluding six smallest		0.055	0.080
Excluding six largest		0.025	0.056

Table 7.8   Mean Reversion in State Residual Wage Inequality

	Dependent Variables	
	Inequality Change, 1970–80	Inequality Change, 1980–90
Intercept	0.536	0.241
	(6.406)	(2.928)
Initial inequality	−0.428	−0.154
	(−6.083)	(−2.272)
R^2	0.429	0.080
N	49	49

Note: Numbers in parentheses are *t*-statistics.

increases in these 6 states. These results suggest that the heterogeneity in state outcomes was an important determinant of national inequality.

7.5.3   Mean Reversion

It is possible that the heterogeneity in state outcomes merely represents a mean reversion to a common level of inequality. Regressing the change in inequality on the initial level, we find that in the 1970s states with higher-than-average initial levels of inequality showed decreases, or smaller increases, while low-inequality states tended to experience more rapid increases (see table 7.8). States with 10 percent higher initial levels in 1970 had, on average, a 4.3 percent lower rise in inequality over the following decade. Initial levels explain over 40 percent of the variation in state performance.[16]

In contrast, in the 1980s initial levels explain only 8 percent of the subsequent movement in inequality across states. The relationship between initial wage differentials and subsequent changes was still negative, but on

16. When additional variables are added to the specification, the coefficient on lagged levels is no longer negative for either decade.

average a 10 percent higher initial wage differential in 1980 was associated with only a 1.5 percent lower increase over the following decade. We can conclude that the variation in state performance in the 1980s was not simply a result of mean reversion in inequality.

7.6   The Explanations

The preceding sections show that shocks to regional labor markets persist over the short and medium run and that states had vastly different outcomes in terms of wage inequality during the 1970s and 1980s. In this section, we reconsider existing explanations of the rise in wage inequality using state-level data. As mentioned at the outset, the dominant explanations for the national inequality increase center on the use of skill-biased technology, changes in product demand due to international trade, supply shifts due to immigration, and shifts in labor market institutions. We construct state-level variables to proxy for each of the explanations.

7.6.1   Skill-Biased Technological Change

One problem with the hypothesis that skill-biased technological change has been the source of the rise in overall wage inequality is the lack of direct evidence. Krueger (1993) argues that the use of computers is associated with a wage premium, but DiNardo and Pischke (1997) offer a compelling argument that computers themselves have not changed the wage structure. Since we do not have direct measures of technology either by state or for individual workers, we follow Berman, Bound, and Griliches (1994) and Bernard and Jensen (1997) in using measures of the capital stock as a proxy for inputs that are complements to skills. A further limitation of these measures is that they are only available for the manufacturing sector from the ASM and Census of Manufactures, and as a result may not capture technology upgrading in other sectors.[17] With these caveats, the hypothesis of skill-biased technological change implies a positive relationship between increases in capital per worker and inequality within the state.

We consider two measures of skill-biased technology for each state, the log levels of machine and equipment stocks per worker in the manufacturing sector in the state (*Machine*) and the log level of computer investment per worker in manufacturing in the state (*Computer*). The data are constructed from the preceding Census of Manufactures (i.e., the 1967 census for 1970, the 1977 census for 1980, and the 1987 census for 1990).[18]

---

17. In an alternative view of skill-biased technological change, Acemoglu (1998) models the increase in skill-biased technology as an endogenous response to the supply of skills. If he is correct, our measures of computers and machines will not correctly proxy for the changes in skill-biased technology.

18. The computer investment data are not available for 1970.

7.6.2   International Trade

Ideally we would be able to measure import and export prices for all goods produced in a state. Instead we use state-level import and export exchange rates (*Import* and *Export*). To calculate the import exchange rate for a state, we start by constructing industry import exchange rates for each four-digit manufacturing industry. The industry import exchange rates are given by the sum of real exchange rates indices (U.S. dollars/foreign currency)[19] across countries weighted by that country's average share in imports in the industry over the preceding 3 years,

$$(3) \qquad EXCHIM_i = \sum_c \frac{IMP_{c,i}}{IMP_i} \cdot EXCH_c.$$

The state import exchange rate is the weighted sum of industry import exchange rates with the weights given by the share of the industry in total shipments from the state, averaged over the sample,

$$(4) \qquad I_{st} = \sum_i \frac{TVS_{s,i}}{TVS_s} \cdot EXCHIM_i.$$

The expected relationship between the state import exchange rate and inequality is negative. A strengthening dollar means cheaper imports in goods that are produced in the state. If a state contains industries that experience substantial import penetration, and imports are generally produced with less-skilled labor, then state-level inequality should rise.

The state export exchange rate is constructed in a comparable fashion:

$$(5) \qquad EXCHEX_i = \sum_c \frac{EXP_{c,i}}{EXP_i} \cdot EXCH_c.$$

The state export exchange rate is the weighted sum of industry export exchange rates with the weights given by the share of the industry in total exports from the state,[20]

$$(6) \qquad X_{st} = \sum_i \frac{EXP_{s,i}}{EXP_s} \cdot EXCHEX_i.$$

If exports are skill-intensive products, as found in Bernard and Jensen (1995, 1997) we should expect to see a positive relationship between the state export exchange rate and inequality.

The main difficulty with both exchange rate measures stems from the

19. The exchange rates are nominal exchange rates deflated by GDP deflators in foreign currency per U.S. dollar normalized to be 100 in 1980.
20. Due to a lack of state industry export data in earlier years, we are forced to use weights based on the 1987 census.

inequality data itself. Since we only observe states in 3 years, our exchange rate measures may not capture the effects of the dollar movements in the first half of the 1980s.

7.6.3 Industry Composition

To capture changes in the composition of output at the state level, we include a measure of durable manufacturing employment for the state. Specifically we calculate the ratio of durable manufacturing employment to total employment in the three census samples (*Durable*). The pictures of the wage inequality changes in figure 7.6 suggest that manufacturing-intensive states saw disproportionate rises in wage inequality. We expect that changes in durable employment would be negatively correlated with inequality changes.

Another measure of product demand is the level of government procurement in the state. The measure is constructed from the government procurement data of Hooker and Knetter (1997) and is given by the log level of government procurement expenditures per capita (*Procure*). Since the government contracts captured in the data tend to be for large skill-intensive products, the expected relationship with inequality is positive.

7.6.4 Immigration

To evaluate the potential role for foreign immigration in depressing low-skilled workers' wages and thus increasing inequality, we include the ratio of recent immigrants to the population (*Immigrant*). Immigrants are those workers who immigrated to the state within the last 5 years of the prior decade.[21] The expected relationship of immigration and inequality is positive if the pool of immigrant labor is generally less-skilled than the existing stock of native workers.[22]

7.6.5 Labor Market Institutions

Recent work by DiNardo, Fortin, and Lemieux (1996) and Fortin and Lemieux (1997) has revived interest in labor market institutions as sources of inequality increases. Lee (1999), using state-level data, argues that all the increase in raw inequality can be attributed to changes in state minimum wages. In particular, the decline in unionization rates and the fall in the real minimum wage are offered as important explanations for the rise in wage dispersion. We construct measures of unionization rates (*Union*) for each state for the 3 years.[23] The data on unionization rates come from

21. For example, for the 1980–90 changes in inequality, the immigration measure is calculated as fraction of the state population who immigrated to the state in 1985–90.
22. Immigrants may have lower apparent skills in the data due to language problems or discrimination even if their actual skill levels are higher than the native population's.
23. Barry Hirsch generously provided files with the unionization data. For early years, some states appear only in groups. We assigned the group unionization rate to the state for those years. Since both sets of data start in 1973, we use the 1973 values for 1970.

Kokkelenberg and Sockell (1985) and Hirsch and Macpherson (1993). The minimum wage data come from Neumark and Wascher (1992). We use the log of the real state minimum wage as our measure (*Minwage*).

7.6.6   Income Levels

To capture the possibility that heterogeneity in state inequality measures is being driven by variations in state income levels, we construct a measure of state economic activity. For each state we calculate the difference between the median income and the national median income (*Cycle*). In our estimation framework, including state fixed effects, we expect that higher state incomes would be correlated with peaks in the state business cycle and associated with lower levels of inequality.

7.7   Explaining State Inequality Changes

Ideally any explanation for the large rise in inequality during the 1980s would be capable of explaining smaller increases in other periods. For our estimation procedure, we choose to pool the data across decades instead of estimating decade-by-decade regressions.[24] We estimate the relationship between our explanatory variables and state residual wage inequality, as measured by the log 90-10 ratio, in levels, pooled across years with state fixed effects.[25]

Table 7.9 contains univariate regressions of state inequality on each of our explanatory variables in columns (1) through (10). Almost all the variables are significantly correlated with inequality changes and have the expected sign. The measure of durable employment share is negatively and significantly correlated with changes in inequality across states (col. [1]) and can explain almost 30 percent of the variance over the 2 decades. A 1 percent change in the fraction of the sample employed in manufacturing is associated with a 1.58 percent increase in the 90-10 ratio.

Both measures of technology deepening, log capital per worker and computer investment per worker, are positively correlated with inequality across states. The capital-intensity measure by itself accounts for over 20 percent of the variation, while for the 1980s computer-investment changes can explain over 40 percent of the total state heterogeneity.[26]

Deunionization is also strongly correlated with increasing inequality. Decline in union membership rates can account for almost 30 percent of the variation in the pooled estimation. The minimum wage measure does the best of all the state-level measures. It is strongly negatively correlated with increases in inequality and accounts for 45 percent of total variation.

24. In table 7.11 below, we also report estimates for changes during the 1980s.
25. Pooled estimation in first differences across the decades does not yield different conclusions.
26. The computer measure is not available before 1980.

Table 7.9   Explaining Changes in State Residual Wage Inequality

					Dependent Variable [log (state 90-10 ratio)][a]					
	(1)	(2)	(3)	(4)	(5)	(6)	(7)	(8)	(9)	(10)
Durable	-1.583*** (0.247)									
Machine		0.098*** (0.019)								
Computer			0.031*** (0.005)							
Import				0.354*** (0.088)						
Export					0.022 (0.104)					
Union						-0.007*** (0.001)				
Minwage							-0.162*** (0.018)			
Immigrant								2.274** (1.153)		
Procure									-0.024*** (0.005)	
Cycle										-0.222** (0.107)
R^2	0.29	0.21	0.42[b]	0.14	0.00	0.29	0.45	0.04	0.18	0.04
N	149	149	99	149	149	149	149	149	149	149

Notes: All regressions were estimated using state fixed effects. South Dakota is missing from the population census for 1980 and Hawaii is missing in all years from the Longitudinal Research Database. Standard errors are given in parentheses.

[a]Residuals from log wage regression.

[b]The computer numbers are not available for 1970.

**Significant at the 5 percent level.

***Significant at the 1 percent level.

Increased immigration also shows up with a positive and significant co-efficient, although its overall explanatory power is low. Similarly, our measure of aggregate state economic activity confirms that states moving from business-cycle troughs to peaks have declines in inequality, although the measure cannot explain much of the cross-state variation in the 2 decades.

Surprisingly, our measures of international trade do not perform well. The import exchange rate has the wrong sign, the appreciation of the dollar on an import basis leads to declines in inequality, and the export exchange rate is not significant.[27] The measure of government purchases per capita is significant, but unexpectedly negatively correlated with inequality.

These univariate results suggest that a wide range of potential explanations may play a role in the increase in inequality. Changes in minimum wage, decreases in durable-manufacturing employment, decreases in unionization, and increases in capital per worker all have substantial explanatory power. However, one drawback of the specification in table 7.9 is that we have neglected to control for time effects; that is, any unobserved aggregate trending variable could be driving movements in both our left-hand-side and right-hand-side variables. We would like to know how robust the univariates are in the presence of time trends.

Table 7.10 reports the same set of regressions with time dummies (i.e., separate time trends for each decade). The differences in the results are quite substantial. Of the previously significant regressors, only durable employment and the business-cycle measure remain statistically significant. In addition, the coefficient on the export exchange rate switches to a negative sign and becomes significant, suggesting that depreciations that stimulate exports may reduce inequality.[28] In other words, only changes in durable employment and business cycles are correlated with differential movements in inequality across states within decades. In particular, the prior significance of the state minimum wage was due almost entirely to its aggregate trend movements and not due to variation across states.

We consider a multivariate specification with all our potential explanatory variables in table 7.11. Columns (1) and (2) report pooled results for both decades without and with time dummies, respectively, while columns (3) and (4) report results just for the 1980s. In all specifications for both time periods, the share of durable-manufacturing employment and the state of the state business cycle enter significantly and with the expected sign. Declines in durable-manufacturing employment are strongly associated with inequality increases, even allowing for the presence of alternative

27. We caution that this does not mean that international trade was unimportant for inequality increases. The decade-long span of our data may hide the role of trade. Preliminary work looking at state-level foreign direct investment shows mixed results.

28. Bernard and Jensen (1997) find that exporters contribute to increases in wage differentials between production and nonproduction workers. However, this may reflect changes in education premia as opposed to changes in residual wage inequality.

Table 7.10   Explaining Changes in State Residual Wage Inequality (with year dummies)

	(1)	(2)	(3)	(4)	(5)	(6)	(7)	(8)	(9)	(10)
	Dependent Variable [log (state 90-10 ratio)][a]									
Durable	-1.047*** (0.007)									
Machine		-0.033 (0.028)								
Computer			-0.001 (0.007)							
Import				-0.012 (0.140)						
Export					-0.311** (0.145)					
Union						-0.002				
Minwage							-0.142 (0.100)			
Immigrant								-1.179 (1.03)		
Procure									0.002 (0.012)	
Cycle										-0.229*** (0.080)
R^2	0.55	0.45	0.67[b]	0.45	0.48	0.45	0.46	0.45	0.45	0.48
N	149	149	99	149	149	149	149	149	149	149

Notes: All regressions were estimated using state fixed effects and time dummies. South Dakota is missing from the population census for 1980 and Hawaii is missing in all years from the Longitudinal Research Database. Standard errors are in parentheses.
[a]Residuals from log wage regression.
[b]The computer numbers are not available for 1970.
**Significant at the 5 percent level.
***Significant at the 1 percent level.

Table 7.11   **Explaining Changes in State Residual Wage Inequality**

	Dependent Variable [log (state 90-10 ratio)][a]			
	(1)	(2)	(3)	(4)
Durable	−1.175***	−1.217***	−0.803***	−0.698***
	(0.224)	(0.228)	(0.238)	(0.243)
Machine	−0.001	−0.011	0.014	−0.009
	(0.024)	(0.025)	(0.027)	(0.030)
Import	−0.011	−0.168	0.259*	0.326**
	(0.114)	(0.139)	(0.144)	(0.148)
Export	0.039	−0.106	0.011	0.005
	(0.121)	(0.140)	(0.109)	(0.108)
Union	0.000	0.000	0.001	0.003
	(0.002)	(0.002)	(0.002)	(0.002)
Minwage	−0.139***	−0.087	−0.151***	−0.045
	(0.031)	(0.095)	(0.042)	(0.079)
Immigrant	−0.198	−0.444	−0.338	−0.837
	(0.911)	(0.932)	(1.307)	(1.322)
Procure	−0.002	0.012	0.010	0.009
	(0.009)	(0.011)	(0.011)	(0.011)
Cycle	−0.255***	−0.217***	−0.267**	−0.312***
	(0.075)	(0.079)	(0.100)	(0.103)
Time dummies		Yes		Yes
R^2	0.64	0.65	0.81	0.82
N	149	149	99	99

Notes: All regressions were estimated using state fixed effects. South Dakota is missing from the population census for 1980 and Hawaii is missing in all years from the Longitudinal Research Database. Standard errors are in parentheses.

[a]Residuals from log wage regression.
*Significant at the 10 percent level.
**Significant at the 5 percent level.
***Significant at the 1 percent level.

explanatory variables. Similarly, state business-cycle expansions are associated with declines in residual inequality, and recessions are times of increasing inequality. The state minimum-wage measure is again significant only in the specifications without time trends. Of the other explanatory variables, measures of capital intensity, immigration, exchange rates, unionization, or government procurement, none is close to being significant, except for the import exchange rate measure in the 1980s, which has the wrong sign.

7.8 Inequality at the Top and Bottom

The preceding results focused on changes in the log 90-10 ratio of residual wages. In this section, we explore what differences, if any, result from looking at changes in the top and bottom halves of the residual wage distribution. Table 7.12 reports specifications for the 90-50 and 50-10 inequality measures with and without time trends. All regressions are pooled over both decades, estimated in levels with state fixed effects.

The results for the 90-50 ratio are in columns (1) and (2) of table 7.12. Increases in inequality in the upper half of the residual wage distribution are significantly negatively correlated with the share of durable-manufacturing employment, although the point estimates are less than one-half those of the entire distribution. In the specification without time trends, we also find significant effects of immigration and the two exchange rates. The exchange rates have the expected sign, a strengthening dollar increases inequality through imports, but a weakening dollar increases inequality through exports. Surprisingly, the minimum-wage mea-

Table 7.12   **Explaining Changes in State Residual Wage Inequality**

	Dependent Variables[a]			
	log (state 90-10 ratio)		log (state 50-10 ratio)	
	(1)	(2)	(3)	(4)
Durable	−0.370***	−0.341***	−0.805***	−0.875***
	(0.101)	(0.103)	(0.185)	(0.189)
Machine	−0.004	−0.011	0.003	0.00
	(0.011)	(0.011)	(0.020)	(0.021)
Import	−0.085*	−0.112*	0.074	−0.056
	(0.051)	(0.063)	(0.094)	(0.115)
Export	0.127**	0.085	−0.088	−0.192
	(0.055)	(0.063)	(0.099)	(0.116)
Union	−0.000	−0.000	0.001	−0.000
	(0.001)	(0.001)	(0.001)	(0.001)
Minwage	−0.112***	−0.032	0.026	−0.055
	(0.014)	(0.043)	(0.026)	(0.078)
Immigrant	1.261***	1.041**	−1.459*	−1.485*
	(0.412)	(0.421)	(0.754)	(0.771)
Procure	0.001	0.004	−0.002	0.008
	(0.005)	(0.005)	(0.007)	(0.009)
Cycle	−0.017	−0.022	−0.238***	−0.194***
	(0.034)	(0.036)	(0.062)	(0.065)
Time dummies		Yes		Yes
R^2	0.79	0.80	0.39	0.42
N	149	149	149	149

Notes: All regressions were estimated using state fixed effects. South Dakota is missing from the population census for 1980 and Hawaii is missing in all years from the Longitudinal Research Database. Standard errors are in parentheses.

[a]Residuals from log wage regression.

*Significant at the 10 percent level.

**Significant at the 5 percent level.

***Significant at the 1 percent level.

sure enters with the expected sign and significantly. We suspect this result is, again, due to decade trends, as most, if not all, economic theories would suggest that changes in the minimum wage should not affect this part of the wage distribution. The state of the business cycle, while significant for changes in the 90-10 differential, does not affect dispersion at the top of the distribution.

Looking at the results for the 50-10 ratio in columns (3) and (4) we find some surprising differences. Overall, our set of variables explains less of the cross-state inequality movements in this part of the distribution. Durable-manufacturing employment, as always, is negative and strongly significant with a much larger coefficient. However, increases in inequality at the bottom of the skill distribution are not significantly correlated with either the measure of technology, the exchange rate measures, or changes in state minimum wages. In addition, the coefficient on immigration has the opposite sign from what we might expect and is marginally significant. The business-cycle measure is now strongly significant with the expected sign.

Taken as a group, these results confirm the importance of durable-manufacturing employment in accounting for inequality changes through the skill distribution. They also highlight the relative importance of business cycles on wage movements in the bottom half of the distribution. The results for state minimum wages largely confirm our earlier findings and suggest that minimum-wage changes are not driving large increases in inequality.

7.9   Conclusion

In this paper, we argue that the previous research on wage inequality in the United States has largely overlooked an important source of information, the heterogeneity of inequality movements across regions.[29] We suspect this oversight stems from an assumption that individuals participate in a single national labor market. If there is one nationwide market setting wages, then there is no reason to look at regional data to understand sources of the rise in wage inequality. If, however, regional labor markets experience idiosyncratic shocks that are only slowly transmitted to other areas, then we can potentially learn about the sources of inequality from the experiences of different regions.

We find that the assumption of a single national labor market fails in the data. Blanchard and Katz (1992) show persistent effects of state employment shocks. In addition, we find that education premia show large, persistent differences across states, suggesting that flows of workers and

---

29. As mentioned earlier, important exceptions are Bound and Holzer (1996), Borjas and Ramey (1994, 1995), and Topel (1993).

firms are not sufficient to eliminate wage differentials. Finally, we show that regional employment shocks have large effects on plant-level wages.[30]

The story that emerges from most of the prior literature on wage inequality in the United States is one of a remarkably consistent increase during the 1970s and 1980s across and within groups (industries, education categories, etc.). The state-level data provide a very different view. Measures of state inequality show a remarkable variety of levels and changes over time. In any given year, numerous states have levels of inequality far from the national average in both directions. More importantly, the relative positions of the states change sharply from decade to decade. Numerous states with above-average inequality in 1970 end up being relatively equal 20 years later, and some states even improve their absolute positions over the period.

This variety of outcomes at the state level provides a natural environment for reexamining the existing theories for the overall inequality rise. To evaluate existing theories of the rise in inequality, we construct state-level measures of industrial composition, skill-biased technology, international trade shocks, and labor market institutions.

Among our results, one fact is clear. The decline in the share of durable-manufacturing employment is negatively correlated with inequality increases in all our specifications, over all periods, and for every segment of the residual wage distribution. By itself, the share of durable-manufacturing employment can account for 30 to 55 percent of the state changes in wage inequality and is especially important for movements in the bottom half of the wage distribution.

The most surprising failure in our state regressions are our measures of international trade and weighted state import and export exchange rate indices, which are not significant and usually are the wrong sign. On the other hand, while immigration is not important for changes in the 90-10 ratio, increased foreign immigration is positively correlated with inequality increases in the upper half of the skill distribution, and negatively correlated in the bottom half.

The evidence collected here is a useful starting point for reconsidering possible explanations for the large increase in inequality in the 1980s, and the smaller but significant increases in the returns to skill in the 1970s. Unlike previous research on inequality increases, we find an important role for the decline of manufacturing employment. These results suggest the importance of understanding the sources of and variation in manufacturing employment declines. While international trade appears not to have played a direct role in the inequality rise, its role in changing the com-

---

30. We encourage further research on the integration of regional labor markets, whether it is increasing, and for which types of workers.

position of production remains to be explored. On a more positive note, the results also suggest that, to the extent that manufacturing employment has stabilized, the increases in residual wage inequality should slow as well.

References

Acemoglu, Daron. 1998. Why do new technologies complement skills? Directed technical change and wage inequality. *Quarterly Journal of Economics* 113 (4): 1055–89.
Berman, Eli, John Bound, and Zvi Griliches. 1994. Changes in the demand for skilled labor: Evidence from the Annual Survey of Manufacturing. *Quarterly Journal of Economics* 109:367–98.
Berman, Eli, John Bound, and Stephen Machin. 1997. Implications of skill-biased technological change: International evidence. NBER Working Paper no. 6166. Cambridge, Mass.: National Bureau of Economic Research.
Bernard, Andrew B., and J. Bradford Jensen. 1995. Exporters, jobs, and wages in U.S. manufacturing, 1976–1987. *Brookings Papers on Economic Activity, Microeconomics,* 67–120.
———. 1997. Exporters, skill-upgrading, and the wage gap. *Journal of International Economics* 42:3–31.
Blanchard, Olivier, and Lawrence Katz. 1992. Regional evolutions. *Brookings Papers on Economic Activity, Microeconomics,* 1–75.
Borjas, George, and Valerie Ramey. 1994. Time series evidence on the source of trends in wage inequality. *American Economic Review* 84 (May): 10–16.
———. 1995. Foreign competition, market power, and wage inequality. *Quarterly Journal of Economics* 110 (4): 1075–110.
Bound, John, and Harry J. Holzer. 1996. Demand shifts, population adjustments, and labor market outcomes during the 1980s. NBER Working Paper no. 5685. Cambridge, Mass.: National Bureau of Economic Research.
Bound, John, and George Johnson. 1992. Changes in the structure of wages during the 1980s: An evaluation of alternative explanations. *American Economic Review* 82:371–92.
DiNardo, John, Nicole M. Fortin, and Thomas Lemieux. 1996. Labor market institutions and the distribution of wages, 1973–1992: A semiparametric approach. *Econometrica* 65:1001–44.
DiNardo, John, and Jorn-Steffen Pischke. 1997. The returns to computer use revisited: Have pencils changed the wage structure too? *Quarterly Journal of Economics* 112 (1): 291–304.
Fortin, Nicole M., and Thomas Lemieux. 1997. Institutional changes and the rising wage inequality: Is there a linkage? *Journal of Economic Perspectives* 11 (2): 75–96.
Gottschalk, Peter. 1997. Inequality, income growth, and mobility: The basic facts. *Journal of Economic Perspectives* 11 (2): 21–40.
Hirsch, Barry T., and David A. Macpherson. 1993. Union membership and coverage files from the Current Population Surveys: Note. *Industrial and Labor Relations Review* 46 (3): 574–78.
Hooker, Mark, and Michael Knetter. 1997. The effects of military spending on economic activity: Evidence from state procurement spending. *Journal of Money, Credit, and Banking* 29 (3): 400–421.

Juhn, Chinhui, Kevin Murphy, and Brooks Pierce. 1993. Wage inequality and the rise in returns to skill. *Journal of Political Economy* 101 (3): 410–42.

Katz, Lawrence, and Kevin Murphy. 1992. Changes in relative wages, 1963–1987: Supply and demand factors. *Quarterly Journal of Economics* 108:33–60.

Kokkelenberg, Edward C., and Donna R. Sockell. 1985. Union membership in the United States, 1973–1981. *Industrial and Labor Relations Review* 38 (4): 497–543.

Krueger, Alan. 1993. How computers have changed the wage structure: Evidence from microdata, 1984–1989. *Quarterly Journal of Economics* 108:33–60.

Krugman, Paul. 1995. Technology, trade and factor prices. NBER Working Paper no. 5355. Cambridge, Mass.: National Bureau of Economic Research.

Lee, David. 1999. Wage inequality in the U.S. during the 1980s: Rising dispersion or falling minimum wage? *Quarterly Journal of Economics* 114 (3): 941–1024.

Levy, Frank, and Richard Murnane. 1992. U.S. earnings levels and earnings inequality: A review of recent trends and proposed explanations. *Journal of Economic Literature* 30 (3): 1333–81.

Neumark, David, and William Wascher. 1992. Employment effects of minimum and subminimum wages: Panel data on state minimum wage laws. *Industrial and Labor Relations Review* 46 (1): 55–81.

Topel, Robert. 1993. Regional labor markets and the determinants of wage inequality. *American Economic Review* 83 (May): 110–15.

Wood, Adrian. 1995. How trade hurt unskilled workers. *Journal of Economic Perspectives* 9 (3): 57–80.

Comment   Lee G. Branstetter

Introduction

This interesting paper is the latest in a series of interesting papers generated by the productive collaboration of Andrew Bernard and Brad Jensen. I found this to be a provocative and well-executed piece of research, and I suspect that this paper may be one of the most important contributions that will emerge in this volume. While, in keeping with the traditional responsibilities of a discussant, I will raise some questions about the authors' approach and results in these comments, I should stress at the outset that I like this paper very much. I should also issue a disclaimer: I am neither a labor economist, nor an "expert" in the debate over the sources of increases in U.S. income inequality. Therefore, the authors and the reader should apply the appropriate discount factor to all that I am about to say.

The authors' starting point is the observation that, while the inequality of income distribution in the United States has widened substantially over the last decade, the direct causes of this increase have eluded the collective research efforts of some of the brightest minds working in economics. The estimated effects of the usual suspects—international trade, deunioniza-

Lee G. Branstetter is assistant professor of economics and director of the East Asian Studies Program at the University of California, Davis, and a faculty research fellow of the National Bureau of Economic Research.

tion, and minimum wage changes—can explain only a portion of this increase. The rest is attributed to "skill-biased technological change," but this attribution has come about more through a process of elimination of alternatives than on the basis of direct evidence.

Can economic analysis at the regional level help us disentangle the causes of changes in the income distribution at the national level? The promise of this idea is that there is considerable variation across states, not only in levels of inequality and their potential determinants, but also in the rates of change of these variables over time, which could be exploited to improve identification. Of course, there are also costs to this approach. One cost comes from the data: The authors have only three cross sections of census data to work with, whereas, for instance, Katz and Murphy (1992) had annual data from the 1960s through the 1980s, which allowed them to look closely at the dynamics of labor market adjustment. Here data availability precludes such an analysis of dynamics. More substantively, U.S. states are really not like miniature countries, nor is the United States like a state within a larger supranational economy.[1] For this and other reasons, extracting lessons for national policy from the experience of individual states may prove problematic.[2]

Nevertheless, a number of researchers have sought to understand changes in the wage distribution by looking at regional economic developments, including Topel (1986, 1994), Bound and Holzer (1996), Borjas and Ramey (1995), and others. These papers have tended to measure inequality by examining the returns to education. Bernard and Jensen make a valuable contribution to this line of research by focusing on state-level changes in residual wage inequality. This approach certainly has promise. After all, international economists and growth specialists have learned much through empirical work at the state and local levels. Such geographic disaggregation may prove to be even more useful in economic analysis of increasing income inequality.

Are States the Appropriate Unit of Analysis?

Given the potential advantages of geographically disaggregating the national economy, the first challenge we come up against is how to define

1. Products and capital move much more freely across state borders than across many national borders, and the associated forces of factor-price convergence are likely to be orders of magnitude stronger within than across countries. Even labor, relatively immobile though it is, is much more mobile within the United States than it is across national borders. Finally, as Paul Krugman (1996) and others have pointed out, for all of the talk of globalization, the U.S. economy remains in many ways a closed system, since the vast majority of goods and services consumed within its borders are also produced there. This is much less true of individual states, even less true if the level of analysis is the MSA.

2. Bernard and Jensen argue that "any theory of the rise in income inequality in the United States as a whole should also be capable of explaining the wide variety of outcomes across individual states." I think this might be asking a bit too much from any theory we are likely to be able to construct, although I agree with their basic message.

regional economies. Are states the appropriate units? To their credit, the authors have obviously thought about this issue, and readily admit the problems of using state data. I think this issue is important enough to merit some additional comment here.

The obvious advantage of states is that much data is available at the state level because states are important political units within the U.S. federal governmental structure. However, there can be considerable diversity within as well as between states. I am not just talking about the obvious differences between urban and rural labor markets (are labor market conditions more similar between San Francisco and the Central Valley than they are between San Francisco and Boston?). In their study of college wage premia at the metropolitan statistical area (MSA) level, Borjas and Ramey (1995) document nontrivial differences across different urban areas within the same state! Moreover, the political boundaries between states often do not correspond very well to the contours of regional economies. Casual empiricism suggests that California contains at least two regional economies, northern California and southern California, with different patterns of specialization in production and possibly different business cycles. At the other extreme, casual empiricism can also identify groups of states that are obviously highly integrated, such as the Tri-State region surrounding metropolitan New York.

Different papers in this literature have taken different approaches to this problem. Robert Topel has looked at agglomerations of states (regions), while Bound and Holzer (1996) and Borjas and Ramey (1995) have looked at MSAs. The fact that these papers have come to different conclusions about the sources of changes in regional income inequality suggests the answers one gets may be somewhat dependent on the level of aggregation at which one conducts empirical analysis. All that being said, I must say that states strike me as a completely logical place to begin.

Do State-Level Labor Markets Exist?

Taking the state as the appropriate unit of analysis, the authors note that looking at state-level data only makes sense if the level of integration across states is limited, at least in the short to medium term. The authors offer three pieces of evidence concerning this claim. First, the authors cite the well-known study by Blanchard and Katz (1992). This study indicates that the migration of workers across state boundaries mediates shocks to employment over horizons of 6–10 years. It seems to indicate that state-level labor markets only exist in the medium run, rather than the long run.

To provide additional support for limited integration across states, the authors show that returns to education differ substantially across states. This is a striking piece of evidence. However, some care needs to be taken in interpreting these numbers. What the coefficients on education actually measure in these regressions are the statistical relationships between schooling and income for a cross section of residents of a particular state at a particular time. The wages of highly educated current residents are measured relative to the less-educated current residents of that state. Of course, many current residents were educated outside the state of current residence.[3] Furthermore, this measure will probably be higher in states with more unequal income distributions.

What these coefficients do not measure are the alternative real wages that could be earned by a given individual with a given level of education and quality, who is contemplating a move to a different state. Imagine an MIT Ph.D. choosing among California, Michigan, and Texas—her decision will be influenced by where her wages are the highest, not where high school dropouts have the lowest relative wages. Another way of thinking about this question is to ask what we might expect a "perfectly integrated" labor market to equalize. The answer is fairly complicated—the after-tax, "cost-of-living" adjusted real wage for individuals with identical education/skill levels (which is not necessarily well captured by "years of schooling"), adjusting for noneconomic amenities (California sunshine or the indignity of being represented by certain politicians in Washington) that are likely to differentially impact utility for different education groups, up to the fixed cost of migrating across states. In other words, it is not clear that even perfectly integrated national labor markets would equalize the education premia that the authors measure. Nevertheless, I do believe that the differences in these measured premia are so large that they are very difficult to reconcile with any notion of a well-integrated national labor market, even in the medium to long run.

For skeptics not convinced by these first two pieces of evidence, the authors undertake some original empirical analysis using the ASM data in defense of their proposition of limited interstate integration of labor markets. They compute the relevant impact of industry and state employment shocks on average wages at the plant level, finding that plant-level wages tend to respond more quickly and to a greater extent to state employment shocks (employment changes outside the two-digit industry of the plant) than to industry shocks (nationwide employment in the same two-digit industry outside the state). I would have thought that plants adjust employment rather than wages, especially in the short term.[4] I also

---

3. These coefficients are also possibly affected by different levels of educational quality across states, as the authors suggest, but they do not measure these levels of quality. In order to do that, one would need information on where a person was educated as well as where they currently lived. David Card and Alan Krueger (1992) present evidence on the returns to education in different states—their evidence suggests that, at least historically, important quality differentials have existed.

4. Given the way plant-level wages are computed, these measured wage changes could reflect changes in the composition of employees rather than a change in the marginal wage paid to a "representative worker."

harbor some reservations about these results due to the fact that many industries are geographically concentrated. Krugman (1996) has suggested that this concentration is evidence of agglomeration externalities. Regardless of the reason, the fact of geographic concentration of industries seems fairly well established. I am therefore a bit surprised that the data seem to have so little trouble differentiating between state employment shocks and industry employment shocks. (It seems that a major downturn in the aerospace industry should have some impact on the state of Washington, just as the oil price declines of the mid-1980s induced a regional slump in Texas and Oklahoma.) Nevertheless, I do not dispute the results—yet more evidence that there is but limited integration of local labor markets in the short to medium run.

Residual Inequality at the State Level and Its Causes

Having offered evidence on limited labor-market integration, the authors then construct measures of "residual inequality" (changes in the log wage ratio of the 90th percentile and the 10th percentile of the wage distribution, controlling for the effects of education and demographic factors) at the state level. These measures have changed over time in dramatically different ways in different states. In fact, for me, the most striking feature of the paper was the contrast between the declining residual inequality in some southern states (-7 percent for Virginia) versus exploding inequality in some northern states in the old manufacturing belt (21.9 percent for Michigan and 20.8 percent for New York) and the West. A whole research agenda could be built around exploring and explaining these differences, which to my knowledge are documented for the first time in this paper. I hope that the authors will proceed full speed ahead in this direction, and I look forward to reading their future papers on this topic.

I have one concern about these numbers, however. Residual income inequality is only one component of the total increase in wage inequality observed in the United States over the last 2 decades. We need to keep this in mind in our subsequent discussion of the authors' results.[5] On a related note, I would like to point out that, as the authors freely admit, they are not weighting by population in any sense. Their striking results may be driven by big changes in small (less populous) states. Not that this is not interesting, but the implications for the U.S. economy as a whole will be different in this case. On the other hand, the authors present evidence in section 7.5.2 that suggests the extreme states are collectively large enough to have had some impact on overall national trends.

The variable that stands out as explaining the changes in residual wage

5. Virginia may have undergone a decline in the level of residual income inequality, but according to the authors' figure 7.3, its advanced degree premium—an alternative measure of inequality—has been persistently high relative to other states.

inequality across states is the (change in) percentage of the state labor force employed in durable-goods manufacturing. Somewhat surprisingly, measures of migration and international exposure seem to matter little, but this measure of changes in the industry composition of employment has very large and very robust effects on local income inequality. The potential implications of this finding are hard to overstate. Careful research at the national level has consistently failed to find any strong relationship between changes in income inequality and changes in the pattern of labor demand across industries.[6] In this paper, at the state level, the authors are able to identify such a linkage in their data. The authors suggest that this is evidence that changes in demand for labor across industries really do have a powerful impact on inequality. They tell a story of manufacturing relocation from the Midwest to the South that is consistent with the data.

An Alternative Explanation?

Does durable-goods manufacturing really move the wage distribution? Perhaps so. I must admit to have been so brainwashed by the accumulated evidence against industry composition being important that I am not easily persuaded. Let me suggest an alternative story, which is actually not my own—rather, it is a restatement of Bound and Holzer's (1996) story based on their analysis of regional labor markets at the SMSA level and the work of Topel (1986). It focuses on labor supply considerations, which are, I think, somewhat in the background in this paper. I should say that I myself do not put too much stock in this alternative scenario, but it is at least worth thinking about.

Let us suppose that Blanchard and Katz (1992) are right—interstate migration does act to smooth shocks. However, the propensity to migrate is quite different for educated/skilled workers than for uneducated/unskilled workers; it is higher for the more-educated and better-skilled workers. This has implications for the wage distribution following a shock to the local economy, whether we measure this by the college wage premium (picking up the returns to educational attainment) or residual wage inequality (picking up, at least in part, the returns to skill, broadly defined). Wage adjustment will fall more heavily on the less-mobile workers. So, less-skilled workers in the southern boomtowns have their wages bid up, less-skilled workers in the North have their wages pushed down. Obviously, expectations about the duration of the shock affect the migration response. But it is not too hard to tell a story of Midwest versus South in which asymmetric responses to different overall demand shocks, rather

---

6. This failure is one important reason why the economics profession has been skeptical about the popular linkage between the rise of manufactured goods imports and the declining economic fortunes of the less educated and less skilled.

than changes in industry composition, tell the story. And the convergence of the southern regional economy toward national levels of income and capital per worker, if nothing else, could drive these kinds of changes. How do I explain the big effects of durable goods? I would have to argue that it is picking up other factors. Durable goods is such a broad aggregate of economic activity that the argument is not impossible to make, but it is not easy either. Furthermore, this alternative explanation may not be consistent with the facts. The authors have told me that a more inclusive measure of immigration from other states proved insignificant in earlier regressions, which would certainly go against this story. Bound and Holzer (1996) have found substantial effects from migration on the college wage premium, using data at the MSA level, but this does not insure that migration would have similar effects on residual inequality at the state level.

Implications for the Increase in Inequality at the National Level

I would like to end this review with the same question I posed in the introduction: Can an examination of changes in income inequality at the regional level help us understand changes in the income distribution at the national level? Here the authors' findings are extremely provocative but, perhaps, not quite conclusive. Nevertheless, as the authors of this paper have measured it, a very large portion of the increase in residual inequality can evidently be explained by changes in industrial structure, and that, in itself, could turn much of what has been written about increasing income inequality on its head.

In fact, the basic message and ultimate impact of this paper may go well beyond the relatively narrow question I posed in my introduction. The balance of the evidence presented in this paper strongly suggests that regional labor markets are much less strongly integrated at the national level than most of the economics profession had previously assumed, despite high levels of interstate migration and more less or less perfectly free trade of goods and services across state lines. At the very least, these findings need to be further explored and explained. Their implications may inform not only our understanding of changes in income inequality, but also our understanding of the roles of distance and political borders in intranational as well as international trade, and the limits this may place on the level of intranational economic integration and, even, the definition of national economic policy. I look forward to the next paper by these authors on this topic.

References

Blanchard, Olivier, and Lawrence Katz. 1992. Regional evolutions. *Brookings Papers on Economic Activity, Microeconomics,* 1–75.

Borjas, George, and Valerie Ramey. 1995. Foreign competition, market power, and income inequality. *Quarterly Journal of Economics* 110 (4): 1075–110.

Bound, John, and Harry Holzer. 1996. Demand shifts, population adjustments, and labor market outcomes during the 1980s. NBER Working Paper no. 5685. Cambridge, Mass.: National Bureau of Economic Research.

Card, David, and Alan Krueger. 1992. Does school quality matter? Returns to education and the characteristics of public schools in the United States. *Journal of Political Economy* 100 (1): 1–40.

Katz, Lawrence, and Kevin Murphy. 1992. Changes in relative wages, 1963–1987: Supply and demand factors. *Quarterly Journal of Economics* 107 (1): 35–78.

Krugman, Paul. 1996. A country is not a company. *Harvard Business Review* 74 (1): 40–51.

Topel, Robert. 1986. Local labor markets. *Journal of Political Economy* 94 (3): S111–430.

———. 1994. Regional labor markets and the determinants of wage inequality. *American Economic Review* 84:17–22.

Exchange Rates and
Local Labor Markets

Linda Goldberg and Joseph Tracy

8.1 Introduction

With the increased internationalization of the U.S. economy, the implications of dollar movements for workers has emerged as a pressing question. A literature has developed that considers this and related themes. First, the exchange rate pass-through literature discusses the degree to which prices of goods—whether exported, imported, or produced domestically for home consumption—are influenced by exchange rates. In the United States export prices tend to be fairly stable in dollar terms. Import prices appear to be more responsive to exchange rate movements, but this responsiveness varies considerably across types of goods and across trading partners. Import-competing product prices show much smaller elasticities of response to exchange rates.[1] Exchange rates also matter for producer profitability, and for decisions about capital spending and employment. Industry features—such as their trade orientation and competitive structure—scale the importance of these exchange rate effects.[2]

Linda Goldberg is assistant vice-president of research at the Federal Reserve Bank of New York and a research associate of the National Bureau of Economic Research. Joseph Tracy is vice-president of research and market analysis at the Federal Reserve Bank of New York.

The views expressed in this paper are those of the individual authors and do not necessarily reflect the position of the Federal Reserve Bank of New York or the Federal Reserve System. Jenessa Gunther and Henry Schneider provided valuable research assistance. The authors appreciate the useful comments of Andrew Rose, Jane Little, Jose Campa, and conference participants.

1. See Goldberg and Knetter (1997) for a survey. The distribution of exchange rate elasticities of the set of U.S. import prices thus far examined appears to be centered around 0.5, but the set of goods studied is by no means exhaustive.

2. See Clarida (1997) and Sheets (1996) on profitability and exchange rates. Campa and Goldberg (1999) show that investment spending is time-varying in accordance with the ex-

The labor market effects of exchange rates are an open question. For the United States, analyses using data through the mid-1980s show that exchange rates have had significant implications for wages (Revenga 1992) and for employment across manufacturing industries (Branson and Love 1988).[3] A recent cross-country, cross-industry study by Burgess and Knetter (1998) found statistically significant effects of exchange rates for employment, with the size of these effects related to industry characteristics such as competitive structure.

However, recent work by Campa and Goldberg (1998) found weaker implications of exchange rates for employment in U.S. industries, but more pronounced effects for wages. This study used a longer time series than previous empirical work (about 25 years of annual data) and focused on two-digit industry employment, wages, overtime activity, and overtime wages. The testing methodology allowed for exchange rate transmission channels to vary over time with industry trade exposures to exchange rates through both revenues and costs. Exchange rate effects were statistically significant mainly for wages, and strongest in industries that were more trade oriented and in industries that generally had lower profit margins.

The combination of significant wage responsiveness to exchange rates without comparable employment effects poses some interesting questions. One possible reconciling argument is that a dollar appreciation, for example, could lead workers to lose their jobs, but then to be reemployed at lower wages within the same broad industry group but in a different, narrower industry definition. Such findings would be consistent with observed patterns of labor force adjustment within an industry to oil-price shocks (Davis and Haltiwanger 1999). If this is the case, a related question is whether workers take new positions in a similar industry within a local labor market, or if they look for opportunities in a similar industry elsewhere in the country. Employment changes can entail worker relocation as well as the type of wage adjustments from moving within and across manufacturing industries that have been detailed by Revenga (1992). Another argument is that under adverse employment conditions from a dollar appreciation, for example, workers may engage in less on-the-job searching for better-paying jobs.[4] Under these conditions, one might observe relatively stable employment with magnified wage restraint. By un-

---

port and imported-input orientation of producers across various industries and across countries and is strongest in industries with low price-over-cost markups (which can be viewed as closer to perfectly competitive market structures).

3. Examining the 1970s into the early 1980s, Branson and Love estimate that durable-goods producers had jobs that were most responsive to exchange rates. Using Revenga's computed elasticities, the estimated effects on jobs are increasing gradually to the extent that import competition exists in an industry.

4. See Mortensen (1986) for a discussion of on-the-job search models.

raveling these issues, we hope to better understand the degree of labor market disruption associated with dollar fluctuations.

The present paper examines more than 2 decades of data on average hourly earnings, hours, and employment for two-digit industries located within the individual states of the United States. This approach has several advantages over prior studies. First, since the trade orientation of industries varies by industry location, we are able to better identify the magnitude of currency shocks hitting local industries. Second, we are able to consider the spillovers of exchange rate effects across local industries. From a local labor market perspective, such spillovers may alter the alternative wage available to workers and help explain the magnified wage and reduced employment sensitivity to exchange rates. Third, by examining state-level data, we capture the adjustments made by workers who might move across state lines, yet remain within the same broad industry.

We find that real exchange rates contribute significant explanatory power to regressions on average hourly earnings, hours, and employment. In pooled industry regressions, dollar appreciations (depreciations) are associated with small but statistically significant declines (increases) in hourly earnings by workers. In individual industry regressions, we observe significant variability across industries in the levels of these earnings implications and even in the sign of these effects. Moreover, even within individual industries, some regions are particularly sensitive to dollar movements. Cross-industry spillovers, which we interpret as providing an indirect means of worker exposure to exchange rates, are significant for average hourly earnings and for employment within high-markup industries.

In contrast to results drawn from nationally aggregated data for industries, the state-level data exhibit more pronounced responsiveness of employment and hours worked within manufacturing industries. On balance, dollar appreciations (depreciations) are associated with employment declines (increases) for high- and low-profit-margin industry groups. As industries increase their export orientation, the adverse consequences of appreciations for employment also increase. However, some of these adverse consequences are counteracted as industries increase their reliance on imported inputs. Both forces are significant in determining the employment effects of exchange rates, and they differ qualitatively and quantitatively across regions and across industries.

Finally, our analysis also focuses on and confirms the type of dynamic patterns of adjustment in local labor markets previously reported by Topel (1986). Using Topel's methodology, we construct state- and industry-specific relative demand shocks, both actual and anticipated. Similar to Topel's finding using microdata, we find that wages increase in response to current relative demand shocks and decrease in response to expected future relative demand shocks.

8.2   The Theory

Our theoretical setup pairs a model of dynamic labor demand and exchange rate exposure (Campa and Goldberg 1998) with a dynamic local labor supply specification. The theory shows clear reasons why industries should be differentially affected by exchange rates. One reason is that industries differ in trade orientation. But, even controlling for these differences, exchange rate effects on wages and employment should vary across industries depending on (1) the industry product demand elasticity at home and abroad, (2) the initial labor share in production, and (3) the elasticity of the labor supply facing the industry in that locality. Industries with high labor-demand elasticity with respect to wages will exhibit more employment response and less wage response to exchange rate movements.

Each industry within each locality (defined as a state in our data) can experience shocks that alter its wages directly or indirectly. Direct effects of exchange rates arise because of own-industry trade orientation. Indirect effects are due to spillovers across local industries via expected alternative wages. Local unemployment rates are important since they influence the probability that a worker will be able to find a job that offers the alternative wage. Some shocks can change the current or future attractiveness of an entire locality and lead to labor-supply shifts through in- or out-migration, as in Topel (1986).

Controlling for direct and indirect effects of exchange rates could help identify the separate channels for wage and employment responsiveness. For example, if an industry is export oriented, in general a dollar appreciation is expected to reduce the competitiveness of its products and, as a consequence, place downward pressure on industry wages and lead to layoffs. However, if other local industries also are export oriented, the dollar appreciation can lower the alternative wage available to workers and locally expand the labor supply to the initial industry. The offsetting direction of movement in labor demand and labor supply to the industry may lead to magnified wage effects and muted employment effects.

8.2.1   Exchange Rates and Labor Demand

We begin with profit-maximizing producers who sell to both domestic and foreign markets. Producers make decisions in a dynamic and uncertain environment, and consider the future paths of all variables influencing their profitability. The unknowns for the producer are aggregate demand in domestic and foreign markets, y and y^*, and the exchange rate e, defined as domestic currency per unit of foreign exchange. Production uses three factors: domestic labor L, other domestic inputs Z, and imported inputs, Z^*. Factor prices are denoted by w, s, and es^*, respectively. Labor is a homogeneous input into production and levels of nonlabor inputs can be adjusted in the short run without additional costs.

Producers optimize over levels of factor inputs and total output in order to maximize expected profits π, equation (1); subject to the constraints posed by the production function, equation (2); and product-demand conditions in domestic and foreign markets, equation (3). Revenues arise from domestic market sales q and foreign market sales q^*. In both markets, the exchange rate influences demand by altering the relative price of home products versus those of foreign competitors. The exchange rate also directly enters costs through the domestic price of imported inputs.

$$(1) \quad \pi(y_t, y_t^*, e_t) = \max_{Q_t, L_t, Z_t^*, Z_t} \sum_{t=0}^{\infty} \phi_t [p(q_t : y_t, e_t) q_t + e_t p^*(q_t^* : y_t^*, e_t) q_t^* - w_t L_t$$

$$- e_t s_t^* Z_t^* - s_t Z_t - c(\Delta L_t)],$$

subject to

$$(2) \qquad\qquad Q = q + q^*, \quad Q = L^\beta Z^{*\alpha} Z^{1-\alpha-\beta},$$

and

$$(3) \quad p(q:y,e) = a(y,e) q^{-1/\eta}, \quad ep^*(q^*:y^*,e) = a^*(y^*,e) q^{*-1/\eta^*}.$$

The time-discount factor is defined by $\phi_t = \Pi_\tau \delta^\tau$. In equations (2) and (3) we have dropped the period t time subscripts for convenience.[5] In equation (3) the parameters η and η^* are the domestic and foreign product-demand elasticities facing producers. The demand curves in domestic and foreign markets include multiplicative demand shifters, $a(y,e)$ and $a^*(y^*,e)$, which capture the influence of real income differences across markets and exchange rates.

It is assumed that an industry's labor input L is costly to adjust. We assume quadratic adjustment costs that are proportional to the prevailing wage in the industry; see equation (4). The parameter b allows for additional industry variation in the cost of adjusting employment levels.

$$(4) \qquad\qquad c(\Delta L_t) = w_t \frac{b}{2} (L_t - L_{t-1})^2.$$

Following Nickell (1986), the solution of this optimization problem is a dynamic equation for optimal labor demand, where labor adjusts toward a target level $\tilde{L}$ that would be optimal in the absence of adjustment costs. The speed of adjustment of labor demand to $\tilde{L}$, $(1 - \mu)$, is reduced when industries face high adjustment costs b and have low wage sensitivity of marginal revenue product. Nickell shows that labor demand in any period can be approximated by

5. A Cobb-Douglas production structure is assumed for simplicity, but our main results also will hold under a more general constant elasticity of substitution production structure.

(5) $$L_t = \mu L_{t-1} + (1 - \mu)(1 - \delta g \mu) \sum_{j=0}^{\infty} (\delta g \mu)^j \tilde{L}_{t+j},$$

where g is the rate of real wage growth for an industry. Solving the optimal labor problem of equations (1)–(4), Campa and Goldberg (1998) show that the labor-demand target $\tilde{L}$ is sensitive to exchange rates, with the effects of exchange rates transmitted through three separate channels—revenues from home market sales, revenues from foreign market sales, and costs of imported inputs into production. The elasticity of response of $\tilde{L}$ to exchange rates is

$$(6) \frac{\partial \tilde{L}}{\partial e} \Big/ \frac{\tilde{L}}{e} = \frac{1}{\beta}[p(\cdot)(1 + \eta^{-1})\eta^{pe}$$

$$+ \chi(ep^*(\cdot)(1 + \eta^{*-1})(1 + \eta^{p^*e}) - p(\cdot)(1 + \eta^{-1})\eta^{pe})$$

$$- \alpha es^*(\partial Q / \partial Z^*)],$$

where $\chi^i = p^* i q^{*i}/(p^i q^i + p^{*i} q^{*i})$ represents the share of export sales in revenues, and η^{pe} and η^{p^*e} are domestic and foreign price elasticities with respect to exchange rates. Observe that the three groups of terms on the right-hand side of equation (6) correspond to the three exposure channels: the sensitivity to exchange rates of labor demand through revenues from domestic sales, revenues from foreign market sales, and the costs of productive inputs. By invoking basic relationships on exchange rate pass-through elasticities and ex ante law of one price, we rewrite this as

$$(6') \frac{\partial \tilde{L}}{\partial e} \Big/ \frac{\tilde{L}}{e} = \frac{p}{\beta}[(1 + \eta^{-1})kM + (1 + \eta^{*-1})\chi - (\partial Q / \partial Z^*)^{-1}\alpha].$$

Equation (6') clearly shows the three channels and industry features that magnify or reduce the degree of industry response to exchange rate movements. First, more import penetration of domestic markets (M) increases the sensitivity of labor demand to exchange rates by increasing the price competitiveness of foreign goods. Second, more export orientation (χ) increases the sensitivity of labor demand to exchange rates, since export revenues are relatively more responsive to exchange rates. Third, greater reliance on imported components (higher α) can offset or even reverse the adverse consequences of a stronger currency (for example) on industry labor demand. Fourth, more-labor-intensive production (high β) is associated with a reduced sensitivity of labor demand to exchange rates. Finally, industries characterized by greater competition among firms (with low η or η^*) are expected to have labor demands that are more sensitive to exchange rates.

Using equations (5) and (6'), and introducing log-linearized terms for domestic and foreign aggregate demand conditions, we generate the following reduced form for optimal labor demand by an industry:[6]

$$(7) \quad L_t^i = \mu^i L_{t-1}^i + (1 - \mu^i)[c_0 + c_1 y_t + c_2 y_t^*$$

$$+ (c_{3,0} + c_{3,1}\chi^i + c_{3,2}M^i + c_{3,3}\alpha^i)e_t + c_4 w_t^i + c_5 s_t + c_6 s_t^*],$$

where all variables other than χ^i, M^i, and α^i are defined in logs.[7] All variables and parameters are specific to an industry except for y_t and y_t^*.[8] Within an industry, state or regional differences in labor demand may arise from local differences in trade exposures.

8.2.2   Labor Supply

Our approach to labor supply focuses on the behavior of forward-looking workers in a local labor market. These workers choose their labor supply to an industry by considering the wages offered by that industry relative to the alternative wage (as offered locally by other industries). Local labor supply also responds to both current and expected future local demand conditions, all relative to conditions outside of the locality. As Topel (1986) demonstrates, these conditions can lead to in-migration to or out-migration from an area.

A reduced-form representation for labor supply to an industry i in a locality r is

$$(8) \qquad L_t^{ir} = a_1^r + a_2^i(w_t^{ir} - \hat{w}_t^{ir}) + a_3^r y_t^r,$$

where y_t^r is a vector of terms for local relative conditions (current relative strength of the locality and expected future relative strength), and $\hat{w}^{ir}$ is the alternative wage in industries outside of industry i in the locality.[9] Exchange rates can shift the labor-supply curve facing an industry in a locality through their impact on the alternative wage, with the magnitude of the shift depending on the trade orientation of the other local industries, $\overline{X}^{ir}$.[10] The

6. Changes in foreign-currency input costs through foreign wages are absorbed into the α term.

7. The actual parameters on the shocks introduced in our equation (7) depend on the perceived degree of permanence of the shock. A shock that is transitory will have a much smaller impact on labor demand than a shock that is viewed as permanent.

8. Real bilateral exchange rates all are exogenous to an industry. These bilateral exchange rates with currencies of individual countries are weighted differently for each industry, depending on the importance of a country as the industry's trading partner.

9. Labor supply is upward sloping in an industry's wage if there is heterogeneity in the workforce, either in terms of preferences for industry job attributes or mobility costs.

10. The alternative wage should be viewed as an equilibrium alternative wage, so that it, in fact, would be a function of all of the variables that shift labor demand, as shown in equation (7). Introducing this full set of terms at this point would complicate the notation and have no bearing on our ultimate estimation structure or our interpretation of the ex-

likelihood that industry i workers could get this alternative wage depends on the tightness of local labor markets. We proxy this tightness as inversely related to the local unemployment rate $Unemp^r$. So, $\hat{w}_t^{ir} \approx a_4^{r\prime} \overline{X}^{ir} e_t + a_5^{r\prime} Unemp_t^r$, and we write the new reduced form equation for labor supply as

$$(9) \qquad L_t^{ir} = a_1^i + a_2^i w_t^{ir} + a_3^r y_t^r + a_4^r \overline{X}^{ir} e_t + a_5^r Unemp_t^r,$$

for industry i in a state/region r.

8.2.3   Labor Market Equilibrium

Setting labor demand by a local industry, equation (7), equal to local labor supply, equation (9), yields equations in industry employment and wages,[11]

$$(10a) \qquad w_t^{ir} = \omega_0^{ir} + \omega_1^i y_t + \omega_2^i y_t^* + \omega_3^i s_t + \omega_6^{ir} Unemp_t^r$$
$$+ (\omega_{5,0}^i + \omega_{5,1}^i X^i + \omega_{5,2}^i M^i + \omega_{5,3}^i \alpha^i + \omega_{5,4}^{ir} \overline{X}^{ir}) \cdot e_t$$
$$+ \omega_6^i y_t^r + \omega_7^i L_{t-1}^i,$$

$$(10b) \qquad L_t^{ir} = \lambda_0^{ir} + \lambda_1^i y_t + \lambda_2^i y_t^* + \lambda_3^i s_t + \lambda_4^{ir} Unemp_t^r$$
$$+ (\lambda_{5,0}^i + \lambda_{5,1}^i X^i + \lambda_{5,2}^i M^i + \lambda_{5,3}^i \alpha^i + \lambda_{5,4}^{ir} \overline{X}^{ir}) \cdot e_t$$
$$+ \lambda_6 y_t^r + \lambda_7^i L_{t-1}^i.$$

Equations (10a) and (10b) form the basis for our tests of exchange rate and local-demand effects on the labor market of industry i operating in region r. The wage and employment response in an industry to local shocks depends on the elasticities of labor demand and supply, as well as the costs of adjusting employment in that industry. When labor-demand or -supply curves are steep—indicating low employment sensitivity to wages—shocks to either demand or supply lead to relatively less employment response and more wage response. When industries have high labor force adjustment costs, the short-run shift in labor demand in response to any given shock is smaller. Given an industry's trade orientation, a more concentrated (and less competitive) industry will experience a smaller labor-demand shift from any given shock.

---

change rate channels. The existence of these other terms would matter for the interpretation of coefficients on the domestic and foreign income and factor-price terms in the regressions, if one were to attempt a semistructural interpretation of these coefficients.

11. The coefficients on the interacted exchange rate terms are interpreted in relation to the individual labor-demand and labor-supply equations in Campa and Goldberg (1998). The main difference between the current system of equations (11) and the prior paper is the inclusion of local labor market effects and the dynamic labor-supply decision.

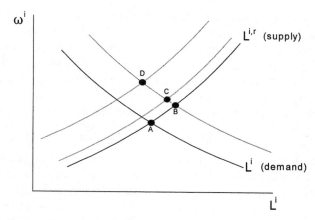

Fig. 8.1   Local labor market equilibrium for industry _i_

The effects of a dollar depreciation on wage and employment in a particular industry are illustrated in figure 8.1. For an industry with external orientation mainly through its export sales, a dollar depreciation increases labor demand. In the absence of a labor-supply shift, labor market equilibrium moves from point _A_ to point _B_. The direct effects of the depreciation are expanded employment and higher wages in the industry. Yet, if other local industries are also trade oriented, labor supply to industry _i_ might contract if alternative wages rise in those other industries. The decline in labor supply to industry _i_ because of the exposure of other local industries moves the equilibrium to point _C_ or point _D_. These indirect effects can be moderate (point _C_), so that local-labor-market spillovers mitigate some of the employment effect of the dollar depreciation, but reinforce the wage effect. However, if the wages of other local industries are very sensitive to exchange rates, employment in the initial industry can be unchanged or even may contract (point _D_). A depreciation generally raises wages, provided that the dominant channels of industry exposure are through favorable revenue effects.

8.3   Data

8.3.1   Labor Market Series

The dependent variables in our study are average employment, hours and wages from the Bureau of Labor Statistics (BLS) _Employment and Earnings_ with all data disaggregated by two-digit Standard Industrial Classification (SIC) industry. We consider the movements in the national data (as a means of generating a set of reference facts), as well as in data disaggregated by states and areas.[12] Firms are classified into industries based on their principal product using 1987 SIC classifications.

The *employment data* capture all persons on establishment payrolls who received pay for any part of the pay period that includes the 12th day of the month. Proprietors, self-employed workers, unpaid volunteers and family workers, and domestic workers are excluded. Workers on paid vacation or sick leave are counted, as are workers who are unemployed or on strike for some but not all of the pay period. The *hours data* reflect hours paid, which may differ from scheduled hours or hours worked. Overtime hours and hours paid to workers on vacation or sick leave are included. Worker absenteeism and work stoppages cause paid hours to fall below scheduled hours and are not included.

The *earnings data* reflect average weekly earnings divided by average weekly hours. Workers who are not paid weekly have their earnings and hours expressed on a weekly basis. Earnings reflect payments for all workers who were on the payroll for any part of the pay period covering the 12th of the month. Gross payroll prior to deductions for social security, life insurance, tax withholding, and union dues is used. Overtime, holiday, and incentive pay as well as regular bonus payments are included, while nonregular bonus payments are excluded. Firm contributions to fringe benefits, such as health insurance and retirement accounts, are not included.

8.3.2   Exchange Rate Series

Our empirical work uses export and import real exchange rates for each industry. These industry-specific real exchange rates are constructed by weighting the bilateral real exchange rates of U.S. trading partners in accordance with the importance of these partners in industry exports or imports in each year. To convert nominal exchange rates into real series, the nominal measures are adjusted by the GDP deflators of the respective trade partners (*International Financial Statistics* data). The resulting real trade-weighted dollar exchange rates follow the empirical convention that an increase in the exchange rate corresponds to an appreciation of the dollar. This convention is opposite that used in our theoretical section.

We use industry-specific exchange rates, rather than a common trade-weighted measure, because these better reflect the actual shocks to individual industries. The industry-specific series are generally highly correlated with the overall real exchange rate for the United States (appendix table

---

12. These data are derived from the Current Employment Statistics survey that is sent out monthly to all employers with at least 250 workers and a random sample of smaller employers. We exclude Alaska, Hawaii, and the District of Columbia from the state data. The data span the years 1971 through 1995. See U.S. Department of Labor (1997) for details. This sampling implies that smaller employer response to stimuli may be less well captured by the data set.

8A.1 provides correlation coefficients). However, for some industries the export exchange rates clearly are more similar to the aggregate real exchange rate measure than are the import exchange rates. The industry for which the export exchange rate is least correlated with the aggregate measure is lumber and wood products, with a 0.63 correlation coefficient. On the import index side, the correlation coefficients between the industry exchange rates and the aggregate real exchange rate were as low as 0.36 for the petroleum and coal industry, 0.50 for paper and allied products, and 0.58 for lumber and wood products. Therefore, our industry-specific series are more appropriate for capturing industry-specific shocks to import competitiveness or imported input providers.

8.3.3   Industry Trade-Orientation Series

In some regression specifications, we interact the real exchange rates with measures of industry export share and imported input share (Campa and Goldberg 1997, constructions based on U.S. Department of Commerce series and U.S. input-output tables). These industry series are not differentiated across states or regions of the United States.

We are able to perform such state differentiation for our export measures by using a shorter time series of export data reported by state of origin and by industry, compiled by the Massachusetts Institute for Social and Economic Research (MISER).[13] These series are only available by two-digit SIC beginning in 1988. For our regressions, we take this information on the relative importance of exports to an industry in a state over this shorter time period, and use it to scale, at the state level, the longer annual series on national export orientation numbers for each industry.

These state-specific data on industry exports make a powerful statement about the diversity of export orientation of industries located in different areas of the United States. To demonstrate this point, figure 8.2 shows the degree of export orientation of production in each state, based on the MISER data.[14] The more export oriented areas include the Pacific region, Texas, Florida, New York, Vermont, and the Carolinas. Indeed, according to these measurements, which use the value of exports to gross state product, Vermont is the most export-oriented state.

---

13. Comparable numbers are not available for imported-input share of industries by state.
14. To construct this map we used MISER data on the export orientation of manufacturing industries in each state, weighted these series by the importance of the specific industry within the state, and assumed a 0 export share on output of nonmanufacturing industries,

$$\left(\frac{\text{manufacturing GSP}}{\text{total GSP}} \right) \cdot \sum_j \left(\left(\frac{\text{state employment in industry } j}{\text{total state manufacturing employment}} \right) \cdot \left(\frac{\text{MISER exports}}{\text{industry } j \text{ GSP}} \right) \right).$$

This measure is computed using data for each year between 1988 and 1994, and averaged over these 7 years of data.

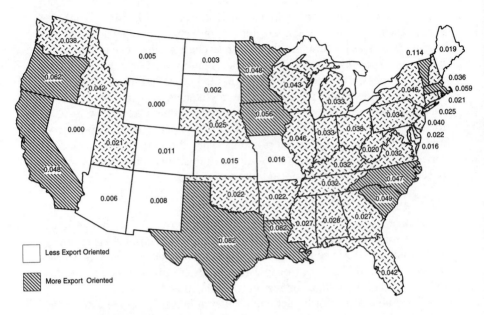

Fig. 8.2   State export orientation, 1988–94 average

Notes: State export orientation is calculated as the weighted sum across manufacturing industries of the MISER export orientation. The MISER export orientation is MISER exports over gross state product (gsp), where each is state and industry specific. The weight that is used to sum across industries is state- and industry-specific employment over state manufacturing employment. The sum is then multiplied by manufacturing gsp over total gsp.

Figure 8.3 shows the biased view of state-export orientation that would arise if one used national export shares for individual industries of individual states. This map presents the ratio of state export orientation as implied by the MISER data versus that implied by the overall national export shares of the industries.[15] A value greater than one on this map indicates that the export orientation of a state (based on MISER data) is greater than that implied using the national data on industry export orientation. The states with dark shading have the most understated export orientation when the national data on industry export shares are used; the states without shading have the most overstated export orientation from national series. For some states this misrepresentation can be enormous. The national aggregates vastly overstate the export orientation of manufacturing industries in the Mountain region and vastly understate the export orientation of various coastal and border areas.

15. Again, we assume that the nonmanufacturing industries within a state have no export orientation. The implied state export share is the weighted average of the industry export shares, where the weights are the industry shares in state output.

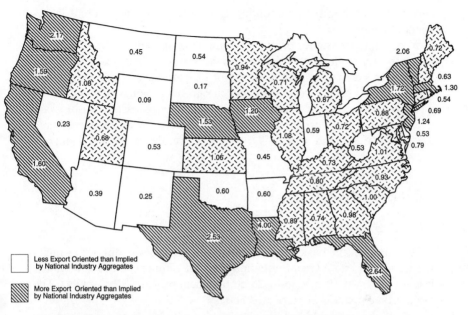

Fig. 8.3   State export orientation, ratio of actual to implied, 1988–94 average

Notes: Ratio of actual to implied state export orientations is calculated as the weighted sum across manufacturing industries of the MISER export orientation over the national industry export orientation. The MISER export orientation is MISER exports over gross state product, where each is state and industry specific. The weight that is used to sum across industries is state- and industry-specific employment over state manufacturing employment.

8.3.4   Other Data

Aggregate demand conditions are proxied by (the change in log) real GDP (IMF International Financial Statistics, line 99b). Other factor costs are captured by (the change in log) real oil prices (line 001) and the (change in log) 10-year T-bill rate deflated by the wholesale price index. The aggregate prime-age-male unemployment rate is our proxy for national labor market tightness. The state prime-age-male unemployment rate is our proxy for local labor market tightness.

Our regressions also include measures of local relative demand shocks. We use an adaptation of Topel's (1986) empirical methodology for measuring current and anticipated relative demand shocks to a local labor market. Like Topel, we use states as our definition of a local labor market. For each industry in a state we adjust the employment in the state by subtracting out the employment for that industry. The current relative demand shock for industry i in state r during year t measures the percentage deviation of the adjusted state employment from its trend relative to the percentage deviation of national employment from its trend in year t (see the appendix for details). This variable captures the extent to which the current local labor-demand conditions deviate from the national labor-demand conditions.

We use the persistence of this measure of local relative demand shocks to control for future local relative demand shocks. We regress the current local relative demand shock measure for a given industry and state on its value lagged 1 and 2 years and on the current national demand shock measure. We use this estimated model to generate forecasts of future relative demand shocks to the locality. Our measure for anticipated future local relative demand shocks is a weighted average of the 1-, 2-, and 3-year forecasts.

8.4 Empirical Results

8.4.1 Regression Method

Starting with the basic forms of equations (10a) and (10b), we estimate the wage and employment equations in first differences using weighted least squares, with lagged industry employment providing the weights. The estimation equations are repeated here.

$$\Delta w_t^{ir} = \omega_0^{ir} + \omega_1^i \Delta y_t + \omega_2^i time + \omega_3^i \Delta s_t + \omega_6^{ir} \Delta Unemp_t^r$$
$$+ (\omega_{5,0}^i + \omega_{5,1}^i X^{ir} + \omega_{5,2}^i M^i + \omega_{5,3}^i \alpha^i + \omega_{5,4}^{ir} \overline{X}^{ir}) \cdot \Delta e_t^i$$
$$+ \omega_6^i \Delta y_t^{ir} + \omega_7^i \Delta L_{t-1}^i,$$

$$\Delta L_t^{ir} = \lambda_0^{ir} + \lambda_1^i \Delta y_t + \lambda_2^i time + \lambda_3^i \Delta s_t + \lambda_4^{ir} \Delta Unemp_t^r$$
$$+ (\lambda_{5,0}^i + \lambda_{5,1}^i X^{ir} + \lambda_{5,2}^i M^i + \lambda_{5,3}^i \alpha^i + \lambda_{5,4}^{ir} \overline{X}^{ir}) \cdot \Delta e_t^i$$
$$+ \lambda_6 \Delta y_t^{ir} + \lambda_7^i \Delta L_{t-1}^i.$$

The implied unit of observation is a worker in manufacturing, not a state or SIC aggregate. All regressions include industry fixed effects, industry time trends, and lagged changes in industry employment. Regressions using state data also include state fixed effects and state time trends. All regressions control for the percentage change in real GDP, the percentage change in real oil prices, the percentage change in real interest rates, and the unemployment rate (at national or state levels, as appropriate). The regressions using state-level data allow the coefficients on these aggregate variables to vary by industry.[16] The interacted-trade-shares for each industry are lagged by one period to avoid simultaneity issues.

---

16. By including the industry-specific coefficients, along with the state and industry fixed effects and trend terms, we reduce the likelihood that our regressions are plagued by the problems caused by combining explanatory variables based on different levels of aggregation.

All of our specifications include both the industry-specific export and import exchange rates. The export exchange rate series proxies the relevant stimuli to export market sales. The import exchange rate series combines the two other trade transmission channels for exchange rates, as shown in our theoretical derivation. Ideally, we would include separate measures for imported-input exchange rates and import-competition exchange rates. However, the import penetration of industries is highly correlated with the imported input shares of industries. Because of this strong correlation, the data do not allow us to effectively distinguish between the import-competition channel and the imported-input channel of exchange rate stimuli. Thus, we include only one import term. We recognize that the estimated parameter on the import exchange rate will combine the two distinct exposure effects. We cannot predict a priori the sign of its coefficient.

8.4.2   Regression Results: Nationally Aggregated Series for Industries

As a first pass through the data, we examine industry data on labor market outcomes collected at the national level. These regressions (shown in appendix table 8A.2) consider whether exchange rate movements are associated with changes in the employment, hours, or wages of workers who are differentiated from each other only in terms of the industries in which they work. In these national data, if a worker changes jobs within a two-digit industry, but moves across state lines, there will not be an observable change in employment. Because of this feature, such data may mask the extent of the possible disruption attributable to exchange rates. Employment changes show up in this data only when a worker moves in or out of a two-digit industry.

The regressions using industry aggregates on wages, hours, and employment impose various parameter constraints. The elasticity of labor market outcomes to exchange rate movements are constrained to be common across all industries, or to differ across industries or over time only due to differences in the industry trade orientation. We do not investigate with the national data differences in elasticities due to other industry-specific features, such as competitive structure (as in Campa and Goldberg 1998), labor market norms, or costs of adjusting the workforce. Given these cross-industry restrictions, it is not surprising that exchange rate implications appear small and generally insignificant for each of our labor market variables.

8.4.3   Regression Results: Data Disaggregated
by States and by Industries

The main body of our empirical work, presented in tables 8.1 to 8.7, uses our full data set on labor market outcomes by industry, by state, and over time for the period 1971–95 (about 8,000 observations). Tables 8.1 to 8.3

Table 8.1   Response Elasticities of Average Hourly Earnings of Workers in Industries in Individual States

	High-Markup Industries			Low-Markup Industries		
	(1)	(2)	(3)	(4)	(5)	(6)
Own industry channels (percent change)						
Export exchange rates	0.053***			−0.009		
	(0.013)			(0.007)		
Import exchange rates	−0.050***			0.004		
	(0.009)			(0.009)		
State/industry export orientation with export exchange rates		0.011	0.011		−0.009***	−0.010***
		(0.008)	(0.009)		(0.003)	(0.003)
State/industry imported-input orientation with import exchange rates		−0.025***	−0.025***		0.007	0.004
		(0.008)	(0.009)		(0.006)	(0.006)
Cross-industry spillovers (percent change)						
Other-industry export orientation with export exchange rates			−0.005			0.002***
			(0.010)			(0.001)
Other-industry imported-input orientation with import exchange rates			.190***			0.011***
			(.041)			(0.004)

	(1)	(2)	(3)	(4)	(5)	(6)
State-specific relative demand shock	0.249***	0.248***	0.271***	0.164***	0.173***	0.166***
	(0.056)	(0.056)	(0.057)	(0.049)	(0.049)	(0.049)
Forecasted state-specific relative demand shock	−0.118**	−0.116*	−0.124**	−0.584***	−0.063	−0.054
	(0.061)	(0.061)	(0.062)	(0.055)	(0.055)	(0.055)
Adjusted R^2	0.387	0.383	0.387	0.347	0.371	0.350
Test for joint significance of exchange rate terms: F-statistic						
Own-industry channels						
Noninteracted	14.64***			0.83		
Interacted with trade orientation		5.07*	4.25*		4.29*	5.35*
Cross-industry spillovers			10.74***			7.57***
Own-industry and cross-industry spillovers			7.92***			5.94

Notes: BLS Employment and Earnings, states and area data. Weighted least squares estimation using prior period's employment levels as weights. Standard errors are given in parentheses. Number of observations is 7,991. Other control variables include industry-specific responses to real GDP changes, real oil-price changes, real interest rate changes, and state unemployment rate. Industry fixed effects, state fixed effects, and industry- and state-specific time trends are included in all specifications. Own-industry and other-industry export orientation measures are adjusted using MISER data to reflect average state/industry differences.

*Significant at the 10 percent level.

**Significant at the 5 percent level.

***Significant at the 1 percent level.

Table 8.2   Response Elasticities of Average Hours of Workers in Industries within Individual States

	High-Markup Industries			Low-Markup Industries		
	(1)	(2)	(3)	(4)	(5)	(6)
Own industry channels (percent change)						
Export exchange rates	−0.031***			−0.029***		
	(0.008)			(0.005)		
Import exchange rates	0.034***			0.019***		
	(0.006)			(0.007)		
State/industry export orientation with export exchange rates		−0.020***	−0.016***		−0.009***	−0.009***
		(0.005)	(0.006)		(0.002)	(0.002)
State/industry imported-input orientation with import exchange rates		0.031	0.001		0.007	0.000***
		(0.005)	(0.000)		(0.005)	(0.000)
Cross-industry spillovers (percent change)						
Other-industry export orientation with export exchange rates			−0.009			−0.001
			(0.007)			(0.001)
Other-industry imported-input orientation with import exchange rates			0.016			−0.001
			(0.026)			(0.003)

	(1)	(2)	(3)	(4)	(5)	(6)
State-specific relative demand shock	−0.015	−0.004	0.005	0.091***	0.096***	0.097***
	(0.036)	(0.036)	(0.037)	(0.038)	(0.038)	(0.038)
Forecasted state-specific relative demand shock	−0.030	−0.036	−0.043	−0.161***	−0.163***	−0.164***
	(0.039)	(0.039)	(0.040)	(0.042)	(0.042)	(0.043)
Adjusted R^2	0.210	0.211	0.211	0.261	0.258	0.258
Test for joint significance of exchange rate terms: F-statistic						
Own-industry channels						
Noninteracted	16.82***	17.11***	17.88***	15.53***	7.08*	6.78*
Interacted with trade orientation						
Cross-industry spillovers			1.10			0.38
Own-industry and cross-industry spillovers			9.11***			3.73

Notes: BLS Employment and Earnings, states and area data. Weighted least squares estimation using prior period's employment levels as weights. Standard errors are given in parentheses. Number of observations is 7,991. Other control variables include industry-specific responses to real GDP changes, real oil-price changes, real interest rate changes, and state unemployment rate. Industry fixed effects, state fixed effects, and industry- and state-specific time trends are included in all specifications. Own-industry and other-industry export orientation measures are adjusted using MISER data to reflect average state/industry differences.

*Significant at the 10 percent level.
**Significant at the 5 percent level.
***Significant at the 1 percent level.

Table 8.3   Response Elasticities of Average Employment of Workers in Industries within Individual States

	High-Markup Industries			Low-Markup Industries		
	(1)	(2)	(3)	(4)	(5)	(6)
Own industry channels (percent change)						
Export exchange rates	0.064***			−0.030***		
	(0.018)			(0.009)		
Import exchange rates	0.033***			0.041***		
	(0.013)			(0.011)		
State/industry export orientation with export exchange rates		−0.035***	−0.051***		−0.003***	−0.003
		(0.011)	(0.012)		(0.004)	(0.004)
State/industry imported-input orientation with import exchange rates		0.118***	0.106***		0.072***	0.072***
		(0.011)	(0.012)		(0.008)	(0.008)
Cross-industry spillovers (percent change)						
Other-industry export orientation with export exchange rates			0.038***			−0.001
			(0.014)			(0.001)
Other-industry imported-input orientation with import exchange rates			0.189***			−0.003
			(0.056)			(0.005)

State-specific relative demand shock	0.110	0.156**	0.142*	0.237***	0.244***	0.245***
	(0.078)	(0.077)	(0.078)	(0.064)	(0.064)	(0.064)
Forecasted state-specific relative demand shock	−0.625***	−0.661***	−0.643***	−0.719***	−0.729***	−0.729***
	(0.085)	(0.084)	(0.084)	(0.072)	(0.072)	(0.072)
Adjusted R^2	0.568	0.575	0.578	0.565	0.567	0.567
Test for joint significance of exchange rate terms: *F*-statistic						
Own-industry channels						
Noninteracted	39.17***		27.62***			
Interacted with trade orientation		69.66***	40.59***		39.76***	39.62***
Cross-industry spillovers			10.71**			0.51
Own-industry and cross-industry spillovers			40.39***			20.13***

Notes: BLS Employment and Earnings, states and area data. Weighted least squares estimation using prior period's employment levels as weights. Standard errors are given in parentheses. Number of observations is 7,991. Other control variables include industry-specific responses to real GDP changes, real oil-price changes, real interest rate changes, and state unemployment rate. Industry fixed effects, state fixed effects, and industry- and state-specific time trends are included in all specifications. Own-industry and other-industry export orientation measures are adjusted using MISER data to reflect average state/industry differences.

*Significant at the 10 percent level.

**Significant at the 5 percent level.

***Significant at the 1 percent level.

separately consider the elasticities of response of real average hourly earnings, weekly hours, and employment, respectively. The industries are grouped together according to their average price-over-cost markups.[17] High-markup industries, all else equal, would be expected to have less responsive labor market outcomes.

For each industry group, tables 8.1 to 8.3 present the results of three specifications of exchange rate effects on the associated labor market outcome. The most constrained specifications are those given in columns (1) and (4) of each table, where the exchange rate effects are constrained to be common across industries in the group and over time. In columns (2) and (5), the exchange rate elasticities are allowed to vary with the size of the export orientation or the import orientation of an industry in a state and at any point in time. The coefficients on the exchange rate terms in these regressions are interpreted as the direct (and contemporaneous) implications for labor markets.[18]

Other useful summaries of the effects of exchange rates on the three dependent variables are given in tables 8.4 to 8.7. Table 8.4 provides independently estimated exchange rate elasticities for each industry. For the results reported in table 8.4, we constrain the industry-specific elasticities to be constant over time and across localities in the United States. In separate tests, we consider whether the data reject equality of the industry exchange rate elasticities across regions of the United States. If the answer is yes (reject equality), we report an r superscript on the associated term in table 8.4. For those industries where the data reject equality across regions, tables 8.5 to 8.7 provide details on the regional variation in the exchange rate effects.

Exchange Rates and Average Hourly Earnings

In state-level data, real exchange rates matter for average hourly earnings (table 8.1), even in the most constrained regression specifications. For both high- and low-markup industries, dollar appreciations generally lower the hourly earnings of workers.[19] For both categories of industries, the estimated magnitudes of the direct effects are small, with an average net effect of at most -0.1 percent from a 10 percent dollar appreciation. Indirect effects, from local industry spillovers, are significant, but on net go in

17. The low-markup group of industries includes primary metal products, fabricated metal products, transportation equipment, food and kindred products, textile mill products, apparel and mill products, lumber and wood products, furniture and fixtures, paper and allied products, petroleum and coal products, and leather and leather products.
18. We averaged the ratio of the MISER industry export orientation (by state) to the aggregate industry export orientation for the years covered by the MISER data. We then adjusted the aggregate industry export-orientation rates in each state and year by this average ratio.
19. The key exception is the positive earnings effect found for dollar appreciations through the export channel in high-markup industries.

Table 8.4   Estimated Industry-Specific Elasticities of Labor Market Outcomes to Exchange Rates

Industry	Real Average Hourly Earnings (percent change)		Weekly Hours (percent change)		Employment (percent change)	
	Export	Import	Export	Import	Export	Import
Food and kindred products	−0.203**	0.233**r	0.005	−0.003r	−0.045	0.087**
	(0.023)	(0.031)	(0.017)	(0.023)	(0.031)	(0.041)
Tobacco products	−0.084	−0.034	−0.036	−0.007	0.103	0.098
	(0.067)	(0.055)	(0.049)	(0.040)	(0.085)	(0.069)
Textile mill products	0.036	−0.073**	−0.114**	0.004	0.005	−0.007
	(0.031)	(0.033)	(0.023)	(0.024)	(0.043)	(0.046)
Apparel and other textile products	0.002	−0.015	−0.044**r	0.065**	0.082**r	−0.036r
	(0.014)	(0.029)	(0.010)	(0.022)	(0.019)	(0.040)
Lumber and wood products	−0.068**	0.129**	−0.006	−0.029	0.074**r	−0.043r
	(0.018)	(0.034)	(0.013)	(0.025)	(0.023)	(0.046)
Furniture and fixtures	0.086	−0.077	0.007	−0.014	0.091	0.000
	(0.053)	(0.073)	(0.039)	(0.054)	(0.072)	(0.099)
Paper and allied products	0.001	0.073**	−0.004	0.020	0.072**	0.009r
	(0.023)	(0.021)	(0.017)	(0.016)	(0.031)	(0.027)
Printing and publishing	0.032	−0.022	0.008	0.005	0.095**	−0.031
	(0.030)	(0.020)	(0.022)	(0.015)	(0.039)	(0.026)
Chemical and allied products	0.144**	−0.101**	0.000r	0.006r	−0.006	0.019
	(0.027)	(0.020)	(0.020)	(0.015)	(0.037)	(0.028)
Petroleum and coal products	0.078	−0.146**	0.106**	−0.061	0.021	−0.011
	(0.057)	(0.062)	(0.042)	(0.045)	(0.059)	(0.060)
Rubber and miscellaneous plastic products	0.042	−0.069*	−0.058**	0.076**	0.065	0.188*
	(0.033)	(0.040)	(0.024)	(0.030)	(0.042)	(0.051)

(continued)

Table 8.4 (continued)

Industry	Real Average Hourly Earnings (percent change)		Weekly Hours (percent change)		Employment (percent change)	
	Export	Import	Export	Import	Export	Import
Leather and leather products	0.036	0.015	−0.061	0.067**r	−0.126r	0.097
	(0.070)	(0.045)	(0.052)	(0.033)	(0.096)	(0.062)
Stone, clay, and glass products	0.139**	−0.118**	−0.037	0.044*	0.153**	0.011
	(0.052)	(0.036)	(0.038)	(0.026)	(0.067)	(0.047)
Primary metal industries	0.095**	−0.139**	−0.065**r	0.060**r	−0.054	0.124**
	(0.032)	(0.032)	(0.023)	(0.024)	(0.041)	(0.041)
Fabricated metal products	0.152**	−0.113**	−0.088**	0.031**	0.010	0.149**
	(0.024)	(0.019)	(0.018)	(0.014)	(0.032)	(0.025)
Industrial machinery and equipment	0.090**	−0.047**	−0.069**	0.052**	−0.097**r	0.129**
	(0.025)	(0.015)	(0.018)	(0.011)	(0.032)	(0.019)
Electronic and other electric equipment	0.043r	−0.049r	−0.088**	0.085**	0.473**	−0.161**
	(0.037)	(0.030)	(0.027)	(0.022)	(0.048)	(0.038)
Transportation equipment	0.235**	−0.126**	0.002r	−0.005	0.235**r	0.048**
	(0.027)	(0.016)	(0.020)	(0.011)	(0.032)	(0.018)
Instruments and related products	−0.124*r	0.066r	−0.077	0.073*	0.116	−0.080
	(0.070)	(0.055)	(0.051)	(0.041)	(0.094)	(0.074)
Miscellaneous manufacturing	−0.273**r	0.334**r	−0.050	0.060	0.157	−0.114
	(0.108)	(0.129)	(0.079)	(0.095)	(0.128)	(0.152)

Notes: Based on specification (1) from tables 8.1 to 8.3, where industry fixed effects were interacted with the percentage change in the industry-specific export and import exchange rates. Standard errors are given in parentheses.

*Significant at the 10 percent level.

**Significant at the 5 percent level.

rStatistically significant regional differences.

Table 8.5   Regional Differences in Exchange Rate Implications for Average Real Hourly Earnings

Industry Name	Reject Equality across Regions?	Combined Regional Coefficient (reported by region only if measurable)								
		Northeast	Mid-Atlantic	East North Central	West North Central	South Atlantic	East South Central	West South Central	Mountain	Pacific
Food (SIC 20)										
XRER	no	−0.24***	−0.28***	−0.27**	−0.21***	−0.18***	−0.26***	−0.23***	−0.22**	−0.26***
		(0.09)	(0.05)	(0.04)	(0.05)	(0.04)	(0.06)	(0.05)	(0.10)	(0.05)
MRER	yes	0.32***	0.43***	0.41***	0.21***	0.21***	0.26***	0.22***	0.31***	0.37***
		(0.11)	(0.06)	(0.06)	(0.07)	(0.06)	(0.08)	(0.07)	(0.07)	(0.06)
Electronics (SIC 36)										
XRER	yes		−0.04	−0.01	−0.11	−0.13	−0.19	−0.35*		−0.42**
			(0.16)	(0.16)	(0.23)	(0.17)	(0.26)	(0.21)		(0.17)
MRER	yes		0.02	0.00	0.04	0.12	0.06	0.31*		0.31**
			(0.12)	(0.12)	(0.17)	(0.12)	(0.20)	(0.16)		(0.13)
Instruments (SIC 38)										
XRER	yes	0.09	−0.16	0.11	0.09	−0.31	0.40	−0.65	0.09	−0.67***
		(0.19)	(0.11)	(0.18)	(0.63)	(0.34)	(0.60)	(0.40)	(0.19)	(0.20)
MRER	yes	−0.15	0.12	−0.13	−0.04	0.23	−0.38	0.49	−0.15	0.52***
		(0.13)	(0.09)	(0.14)	(0.49)	(0.27)	(0.46)	(0.31)	(0.36)	(0.16)
Miscellaneous manufacturing (SIC 39)										
XRER	yes	−0.81*	−0.18	−1.00***	−0.02	−0.01	−0.81	−1.14***	−0.81*	0.19
		(0.40)	(0.12)	(0.23)	(0.44)	(0.37)	(0.40)	(0.35)	(0.40)	(0.19)
MRER	yes		−0.53	0.14	−0.39	−0.74		0.81	0.00	−0.83
			(0.49)	(0.55)	(0.67)	(0.62)		(0.63)	(0.63)	(0.52)

Notes: XRER, industry-specific export real exchange rates; MRER, industry-specific import real exchange rates. Standard errors are given in parentheses.
*Significant at the 10 percent level.
**Significant at the 5 percent level.
***Significant at the 1 percent level.

Table 8.6   Regional Differences in Exchange Rate Implications for Average Weekly Hours

Industry Name	Reject Equality across Regions?	Combined Regional Coefficient (reported by region only if measurable)								
		Northeast	Mid-Atlantic	East North Central	West North Central	South Atlantic	East South Central	West South Central	Mountain	Pacific
Food (SIC 20)										
XRER	no	0.04 (0.06)	−0.01 (0.03)	0.07** (0.03)	0.04 (0.04)	−0.01 (0.03)	0.03 (0.04)	−0.07* (0.04)	0.01 (0.07)	0.01 (0.03)
MRER	yes		−0.05 (0.08)	−0.11 (0.08)	−0.09 (0.08)	−0.03 (0.08)	−0.01 (0.09)	0.07 (0.09)	−0.09 (0.09)	−0.05 (0.08)
Apparel and fabric (SIC 23)										
XRER	yes	0.05 (0.05)	−0.00 (0.02)	0.01 (0.06)	0.02 (0.16)	−0.07*** (0.02)	−0.08*** (0.03)	−0.14*** (0.04)	0.05 (0.05)	−0.10** (0.04)
MRER	no	0.08 (0.10)	0.03 (0.04)	−0.03 (0.11)	−0.20 (0.30)	0.08* (0.05)	0.10* (0.06)	0.19** (0.09)	0.08 (0.16)	0.03 (0.07)
Chemicals and products (SIC 28)										
XRER	yes	0.01 (0.07)	0.04 (0.03)	0.00 (0.04)	−0.21* (0.10)	−0.08** (0.04)	−0.09 (0.06)	0.01* (0.06)	0.01 (0.07)	0.02 (0.07)
MRER	yes	−0.02 (0.05)	−0.01 (0.02)	0.00 (0.03)	0.17** (0.08)	0.07** (0.03)	0.05 (0.05)	−0.06 (0.04)	−0.02 (0.08)	0.01 (0.05)

Leather and products (SIC 31)										
XRER	no	0.03 (0.07)	0.01 (0.07)	−0.31** (0.15)	−0.14 (0.13)	−0.10 (0.23)	−0.23* (0.13)	−0.32** (0.14)	0.03 (0.07)	−0.09 (0.18)
MRER	yes	0.02 (0.05)	0.02 (0.04)	0.35*** (0.12)	0.14 (0.10)	0.06 (0.16)	0.19* (0.10)	0.36*** (0.11)	0.02 (0.13)	0.10 (0.14)
Primary metal products (SIC 33)										
XRER	yes	0.09 (0.10)	0.09 (0.10)	0.04 (0.10)	−0.20 (0.15)	−0.10 (0.11)	−0.17 (0.12)	−0.09 (0.13)	−0.10 (0.18)	−0.06 (0.12)
MRER	yes	0.08 (0.08)	0.04 (0.04)	−0.01 (0.03)	0.19* (0.11)	0.18* (0.06)	0.11 (0.07)	0.19** (0.08)	0.16* (0.08)	0.17** (0.08)
Transportation equipment (SIC 37)										
XRER	yes	−0.15 (0.10)	−0.10 (0.09)	0.12** (0.05)	0.00 (0.12)	−0.10 (0.11)	−0.05 (0.15)	−0.21* (0.12)	−0.06 (0.37)	−0.15** (0.07)
MRER	no	−0.05 (0.07)	−0.05 (0.07)	−0.15** (0.06)	−0.10 (0.09)	−0.02 (0.08)	−0.10 (0.11)	0.06 (0.09)	−0.02 (0.09)	−0.06 (0.07)

Notes: XRER, industry-specific export real exchange rates; MRER, industry-specific import real exchange rates. Standard errors are given in parentheses.

*Significant at the 10 percent level.

**Significant at the 5 percent level.

***Significant at the 1 percent level.

Table 8.7   Regional Differences in Exchange Rate Implications for Average Employment

Industry Name	Reject Equality across Regions?	Combined Regional Coefficient (reported by region only if measurable)								
		Northeast	Mid-Atlantic	East North Central	West North Central	South Atlantic	East South Central	West South Central	Mountain	Pacific
Apparel and fabric (SIC23)										
XRER	yes	0.07 (0.07)	0.04 (0.03)	0.11 (0.07)	−0.07 (0.19)	0.06* (0.03)	−0.01 (0.04)	0.03 (0.06)	0.22 (0.28)	0.20*** (0.05)
MRER	yes		−0.18 (0.14)	−0.45** (0.18)	−0.12 (0.39)	−0.16 (0.15)	−0.21 (0.16)	−0.36** (0.17)	−0.35** (0.17)	−0.61*** (0.17)
Lumber and wood (SIC 24)										
XRER	yes	0.09 (0.08)	0.06 (0.06)	−0.01 (0.04)	0.10 (0.12)	0.12*** (0.04)	0.09** (0.04)	0.10** (0.05)	−0.01 (0.08)	−0.03 (0.03)
MRER	yes	0.31* (0.18)	−0.32** (0.13)	−0.02 (0.08)	−0.28 (0.31)	0.13* (0.08)	−0.14 (0.10)	0.15 (0.10)	−0.07 (0.10)	−0.41*** (0.07)
Paper products (SIC 26)										
XRER	no	0.02 (0.05)	0.07** (0.04)	0.01 (0.03)	0.05 (0.05)	0.06 (0.04)	0.09* (0.05)	0.01 (0.06)	0.03 (0.31)	0.14*** (0.05)
MRER	yes	−0.03 (0.04)	0.06** (0.03)	0.00 (0.03)	0.06 (0.08)	0.02 (0.05)	−0.06 (0.07)	0.01 (0.08)	−0.06 (0.08)	−0.16** (0.07)

Leather and products (SIC 31)										
XRER	yes	0.09	−0.05	−0.49*	−0.39	0.31	−0.76***	−0.10	0.09	−0.17
		(0.15)	(0.15)	(0.28)	(0.27)	(0.44)	(0.26)	(0.30)	(0.15)	(0.37)
MRER	no	0.02	0.05	0.41*	0.26	0.12	0.39*	0.24	0.02	0.10
		(0.10)	(0.09)	(0.22)	(0.21)	(0.30)	(0.20)	(0.23)	(0.27)	(0.29)
Industrial machinery (SIC 35)										
XRER	yes	−0.17	0.05	−0.09	−0.26***	0.07	0.10	−0.36***	0.03	0.20*
		(0.13)	(0.09)	(0.07)	(0.13)	(0.12)	(0.18)	(0.13)	(0.35)	(0.11)
MRER	no	0.12	0.05	0.16***	0.26***	0.13	0.08	0.27***	−0.02	0.09
		(0.08)	(0.05)	(0.04)	(0.08)	(0.08)	(0.12)	(0.08)	(0.08)	(0.08)
Transportation equipment (SIC 37)										
XRER	yes	−0.16	0.03	0.55***	0.22	0.15	0.40*	−0.64***	−0.07	−0.04
		(0.19)	(0.16)	(0.08)	(0.20)	(0.18)	(0.24)	(0.21)	(0.48)	(0.12)
MRER	no	−0.17	−0.28**	−0.23	−0.24	−0.26	0.09	−0.20	−0.14	
		(0.13)	(−0.28)	(0.16)	(0.15)	(0.18)	(0.17)	(0.17)	(0.13)	

Note: XRER, industry-specific export real exchange rates; MRER, industry-specific import real exchange rates. Standard errors are given in parentheses.

*Significant at the 10 percent level.

**Significant at the 5 percent level.

***Significant at the 1 percent level.

the opposite direction to that expected from the alternative wage arguments.

The first two columns of table 8.4 report the industry-specific estimates of average hourly earnings elasticities with respect to export and import exchange rates. Exchange rates enter significantly in 14 of the 20 industries. The separate channels for exchange rate effects can be large and sometimes offsetting. Clear examples of these counteracting forces are found in the food, chemical, and transportation equipment industries. In 8 industries the net elasticities of hourly earnings responses to exchange rates are significantly different from 0, but the sign pattern is mixed.

Table 8.5 shows the pattern of regional differences in earnings sensitivity for food, electronics, instruments, and miscellaneous manufacturing. For electronics, the West South Central and Pacific regions are most significantly effected by changes in the real exchange rates of export and of imported-input partners.

Exchange Rates and Average Weekly Hours

Dollar movements have significant implications for average weekly hours in manufacturing (table 8.2). When the dollar appreciates against the currencies of U.S. export partners, hours worked decline for both high- and low-markup industries. Symmetrically, when the dollar appreciates against the currencies of countries from which U.S. industries purchase inputs, hours worked expand. These two effects largely offset each other, so that the net effect of dollar movements on hours is small. We find no important cross-industry spillover effects of exchange rates on hours.

Estimates of industry-specific coefficients for the two transmission channels tell a similar story (table 8.4, cols. [3] and [4]). In 11 of the 20 industries, average weekly hours respond significantly to dollar movements through either the export or the import channels. While both channels for the exchange rate effects often are significant, the net effect on hours is significantly different from 0 only in the case of textile mill products and fabricated metal products (where a 10 percent appreciation reduces average weekly hours by 1.1 percent and 0.6 percent, respectively). Regional differences in the responsiveness of hours to dollar movements are evident for 6 of the 20 manufacturing industries. As shown in table 8.6, no single region has industry hours that are uniformly more responsive to exchange rates.

Exchange Rates and Average Industry Employment

The data show that exchange rate movements are clearly correlated with changes in industry employment (table 8.3). For high- and low-markup industries, these regressions support the expected pattern of direct effects through export and imported-input channels. Dollar appreciations against export partners are associated with employment declines (both through direct and indirect industry effects), while appreciations against input providers are associated with employment expansion.[20]

There is considerable heterogeneity across industries in the effect of dollar movements on employment (table 8.4). In 13 of the 20 industries, employment is responsive to exchange rates through at least one of the trade channels. At the state level, some of these local employment effects are very large, even in net terms. Regional differences in employment elasticities are important for 6 of the 20 manufacturing industries (see table 8.7).

During the full time period (1971–95), the net effect of a dollar appreciation appears to be expansion of employment. However, tests of the stability and robustness of the regression coefficients across different subperiods suggest that caution is warranted. The coefficient estimates are fairly stable or sign-consistent into the mid-late 1980s, but for the late 1980s and early 1990s the fit of the regression equations significantly deteriorates. In many cases, there are even sign reversals on many estimated coefficients.

Actual versus Anticipated Shocks, and Local Labor Markets

Finally, the results from our constructed measures of state relative demand shocks are of independent interest for understanding the dynamics of labor market adjustment to stimuli. Using Current Population Survey data from 1977–79, Topel (1986) finds that an increase in his current relative demand-shock measure leads to significantly higher average weekly wages. In contrast, an increase in his expected future relative demand shock measure leads to significantly lower average weekly wages. Topel interprets the positive wage response to the current shock as consistent with a labor-demand shift with a stable labor supply, and the negative wage response to expected future shocks as consistent with a labor-supply shift with a stable labor demand. The current labor supply shifts in advance of expected future labor-demand shifts as workers attempt to arbitrage lifetime earnings differentials across separate labor markets.

While our study uses aggregate data and not microdata and controls for a different set of variables, our results nonetheless confirm Topel's pattern of wage adjustments to these state relative demand shock measures. Average weekly wages show a large positive and statistically significant response to current relative demand shocks. In addition, average weekly wages fall in response to expected future relative demand shocks (table 8.2). For both high- and low-markup industries, the elasticity with respect to the current shock is more than double the elasticity with respect to the expected future shock.

If the local market experiences a demand shock that is large relative to

20. Again, the exception is for dollar appreciations through the export channel for high-markup industries where we find a positive employment effect. However, when we interact the export exchange rate with the industry export intensity we find the predicted negative employment effect.

the shocks experienced by other localities, we also expect local employment and hours to increase.[21] From table 8.2, we observe a significant qualitative difference across high- versus low-markup industries on the response of hours worked. Hours worked in low-markup industries are very sensitive to relative local demand conditions: Hours increase in response to the current (favorable) shocks, and decrease in anticipation of future (favorable) shocks. Table 8.3 confirms the same sign pattern of employment adjustment to these shocks, and suggests that market structure may play a role in determining the magnitude of responsiveness to current shocks. Although wages were more responsive to current shocks, hours and employment are more responsive to perceived future conditions.

8.5   Conclusion

In this paper we have used labor market data disaggregated by industry and by state to explore the labor market implications of exchange rates. This approach offers several potential advantages over prior studies. First, we can better specify the alternative wage by using data at the state versus the national level. Second, given the nonrandom distribution of industry employment across labor markets, aggregate industry-level data may pick up spurious state- or region-specific labor market effects. Third, we are able to introduce state- and industry-specific export-orientation data and can consider spillovers within and across labor markets. Finally, and importantly, if exchange rate movements lead to reallocation of workers and jobs across state lines, but still within similar industries, we are likely to pick up some effects that may be missed in industry data aggregated from the state to the national level.

We find that local industries differ significantly in their earnings, hours, and employment responses to exchange rates. Industry wages unambiguously respond to dollar movements in 8 of the 20 manufacturing industries, with possible effects surfacing in 14 of the 20 industries. A dollar depreciation is sometimes associated with earnings growth, but sometimes with wage restraint. In some industries, there are significant regional differences in these elasticities. Employment is unambiguously responsive to exchange rates in 12 of the 20 manufacturing industries. The employment effects of exchange rates are much more easily discerned in the local labor markets than in nationally aggregated series. However, there are clear issues of the stability of empirical specifications that become especially pronounced by the late 1980s. This lack of stability leads us to suggest caution in interpreting and identifying industry-specific responses of labor market outcomes to dollar movements.

---

21. Topel (1986) only looks at the impact on average weekly earnings.

Appendix
Local Relative Demand Conditions and Forecast

For each state r and industry i, we construct a time series of private-sector nonagricultural employment excluding employment in that industry[22] and regress its logarithm on a quadratic time trend. The residuals from these regressions, ε_t^{ir} measure the deviations from trend employment in state r exclusive of industry i at time t. Similarly, we regress the logarithm of national private sector nonagricultural employment in year t on a quadratic time trend. The residuals from this regression, ε_t, capture the aggregate business cycle. Relative local demand shocks in state r and industry i in year t are defined as

$$\text{(A1)} \qquad \Delta y_t^{ir} = \varepsilon_t^{ir} - \varepsilon_t,$$

so that the relative demand shock measures the local employment shock as a deviation from the national employment shock.

We use the persistence of these relative demand shocks to develop a measure of the expected future relative shock to a state/industry. Specifically, for each state/industry we estimate the following regression:

$$\text{(A2)} \qquad \Delta y_t^{ir} = \alpha_1^{ir} \Delta y_{t-1}^{ir} + \alpha_2^{ir} \Delta y_{t-2}^{ir} + \beta^{ir} \varepsilon_t.$$

The relative demand shock for industry i in state r is modeled as a function of two lags of the relative demand shock and the current national shock. If β^{ir} is positive, then this industry/state experiences relative cycles that are magnified by the aggregate cycle. This empirical model is used to generate 1- to 3-year forecasts of the relative demand shocks for each industry/state. We use a second-order autoregressive model to forecast the national employment shocks. Following Topel (1986), we summarize these forecasts into a single weighted average of the forecasts, with weights declining linearly over the forecast horizon.

---

22. Here is where we deviate from Topel's methodology. Since we are interested in explaining the impacts of relative demand shocks on the wage, hours, and employment in an industry/state, we must remove any direct contribution of that industry/state from our measure of the relative demand shock. We do this by subtracting the employment movements in that industry from our time series on state employment. This implies that each manufacturing industry in a state will have a slightly different series of estimated relative demand shocks.

Table 8A.1   **Correlation Coefficients between Industry-Specific Real Exchange Rates and an Aggregate Real Exchange Rate**

Industry Name (code)	XRER with RER	MRER with RER	XRER with MRER
Food and kindred products (20)	0.89	0.93	0.92
Tobacco products (21)	0.88	0.76	0.56
Textile mill products (22)	0.88	0.85	0.75
Apparel and other textiles (23)	0.77	0.82	0.61
Lumber and wood products (24)	0.63	0.58	0.48
Furniture and fixtures (25)	0.79	0.82	0.71
Paper and allied products (26)	0.92	0.50	0.45
Printing and publishing (27)	0.91	0.81	0.76
Chemical and allied products (28)	0.93	0.89	0.92
Petroleum and coal products (29)	0.90	0.36	0.34
Rubber and miscellaneous plastic (30)	0.83	0.87	0.68
Leather and leather products (31)	0.91	0.65	0.55
Stone, clay, and glass (32)	0.85	0.86	0.76
Primary metal industries (33)	0.90	0.82	0.81
Fabricated metal products (34)	0.84	0.80	0.60
Industrial machinery and equipment (35)	0.92	0.85	0.85
Electronic and other equipment (36)	0.88	0.76	0.67
Transportation equipment (37)	0.90	0.75	0.73
Instruments and related products (38)	0.91	0.81	0.89
Miscellaneous manufacturing (39)	0.90	0.88	0.90

Notes: The industry-specific export real exchange rates are denoted by XRER; industry-specific import real exchange rates are denoted by MRER; the trade-weighted aggregate real exchange rate is the Federal Reserve Bank of Dallas series.

Table 8A.2   Nationally Aggregate Industry Data on Earnings, Hours, and Employment, 1971–95

	Real Average Hourly Earnings (percent change)		Average Weekly Hours (percent change)		Average Employment (percent change)	
	(1)	(2)	(3)	(4)	(5)	(6)
Export exchange rates	0.018		0.002		0.072**	
	(0.018)		(0.008)		(0.027)	
Import exchange rates	−0.014		−0.008		0.023	
	(0.014)		(0.007)		(0.022)	
Industry export orientation with export exchange rates		−0.008		−0.011		0.016
		(0.016)		(0.007)		(0.022)
Industry imported-input orientation with import exchange rates		0.003		−0.002		0.046**
		(0.014)		(0.006)		(0.021)
Real GDP	0.104**	0.108**	0.236**	0.237**	0.879**	0.921**
	(0.037)	(0.037)	(0.017)	(0.017)	(0.055)	(0.054)
Real oil prices	−0.035**	−0.035**	0.004**	0.004**	0.016**	0.017**
	(0.004)	(0.004)	(0.002)	(0.002)	(0.006)	(0.006)
Real interest rates	−0.009	−0.011	0.010*	0.009*	0.081**	0.090**
	(0.012)	(0.012)	(0.006)	(0.005)	(0.018)	(0.017)
National unemployment rate	0.003*	0.002*	0.001	0.001	−0.009**	−0.007**
	(0.001)	(0.001)	(0.001)	(0.001)	(0.002)	(0.002)
Lag employment growth	−0.094**	−0.094**	−0.164**	−0.164**	0.106**	0.137**
	(0.029)	(0.029)	(0.013)	(0.013)	(0.043)	(0.041)
Adjusted R^2	0.629	0.628	0.586	0.589	0.570	0.567
Test for joint significant of exchange rate terms: F-statistics, [Change in adjusted R^2]						
Noninteracted	0.69		0.66		5.87**	
	[−0.0007]		[−0.0008]		[0.0122]	
Interacted with trade orientation		0.013		1.91		4.79**
		[−0.0019]		[0.0022]		[0.0093]

Notes: BLS Employment and Earnings, national data. Weighted least squares estimates with the weight being last period's employment level. Standard errors are given in parentheses. Specifications include a time trend and industry fixed effects. Number of observations is 368 for average hourly earnings and average weekly hours, and 400 for average employment.

*Significant at the 10 percent level.

**Significant at the 5 percent level.

References

Branson, W., and J. Love. 1988. United States manufacturing and the real exchange rate. In *Misalignment of exchange rates: Effects on trade and industry,* ed. R. Marston, 241-70. Chicago: University of Chicago Press.

Burgess, S., and M. Knetter. 1998. An international comparison of employment adjustment to exchange rate fluctuations. *Review of International Economics* 6 (1): 151–63.

Campa, J., and L. Goldberg. 1997. The evolving external orientation of manufacturing: Evidence from four countries. *FRBNY Economic Policy Review* (July): 53–81.

———. 1998. Employment versus wage adjustment and the U.S. dollar. NBER Working Paper no. 6749. Cambridge, Mass.: National Bureau of Economic Research.

———. 1999. Investment, pass-through and exchange rates: A cross-country comparison. *International Economic Review* 40 (2): 287–314.

Clarida, R. 1997. The real exchange rate and U.S. manufacturing profits: A theoretical framework with some empirical support. *International Journal of Finance and Economics* 2 (3): 177–88.

Davis, S., and J. Haltiwanger. 1999. Sectoral job creation and destruction responses to oil price changes and other shocks. NBER Working Paper no. 7095. Cambridge, Mass.: National Bureau of Economic Research, April.

Goldberg, P., and M. Knetter. 1997. Goods prices and exchange rates: What have we learned? *Journal of Economic Literature* 35 (3): 1243–72.

Mortensen, D. 1986. Job search and labor market analysis. In *Handbook of labor economics,* ed. O. Ashenfelter and R. Layard, vol. 2, 848–919. Amsterdam: North-Holland.

Nickell, S. J. 1986. Dynamic models of labour demand. In *Handbook of labor economics,* ed. O. Ashenfelter and R. Layard, 473–522. Amsterdam: North-Holland.

Revenga, A. 1992. Exporting jobs? The impact of import competition on employment and wages in U.S. manufacturing. *Quarterly Journal of Economics* 107 (1): 255–84.

Sheets, N. 1996. The exchange rate and profit in developed economies: An intersectoral analysis. Washington, D.C.: Board of Governors of the Federal Reserve System. Working paper.

Topel, R. 1986. Local labor markets. *Journal of Political Economy* 94 (3): S111–43.

U.S. Department of Labor. Bureau of Labor Statistics. 1997. *BLS handbook of methods.* Bulletin no. 2490, chap. 2 (Employment, hours, and earnings from the Establishment Survey). Washington, D.C.: U.S. Government Printing Office.

Comment   Andrew K. Rose

To Begin

In this paper, Goldberg and Tracy perform exactly the sort of careful empirical work which I like to see done. I'm happy someone did it. More precisely, I'm happy someone *else* did it. There are two reasons. First, they did it very well. This paper was very thorough and very careful, and the results are completely believable. But those results can, I think, be reasonably described as being "less than completely successful." There's a reason why economists differentiate between doing "theory" and "empirical work," rather than "theory work" and "empirics." It sometimes takes remarkable effort (and this paper clearly represents a lot of work) before one can run the regressions that disclose remarkably little.

This paper had to be written; it addresses a question of enormous policy import. We certainly want to know what the impacts of exchange rate changes are on labor markets, and we want to know if they differ substantially by region and industry. So Goldberg and Tracy are clearly asking a good question. What is their answer? The message I personally take away is that the effects of exchange rates on wages, employment, and hours are surprisingly small at both aggregate and disaggregated levels. While they find statistically significant differences in these impacts across regions and industries, those effects don't appear to be that economically important. Their meticulous work does not uncover economically important effects that were hidden by aggregation. Since I think that this result is probably robust (I find it hard to believe that it could be overturned by an even more disaggregated look at the data), it's a strong but negative statement. Negative results are important in this case, since they make our lives easier in a nontrivial way; it is much easier to stay at the aggregate level, if one can. So I don't want to underplay the importance of their nonresults. But they are still nonresults. We still haven't found the illusive strong sensible effects of exchange rates on labor markets.

The Question

Goldberg and Tracy are interested in seeing whether the exchange rate affects regions and industries differently across the country, and whether these effects come in the form of wage adjustments, employment growth, or changes in hours. Why is this an important issue? Industries are subject to different effects from the exchange rate depending on how export oriented they are, who their competitors are, and whether their inputs come

Andrew K. Rose is the B. T. Rocca Jr. Professor of International Trade, Economic Analysis, and Policy in the Haas School of Business at the University of California, Berkeley; acting director of the NBER International Finance and Macroeconomics Program; and a research fellow of the Centre for Economic Policy Research, London.

from abroad. And regions differ in their industrial composition. Suppose particular geographic constituencies are more dramatically affected by exchange rate pressures than others. Then political bodies that are geographically formed (e.g., the U.S. Senate) might be more willing to pass protectionist legislation than ones that are based on population (e.g., the House of Representatives). Similarly, if exchange rate changes have important industrial effects, one might expect lobbyists and pressure groups to be industrial rather than regional. For these reasons, and a hosts of others, disaggregating the effects of exchange rate changes is of great intellectual interest.

This is a formidable task, and a worthy one; the authors are clearly ambitious. At least two substantial tasks are entailed. First, the authors need to create a theoretical framework in which to construct their empirical work. Second, they have to create a data set that is disaggregated in three dimensions—time, location, and industry. Exploiting this data set is a lot easier than creating it, and unfortunately one has no clear idea of whether it will be worth all the trouble until the costs have been borne.

The theoretical part of the paper is reasonable and relatively straightforward. It forms a good framework for the paper and allows us to understand the results. It is a necessary part of the paper, but not, in my judgment, where most of the value added lies. The second part of the paper is empirical, and it is the chief contribution, so I will discuss it at greater length.

A caveat before I begin. This study is concerned with the impact of exchange rates on manufacturing trade. While historically most trade has been in goods, my home state of California is home to a large growing export-oriented service industry. The 1997 *Economic Report of the President* (table B-104) shows that in 1995, exports of services were worth $211 billion; exports of goods were valued at $576 billion. The authors are limited by the available data, but it is still important to remain aware of these limitations. And manufacturing is only around 15 percent of American employment in any case.

The Answer

The authors have some of the standard problems of using microdata. For instance, they frequently have results that are difficult to summarize (since they seem to be contradictory), for instance, exchange rate effects that differ by time period. On the other hand, they don't have one standard problem that plagues most applied economists working with large data sets. "Left-handed labor economists" earned that nickname because in a regression of 10,000 observations of anything on anything, everything is usually significant (including being left-handed). As a result, most people who do such things are informal Bayesians; they tighten significance levels with degrees of freedom. Yet in this paper, remarkably few effects are significant (manifest in the use of an asterisk to denote significance at the 10 percent level).

This is the heart of the matter. Consider table 8.1, which portrays the effects of exchange rates on wages. The estimation uses thousands of observations in an extensive panel disaggregated by time, industry, and state, split into different classes (by markups), with many controls, and both direct and indirect channels for exchange rate effects. This setup is not only theoretically sensible, but it seems to deliver the empirical goods in some dimensions; the effects of GDP are large in both economic and statistical terms. But the exchange rate effects are simply not, as the authors acknowledge. The elasticities are small, vary in sign, and cannot easily be summarized. While somewhat larger effects are found for employment, the effects essentially remain economically very small. They also seem to vary a lot over time and are often counterintuitive. Hours look even worse. Tables 8.1 through 8.3 don't present a strong prima facie case for disaggregating by region.

Table 8.4 is the crux, which reports the effects of exchange rate changes on labor market outcomes by industry. In only 8 of the 20 industries do exchange rates affect wages; 4 with positive elasticities, 4 negative, and none large. Hours and employment look similar. I interpret this evidence as saying that the effects that we all believe are buried somewhere in the data are illusive.

To Conclude

In the end, I ask myself: Have Goldberg and Tracy made the case for disaggregation? In my opinion, the answer is no. In some sense this is a negative result; a lot of careful work turned out not to deliver big results. But in an important sense, this negative result is very useful to us all. Dealing with disaggregated models and data is a pain. Finding out that aggregating across industries doesn't seem to do enormous violence is an extremely useful simplification, and we owe them a debt for discovering it.

Reference

Economic report of the president. 1997. Washington, D.C.: U.S. Government Printing Office.

Trade Flows and Wage Premiums
Does Who or What Matter?

Mary E. Lovely and J. David Richardson

9.1 Introduction

In this paper we investigate relationships between trade, wages, and the rewards to skill for U.S. workers during the period 1981–92. We isolate correlations between several types and measures of international trade and several types and measures of wage premiums, controlling for other important correlates. We find very different empirical patterns for trade with newly industrialized countries than for trade with traditional industrial partners. We also find very different empirical patterns for premiums paid to low-skilled workers than for those paid to high-skilled workers.

The broadest summary of our results is as follows. Greater U.S. trade with newly industrialized countries is associated with increased rewards to skill and reduced rewards to pure labor, consistent with heightened wage inequality and distributional conflict. The opposite association appears for trade with traditional industrial countries. It is associated with lower rewards to skill, higher rewards to pure labor, and lessened distributional conflict.

Our interpretation of these results rests on two models. The first model distinguishes intraindustry trade between two fully integrated northern countries from the intraindustry trade between them and a southern region whose factor prices vary from those in the north. North-north intra-

Mary E. Lovely is associate professor of economics at Syracuse University. J. David Richardson is professor of economics at Syracuse University, a research associate of the National Bureau of Economic Research, and a visiting fellow at the Institute for International Economics, Washington, D.C.

The authors are indebted to Donald Bruce and Chi Zhang for outstanding research assistance; to George Borjas, Robert C. Feenstra, and Alan B. Krueger for helpful comments; and to conference participants for stimulating discussion.

industry trade is entirely in differentiated, skill-intensive producer inputs. North-south intraindustry trade is the vertical exchange of labor-intensive intermediates for skill-intensive producer inputs or finished manufactures. The second model is a partial equilibrium model of industry wage premiums that are rewards for loyalty, firm-specific knowledge, or (dis)amenities. We posit different premiums for skilled and less-skilled workers, as we assume that these labor markets are segmented from each other. We use this conceptualization to predict the movement of wage and skill premiums in response to industry-specific trade surges from industrial and newly industrialized partners.

Our paper relates to several recent contributions to the literature. One group studies how wages may be affected distinctively by trade with poorer countries and by trade in inputs (international outsourcing).[1] Another group conceives and estimates industry wage premiums and the way such premiums correlate with measures of international trade.[2] Because the literature on trade and wages has been surveyed extensively elsewhere, and because our empirical approach focuses on industry wage premiums, we review here only previous research investigating the relationship between trade and these premiums.

Dickens and Katz (1987), Krueger and Summers (1988), and Helwege (1992) find that industry premiums persist over time. Dickens and Lang (1988) and Katz and Summers (1989a) find that despite the stability of the ranking of these premiums across industries, they are correlated with trade flows: Wage premiums are negatively correlated with imports and positively correlated with exports. Using more detailed data on trade protection and allowing for endogenous protection, Gaston and Trefler (1994) confirm the positive wage effect of exports and the negative effect of imports.

Recent contributions to the literature ask whether all trade flows have similar effects. For example, Fung and Huizinga (1997) find evidence from Canada that freer intraindustry, as opposed to interindustry, trade raises workers wages. Anderton and Brenton (1998) take a different approach, distinguishing trade flows by characteristics of the source country. They find that increased imports from low-wage countries explain some of the rise in inequality among low-skill-intensive industries.

We make several contributions to this literature in models, measurement, and methods. Our theoretical models reveal that there are no obvious correlations between wages and global outsourcing and price trends, once one allows for inter- and intraindustry trade between and within a

---

1. Lawrence (1996), Sachs and Shatz (1998), Feenstra and Hanson (1996a, 1996b, 1997), Campa and Goldberg (1997), and Feenstra (1997).
2. Topel (1994), Borjas and Ramey (1995), Krueger and Summers (1988), Gibbons and Katz (1992), Kahn (1997), and Richardson and Khripounova (1998).

primary-producing "southern" tier of countries that also can assemble final manufactures and a "northern" tier of countries that assemble final manufactures and produce the intermediate components from which they are assembled. By measuring trade with three groups of trading partners—industrial countries, newly industrialized countries, and primary-product producers—we are able to estimate the correlation of trade flows from each partner group with wage premiums. Moreover, using econometric methods that separate pure wage premiums from the return to an individual worker's education, we are able to estimate the relationship between different types of trade flows and the skill differential. Thus, the paper broadens the existing literature by looking simultaneously at the distributional effects of trade with both developing- and developed-country partners.[3] In the sections that follow, we discuss measurement, and then move on to models, specification, results, and conclusions.

9.2   U.S. Trade Patterns by Trading-Partner Aggregates

Much of the concern expressed in the trade and wages debate (e.g., Lawrence 1996; Sachs and Shatz 1998) has focused on increased trade with newly industrialized countries and the ability of imports to displace U.S. production in industries that pay wage premiums, especially to blue-collar employees. These imports may take the form of finished goods that displace domestic production directly. Alternatively, the imports may take the form of outsourcing, defined as the import of components or assembly by firms who previously may have produced these inputs internally. As noted by Feenstra and Hanson (1996b), certain industries have a high propensity to outsource because their production processes can be separated into self-contained stages that vary considerably in the relative intensity with which they use labor of different skill types. These features of production and the search for low-cost workers are widely believed to be the impetus behind the outsourcing of activities, such as product assembly, to newly industrialized countries.

We investigate differences in industrial and newly industrialized countries' trade patterns with the United States by dividing countries into three broad groups on the basis of level of industrialization. These groupings are the industrialized countries (I countries), newly industrialized countries (N countries), and a group of primary producers (P countries). The appendix contains a list of countries in each grouping. The trade data

---

3. Rodrik (1998) notes that virtually all of the empirical studies in the literature looking at the labor market consequences of trade have focused on trade with developing countries, but argues that trade with developed countries matters for U.S. wages. Our findings support the view that attention to trade with traditional partners is clearly warranted. However, the nature of this trade, and its wage effects, may be quite different from those found for trade with developing countries.

come from the Statistics Canada compilation of United Nations bilateral trade by commodity, classified according to the Standard International Trade Classification (SITC), revision 3. Trade values are expressed in millions of (current) U.S. dollars. We aggregate data on U.S. exports and imports, annually from 1980 through 1994, across products and trading partners in ways described later and in the appendix. Virtually all U.S. merchandise trade is covered, although it is "allocated" among manufacturing subindustries in the United States.

For each group of trading partners, we also divide industries into three categories—producer nondurables, producer durables, and consumer goods—as described in detail in the appendix.[4] The producer-goods breakdown into nondurables and durables conforms very roughly to a distinction between industries producing intermediates and those producing capital goods. Raw materials, agricultural, and mineral products are associated with manufacturing sectors that use them as intermediate inputs; for example, raw crops are associated with manufactured foods. Capital goods, which are all manufactures, are assigned to the manufacturing sector in which they are produced.[5]

Several aspects of the trade data are noteworthy.

- The United States typically trades inputs, not outputs. In 1994, U.S. exports of producer goods swamped U.S. exports of consumer goods; they are typically three to four times as large.[6] More surprisingly, the same is true of U.S. imports, although the corresponding ratio is smaller, roughly two to one.

- By 1994, the cross-sector pattern of input trade with newly industrialized countries was very similar to the patterns with traditional industrial trading partners, and roughly one-half the size in the typical manufacturing sector. In electrical equipment (SIC 36), however, newly industrialized and industrial countries had become equally important.[7]

---

4. In our empirical research, however, category trade rarely correlated in any significant way with wages or returns to skill, suggesting perhaps that our category disaggregation was simply too crude. These results are not reported here.

5. As if the "own-sector" were the major purchaser of these capital goods. The same is done for intermediate manufactures, such as leather. Thus, imports of passenger railway cars are assigned to transport equipment (SIC 37), even if they are purchased and used by mass-transit service providers, and purchases of leather are assigned to leather products (SIC 31), even if they are purchased and used by apparel makers. That this assignment is closer to the typical case than one might imagine is demonstrated in Feenstra and Hanson (1997, 18).

6. The producer-goods breakdown into intermediates and capital conforms roughly to manufacturing distinctions between nondurables and durables. Fabricated metal products (SIC 24) was the only two-digit SIC sector where SITC trade in producer goods was subdivided into nondurables (SITC 69) and durables (SITC 81). Computers and office machines (SITC 75) were divided in half between capital equipment and consumer goods.

7. The exceptions are food (SIC 20), where U.S. trade in final and intermediate goods is about the same size, and apparel, footwear, and transport equipment (SIC 23, 31, and 37), where U.S. imports of consumer goods bulk somewhat larger than the norm in other sectors.

- Trade growth was strong with all types of countries, but transactions with industrial and newly industrialized countries swamped those with primary producers; they were five to eight times as large (except in imports of oil, apparel, and footwear, where transactions with primary producers either swamped or rivaled those with others in size).

- Two-way trade was, in 1994, a very prominent feature of U.S. trade in producer goods with industrial and newly industrialized countries. That was also true in 1980 for nondurables. But for capital goods in 1980, two-way trade characterized U.S. transactions only with its traditional industrial partners. Large net exports (one-way trade) characterized transactions with the N countries—that were only partway to becoming newly industrialized in that year, of course.

- One-way (interindustry) trade characterizes the relatively small amount of U.S. trade in producer goods with primary producers; oil flows one way and intermediates and capital goods flow the other. They also finance modest net U.S. imports in two final goods, apparel and footwear. With primary producers, two-way U.S. trade characterizes only food, both input trade and output trade.[8]

We use these data, scaled by industry shipments, as one measure of trade, "trade intensity," and examine its correlations with wage and skill premiums. We also use these data to create a variety of Grubel-Lloyd indices (GLIs) of intraindustry trade.[9]

Figure 9.1 presents the GLI breakdown by industry type and by goods type. In panel A, one can see that intraindustry trade is a large share of trade with all three groups of countries.[10] Panel B shows a breakdown by goods type, with intraindustry trade in producer goods of both types, durables and nondurables, being very high. Two-way trade in consumer goods is much less important than it is for producer goods.

Figure 9.2 shows Grubel-Lloyd indices for 19 industries. The industries show a great deal of variation in the importance of intraindustry trade. Almost all trade is intraindustry in SIC 24 (lumber), but less than one-half of trade is intraindustry in SIC 21 (tobacco), SIC 23 (apparel), SIC 29 (petroleum), and SIC 31 (leather). Although intraindustry trade fell in some industries during the mid-1980s, it rose in others and shows no discernible pattern in many others.

---

8. In 1980, U.S. capital-goods trade with the N countries had the same size and pattern as U.S. capital goods trade with the P countries. By 1994, the former had left the latter in the dust, especially in electrical and scientific/professional equipment (SIC 36 and 38).

9. We control for other variables, including industry price indexes, which some argue are better measures of global pressure than trade-intensity variables, as the debate over "factor content" calculation illustrates.

10. Grubel-Lloyd indices are defined as $GLI_j = 1 - [|X_j - IM_j| / (X_j + IM_j)]$, where X_j is the value of exports from country group j, and IM_j is the value of imports from j. See Grubel and Lloyd (1971).

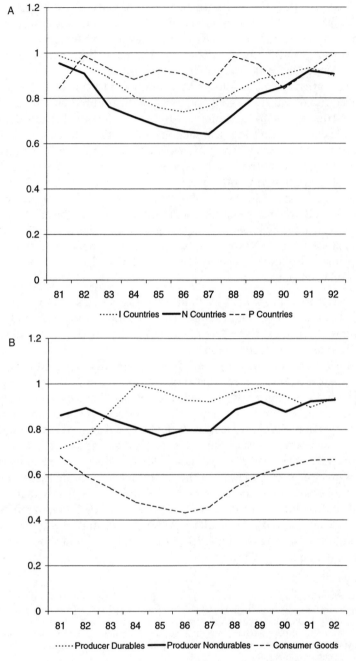

Fig. 9.1 Grubel-Lloyd index, 1981–92: (*A*) by country type; (*B*) by goods type

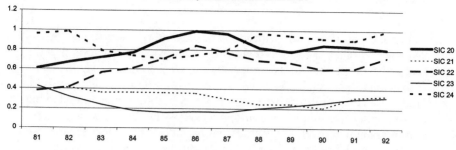

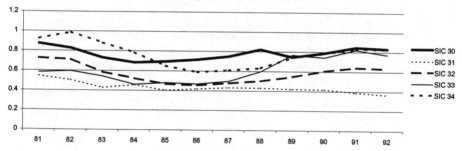

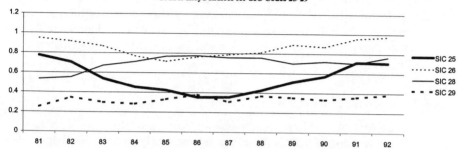

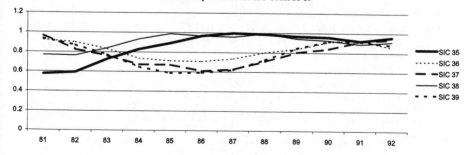

Fig. 9.2   Grubel-Lloyd indices for 19 industries

Although by 1994 trade with industrial and newly industrialized partners seems similar at the two-digit level, other evidence suggests that the skill intensity of the goods traded may differ.[11] Industry classifications span subproducts and processes with widely differing skill intensities. Trade with newly industrialized countries may be more concentrated in the less-skill-intensive subproducts and processes within the broad aggregates than is trade with traditional industrial partners. In the next section, we present a model of trade in which an industry consists of two distinct processes. The home country trades manufactures with both industrial and newly industrialized partners, but the factor contents of these trade flows are quite different. In this context, we see that shocks to the trading system have different wage and distributional implications depending on whether they originate in the economies of industrial or newly industrialized partners.

9.3 Theoretical Considerations

We explore two separate theoretical approaches to understanding the wage implications of trade with industrial and newly industrialized countries. First, we consider a model that maintains many of the standard assumptions of neoclassical trade theory with intermediate goods, including perfect intersectoral factor mobility. This model provides a basis for understanding why the relationship between trade flows, outsourcing, and the skill differential is more complex than simple intuition and popular alarm allow. Similar changes in the volume and country source of trade can arise from alternative causes and may be correlated with either positive or negative movements in the relative return to skill. The model provides some cautionary lessons for our empirical work, which correlates wage changes with volume of trade measures and with intraindustry trade.

Second, we deviate from the standard neoclassical assumptions to permit industry wage premiums. Using a general form of compensating differentials to explain the existence of industry-specific wages, we present a framework for thinking about the effect of trade shocks on industry-specific returns to skilled and unskilled labor.[12] We use this framework to develop methods for estimating the relationship between wage premiums and trade flows.

11. Grossman (1982) and Bailey and Sandy (1998).
12. Anderson (1998, 6) concludes in a recent survey paper that this conception explains, at least, an important part of measured interindustry wage differentials. The other important part is thought to spring from unobservable worker characteristics that are valued differently by different industries in matching (sorting) equilibria, as modeled, for example, by Gibbons and Katz (1992). We do not attempt to explore this explanation, nor do we address the econometric selection problems it raises.

9.3.1 A General Equilibrium Model with Outsourcing

We review here the main findings of the model presented in Lovely (1999). The purpose of this formal modeling effort is to capture the response to shocks of a human-capital-abundant economy that trades with both developed and developing countries. The economy is simultaneously engaged in the outsourcing of labor-intensive production activities to relatively labor abundant countries and in intraindustry trade in producer inputs with other human-capital-abundant countries. This model of intraindustry trade in horizontally and vertically differentiated inputs is built on Ethier's (1982) model of the international division of labor and Feenstra and Hanson's (1996a) model of outsourcing.

There are two regions of the world, distinguished by their proportionate endowments of pure labor and human capital. The "South"—representing the newly industrialized countries—is labor abundant relative to the "North"—representing the traditional industrial countries. Production patterns differ between the two regions and factor-price equalization between the South and the North does not obtain. The South produces a traditional good, grain, and engages in assembly of bundles of northern-producer intermediates into final manufactures. While assembly is human capital intensive relative to grain, it is labor intensive relative to producer intermediates.[13] Comparative North-South factor endowments are such that producer intermediates are produced only in the North. This relative intensity ranking and specialization pattern capture in a simple way the relative intensity continuum developed by Feenstra and Hanson (1996a).

The North consists of two countries, "East" and "West," with the West designated as the home country. These countries have similar proportions of labor to human capital, in the sense that both produce positive quantities of assembly activities and producer intermediates in equilibrium. Producer intermediates and assembly use labor and human capital. As in Ethier's (1982) division-of-labor model, there is an international external economy from diversity in producer intermediates. Because we assume that there is free trade in producer intermediates, the productivity of intermediates in final manufactures will be the same in the East and the West and, as shown by Ethier (1982, 396), factor-price equalization will obtain in equilibrium. For this reason, we are able to treat the North as an integrated equilibrium.

The equilibrium is characterized by two-way trade between northern countries (East-West trade) in producer intermediates and by outsourcing, which we define as southern assembly of northern-producer intermediates into final manufactures. Intermediate varieties of differentiated inputs are

---

13. We assume there are no factor-intensity reversals.

exchanged by the East and West, generating an intraindustry flow in producer inputs. The direction of trade in final manufactures is indeterminate, as it depends on the equilibrium location of assembly activities. If the East, for example, produces a larger share of world assembly activities than its share of world income, it will be a net exporter of assembly services, visible as net exports of final manufactures. North-South intraindustry trade, in contrast, does not involve the exchange of intermediate varieties but, rather, reflects stages of production. The South assembles producer intermediates, which are produced and exported by the North. Again, the direction of net trade in final manufactures is indeterminate. We assume that the South is a net exporter of assembly activity and that final manufactures flow from South to North. The South also exports the traditional good, grain. Its exports of grain and assembly activities fund its net imports of producer intermediates, which are embodied in its consumption of final manufactures. Thus, the model is characterized by both conventional interindustry trade and by horizontal (East-West) and vertical (North-South) intraindustry trade. We turn now to a more detailed description of the model.

Production in the South

The South produces grain (G) and assembly activities (A_S) with production functions that we assume are linearly homogenous. Grain is chosen to be the numeraire and it is produced using labor only. Because of this production technology, the grain sector determines the southern wage. Assembly activities require both labor and human capital. We assume that the production technology for assembly is linearly homogeneous and twice differentiable. Because human capital is used only in assembly in the South, it has the characteristics of a sector-specific factor. Southern labor is fixed in total supply and is allocated so that its value of marginal product is equalized across sectors. Thus, a change in the stock of human capital will lead to a reallocation of labor across sectors without altering the southern wage.

Production in the North

Because the two countries of the North have similar endowments and engage in free trade in producer intermediates, we treat the East and West as an integrated equilibrium. The North produces two goods, assembly (A_N) and producer intermediates, (x_i), where i indexes intermediate varieties. We assume that both are freely and costlessly traded. Assembly activities are supplied by perfect competitors using human capital (H_A) and unskilled labor (L_A) in a constant-returns-to-scale technology. These factors may also be combined, again in a constant-returns-to-scale technology, to produce factor bundles (f), which are used to produce intermediates. In the final stage, intermediates and assembly combine to form the finished manufactured good (M). Both factors are intersectorally mobile and internationally immobile.

The production technology for assembling the manufactured good M is given by

$$(1) \qquad M \;=\; \min\left[A, \left(\sum_{i=1}^{n} x_i^{\beta} \right)^{(1/\beta)} \right],$$

where A is assembly activities, which may be performed in the North or outsourced to the South ($A = A_S + A_N$). Intermediate varieties are imperfect substitutes; β measures the degree of differentiation of intermediates ($0 < \beta < 1$). The productivity of intermediates exhibits constant returns to scale for a given number of intermediate varieties and increasing returns with higher degrees of specialization, as measured by the number of intermediate producers n. These economies are external to the finished manufactures industry and each competitive firm assembling finished manufactures takes n as given.

As does Ethier (1982), we assume that all intermediates have identical homothetic cost functions, implying that in equilibrium any produced variety will be produced in the common quantity x. The properties of the monopolistically competitive sector are well known.[14] Intermediates producers equate marginal cost and marginal revenue, setting a price for intermediates that is proportional to the price of factor bundles. Free entry implies zero profits in equilibrium and that the common value of x will be a constant. The price of finished manufactures is the international trading price, P_M. Free entry generates zero profits in the assembly of intermediates into final goods, implying that the value of finished manufactures equals the value of total factor bundles embodied in intermediates plus the value of total assembly activity.

Market Equilibrium

The free-trade relative price of manufactures to grain, the two final goods in the model, equates world supply and demand. We assume that demand is identical across countries and individuals and that it takes a simple Cobb-Douglas form, so that world expenditure on final manufactures is a constant share of world income.

The demand for assembly activities must equal the supply of assembly activities. Given the Leontief technology for creating final manufactures from assembly and producer inputs, clearance in the market for assembly

---

14. Because intermediate varieties are imperfect substitutes, each producer experiences some market power. There is free entry into the industry and the number of firms is large enough so that each firm behaves as a monopolistic competitor. Each intermediate producer takes the price of factor bundles as given.

activities may be written as $A = M$. Similarly, clearance in the market for producer intermediates may be written as $n^{\alpha}x = M$.[15]

The comparative-static exercises that we review here reflect our judgment about the most important changes in the trading environment during the time period of our empirical analysis, 1981–92. We consider three shocks to the international trading system. The first is an increase in human capital in the South, which in the model is used only in manufacturing. This simple exercise is meant to capture the response of the economy to a variety of shocks that enhance the South's ability to perform outsourcing activities, including increasing human-capital-to-labor proportions, particularly among the newly industrialized countries; the development of local technology and managerial stocks; and the provision of supporting public infrastructures. Our second comparative-static exercise considers an increase in the relative abundance of human capital in the North. As documented by Baldwin and Cain (1997) the share of the U.S. labor force completing 13 or more years of education rose from 38 percent of the labor force in 1980 to 53 percent in 1992. Our third exercise considers demand shocks to the manufacturing sector, reflecting the growing demand for capital goods and other manufactures as developing countries have pursued growth and liberalization of restrictions on manufactured imports, as documented by Rodrik (1994).

An Increase in Southern Human Capital

This first exercise shows how growth in the southern human capital endowment concentrates assembly in the South, increasing the extent of outsourcing between the South and the North. An increase in human capital in the South raises the share of southern labor devoted to assembly activity, so as to ensure equal-value marginal products across sectors in the South. The additional southern assembly places downward pressure on the world price of assembly services relative to intermediates, inducing the North to increase production of and intraindustry trade in producer intermediates. These changes alter northern factor prices, driving up the return to human capital and driving down the return to pure labor, while increasing the East-West exchange of producer input varieties. These changes occur even though the relative price of manufactures falls relative to the southern traditional good, grain, to ensure international final-goods market clearance.[16] This case illustrates the effect of an increase in the

---

15. The same results obtain from a more general Leontief technology in which one or both inputs are multiplied by a scalar, which would in turn scale the relationship between $n^{\alpha}x$ and A. Throughout our analysis of the model, we assume that the northern price-output response is normal (in Ethier's terminology, the intersectoral effect outweighs the scale effect) and that this assumption implies that the relative supply curve for manufactures is upward sloping.

16. If final-goods prices are held fixed, the proportionate change in the skill differential will be larger. Of course, such a conditional exercise ignores market clearance.

southern supply of assembly—it will result in an increase in intraindustry trade that is accompanied by an increase in the northern skill differential, defined as the return to skill relative to the return to pure labor.

An Increase in Northern Human Capital

A second exercise examines an increase in the northern human capital endowment. An increase in human capital raises the production of intermediates and reduces assembly activity in the North, holding the relative price of factor bundles fixed (a Rybczynski effect), raising productivity of intermediates in manufacturing. Taken by itself in isolation from price adjustments and other endogenous responses, this boost in productivity would raise the return to human capital and reduce the return to pure labor. The increase in producer intermediates, however, calls forth an increase in global assembly activity. In both the North and the South, the relative price of assembly must rise to induce this new activity. In the North, the price of assembly rises relative to the price of intermediates (factor bundles); in the South, it rises relative to the price of grain. But in the world as a whole, the price of assembly-and-intermediates combined into final manufactures must fall relative to the price of grain. That is, world market clearance requires a decrease in the relative price of final manufactures. These effects may combine to decrease the relative price of human-capital-intensive factor bundles and the return to human capital relative to labor. For our purposes, we emphasize that this decrease in the skill differential may occur even though intraindustry trade between the South and the North has risen due to greater outsourcing of assembly activity. This case illustrates the effect of an increase in the global demand for assembly—it can result in an increase in intraindustry trade that is accompanied by a decrease in the northern skill differential.

Demand Shocks

Shocks to the demand for final manufactures can be treated in the model as an exogenous increase in the share of income spent on finished manufactures. A positive shock of this sort raises the price of final manufactures relative to grain, bringing forth greater northern output of producer intermediates and reducing northern assembly activity. In the South, resources are transferred from the traditional sector, grain, to the assembly of northern inputs as the price of assembly activity relative to grain increases. These adjustments raise the relative price of factor bundles used in producer intermediates in the North, increasing the relative return to human capital there. Thus, a positive shock to manufacturing demand raises the extent of outsourcing from the South and the skill differential in the North. When the source of the disturbance is a finished-manufactures demand shock, then outsourcing and the skill differential will be positively correlated.

Summary of Comparative-Statics Results

These comparative-statics exercises have a number of lessons concerning the relationship between the northern skill differential and trade with industrial and newly industrialized countries.

• Final-goods price changes do not tell the whole story when we move away from the two-by-two Heckscher-Ohlin framework. Skill-intensive final-goods prices may be negatively correlated with the skill differential.
• Neither an increase in outsourcing nor an increase in North-South trade intensity is always associated with a larger skill differential. Since both trade flows and factor prices are endogenously determined, unless the production structure ties outsourcing directly to factor-price movements, there is no reason that outsourcing and wages need move together in one direction or the other.
• The sign of the correlations between North-South trade volumes or intraindustry trade and the skill differential depends on the source of the shock. These exercises suggest that shocks that raise the supply of assembly in the South raise the northern skill differential. The initial excess supply of assembly induces a reduction of these activities in the North and an expansion of complementary producer inputs. These production responses bid up the price of human capital relative to pure labor in the North.
• Shocks that raise the global demand for assembly lead to different results for the skill differential. An increase in the northern human capital endowment creates an excess supply of producer inputs and excess demand for assembly activities, at initial prices. The demand for southern assembly rises, raising outsourcing in manufacturing, but the skill differential decreases as prices adjust to obtain market clearance in producer intermediates and final manufactures.
• An increase in the global demand for final manufactures raises the relative return to the factor used intensively (skilled labor in the North) or exclusively (skilled labor in the South) in that sector.

These observations reflect the fact that outsourcing is one endogenous piece in the system, just as prices are another. The most direct formal testing of the model's implications would require time-series data on relative wages for a group of countries and measurement of the true underlying shocks to endowments, demand parameters, and so on.

Given the enormous data requirements of such an approach, we consider a second approach that uses the interindustry variation in wages to assess the relationship between trade with industrial and newly industrialized countries and the relative return to skill. This second approach has the advantage of being both empirically tractable and policy relevant. Much of the concern about heightened trade with newly industrialized countries is its effect on "good jobs"—manufacturing jobs that pay above-average wages[17]—an issue that requires one to deviate from models in which all similar workers receive the same return, regardless of the sector in which they are employed. Indeed such industry wage premiums for comparable workers are a ubiquitous fact of life for both industrial and newly industrialized countries (Anderson 1998; Cragg and Epelbaum 1996; Kahn 1997; Krueger 1998; Robertson 1998).

9.3.2   A Model with Interindustry Wage Premiums

The existence of interindustry wage premiums remains a puzzle for labor economists. Wage premiums may be attributable to the fact that the industry of affiliation is important per se, as in the case of compensating differentials, or it may be that industry affiliation is systematically correlated with unobserved worker attributes (as would result from a worker-sorting process based on unobserved ability), or both.[18] We take a broad version of the former approach, treating industry premiums as compensation for particular industry characteristics.

We model the labor market in a partial equilibrium context, incorporating the pattern of specialization used in the previous general-equilibrium model. Each firm takes the outside wage as given, but pays a premium to compensate workers for loyalty, firm-specific skill acquisition, or for the disutility from higher effort, longer work weeks, unpleasant or risky working conditions, and so on, associated with employment in the industry. Firms are assumed to face two distinct labor markets, one for unskilled workers and another for skilled workers, and may pay a different premium above the outside wage to each type of worker. We assume that the (dis)utility arising from employment in the industry varies within the population and that workers in each labor market can be arrayed from those who experience low to those who experience high (dis)utility from working in a given industry. Based on these supply conditions, a firm in a particular industry faces an upward-sloping supply curve for labor of either type.

We assume that the demand curve for each type of labor for a given industry is downward sloping. We conceive changes in the volume of trade as shocks to the demand for labor. Changes in the volume of trade arise outside the industry from fundamental shocks such as endowment changes in the South or in other northern partners, or in the global demand for industry output, as previously described.

The pattern of specialization in our general-equilibrium model provides grounds for reasoning differently about volume-of-trade shocks for north-

17. For an expression of this concern, see, for example, Borjas and Ramey (1995).
18. Once again, a more direct approach would measure the true underlying shocks to endowments, demand parameters, and so on, rather than the admittedly endogenous trade volumes. The further assumption we are making is that the volume of trade shocks is uncorrelated with shocks to industry labor-supply curves.

ern and southern trading partners. Northern countries form an integrated market equilibrium in which relative wages and returns to skill are everywhere comparable, whereas southern factor returns differ from those in the North.[19] Trade among northern countries involves significant "horizontal" two-way trade in intermediate goods; North-South trade involves "vertical" trade of skill-intensive intermediates for labor-intensive finished manufactures.

Trade between northern partners involves the two-way exchange of skill-intensive inputs as well as trade in products of different skill intensity. We thus conceive an increase in imports in the same industrial classification from industrial countries as a negative shock to the demand for skilled labor.[20] Northern imports are substitutes for skill-intensive inputs or processes, reducing the demand for skills in the domestic industry. This shift in the demand curve for skilled labor moves the industry down the labor-supply curve, reducing the premium paid to skilled workers. If the size of the industry is held fixed (i.e., controlling for the value of industry shipments), the composition of domestic production shifts away from skill-intensive activities toward labor-intensive activities. Thus, when shipments are held constant, an increase in northern imports should be associated with an increase in the premium paid to pure labor in the industry. The increased premium is necessary to draw additional workers (who have a higher (dis)utility from industry characteristics) into the industry.

Conversely, industry exports to northern partners are assumed to correspond to increased demand for skilled workers and lower demand for unskilled workers, again holding shipments fixed. Thus, a larger volume of exports to I-country partners should be associated with a higher premium for skilled workers and a lower premium for labor.

In contrast, exports and imports from southern newly industrialized countries reflect vertical-chain trade based on differences in factor proportions, and reflected in North-South factor-price differences. Imports from southern partners are assumed to substitute for labor-intensive activities within the industry, such as assembly. Consequently, we view an increase in southern imports as a negative shock to the demand for unskilled labor. Given an upward-sloping supply of labor to the industry, this shock should result in a reduced premium for unskilled workers. Holding industry shipments constant, increased southern imports imply a shift within the domestic industry toward skill-intensive activities. Thus, we expect increases in N-country imports to be associated with a higher premium for skilled workers.

---

19. Even interindustry wage differentials are similar in rank ordering, although less similar in size, among industrialized countries (Kahn 1997).

20. For example, one northern country's increased northern imports would be the expected consequence of human capital growth in the other northern country.

Exports to southern partners are expected to raise the relative demand for skilled workers, just as southern imports do. An increase in exports to newly industrialized partners is likely to be based on comparative advantage and, thus, to raise the relative demand for high-skilled intermediate inputs or processes within the industry. Using this reasoning, we expect an increase in N-country exports, as well as N-country imports, to be associated with a lower premium for labor and a higher premium for skilled workers. We note again the asymmetry between our treatment of I-country and N-country trade.

In the next section, we use this framework to develop a method for estimating the correlation between premiums for skilled and unskilled workers and trade flows distinguished by trading-partner aggregates.

9.4 Estimating the Correlation among Wage Premiums, Skill Premiums, and Trade Flows

To estimate the correlation among wage premiums, skill premiums, and trade flows, we use two approaches. The first approach modifies a standard two-step procedure for estimating industry wage premiums and their correlation with trade flows, by distilling a pure wage premium and a separate industry-specific premium to skill. The second approach estimates the wage and skill premiums and their relationship to trade flows in a one-step procedure. We are able to account for individual fixed effects in this second approach, thereby controlling in some measure for the way that industry premiums may reflect industry selection by heterogeneous workers who sort themselves according to unmeasured characteristics. In both approaches, we associate skill with years of formal education.

9.4.1 Cross-Sectional Estimation

To estimate the premium paid to unskilled and skilled workers, we modify an approach used by Dickens and Katz (1987), Dickens and Lang (1988), Katz and Summers (1989a), Gaston and Trefler (1994), and Richardson and Khripounova (1997) to estimate interindustry wage premiums and their correlations with trade flows. In the first stage of this procedure, industry wage premiums are estimated. Our modification of the procedure is to simultaneously estimate an industry premium to pure labor and an industry-specific return to education (skill).

Let $i = 1, 2, \ldots, I_j$ index workers in industry j. Let $\ln(w_{ij})$ be the natural logarithim of the hourly wage of individual i in industry j, X_{ij} be a vector of individual characteristics that affect wages, and S_{ij} the years of schooling of individual i in industry j. In the first stage of our procedure, we estimate the following set of equations for each year in the sample period:

$$(2) \quad \ln(w_{ij}) = X_{ij}\beta_X + D_j w_L^* + D_j S_{ij} w_S^* + \varepsilon_{ij}, \quad i = 1, \ldots, I_j, j = 1, \ldots, J,$$

where D_{ij} is a dummy for industry j, β_X, w_L^*, and w_S^* are vectors of estimated coefficients and ε_{ij} is an error term assumed to be independent and identically distributed. We interpret w_L^* as the premium to pure labor in industry j, and w_S^* as the premium to skill (education) in industry j. Because our data include 20 industries[21] and 12 sample years, we estimate 240 premiums to labor and 240 premiums to skill.

We use these sets of estimated premiums as dependent variables in a second-stage regression, designed to estimate the relationship between unskilled and skilled premiums and industry-specific trade flows. Let Z_j be a vector of industry characteristics other than trade and T_j be a vector of measures of trade flows. The second-stage regressions take the form

$$(3) \quad w_L^* = Z_{jt}\rho_L + T_{jt}\beta_L + \mu_{jt}, \qquad j = 1,\ldots,J,\ t = 1,\ldots,T,$$

$$w_S^* = Z_{jt}\rho_S + T_{jt}\beta_S + v_{jt}, \qquad j = 1,\ldots,J,\ t = 1,\ldots,T,$$

where μ_{jt} and v_{jt} are random error terms. As discussed by Dickens and Katz (1987) and Borjas (1987), the dependent variables in the second-stage regressions are themselves estimated regression coefficients. Hence, the disturbances in these regressions are heteroskedastic. Because the exact form of the heteroskedasticity in these regressions is not known, we use White's (1980) method to estimate robust standard errors for the second-stage coefficients.

To control for economywide changes in the return to labor and skills, and general-equilibrium factor return changes due to product-price changes, we include year dummies and industry producer price indexes among the elements of Z_j. The elements of the estimated coefficient vectors β_L and β_S indicate the relationship between our measures of trade and the premium paid to labor and skill, respectively. We estimate this relationship for several trade measures. One is trade intensity—industry imports and exports, expressed as a share of industry shipments. A second disaggregates by partner, distinguishing industry imports and exports with countries in each of the three groups, industrial, newly industrialized, and primary-producer countries, also expressed as a share of industry shipments. A third measure employs GLIs of the extent of two-way intraindustry trade in the industry, and a fourth measure defines GLIs for each of the three partner groups.

9.4.2   Fixed-Effects Estimation

In the second approach, we estimate the correlations between trade flows and the skill differential, taking advantage of the panel nature of our individual data and controlling to some degree for worker heterogeneity.

---

21. Nonmanufacturing is the base industry against which the 20 premiums are measured.

We regress the log of hourly earnings on years of education and other individual controls, interpreting the industry-specific intercepts as the return to pure labor and the industry-specific coefficients on educational attainment as the premium to skill. We look for correlations between these premiums and trade measures by adding two sets of trade variables to the standard wage equation, T_j, and T_j interacted with S:

$$(4) \quad \ln(w_{ijt}) = X_{ijt}\beta_X + D_{ijt}w_L^* + D_{ijt}S_{ijt}w_S^* + T_{ijt}\beta_L^* + T_{ijt}S_{itj}\beta_S^* + \eta_{it},$$

$$i = 1,\ldots,I_j, \; j = 1,\ldots,J, \; t = 1,\ldots,T,$$

where all variables are as previously defined and η_{it} is an error term assumed to be independent and identically distributed. We interpret w_L^* as the average premium to pure labor in industry j, and w_S^* as the average premium to skill (education) in industry j paid during the whole sample period. The interaction terms β_L^* and β_S^* indicate the correlation of these premiums with trade measures.[22] The trade measures we use are the same set we use in the two-stage procedure, imports and exports, expressed as a share of industry shipments, in the aggregate and by trading partner group. We also use the aggregate and partner-specific GLIs of intraindustry trade. As before we control for time-dependent changes in relative prices, which themselves may be correlated with trade volumes in general equilibrium (including as controls an industry-specific producer price index, PPI_{jt}, and the interaction of this variable with education) and for trends in the return to labor and human capital that affect the economy as a whole, but are not related to trade patterns in particular industries (including dummy variables for year, Y_t, both directly and interacted with education).

In this approach, wages could clearly be affected by unobserved characteristics of each individual. These individual effects could be random or fixed. If they are random, an ordinary least squares (OLS) estimation of equation (4) will understate the standard errors, perhaps substantially. If they are fixed and correlated with the trade variables, then our estimated coefficients for these variables are subject to omitted variable bias. For example, individuals with high motivation or high-quality schooling might be the first ones attracted to (or recruited by) industries with strong export growth. We follow the standard approach to this issue. We estimate both a random- and a fixed-effects model and then use a Hausman test to determine which one applies.[23] The test results always support the use of a fixed-

---

22. Including industry dummy variables reduces the extent of problems caused by correlation across errors from individuals in the same industry, but it also causes collinearity with the trade-volume measures, making estimation of these effects difficult.

23. To be specific, we use the "xthaus" procedure in Stata (1995 release). In our case, this procedure uses the Baltagi (1985) generalization of the Hausman test for an unbalanced panel.

effects specification, so we use that as the basis of the results presented here.

The use of a fixed-effects model is not without cost. This model effectively eliminates variation in initial education across individuals, and may therefore make it difficult to estimate β_S with precision. However, fixed effects do not eliminate all variation in the interaction between individual education and the trade measures, which is the variation needed to estimate β_S. Some variation remains both because individuals obtain more education and because trade flows change over time.[24]

9.5   Data and Base Regressions

Our data on individuals and their personal and employment characteristics were drawn from the Panel Study on Income Dynamics (PSID). We selected the PSID because it is a longitudinal panel, permitting us in our second approach to control for individual fixed effects when we estimate the return to skill (measured as years of formal education).[25]

To rule out people with long-term employment problems, we include those individuals in the data set only for years in which they had earnings and that were preceded or followed by another sample year in which they had earnings. Following standard practice with the PSID (see, e.g., Abraham and Farber 1987), we also restrict our sample to individuals between 18 and 60 years old who are not retired, permanently disabled, self-employed, employed by the government, or residents of Alaska, Hawaii, or Washington, D.C. The sample includes workers from all industries, including those employed outside the manufacturing sector. We begin with information on 6,606 individuals. After deleting years with no earnings or missing information for job tenure or education, we are left with 6,477 individuals and 41,834 observations for these individuals. Following standard practice with the PSID, our dependent variable is the log of average hourly earnings, defined as total earned income during the previous year divided by total hours worked during the previous year, divided by the GNP implicit price deflator for consumption. Table 9.1 describes our individual control variables. Table 9.2 reports typical cross-sectional estimates of coefficients for the control variables used in equation (2), almost all significant and of familiar size from studies of this sort.

The control variables listed in table 9.1, along with year dummies, were used to estimate a base version of equation (4) that omits measures of trade. Figure 9.3 displays these fixed-effects estimates of the industry-

24. The years-of-education variable in the Panel Study on Income Dynamics has some implausible entries. We developed an error-correction procedure designed primarily to eliminate cases in which an individual's education declined over time.

25. As shown by Haisken-DeNew and Schmidt (1998), about one-half of the cross-sectional variation in wages can be accounted for by individual effects.

Table 9.1 **Definitions of Control Variables and Summary Statistics**

Variable	Definition	Mean	(Std. Dev.)
Food	Individual is employed in SIC 20	0.015	(0.120)
Tobacco	Individual is employed in SIC 21	0.001	(0.034)
Textile	Individual is employed in SIC 22	0.004	(0.060)
Apparel	Individual is employed in SIC 23	0.010	(0.101)
Lumber	Individual is employed in SIC 24	0.009	(0.094)
Furniture	Individual is employed in SIC 25	0.005	(0.073)
Paper	Individual is employed in SIC 26	0.005	(0.069)
Printing	Individual is employed in SIC 27	0.016	(0.126)
Chemical	Individual is employed in SIC 28	0.012	(0.111)
Petroleum	Individual is employed in SIC 29	0.002	(0.039)
Rubber	Individual is employed in SIC 30	0.006	(0.080)
Leather	Individual is employed in SIC 31	0.008	(0.088)
Stone	Individual is employed in SIC 32	0.005	(0.069)
Primary metals	Individual is employed in SIC 33	0.005	(0.071)
Fabricated metals	Individual is employed in SIC 34	0.012	(0.110)
Machinery	Individual is employed in SIC 35	0.029	(0.168)
Electronics	Individual is employed in SIC 36	0.021	(0.144)
Transport equipment	Individual is employed in SIC 37	0.028	(0.165)
Instruments	Individual is employed in SIC 38	0.005	(0.067)
Other manufactures	Individual is employed in SIC 39	0.005	(0.069)
Age	Individual's age	36.362	(10.198)
Age^2/100	Age×Age divided by 100	14.262	(8.048)
Tenure	Length of present employment, in months	77.713	(88.643)
Tenure^2/1,000	Tenure×Tenure divided by 1,000	13.897	(28.390)
Education	Highest grade completed up to that year	13.226	(2.283)
Black	Head of household is African American	0.074	(0.261)
American Indian	Head of household is Native American	0.016	(0.126)
North central	Individual lives in the north-central region	0.290	(0.454)
South	Individual lives in the southern region	0.326	(0.469)
West	Individual lives in the western region	0.175	(0.380)
Work limitation	Individual has a work-limiting disability	0.040	(0.196)
Gender	Individual is female	0.489	(0.500)
Union	Individual is a member of a union	0.153	(0.360)
Number of children	Number of children under age 18 in household	1.070	(1.153)
Married	Individual is married	0.809	(0.393)
Head of HH	Individual is a PSID household head	0.622	(0.485)
MSA residence	The nearest city has more than 50,000 people	0.532	(0.499)
Local unemployment rate	County unemployment rate	6.468	(2.850)
Ship	Total shipments, by industry and year (millions of dollars)	35,418.99	(84,787.78)
PPI	PI, by industry and year	21.484	(42.908)
ED×PPI	Education×PPI	272.718	(556.712)

Notes: Means and standard deviations are for pooled regression sample used in fixed-effects estimation ($n = 41,834$). Ship and PPI (producer price index) are set equal to 0 for nonmanufacturing industries.

Table 9.2   **Typical Cross-Section Regression Results for Control Variables**

	1982		1992	
	Coefficient	Standard Error	Coefficient	Standard Error
Age	0.056**	0.007	0.042**	0.008
Age^2/100	−0.0650**	0.00876	−0.0436**	0.009790
Tenure	0.003**	0.000	0.004**	0.000
Tenure^2/1,000	−0.00563**	0.0008420	−0.00664**	0.0009420
Education	0.081**	0.005	0.116**	0.005
Black	−0.169**	0.033	−0.170**	0.038
American Indian	−0.076	0.057	0.037	0.080
North central	−0.026	0.025	−0.186**	0.027
South	−0.007	0.026	−0.148**	0.027
West	0.039	0.028	−0.099**	0.030
Work limitation	−0.112**	0.047	−0.137**	0.046
Gender	−0.197**	0.039	−0.146**	0.042
Union	0.205**	0.025	0.123**	0.029
Number of children	−0.024**	0.009	−0.023**	0.009
Married	0.169**	0.034	0.159**	0.035
Head of HH	0.218**	0.044	0.185**	0.046
MSA residence	0.139**	0.019	0.126**	0.019
Local unemployment rate	−0.002	0.002	−0.005	0.004
N	3,506		4,310	
R^2	0.42		0.37	
$F_{(45, 4251)}$	43.7200		42.4400	
Probability value (F-test)	0.0000		0.0000	

Notes: Dependent variable is log of hourly wage. Regressions also contain industry dummies and education-industry interactions.

*Statistically significant at the 10 percent level.

**Statistically significant at the 5 percent level.

specific skill premiums attached to different amounts of education. The skill premium declines in most industries as the years of formal schooling of the employee increase. This declining premium could reflect a variety of factors, including lower industry-specific (dis)utility experienced by more highly skilled workers, greater locational mobility of more highly educated workers, or greater intersectoral mobility of educated workers.[26]

Together, these profiles suggest that an important piece of an explanation of industry wage premiums is differing labor market conditions for skilled and unskilled workers. In several industries there is no premium for workers with some education beyond high school and in most industries there is no premium for workers with a college degree. The existence of industry wage premiums, therefore, may be less a phenomenon of

26. Only three industries have rising premiums—petroleum, primary metals, and stone—while one industry—tobacco—has a profile that is essentially flat.

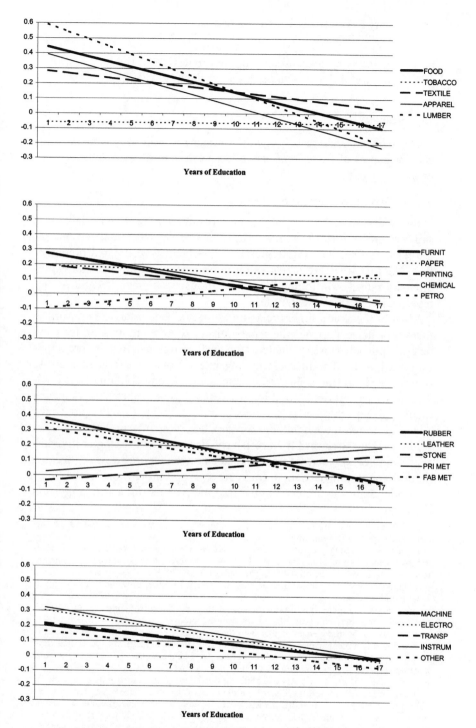

Fig. 9.3   Industry wage premiums by education level (deviations from employment-weighted average log real wage)

particular industry structure and more a reflection of the local industry-specific nature of the labor market facing the less skilled.

9.6 Results

Our particular interest is how these wage and skill premiums correlate with measures of trade, both as an aggregate and disaggregated by type of trading partner.

9.6.1 Two-Stage Regression Results

In the first stage of our cross-sectional approach, we estimate labor and skill premiums for each industry in each sample year. Table 9.3 records the results of second-stage regressions in which the estimated premiums from the first stage are regressed on import penetration rates and export intensity rates,[27] controlling for overall industry shipments,[28] and on our measures of intraindustry trade.

Most of the extant literature assumes that skilled and unskilled workers in an industry experience the same industry wage premiums. So for comparison purposes, we estimated standard premiums (that is, premiums estimated without industry-schooling interactions) and related them to our measures of trade. The results appear in the first column of table 9.3. The upper-left results ("Total imports" and "Total exports") replicate the qualitative results other researchers have found (e.g., Gaston and Trefler 1994), although the magnitudes are smaller.[29] One interpretation of these results is that the reward to industry-specific experience is larger in industries (and years) where comparative advantage is more relevant (because natural and policy barriers to trade are low) and more pronounced.

Subdividing the influences by trading partner indicates important

27. The import penetration rate and export intensity rates are defined as the ratio of imports and exports to shipments, respectively.

28. The second-stage regressions also contain year dummies, producer price indexes, and shipments, as previously outlined. The year dummies, although largely insignificant, tend to peak in size in the mid-1980s. The pattern of results is similar whether unweighted or employment-weighted least squares is used. Table 9.3 reports only the results from unweighted least squares.

29. The year dummies bleed away the size of these coefficients. Comparable workers in two similar industries or years that differ only in import penetration, with one import-penetration rate being 5 percent higher than the other, have wage premiums that are smaller by roughly 0.1 percent. Comparable workers in two similar industries or years that differ only in export intensity, with one export-intensity rate being 5 percent higher than the other, have wage premiums that are larger by a little more than 0.3 percent. Comparable workers in two similar industries or years that differ in both import and export intensity, with one industry's rates being 5 percent higher than the rates of the other, have wage premiums that differ by somewhat more than 0.2 percent, with the more globally engaged industry having the larger wage premiums. Richardson and Khripounova (1997) show that these cross-industry patterns also characterize socioeconomic subsamples of manufacturing workers. Thus, for example, industries with higher export intensity, lower import penetration, and greater trade engagement have larger wage premiums, ceteris paribus, for both women and men, and for ethnic minorities and majorities.

Table 9.3   **Selected Coefficients (Standard Errors) from Pooled Regressions of Differentials on Various Trade Measures**

	Standard IIWD		Distributional IIWD			
			Labor Premium		Skill Premium	
A. Total Trade						
Total imports	−0.243	(0.0479)**	0.0790	(0.172)	−0.0237	(0.0135)*
Total exports	0.586	(0.104)**	−1.37	(0.544)**	0.151	(0.0426)**
R^2	0.48		0.14		0.13	
$F_{(16, 224)}$	20.17		3.08		2.67	
B. Trade by Trading Partner						
I-country imports	0.544	(0.186)**	3.31	(1.15)**	−0.206	(0.0902)**
I-country exports	−0.192	(0.288)	−3.31	(1.62)**	0.235	(0.128)*
N-country imports	−0.824	(0.121)**	−0.375	(0.689)	−0.0321	(0.0529)
N-country exports	3.30	(0.548)**	−4.25	(3.55)	0.578	(0.277)**
P-country imports	−0.0193	(0.266)	0.0896	(1.10)	−0.0109	(0.0876)
P-country exports	−1.05	(1.10)	2.37	(5.25)	−0.262	(0.422)
R^2	0.55		0.17		0.16	
$F_{(20, 200)}$	28.99		4.32		3.00	
C. Intraindustry Trade						
Overall GLI	121	(33.4)**	183	(171)	−4.31	(13.7)
R^2	0.43		0.11		0.08	
$F_{(15, 225)}$	17.36		3.03		1.73	
D. Intraindustry Trade, by Trading Partner						
I-country GLI	−93.5	(35.5)**	−112	(184)	0.617	(13.9)
N-country GLI	173	(41.6)**	262	(167)	−7.41	(13.5)
P-country GLI	−17.8	(30.4)	251	(130)*	−21.1	(9.93)**
R^2	0.45		0.13		0.10	
$F_{(17, 223)}$	14.44		2.56		1.63	

Notes: Dependent variable is the etimated coefficient on industry dummy variables (labor premium) or their interaction with education (skill premium) from cross-sectional wage regressions, pooled across all years. Regressions also contain year dummies, PPI, and Ship. Standard errors are in parentheses, calculated using White's (1980) method. IIWD = interindustry wage differentials.

*Statistically significant at the 10 percent level.

**Statistically significant at the 5 percent level.

differences. First, looking at the left-column results by country type (panel B), we find that the familiar aggregate coefficients are driven almost entirely by trade with newly industrialized countries. In fact, imports from traditional industrial trading partners are positively correlated with U.S. wage premiums (and exports negatively, although insignificantly correlated).[30] Second, the coefficients for trade with newly industrialized coun-

30. We do not discuss the panels for trade with primary-producing (P) countries, where trade is low and coefficients are uniformly insignificant. In trade with primary-producing countries, skilled workers appear to "lose" from deeper export intensity, while unskilled

tries suggest large effects. Comparable workers in two similar industries that differ only in export intensity with newly industrialized countries by 5 percent would have wage premiums that differ by as much as 1.2 percent.

Distinguishing skilled from less-skilled workers provides some insight into these results. The right-column results, under the heading "Distributional IIWD" (interindustry wage differential) suggest that trade has opposing effects on the return to pure labor and the return to skill. While increased trade (larger import and export shares of shipments) is associated with a higher return to skill, it is associated with a lower return to pure labor, as seen by the signs and magnitudes of the estimated coefficients. Shifting down those same right columns, it can be seen that skilled workers are the ones who enjoy strongly positive wage premiums in industries or years with high export intensity and low import penetration, whether traditional or newly industrialized partners are concerned. In contrast, the industry wage premiums earned by less-skilled workers are insignificantly related to trade with newly industrialized countries, and oppositely related to trade with traditional industrial partners—higher where import penetration ratios are higher, lower where export intensity is higher. These results are consistent with a model in which import surges displace high-skilled workers in home intermediates and increase the demand for lower-skilled workers; export surges of intermediates to fellow northern countries require more high-skilled workers and reduce demand for the less skilled.[31] These results suggest broadly that distributional conflict is more likely from trade with newly industrialized countries than with traditional partners, as popular debate often assumes.

The results for the GLIs of intraindustry trade[32] maintain the conclusion that trade with traditional and newly industrialized countries has differently signed strong impacts on wage premiums. But they do not suggest any significant distributional conflict. The aggregate GLI is significantly, positively correlated with the standard premium measure (undifferentiated by skill) in the first column, panel C, due largely to trade with the newly industrialized countries. The correlation with newly industrialized–partner trade overwhelms the tendency for higher intraindustry trade with industrial partners to be negatively associated with the standard wage premium (first column, panel D). However, the distributional effects in the "Labor Premium" and "Skill Premium" columns are all insignificant.[33]

---

workers "gain." Unreported results suggest that this correlation is driven by foods and beverages, and in any case P-country trade is much smaller than I- and N-country trade.

31. Seven of the eight estimated coefficients have coefficients with the signs predicted by the partial equilibrium model of compensating differentials presented previously. Only the correlation of N-country imports and the skill premium has an unexpected sign.

32. Such indices cannot be meaningfully included in the same regression with export intensity and import penetration ratios; these measures are nonlinear transformations of the others. One cannot meaningfully hold two constant and let the third vary.

33. Unreported regressions that distinguish the wage effect of trade by industry indicate

9.6.2   Single-Stage Fixed-Effects Regression Results

In the single-stage approach, we estimate labor and skill premiums and their relation to our trade measures across all years, controlling for the appearance of the same worker multiple times in our sample.[34] We regress log real wages on the individual control variables listed in table 9.2, industry dummy variables, industry-education interactions, industry shipments, an industry producer price index, and various trade measures. We interpret the sign of the coefficient on a trade measure as the sign of the correlation between that flow and the return to pure labor (given by the industry-specific intercepts). Similarly, we interpret the sign of the coefficient on the interaction between education and a trade measure as the sign of the correlation between that flow and the return to skill.

Table 9.4 records results for the one-stage estimates that account for individual fixed effects. In the first two columns, we report results without the inclusion of year dummies; we report results including year dummies in the last two columns. The year dummies are entered to account for economywide, rather than industry-specific, trends. The inclusion of the year dummies absorbs most of the temporal variation in the trade measures, however, reducing their magnitude and generally eliminating their significance.

The results in panel B estimate the correlation between total import penetration, total export intensity, and the returns to pure labor and to skill. The sign pattern is reversed from the pattern that appeared in the cross-sectional two-stage results in table 9.3, but none of the estimated coefficients in table 9.4 are significant. Taken by itself, this seems to suggest that the distributional conflict described in the previous results is accounted for by sorting of workers with unmeasured productivity (whatever their measured skills) into industries with strong comparative advantage (high exports, low imports).

But this conclusion would be premature. When trade is broken down by trading partner (panel C), the distributional conflict seen in the cross-sectional results reappears, although not significantly in the right-column results with year dummies. As found in the two-stage results, skilled workers in industries with high export intensity to newly industrialized

---

that the significant P-country distributional results reflect conditions in the food sector alone. Greater intraindustry trade in that sector is correlated with lower premiums for skilled workers and higher premiums for less-skilled workers.

34. Incorporating individual fixed effects eliminates much of the variation in education, forcing identification of the education-industry interactions through those individuals who change industry or acquire more education during the period. (As noted previously, the education-trade interactions, which are our focus here, are also identified through changes over time in trade flows.) Some of the "industry switchers" in the PSID sample may be individuals whose industry is misidentified in one or more sample years; research on this same misidentification in the Current Population Surveys by Rothgeb and Cohany (1992) shows that many, not only a few, industry switchers are misidentified. Reducing this source of error, however, is our use of broad (two-digit) industry classifications.

Table 9.4 **Selected Coefficients (Standard Errors) from Fixed-Effect Regression of Real Log Wage on Various Trade Measures**

	No Year Dummies		With Year Dummies and Year-Education Interactions	
	Labor Premium	Skill Premium	Labor Premium	Skill Premium
A. Producer Price Index				
PPI	−14.0	1.05	0.467	−0.0378
	(2.62)**	(0.201)**	(2.85)	(0.218)
F (6476, 35299)		8.118		8.185
B. Total Trade				
Total industry imports	−0.465	0.0426	−0.269	0.0200
	(0.374)	(0.0295)	(0.384)	(0.0302)
Total industry exports	0.353	−0.0429	0.993	−0.0752
	(0.821)	(0.0632)	(0.851)	(0.0653)
PPI	−13.2	1.00	−0.328	0.0260
	(3.01)**	(0.231)**	(3.18)	(0.243)
F (6476, 35295)		8.114		8.183
C. Trade by Trading Partner				
I-country imports	0.756	−0.0268	2.42	−0.148
	(1.52)	(0.115)	(1.54)	(0.117)
I-country exports	1.23	−0.0791	0.542	−0.0645
	(1.88)	(0.146)	(1.90)	(0.147)
N-country imports	1.13	−0.0710	−0.102	0.000201
	(1.11)	(0.0861)	(1.12)	(0.0869)
N-country exports	−10.3	0.736	−5.36	0.461
	(4.24)**	(0.328)**	(4.28)	(0.331)
P-country imports	−0.789	0.000593	0.345	−0.0760
	(1.92)	(0.155)	(1.92)	(0.154)
P-country exports	22.6	−1.83	20.0	−1.57
	(5.54)**	(0.430)**	(5.63)**	(0.437)**
PPI	−9.18	0.730	2.00	−0.119
	(3.19)**	(0.245)**	(3.32)	(0.255)
F (6476, 35287)		8.118		8.184
D. Intraindustry Trade				
Overall GLI	−879	61.9	−602	41.8
	(234)**	(18.4)**	(236)**	(18.4)**
PPI	−12.8	0.967	1.03	−0.0788
	(2.62)**	(0.203)**	(2.87)	(0.220)
F (6476, 35297)		8.117		8.184
E. Intraindustry Trade, by Trading Partner				
I-country GLI	−461	20.0	−343	13.2
	(305)	(24.6)	(311)	(25.0)
N-country GLI	−357	32.8	−169	17.1
	(200)*	(15.8)**	(202)	(16.0)
P-country GLI	−116	9.18	44.7	−3.31
	(202)	(16.0)	(202)	(16.0)
PPI	−11.8	0.904	1.25	−0.0805
	(2.74)**	(0.211)**	(2.93)	(0.224)
F (6476, 35293)		8.119		8.185

Notes: Dependent variable is log of real hourly wage. Regressions also include the individual control variables listed in table 9.2, industry dummies, industry-education interactions, and Ship. Estimated with individual fixed effects. Based on 41,834 observations, 6,477 individuals. Standard errors are in parentheses.

*Statistically significant at the 10 percent level.

**Statistically significant at the 5 percent level.

countries enjoy higher-than-average wage premiums; unskilled workers in such industries receive lower premiums. Moreover, in keeping with the predictions of our partial equilibrium model, we find that skilled workers in industries with high import penetration from newly industrialized countries enjoy higher-than-average premiums; unskilled workers receive lower premiums. Conversely, and as predicted, high import penetration from traditional partners is associated with larger premiums for unskilled workers and lower premiums for skilled workers.

The results for the GLIs of intraindustry trade in panels D and F have a very similar interpretation. Industries with strong two-way trade links pay significantly higher premiums to skilled workers, and lower premiums to unskilled workers. The size of these effects is quite large. But it is precisely accounted for by two-way intraindustry trade with newly industrialized countries; other trading partners have insignificantly (although similarly signed) coefficients.

9.7 Conclusion

Distributional issues in the globalization debate are surging in importance. At the same time that consensus has grown that global engagement has positive overall effects on average living standards and growth, suspicion has grown that the averages hide great unevenness, with some identifiable groups even losing from global engagement. In the United States, the suspicions seem greatest when trade-liberalizing initiatives are aimed at poorer, developing countries, and are more subdued when perceived peer countries are involved. In other words, the distribution of our trading partners may matter to the distribution of our gains from trade.

This paper has examined these distributional issues for American workers in the 1980s and early 1990s. In general, we find that the suspicions are supported by evidence, once we control for the usual correlates of wages (including unobserved worker characteristics). We find that skilled (educated) American workers seem to have received higher rewards for their skill in industries and years with high export dependence on newly industrialized–country markets, and even when two-way, intraindustry trade with them is high (that is, both exports and imports). Workers with little education seem correspondingly to have lower industry-specific wage premiums (rewards for specific training or compensation for industry amenities or disamenities) in industries and years where exports to newly industrialized countries were large, or where intraindustry trade with them was large. Trade with established industrial countries appears to have a different relationship to wages and rewards to skills. Skilled workers in industries or years in which export intensity was high and import penetration low received larger-than-average premiums. Conversely, low export intensity and high import penetration with traditional partners is associated with larger-than-average premiums for unskilled workers.

We interpret these results in the light of models that assume differences in the types of trade that the United States conducts with traditional industrial and newly industrialized trading partners and differences in the types of labor markets that less-skilled and more-skilled workers face. Our empirical results are largely consistent with variegated outsourcing—horizontal intraindustry trade in specialized, skill-intensive intermediate producer goods between highly integrated industrial economies, but vertical intraindustry trade of those same intermediates for less-skill-intensive assemblies and finished manufactures between industrial and newly industrialized economies that are not yet fully integrated. The results also support a view of labor markets that is to some extent industry specific, generating different industry-specific components to wages and the return to education. The data show pronounced differences in the size of these industry wage premiums across industries and between workers, and in turn, pronounced differences in the way trade affects them. Industry wage premiums for less-educated workers are, in particular, far larger than for more-educated workers (for whom they are sometimes 0).

In sum, our results suggest that both what we trade and with whom we trade seem to matter for U.S. wage inequality. The way in which "what" and "whom" matter, however, is complex, and we do not claim to have provided more than a beginning interpretation. But we believe that this paper suggests both interesting new answers and nuanced new questions for the debate about trade and wages.

Appendix

Trade Data: Product Aggregation, Concordance, Assignment

Trade data are a reaggregation from the Statistics Canada compilation of United Nations bilateral trade by commodity, Standard International Trade Classification, revision 3.[35] As described previously data were first aggregated across products and then across trading partners. The product aggregation constructed three broad types of goods: intermediate inputs (raw materials, primary products, and producer nondurables), capital-goods inputs (producer durables), and consumer goods. The three types were allocated to the 20 two-digit manufacturing sectors in the Standard Industrial Classification, either according to end use (raw materials and primary products) or according to the corresponding manufacturing sector (producer nondurables and durables).

---

35. Omitted SITC categories included 27xx, 29xx, and 9xxx, mostly miscellaneous products.

Intermediate Inputs (Raw Materials, Primary Products, and Producer Nondurables)

SIC sector	SITC categories
20	0xxx minus (01xx + 02xx + 03xx + 05xx + 09xx)
	22xx
	4xxx
21	121x
22	26xx
	65xx minus (652x + 653x + 654x + 655x)
23	652x + 653x + 654x + 655x
24	24xx + 63xx
26	25xx + 64xx
28	5xxx
29	3xxx
30	23xx + 62xx
31	21xx + 61xx
32	66xx
33	28xx + 67xx + 68xx
34	69xx

Capital-Goods Inputs (Producer Durables)

SIC sector	SITC categories
25	82xx
34	81xx
35	71xx + 72xx + 73xx + 74xx + (0.5)75xx[36]
36	764x + (77xx minus 775x)
37	7621 + 782x + 783x +784x + 786x + 79xx
38	87xx + (88xx minus 885x)

Consumer Goods

SIC sector	SITC categories
20	01xx + 02xx + 03xx + 05xx + 09xx
	11xx
21	122x
23	84xx
31	83xx + 8510
35	(0.5)75xx
36	76xx minus 7621 minus 764x

36. Computers and office machines (SITC 75xx) were divided equally between producer goods and consumer goods.

37	7810 + 785x
38	885x
39	89xx

Trade Data: Trading-Partner Aggregation

Aggregation across trading partners created three groups: traditional industrial trading partners (the I group), newly industrialized trading partners (the N group), and primary-product producers (the P group). The groups are detailed in table 9A.1 and were based loosely on per capita income and judgment about product mix.

Table 9A.1   **Country Categories**

I Countries (Traditional Industrial)				
Australia	Canada	Germany	Netherlands	Sweden
Austria	Denmark	Ireland	New Zealand	Switzerland

Belgium-
    Luxembourg
	Finland
	France
		Italy
		Japan
			Norway
			Spain
				United
				    Kingdom

N Countries (Newly Industrialized)			
Argentina	Greece	Korea Rp.	Singapore
Brazil	Hong Kong	Malaysia	South Africa
Chile	Hungary	Mexico	Taiwan
Czechoslovakia	Israel	Portugal	Uruguay

P Countries (Primary Producers)				
Afghanistan	Comoros	Iraq	Oman	Trinidad and
Albania	Congo	Jamaica	Pakistan	Tobago
Algeria	Costa Rica	Jordan	Panama	Tunisia
Angola	Côte d'Ivoire	Kenya	Papua New	Turkey
Bahamas	Cyprus	Korea D.P.Rp.	Guinea	Uganda
Bahrain	Dominican	Kuwait	Paraguay	United Arab
Bangladesh	Republic	Laos P.D.R.	Peru	Emirates
Barbados	Ecuador	Lebanon	Philippines	USSR (former)
Belize	Egypt	Liberia	Poland	Venezuela
Benin	El Salvador	Madagascar	Qatar	Vietnam
Bermuda	Ethiopia	Malawi	Romania	Yemen
Bhutan	Fiji	Maldives	Rwanda	Yugoslavia
Bolivia	Gabon	Mali	Saudi Arabia	(former)
Brunei	Gambia	Malta	Senegal	Zaire
Bulgaria	Ghana	Mauritania	Sierra Leone	Zambia
Burkina Faso	Guatemala	Mauritius	Somalia	Zimbabwe
Burundi	Guinea	Mongolia	Sri Lanka	
Cambodia	Guinea-Bissau	Morocco	Sudan	
Cameroon	Guyana	Mozambique	Suriname	
Central African	Haiti	Myanmar	Tanzania	
Republic	Honduras	Nepal	(United	
Chad	India	Nicaragua	Republic of)	
China	Indonesia	Niger	Thailand	
Colombia	Iran	Nigeria	Togo	

References

Abraham, Katherine G., and Henry S. Farber. 1987. Job duration, seniority, and earning. *American Economic Review* 77 (June): 278–97.

Anderson, Patricia, M. 1998. Defining the scope of the labor market: Who competes with whom? Paper prepared for the NBER Conference on Trade and the U.S. Labor Market, April.

Anderton, Bob, and Paul Brenton. 1998. The dollar, trade, technology and inequality in the USA. London: National Institute of Economic and Social Research. Manuscript.

Bailey, Thomas, and Carola Sandy. 1998. Pret-à-porter, pret-à-partir: The effects of globalization on the U.S. apparel industry. Paper prepared for the NBER Conference on Trade and the U.S. Labor Market, April.

Baldwin, Robert E., and Glenn G. Cain. 1997. Shifts in U.S. relative wages: The role of trade, technology and factor endowments. NBER Working Paper no. 5934. Cambridge, Mass.: National Bureau of Economic Research.

Baltagi, Badi H. 1985. Pooling cross-sections with unequal time-series lengths. *Economic Letters* 18:133–36.

Borjas, George J. 1987. Self-selection and the earnings of immigrants. *American Economic Review* 77:531–53.

Borjas, George J., and Valerie A. Ramey. 1995. Foreign competition, market power, and wage inequality. *Quarterly Review of Economics* 110:1075–110.

Campa, Jose, and Linda S. Goldberg. 1997. The evolving external orientation of manufacturing: A profile of four countries. *Economic Policy Review* 3:53–81.

Cragg, Michael I., and Mario Epelbaum. 1996. Why has wage dispersion grown in Mexico? Is it the incidence of reforms or the growing demand for skills? *Journal of Development Economics* 51:99–116.

Dickens, William T., and Lawrence F. Katz. 1987. Inter-industry wage differences and industry characteristics. In *Unemployment and the structure of labor markets,* ed. Kevin Lang and Jonathan S. Leonard, 48–89. New York: Basil Blackwell.

Dickens, William T., and Kevin Lang. 1988. Why it matters what we trade: A case for active policy. In *The dynamics of trade and employment,* ed. Laura D'Andrea Tyson, William T. Dickens, and John Zysman, 87–112. Cambridge, Mass.: Ballinger.

Ethier, Wilfred J. 1982. National and international returns to scale in the modern theory of international trade. *American Economic Review* 72:388–405.

Feenstra, Robert C. 1997. Integration and disintegration in the global economy. Davis: University of California, Department of Economics. Manuscript.

Feenstra, Robert C., and Gordon H. Hanson. 1996a. Foreign investment, outsourcing, and relative wages. In *The political economy of trade policy: Essays in honor of Jagdish Bhagwati,* ed. Robert C. Feenstra, Gene M. Grossman, and Douglas A. Irwin, 80–127. Cambridge, Mass.: MIT Press.

———. 1996b. Globalization, outsourcing, and wage inequality. *American Economic Review* 86 (March): 240–45.

———. 1997. Productivity measurement and the impact of trade and technology on wages: Estimates for the U.S., 1972–1990. NBER Working Paper no. 6052. Cambridge, Mass.: National Bureau of Economic Research.

Fung, K. C., and Harry Huizinga. 1997. Can freer intra-industry trade raise wages? Evidence from Canada. Santa Cruz: University of California. Manuscript.

Gaston, Noel, and Daniel Trefler. 1994. Protection, trade, and wages: Evidence from U.S. manufacturing. *Industrial and Labor Relations Review* 47 (July): 574–93.

GATT (General Agreement on Tariffs and Trade). 1996. *Annual report,* volume 2. Geneva: GATT Secretariat.

Gibbons, Robert, and Lawrence F. Katz. 1992. Does unmeasured ability explain inter-industry wage differentials? *Review of Economic Studies* 59 (July): 515–35.

Grossman, Gene M. 1982. Import competition from developed and developing countries. *Review of Economics and Statistics* 64:217–81.

Grubel, Herbert G., and Peter J. Lloyd. 1971. The empirical measurement of intraindustry trade. *Economic Record* 47 (December): 494–517.

Haisken-DeNew, John P., and Christoph M. Schmidt. 1998. Interindustry wage differentials revisited: A longitudinal comparison of Germany and USA (1984–1996). Berlin: Deutsches Institut für Wirtschaftsforschung. Manuscript.

Helwege, Jean. 1992. Sectoral shifts and interindustry wage differentials. *Journal of Labor Economics* 10:55–84.

Kahn, Lawrence M. 1997. Collective bargaining and the inter-industry wage structure: International evidence. *Economica* 65:507–34.

Katz, Lawrence F., and Lawrence H. Summers. 1989a. Can inter-industry wage differentials justify strategic trade policy? In *Trade policies for international competitiveness,* ed. Robert C. Feenstra, 85–116. Chicago: University of Chicago Press.

———. 1989b. Industry rents: Evidence and implications. *Brookings Papers on Economic Activity, Microeconomics,* 209–90.

Krueger, Alan B. 1998. Thoughts on globalization, unionization, and labor market rents. Paper prepared for the NBER Conference on Trade and the U.S. Labor Market, April.

Krueger, Alan B., and Lawrence H. Summers. 1988. Efficiency wages and the inter-industry wage structure. *Econometrica* 56 (March): 259–93.

Lawrence, Robert Z. 1996. *Single world, divided nations? International trade and OECD labor markets.* Washington, D.C.: Brookings Institution.

Lovely, Mary E. 1999. Outsourcing and the skill differential. Syracuse, N.Y.: Syracuse University. Manuscript.

Richardson, J. David, and Elena Khripounova. 1997. Inequality in U.S. inter-industry wage differentials and their relation to international trade. Syracuse, N.Y.: Syracuse University. Manuscript, July.

———. 1998. U.S. labor market power and linkages to international trade: Identifying suspects and measures. Syracuse, N.Y.: Syracuse University. Final Report to the U.S. Department of Labor.

Robertson, Raymond. 1998. Are inter-industry wage differentials similar and stable? The case of the United States and Mexico. Syracuse University Discussion Paper no. 85. Syracuse, N.Y.: Syracuse University, January.

Rodrik, Dani. 1994. The rush to free trade in the developing world: Why so late? Why now? Will it last? In *Voting for reform: Democracy, political liberalization, and economic adjustment,* ed. S. Haggard and S. B. Webb, 61–88. New York: Oxford University Press.

———. 1998. The debate over globalization: How to move forward by looking backward. In *Launching new global trade talks: An action agenda,* ed. Jeffrey J. Schott, 25–38. Washington, D.C.: Institute for International Economics.

Rothgeb, Jennifer M., and Sharon R. Cohany. 1992. The revised CPS questionnaire: Differences between the current and proposed questionnaires. Paper presented at the Annual Meetings of the American Statistical Association, August.

Sachs, Jeffrey D., and Howard J. Shatz. 1998. International trade and wage inequality in the United States: Some new results. In *Imports, exports, and the American worker,* ed. Susan M. Collins, 61–88. Washington, D.C.: Brookings Institution.

Topel, Robert. 1994. Regional labor markets and the determinants of wage inequality. *American Economic Review* 84:17–22.

White, H. 1980. A heteroskedasticity-consistent covariance matrix estimator and a direct test for heteroskedasticity. *Econometrica* 48:817–30.

Comment   George J. Borjas

This paper addresses the interesting question of whether intraindustry trade matters. In their theoretical discussion, Lovely and Richardson note that intraindustry trade can occur when developed countries (the North in their exposition) export intermediate products to developing countries (the South). The labor-abundant South takes these intermediate products and converts them into final products, which it then exports back to the North. Intraindustry trade can also occur when the same types of finished products are traded between countries.

Lovely and Richardson's concern is not with estimating the volume of intraindustry trade, but with measuring the effect of this trade on the U.S. wage structure. To formalize their ideas, the authors develop a general-equilibrium model that allows for various types of trade flows between industrialized and developing economies. The main lesson of the model is that there may be a positive correlation between measures of intraindustry trade and the rate of return to skills in the United States. Put differently, an increase in intraindustry trade may widen the wage gap between skilled and less-skilled workers in the United States. This is the theoretical implication that the authors test in their empirical work.

Because of the general-equilibrium nature of the model, the link between the measure of intraindustry trade and the rate of return to skills in the United States is simply a correlation, not a causal relationship. The authors suggest two channels through which this positive correlation can arise: an increase in human capital in the South (which raises the share of southern labor devoted to assembly activity, inducing the North to increase production of intermediate products, which raises the return to human capital); and demand shocks such as an increase in the demand for finished manufactures (which also raises northern production of intermediate products). The authors also note, however, that different comparative-statics exercises (such as an increase in northern human capital) would generate a negative correlation between intraindustry trade and the rate of return to skills in the North. In the end, the sign of the link between intraindustry trade and the skills wage gap remains an empirical question.

The main contribution of the paper, therefore, is simply to establish empirically the sign of this correlation. So I will devote most of my comments to the empirical work. Let's first start out with the Grubel-Lloyd index, the measure of intraindustry trade that Lovely and Richardson use in the analysis. This index is given by

George J. Borjas is the Pforzheimer Professor of Public Policy in the John F. Kennedy School of Government at Harvard University and a research associate of the National Bureau of Economic Research.

(1) $$GLI = 1 - \frac{|X_N - IM_N|}{X_N + IM_N},$$

where X_N gives the value of manufacturing exports from the North to the South, and IM_N gives the value of manufacturing imports from the South to the North. GLI takes on a value of 1 if exports and imports are exactly equal to each other, and takes on a value of 0 if the North only exports the manufacturing good or only imports it. The higher GLI, therefore, the greater the importance of intraindustry trade. The calculation of GLI for the United States generates one interesting result: To a large extent, the United States trades inputs, not outputs.

From the perspective of analyzing changes in the U.S. wage structure, I think this particular index is somewhat problematic for the analysis. Suppose that the value of the manufacturing exports is exactly half the value of the imports, $X_N = \frac{1}{2}(IM_N)$. It is easy to work out that $GLI = \frac{1}{3}$. In contrast, suppose that the value of the manufacturing imports is exactly half the value of exports, $IM_N = \frac{1}{2}(X_N)$. In this case, the index also takes on a value of $\frac{1}{3}$.

The point is that the index is symmetric in terms of the importance of imports and exports. Moreover, the index is invariant to the actual volume of trade. Although I can appreciate that there may be sound theoretical reasons as to why, in a general-equilibrium setting, such a distinction might not matter, we know that the difference between imports and exports does matter, and that the volume of exports and imports also matters. Toward the end of the paper, for example, Lovely and Richardson report empirical evidence that a higher volume of exports greatly increases the wage in the industry, while a higher volume of imports reduces (but by a smaller absolute amount) the wage in the industry. The use of the GLI masks the potentially important distinction between imports and exports. I conjecture that the rate of return to skills is substantially different in a manufacturing industry, where all the intraindustry trade is composed of exports, than in one where all the intraindustry trade is composed of imports.

The authors calculate the GLI for manufacturing industries over the period 1981–92, and they link these industry- and time-specific data with individual-level data from the Panel Study of Income Dynamics (PSID). The empirical analysis presented in the paper often disaggregates the measure of the GLI across different types of countries (industrialized, newly developing, and primary producers), as well as among different types of goods trade (e.g., durables and nondurables), but I will tend to focus my remarks on the simplest calculations.

A general specification of the regression model that Lovely and Richardson use in their empirical analysis is

$$(2) \quad \log w_{ij}(t) = X_{ij}(t)\beta_1 + \beta_2 s_{ij}(t) + \delta_1 GLI_j(t) + \delta_2(s_{ij} \times GLI_j(t))$$
$$+ \kappa_i + \gamma_t + \varepsilon_{ij}(t),$$

where $w_{ij}(t)$ gives the wage of work i employed in industry j at time t; X_{ij} gives a vector of socioeconomic characteristics of the worker; $s_{ij}(t)$ gives the worker's educational attainment at time t; κ_i gives a fixed effect for the worker; and γ_t gives a fixed effect for the period. The standardizing vector X contains a large number of variables—perhaps too many. For example, the regressions control for a worker's occupation. If one wants to estimate the impact of trade on the rate of return to skills, it seems to me that controlling for occupation nets out a substantial part of what higher skill levels do for a particular worker.

The authors report the initial estimates of their regression model in table 9.3. In this table, the specification in equation (2) is simplified in a number of important ways. First, they omit the period fixed effects (γ_t) from the regressions. Second, they aggregate over all manufacturing industries in the economy at time t to obtain a single measure of intraindustry trade at that time, GLI_t. Lovely and Richardson motivate this particular specification by noting that there may be perfect factor mobility in the U.S. labor market, and the impact of intraindustry trade in a particular industry would then be diffused throughout the entire economy.

The results in table 9.3 are among the strongest presented in the paper. Intraindustry trade has significant impacts on the wage structure both in terms of wage levels (δ_1) and on the return to skills (δ_2). The sign of these coefficients, however, is not consistent from one specification to the next. The analysis reports one particular sign pattern when intraindustry trade is with industrialized economies, and the opposite sign pattern when the trade is with the newly developing countries. I am not sure I understand precisely why this sign inconsistency occurs, and the authors' attempt at explaining the results (which relies on the possibility that increases in intraindustry trade occur for different reasons across different countries) is not fully convincing. At the very least, some type of reduced-form estimation seems to be required to explain the sign pattern, where the wages of U.S. workers are related to the factors that actually changed in the particular countries (rather than to the GLI).

Even if one accepts the authors' explanation, I have a number of questions about the regression model. First, the regressions in table 9.3 ignore period effects. We know, for example, that there were dramatic changes in the U.S. wage structure during the sample period, particularly in the wage gap between skilled and less-skilled workers. Admittedly, part of these changes in the U.S. wage structure may be due to intraindustry trade, but there are many other factors that are probably at work—and none of these factors are controlled for.

A second potential problem—and one that continues throughout the empirical analysis—is the authors' use of the PSID data to analyze the link between intraindustry trade and the U.S. wage structure. In particular, I am concerned about using regressions that control for individual fixed effects to analyze these types of questions. The parameter δ_2 can be identified if the worker's educational attainment is changing within the sample period. There is nothing inherently wrong with this procedure, except that the parameter of interest to the study is being identified from a very small sample. Moreover, many of the changes in schooling reported by a particular worker can probably be attributed to measurement error. Why not just estimate the returns to schooling and the industry wage levels from Current Population Surveys (CPS)? This type of analysis—which is the standard in the wage-structure literature—would probably give a much more robust answer to the questions that Lovely and Richardson ask.

Finally, the estimation procedure essentially regresses individual-level data (the worker's log wage) on an aggregate variable (the GLI) that takes on the same value for a subset of the individuals in the sample. It is well known that this type of regression leads to downward-biased standard errors if the estimation ignores the possibility that there may be an inter-correlation among individuals who share the same value of the GLI. I suspect that some of the statistically significant results reported in the paper would disappear if the estimation allowed for this type of random-effects stochastic structure.

Table 9.4 generalizes the regression model by allowing for variation in the GLI measure across manufacturing industries and by adding in the period effects. For the most part, this specification does not provide many statistically significant findings. Moreover, this regression introduces an alternative problem into the estimation. Throughout the individual-level analysis of the PSID data, Lovely and Richardson use a sample of workers, ages 18–60, who, among other things, are not retired, disabled, self-employed, or employed by the government. By construction, the sample includes workers in both manufacturing and nonmanufacturing industries. In these regressions, the GLI is set to 0 for workers not employed in manufacturing at time t, and the regressions include an industry fixed effect to capture the "main effect." It is not clear to me why workers employed in nonmanufacturing are in the analysis in the first place. A much cleaner approach would exclude these workers from the study—since they cannot contribute any information whatsoever to the estimation of the impact of interindustry trade. Moreover, it is unclear why one would want to impose the restriction that the other parameters of the model are the same for production and nonproduction workers.

Lovely and Richardson shift gears toward the end of the paper, and do, in fact, conduct part of the "cleaner" analysis that I have been advocating. In particular, using the PSID data, Lovely and Richardson estimate the adjusted industry wage for each manufacturing industry in each year between 1981 and 1992, and "stack" these industry fixed effects. The analysis is conducted only for manufacturing industries. They then relate these adjusted industry wages to measures of exports, imports, and the index of intraindustry trade. Generally, industry wages are higher in manufacturing industries with more exports, fewer imports, and more intraindustry trade. This part of the analysis, however, does not investigate the link between the rate of return to skills and intraindustry trade (or exports or imports). I suspect that a much clearer picture would be obtained if the authors conducted this type of analysis with CPS data.

Overall, Lovely and Richardson have embarked on a very interesting (and important) research path. Although the preliminary results reported in this paper are not conclusive, they are suggestive that intraindustry trade may be playing an important role in the U.S. labor market.

Trade and Job Loss in U.S. Manufacturing, 1979–1994

Lori G. Kletzer

10.1 Introduction

Since the late 1970s, millions of workers have lost their jobs following plant closures, plant relocations, or large-scale reductions in operations. Job insecurity remains at the forefront of public discourse, a stubborn reminder that even a prolonged economic expansion and a steadily falling national unemployment rate cannot erase perceptions created by widespread experiences of permanent job loss. Today, globalization and technological change are often cited as key factors in changes in employment stability.

This paper examines the relationship between increasing foreign competition and job displacement in U.S. manufacturing during the period 1975–94.[1] This was a period of increased trade flows, large swings in the value of the dollar, and falling trade barriers in developing countries.[2] This period was also characterized by widespread permanent job loss, particularly in manufacturing.[3]

Labor reallocation is a likely implication of a move to freer trade, and there is a sizable empirical literature that examines the link between in-

Lori G. Kletzer is professor of economics at the University of California, Santa Cruz.

This research is supported by the W. E. Upjohn Institute for Employment Research. Jeannine Bailliu and Ivy Kosmides provided excellent research assistance. The author appreciates the helpful comments and suggestions of Lisa Lynch, J. David Richardson, and seminar participants at UC Berkeley, the University of Arizona, and Stanford University.

1. As commonly understood, job displacement is an involuntary (from the worker's perspective) termination of employment based on the employer's operating decisions and not on a worker's individual performance.

2. For a discussion of the last of these three events, see Sachs and Warner (1995).

3. See Fallick (1996) and Kletzer (1998a) for reviews of the literature on the incidence and consequences of job displacement.

creasing trade and changes in industry net employment and wages. These net employment changes are a result of changes in the gross flows of new hires, recalls, quits, displacements, temporary layoffs, and retirements. My focus here on displacement is motivated by the perspective that the amount of social and private adjustment to freer trade depends in an important way on gross employment changes, and it is the job-loss component of employment change that most concerns workers, the general public, and policymakers. There is no doubt that the assertion "trade costs jobs" plays an important role in the domestic political economy of free trade.

This paper extends earlier research, first reported in Kletzer (1998b, 1998c), that found evidence that as imports become more competitive, domestic industry displacement rises.[4] The research is motivated by the expectation, based on theory and previous empirical work, that trade liberalization will lead to labor reallocation, with jobs moving away from import-competing industries and toward export industries. From that starting point, several questions are posed. Descriptively, how does the survey evidence on job displacement accord with standard measures of increasing foreign competition? Causally, is the incidence of job displacement across and within industries related to changes in foreign competition? Such changes may occur with developments such as the North American Free Trade Agreement (NAFTA) and the General Agreement on Tariffs and Trade (GATT). Finally, what does the pattern of labor reallocation look like, based on individual-level data? Do workers displaced from import-competing industries become reemployed in export industries or do they move to services (where average wages are lower)?

This paper is organized as follows. Section 10.2 reviews recent studies of the relationship between increasing foreign competition and changes in U.S. employment and wages, and the more recent studies of trade and job loss. Theoretical issues related to measures of industry trade sensitivity are discussed in section 10.3, followed by a discussion of the various data sources in section 10.4. Section 10.5 presents a descriptive analysis of the link between trade and job loss. The empirical model and estimation strategy are discussed in section 10.6. Results from the econometric analysis are presented in section 10.7. Individual-level data from the Displaced Worker Surveys are used in section 10.8 to examine the pattern of reemployment following job displacement. Section 10.9 offers concluding remarks.

10.2 A Brief Background from Previous Research

This examination of trade and job loss joins and complements recent work on trade, wages, and employment. This literature is motivated by

---

4. See also Haveman (1998) and Addison, Fox, and Ruhm (1995).

standard theories of international trade that predict trade liberalization will reduce lower-skill domestic employment and widen the wage gap between skilled and unskilled workers. The effects of trade on U.S. changing employment patterns and wage inequality is a subject of considerable debate. Over the years, the debate has ranged widely, and there are several reviews that help summarize this extensive and diverse literature. Dickens (1988), with a focus on trade and employment, assessed the literature up to the mid-1980s as reaching a common conclusion that import competition caused only a small fraction of employment losses. Most employment change was judged to result from changes in domestic demand, real wages, and productivity.[5] In their review of more recent studies, Belman and Lee (1995) reach a different assessment, that increased import competition affects negatively both employment and wages, with the employment effects several times larger than the wage effects.[6] Revenga (1992) is particularly notable. She shows that for a sample of manufacturing industries during the period 1977–87, changes in import prices have a sizable effect on employment and a smaller yet significant effect on wages. She concludes that most of the adjustment in an industry to an adverse trade shock occurs through employment. Revenga takes these results to suggest that workers are mobile across industries. This mobility implies that the effects of trade on the manufacturing sector are not limited to that sector, as workers seek new jobs in nonmanufacturing industries.

Richardson (1995, 51) sees trade as making a moderate contribution to increasing income inequality that warrants attention.[7] Cline (1997) offers a detailed, comprehensive, and critical survey of the trade and wage inequality literature. He concludes that about 20–25 percent of the rise in the skilled/unskilled wage gap over the past 20 years has been due to the combined forces of trade and immigration.

U.S. trade with developing countries is the most recent focus, in part due to 1980s trade liberalization in these countries. To date, there is an emerging consensus, both theoretical and empirical, that U.S.–developing country trade lowers the employment and wages of U.S. lower-skilled workers. Sachs and Shatz (1998) emphasize skill differences between the manufacturing and nontraded sectors, noting that a reduction in manufacturing employment, particularly import-competing manufacturing, will release relatively unskilled workers into the nontraded (service) sector, leading to a fall in the relative wage of unskilled workers.

---

5. Grossman (1986, 1987) is widely cited on this point.

6. See Borjas, Freeman, and Katz (1992); Freeman and Katz (1991); Murphy and Welch (1991); Revenga (1992); Sachs and Schatz (1994); and Davis, Haltiwanger, and Schuh (1996). Not all studies agree. A number of studies written in the late 1980s and early 1990s concluded that trade plays a small role; see Mann (1988), Krugman and Lawrence (1994), Lawrence and Slaughter (1993), and Lawrence (1994). Berman, Bound, and Griliches (1994) conclude that trade plays a small role in increasing the relative employment of skilled workers.

7. Leamer (1993, 1994) and Wood (1994) conclude more strongly about the role of increasing globalization in increasing income inequality in the United States.

Using a factor proportions model, Borjas, Freeman, and Katz (1997) find that the growth of U.S. imports of less-developed-country (LDC) manufacturing goods has increased the effective supply of less-skilled labor, lowering relative earnings of low-wage workers. They conclude that increased trade has a substantially smaller effect on relative wages than increased immigration.

None of these studies deny the role of increasing trade. The debate is over how large a role trade plays in changing employment patterns and relative wages, and whether trade or technological change is more important.[8]

10.3 Measuring Industry Trade Sensitivity

There are different ways in the trade and employment literature to measure changes in international trade. Some studies measure trade changes and increasing foreign competition as changes in import prices, and other studies use changes in import share. Kletzer (1998b) discusses in detail the various measures available and how the measures may (or may not) be related to changes in employment and job loss. Here, I summarize that discussion to provide a background for the empirical research that follows.

Import penetration ratios (or import shares) provide an intuitively appealing way to categorize industries facing significant foreign competition. More generally, industries with a large (or rising) share of output (or supply) internationally traded are often labelled trade-sensitive (or import/export-sensitive) on the basis of calculated import and export penetration ratios. If the flow of imports reduces domestic employment, industries with high import penetration ratios are where that result is most likely to be found.[9]

From a theoretical perspective, there is no simple causal link between the volume of trade and employment changes because the rise in import share could indicate a number of foreign or domestic developments. A few examples may be illustrative.[10] Take the case of perfect competition, increasing but different marginal costs of production for both domestic and foreign firms, with substitutability between domestic and foreign goods. Let foreign supply expand, perhaps from technological diffusion (or an export promotion scheme) that lowers foreign costs while domestic

---

8. See also Berman, Bound, and Machin (1997).

9. An import penetration ratio is calculated by dividing industry imports by the sum of industry output plus imports (the denominator is industry supply). An export penetration ratio is calculated by dividing industry exports by industry output. See Schoepfle (1982) for classifications over the period 1972–79 and Bednarzik (1993) for the period 1982–87. Davis, Haltiwanger, and Schuh (1996) find high rates of job destruction for plants in industries with very high import penetration ratios during the period 1972–88. Plants in the top quintile of industries ranked by import penetration ratios had average annual employment reductions of 2.8 percent.

10. See also the discussion in Richardson (1995).

costs remain unchanged. This reduces the foreign good price and imports rise. With constant demand, the rise in imports reduces price, domestic output, and domestic employment. With declining domestic output, import share also rises. How much the import share rises depends on the elasticity of domestic supply. As domestic supply becomes more elastic, a given increase in imports produces a bigger reduction in domestic quantity (and presumably employment) and a rising import share.

When trade is measured as quantity flows, it is important also to consider the role of domestic demand. In the perfectly competitive case, imports may also rise if domestic demand increases. Price moves accordingly, and if foreign supply is more elastic than domestic supply, import share will also rise because the increase in imports will exceed the increase in domestic output. Alternatively, if domestic supply is more elastic than foreign supply, the rise in imports will be accompanied by a decline in import share. Here, the use of quantities reveals an ambiguity: Rising imports and import share are associated with increased domestic employment and presumably less displacement, and rising imports may not be associated with rising import share. These two cases imply that, over time, industry import shares will differ as a result of differences in supply elasticities as well as differences in the competitiveness of domestic firms relative to foreign firms.

In a standard Heckscher-Ohlin model, industries face increasing import-price competition when import prices fall, thus the appeal of using a price measure to examine whether job loss occurs when imports become more competitive. The link between import-price competition and industry employment is fairly straightforward. If the price of an imported (substitutable) good falls, labor's marginal revenue product falls. This drop in the derived demand for labor reduces employment (on an upward-sloping labor-supply curve). Flexible wages dampen the fall in employment. If wages adjust fully to equate labor demand and labor supply (a competitive labor market), employment falls to desired levels through (employee-initiated) quits. How much wages and employment change will depend on supply and demand elasticities, but there will be no displacement. Only if prices fall enough that firms find it more profitable to shut down than to continue to operate will displacements occur (through plant closings).

In a market where wages differ from market clearing, the likely consequences of increasing import competition are a bit more complicated. In unionized labor markets, if current wages exceed opportunity wages, the presence of rents may leave room for wage concessions. These concessions may dampen employment loss. If wages diverge from market clearing for efficiency-wage reasons, firms may be reluctant to impose wage reductions if they anticipate negative productivity consequences. Alternatively, senior union members may prefer to maintain wages (and their jobs), with layoffs reducing the employment of junior workers.

There are at least two reasons to think that price, arguably the preferred measure, is not completely informative about the effect of changes in trade policy or foreign supply. The first is that during some of the time period studied here some industries had quota protection (apparel, footwear, radio and television). Import-price changes will not necessarily reflect these quantity restraints. More importantly, these quota restraints imply that market share (import share) is likely to be a determinant of foreign and domestic supply.

The second difficulty with price alone is more fundamental. Using a monopolistically competitive dominant/fringe model, Mann (1988) shows how market share is likely to be a determinant of both foreign and domestic supply. She notes that quantity is a key variable in monopolistic competition with heterogeneous outputs. Furthermore, in the context of a three-factor Cobb-Douglas production function with no restrictions on returns to scale and with capital fixed in the short run, she discusses how increasing returns to scale are an important determinant of price. In her empirical analysis, covering the period 1974–81 for a subset of import-sensitive industries, Mann finds that foreign competition, measured as both import prices and import share, plays a small role in determining employment relative to the role played by domestic demand and prices for most industries.

10.4   Data: Measuring International Trade and Job Displacement

10.4.1   Trade Indicators

Data on U.S. import and exports by four-digit Standard Industry Classification (SIC) category, for the period 1958–94, are available as part of the NBER Trade Database. The import and export data file, available online, also reports the 1958–94 value of domestic shipments from the NBER Productivity Database.[11]

Import-price data are available for many four-digit SIC manufacturing industries starting in 1983–84 and currently ending with 1992, with coverage of a small number of industries available from 1978. The price measure is a fixed-weight Laspeyres index with a 1985 base period.[12] Relative import prices are obtained by deflating by the producer price index (PPI) as a proxy for the aggregate price level.

The SIC-based industry trade data must be aggregated up to a three-

11. The 1958–94 file combines data from the earlier NBER Trade and Immigration data file (described in Abowd 1991) with the NBER Trade Database (see Feenstra 1996).
12. These indexes are described in more detail in U.S. Bureau of Labor Statistics (1992). They are based on a survey of actual transactions prices, and, to the degree possible, they reflect c.i.f. (cost, insurance, freight) prices. The NBER Trade data were used to aggregate up to three-digit CIC industry. When aggregation was needed, the SIC indexes were weighted by their relative shares in total imports.

digit Census Industrial Classification (CIC) industry level to combine trade information with information on job displacement. Aggregating up from four-digit SIC to three-digit CIC is somewhat "costly" for the import-price data. Coverage is not complete for all manufacturing industries, so that not all the four-digit SIC industries within a three-digit CIC industry have information available for constructing an aggregate three-digit CIC industry price index.

10.4.2 Job Loss

The Displaced Worker Surveys (DWS) provide information on displacement. Available surveys, administered biennially as supplements to the Current Population Survey (CPS), cover displacements occurring during the period 1979–95. In each survey, adults (of ages 20 years and older) in the regular monthly CPS were asked if they had lost a job in the preceding 5-year period due to "a plant closing, an employer going out of business, a layoff from which he/she was not recalled, or other similar reasons." If the answer was yes, a series of questions followed concerning the old job and period of joblessness.

A common understanding of job displacement is that it occurs without personal prejudice; terminations are related to the operating decisions of the employer and are independent of individual job performance. In the DWS, this definition can be implemented by drawing the sample of displaced from individuals who respond that their job loss was due to the reasons noted previously. Other causes of job loss, such as quits or firings, are not considered displacements.[13] This operational definition is not without ambiguity: The displacements are job displacements, in the sense that an individual displaced from a job and rehired into a different job with the same employer is considered displaced.

Some of the distinctions may be too narrow or arbitrary. The distinction between quits and displacements is muddied by the ability of employers to reduce employment by reducing or failing to raise wages. Wage changes may induce some workers to quit (and not be in the sample), while others opt to stay with the firm (and they get displaced and enter the sample).[14] This distinction means that the displaced-worker sample will underestimate the amount of job change "caused" by trade. In addition, if the workers who stay on with the firm until displacement are those who face the worst labor market outcomes of all those at risk of displacement, then the displaced sample will be potentially nonrandom and it will overstate the costs of job loss. Without data on quits, these issues cannot be addressed.

13. Individuals may also respond that their job loss was due to the end of a seasonal job or the failure of a self-employed business. These individuals are not considered displaced.
14. Jacobson, LaLonde, and Sullivan (1993) show that wages fall for displaced workers before they are displaced.

The sample here is limited to workers displaced from manufacturing industries who are ages 20 to 64 at the time of displacement. Because the information is retrospectively gathered, it has potential recall error. Problems of recall are compounded by the overlapping coverage of years of displacement by surveys, with some years covered in two or three surveys.[15] This bias is believed to be significant. As Topel (1990) and Farber (1993) show, it is likely that the surveys seriously underestimate job loss that occurred long before the survey date due to inaccuracies in recall as well as question design.[16] This makes it desirable to have nonoverlapping recall periods (that is, each year of displacement drawn from only one survey). For this analysis I restrict the sample to displacements occurring in the 2-year period prior to each survey. This makes recall periods shorter and eliminates overlapping year coverage. I drew a larger sample from the 1984 survey by also including workers displaced during 1979–80.

I calculated industry displacement rates by dividing the number of workers displaced from a three-digit CIC industry in a year by the number of workers employed in that industry in that year. The annual industry employment numbers were calculated from merged CPS Outgoing Rotation Group data files, and they are a proxy for industry workers at risk of displacement.

10.5 A Descriptive Look at Trade and Job Loss, 1979–94

10.5.1 Job Loss

Based on calculations from sample described, drawn from the DWS, 32 million workers reported experiencing at least one permanent job loss during the period 1979–94 (excluding agriculture). Manufacturing accounted for 35.5 percent of total job loss, with 10.2 million workers reporting a job loss from that sector. Averaging over the 16-year time period, manufacturing accounted for 18–19 percent of total nonagricultural employment, starting with 23.4 percent in 1979 and ending at 16.0 percent in 1994.

For the period as a whole, the top job-loss manufacturing industries, measured by total workers displaced, are shown in table 10.1. In part, these industries accounted for much of the job loss because they are large industries in terms of employment. By adjusting for employment, the displacement rate offers a proxy for the "risk of job loss." All these industries were near or below the average job-loss rate for manufacturing industries.

Figure 10.1 plots the total and manufacturing displacement rates during the period 1979–94. The rate of job loss from manufacturing is consider-

15. The 1984 DWS covered the period 1979–83; the 1986 survey, 1981–85; the 1988 survey, 1983–87; the 1990 survey, 1985–89; the 1992 survey, 1987–91; the 1994 survey, 1991–93; and the 1996 survey, 1993–95.
16. If more than one job was lost, information is gathered only for the job held longest. See Topel (1990) and Farber (1993).

Table 10.1   **Number of Workers Displaced by Industry with Industry Displacement Rates**

Industry (CIC)	Workers Displaced ($\times 10^3$)	Average Annual Displacement Rate
Electrical machinery, nec (342)	688.3	0.038
Motor vehicles (351)	618.9	0.051
Apparel (151)	617.7	0.052
Printing, publishing (excl. newspapers) (172)	522.1	0.038
Machinery (excl. electrical) (331)	509.2	0.044
Electronic computing equipment (322)	337.9	0.045
Fabricated structural metals (282)	313.3	0.056
All manufacturing industries	11,380	0.051

Note: nec = not elsewhere classified.

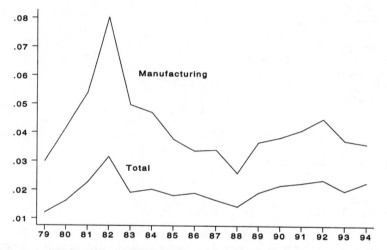

Fig. 10.1   Manufacturing and total displacement rates, by year
Source: Author's calculations from the 1984–96 Displaced Worker Surveys.

ably higher than for all industries. The manufacturing displacement rate rose to 8 percent in the early 1980s recession and then fell sharply until the late 1980s. It rose steadily through the prolonged early 1990s recession and then fell. Although the rate of job loss is down from its 1992 peak, it remains high given the extent of the 1990s expansion. The total displacement rate follows a similar, although dampened, pattern. The overall rate of job loss was high in 1994, given the strength of the economy (for more on the pattern of job loss over the 1980s and 1990s, see Farber 1997).[17]

17. My estimates of the rate of job loss are lower than Farber's due to differences in sample construction.

Table 10.2   **Top Quartile, Mean Annual Displacement Rate, > .061**

Industry	CIC	Mean Displacement Rate	Mean Import Share	Mean Change in Import Share
Leather products	222	.142046	.4079864*	.0238756*
Optical and health supplies	372	.1262741	.0801311	.003507
Radio, television	341	.1259439	.1957753*	.0081509*
Railroad locomotives	361	.1077487	.0925145	.0067265
Wood buildings and mobile homes	232	.0972105	.0434898	.0001035
Cycles and miscellaneous transport	370	.093942	.2542767*	−.0068314
Watches, clocks	381	.0913399	.5229867*	.0278894*
Footwear	221	.0906134	.4954904*	.0241364*
Structural clay products	252	.083527	.1209288	.0060668
Guided missiles	362	.0803838	.0256684	.0021725
Other primary metals	280	.0775787	.1853473*	.0038447
Ship and boat building	360	.0746358	.027272	.0012961
Leather tanning	220	.0739732	.2082242*	.00799*
Miscellaneous petroleum and coal	201	.0720061	.064999	−.0013748
Pottery and related products	261	.0717307	.3800826*	.0105394*
Primary aluminum	272	.0702517	.0828264	.0063072
Toys	390	.0677491	.3408123*	.0177078*

Source: Author's calculations from the Displaced Worker Surveys and U.S. Import and Export Data, 1958–94.
*Top quartile of respective distribution.

10.5.2   Trade and Job Loss by Industry

The previous discussion highlights the widespread job displacement of the last 16 years. Are high rates of job loss associated with import competition? Are import-competing industries characterized by high rates of job loss? As a preliminary, I stay within the tradition of using import shares to classify industries as "import competing." The mean annual import share across the industries in the sample was 0.117 during the period 1975–94, ranging from 0.002 to 0.523. The mean annual displacement rate across the industries in the sample was 0.052, ranging from 0.0078 to 0.142. If industries are ranked by mean annual displacement rates, the top quartile is listed in table 10.2, along with their mean displacement rate, mean import share, and mean change in import share. Overall, the industry list is consistent with the perception that import-competing industries have experienced high rates of job loss. The list has the "usual suspects:" footwear, leather products, pottery, radio and television, watches and clocks, and toys. For the most part, these high-job-loss-rate industries are either high import share (traditionally import-competing) or have experienced a large (positive) change in import share (increasing import competition), or both.

Table 10.3 contains additional summary univariate classifications of trade and job loss. Panel A reports the mean annual displacement rate for each quartile of the industry mean import-share distribution. The highest import-share industries have, on average, the highest job-loss rate, but from below the top quartile, job-loss rates are relatively uniform. Within each quartile, the distribution of job-loss rates is fairly similar. Panel B reports mean job-loss rates by industry mean change in import share. In this panel, lob-loss rates are higher for industries with above-average changes in import share.

At this level of industry aggregation, industries are both importers and exporters, and panel C reports the mean annual displacement rate for each quartile of the industry mean annual change in net export share, calculated as (Exports − Imports)/Shipments. Here, we might expect declining job loss with a positive change in net exports, so that from the top quartile to the bottom, job-loss rates would rise. This is the pattern in panel C, although the decline in job loss as net exports rise is not smooth, and the range of job-loss rates within each quartile is fairly similar. Last, panel D reports a mean import share for the full job-loss industry distribution.

Table 10.3   Trade and Job Loss by Industry

	Bottom Quartile	Second Quartile	Third Quartile	Top Quartile
A. By mean import share	<.043	.044 to .087	.088 to .1537	>.154
Mean annual displacement rate	.046	.045	.045	.065
[Min, Max]	[.024, .097]	[.021, .126]	[.016, .108]	[.008, .142]
B. By mean change in import share	<.0007	.0007 to .003	.003 to .0075	>.0075
Mean annual displacement rate	.045	.042	.055	.059
[Min, Max]	[.021, .097]	[.021, .080]	[.024, .126]	[.008, .142]
C. By mean change in net exports/ shipments	<−.0029	−.003 to −.0008	−.0008 to .00059	>.00059
Mean annual displacement rate	.059	.044	.053	.044
[Min, Max]	[.008, .142]	[.015, .080]	[.022, .126]	[.021, .094]
D. By mean annual displacement rate	<.031	.031 to .044	.045 to .061	>.061
Mean import share	.087	.081	.084	.207
[Min, Max]	[.002, .209]	[.01, .179]	[.007, .264]	[.025, .522]

Source: Author's calculations from the Displaced Worker Surveys and U.S. Imports and Exports, 1958–94.

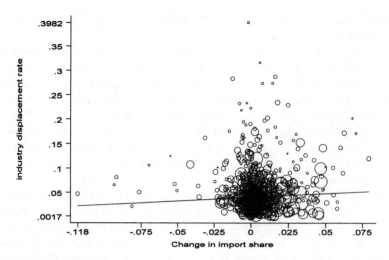

Fig. 10.2   Industry displacement rates and changes in import share, 1979–94
Source: See table 10.4.

Similar to table 10.2, import share is highest among the high-job-loss-rate industries, and the top half of the job-loss rate distribution has a distinctly higher import share than the lower half of the distribution. For the four measures used in table 10.3, appendix tables 10A.1 to 10A.4 report a full industry listing by quartile.

One suggestion from these univariate classifications is that the combination of "trade with job loss" arises from continued, sustained import competition. That is, high rates of job loss are found for industries with high import share and large (positive) changes in import share. For the most part, increasing import competition (positive changes in import share), from a lower level of import share, is associated with below-average job loss (e.g., photographic equipment, scientific and controlling instruments, and pulp and paper).

To examine the full industry-by-year range of observations, figures 10.2 and 10.3 are scatter plots of annual industry displacement rates and percent changes, from the previous year, in import penetration ratios (fig. 10.2), or real import prices (fig. 10.3). In each scatter plot, the circles are scaled to reflect industry employment size. Each plot contains a regression line for the simple regression of the displacement rate on the chosen trade indicator (and a constant term).

Figure 10.2 contains the scatter plot for displacement rates and import share for the period 1979–94. There are a number of industry-year observations where import share changes very little and displacement is high. At the same time, there are enough industries where positive (negative) changes in import share are associated with high (low) displacement rates,

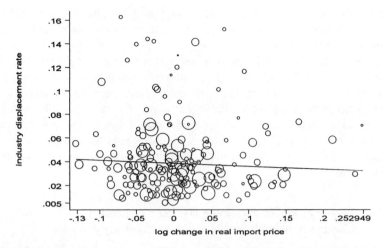

Fig. 10.3   Industry displacement rates and changes in import prices, 1983–92
Source: See table 10.4.

so that the regression line has positive slope (with *t*-statistic of 1.907 for the estimated slope coefficient).[18] A few traditionally trade-sensitive industries, such as footwear, leather products, apparel, and steel, are important in determining the slope of the regression line.

In figure 10.3, it is important to note that the price coverage is less comprehensive than the trade-flow coverage (only 20 three-digit CIC industries are included), and the period of coverage is 1983–92. This scatter plot seems to reveal little evidence of a negative correlation between import prices and job-loss rates. There are a few industry-year observations where an increase in import prices (a reduction in import competition) is associated with lower displacement rates. The regression line has a negative slope, with a *t*-statistic of −0.813.[19] There are also a number of industry observations with high displacement rates and little change in relative import prices.

A few observations stand out from these descriptive figures and tables. There is a set of industries facing sustained import competition, those

18. The estimated regression, using industry employment weights, with standard errors in parentheses, is

$$\text{Displacement rate} = \underset{(0.0011)}{0.0401} + \underset{(0.0805)}{0.1534} \ (\% \ \Delta \ \text{Import penetration ratio}).$$

19. The estimated regression, using industry employment weights, with standard errors in parentheses, is

$$\text{Displacement rate} = \underset{(0.0019)}{0.0387} - \underset{(0.0312)}{0.0254} \ (\text{log Difference real import price}).$$

with both high levels of import share and positive changes in import share where the rate of job loss is high. The scatter plots provide additional evidence, revealing industries where decreases in import prices are associated with high rates of job loss. These industries are consistent with the perception that "trade costs jobs," although inferences about causality should not be made based on the descriptive evidence. At the same time, the scatter plots reveal a considerable amount of variation in job displacement across industries. There are numerous industry-year observations where job loss is high in the absence of changes in foreign competition. Thus trade itself can explain only a small share of the variation in job displacement.

10.6   Empirical Model: Increasing Foreign Competition, Changes in Industry Employment, and Industry Job Loss

This section presents a simple empirical framework for examining the relationship between international trade and job displacement that follows Kletzer (1998b). It starts with a discussion of trade and employment change that follows Revenga (1992). A model of labor turnover is used to relate employment change to displacement.

To simplify the analysis, assume wages adjust to equate labor supply and labor demand. Using first differences, the demand for labor in industry i in year t (N_{it}) can be written as

$$(1) \qquad d\ln N_{it} = \beta_1 d\ln W_{it} + \beta_2 d\ln X_{it}^1 + \beta_3 d\ln X_{it}^2 + v_{1it},$$

where W_{it} is the industry wage, X_{it}^1 is a vector of trade-related factors (discussed in more detail later) that shift labor demand for industry i in year t, X_{it}^2 is a vector of non-trade-related factors, and v_{1it} is the error term. Also in first differences, labor supply can be written as

$$(2) \qquad d\ln N_{it} = \alpha_1 d\ln W_{it} + \alpha_2 d\ln H_{it} + v_{2it},$$

where H_{it} is a vector of factors that shift labor supply and v_{2it} is an error term. Labor market clearing implies

$$(3) \qquad d\ln N_{it} = \gamma_1\beta_2 d\ln X_{it}^1 + \gamma_2\alpha_2 d\ln H_{it} + \gamma_3\beta_3 d\ln X_{it}^2 + \varepsilon_{it},$$

$$(4) \qquad d\ln W_{it} = \lambda_1\beta_2 d\ln X_{it}^1 + \lambda_2\alpha_2 d\ln H_{it} + \lambda_3\beta_3 d\ln X_{it}^2 + u_{it}.$$

Equation (3) is a basic reduced-form equation for net changes in employment. A simple model of turnover can be used to modify and narrow the focus to just one of the gross flows, job displacement. Firms implement net employment reductions through the use of displacements and unreplaced attritions. Attritions are separations due to quits, discharges (for cause), retirements, and deaths. Attritions that are not replaced by employers are called unreplaced attritions. For an industry, net employment change in year t can be written as

$$(5) \qquad\qquad DIS + UA = -\Delta N,$$

where DIS is displacements, and UA is unreplaced attritions (other non-displacement separations minus accessions).[20] This net change in employment can be expressed as a proportion of total employment,

$$(6) \qquad \frac{DIS}{N_{t-1}} = \text{Displacement rate} = \frac{-(N_t - N_{t-1})}{N_{t-1}} - \frac{UA}{N_{t-1}}.$$

Relying on the approximation of the rate of change of employment $(N_t - N_{t-1})/N_{t-1}$ to the change in log employment $\ln N_t - \ln N_{t-1}$, for small changes, equation (6) is approximately equal to

$$(7) \qquad\qquad \text{Displacement rate}_t = d\ln N_t - \text{UA rate},$$

where UA rate $= UA/N_{t-1}$.

Equations (3) and (7) can be combined to yield a reduced-form equation for industry i displacement:

$$(8) \quad \text{Displacement rate}_{it} = \gamma_1\beta_2 d\ln X_{it}^1 + \gamma_2\alpha_2 d\ln H_{it} + \gamma_3\beta_3 d\ln X_{it}^2$$
$$+ \gamma_4 \text{UA rate}_{it} + (\varepsilon_{it} + \eta_{it}),$$

where η_{it} reflects unobservable factors related to displacement.

In the context of a turnover model, it is inappropriate to include quits, discharges, and accessions (summed here as the UA rate) as independent variables in a displacement relationship. Quits are very likely to be influenced by conditions within the industry.[21] Firms and industries are likely to differ in their use of the various components of turnover to implement desired changes in employment.

The elements of the vector X^1 need to be specified. There are two alternatives. The first, using relative import prices, yields

$$(9) \qquad \text{Displacement rate}_{it} = \delta_1 d\ln P_{it}^m + \delta_2 d\ln X_{it}^2 + \Gamma_i + e_{it}^1,$$

where P_{it}^m is the domestic price (in dollars) of the import good (relative to the aggregate price level). Elements of H are subsumed in X^2 and the UA rate is now subsumed in the industry fixed effect Γ_i; δ_1 and δ_2 are coefficients to be estimated, and e_{it}^1 is the error term.

---

20. "Accessions" are new hires and rehires. The term "unreplaced attritions" appears in Brechling (1978).

21. Brechling (1978) presents a model of turnover with endogenous quits. In that model, quits rise and fall with industry employment growth and the state of the overall economy. In depressed industries, workers are much less likely to quit; therefore, normal attrition cannot be counted on to reduce employment.

At this point, it is important to note what is measured by industry relative import price. In the previous discussion, it was noted that falling relative import prices increase the competitiveness of final-good imports. From this there may follow a reduction in labor demand and desired employment and increased job loss. A reduction in import price, however, can also mean lower prices of imported intermediate inputs. The import-price data used here do not allow a distinction between the two types of imports. By including just one industry import price, the estimated parameter on import price combines the two different effects.

An alternative specification uses import share and exports. The previous discussion suggests that import share be used along with measures of domestic demand. Total sales can be decomposed into its component parts: the domestic market (Domestic = Sales − Exports + Imports); exports; and import share. A first-order approximation gives

$$(10) \qquad d \ln \text{Sales} = w_1 d \ln(\text{Domestic}) + w_2 d \ln(\text{Exports})$$
$$- w_3 d(\text{Import share}),$$

where w_1 = (Sales − Exports)/Sales, w_2 = Exports/Sales, and w_3 = Domestic/Sales. The weights adjust changes in the three components for the difference in the absolute magnitude of sales generated by the domestic side as compared to the trade side.[22] The following equation relates changes in sales to displacement:

$$(11) \quad \text{Displacement rate} = \delta_3 w_1 d \ln(\text{Domestic}) + \delta_4 w_2 d \ln(\text{Exports})$$
$$+ \delta_5 w_3 d(\text{Import share}) + \delta_6 d \ln X_{it}^2 + \Pi_i$$
$$+ e_{it}^2,$$

where the δ are coefficients to be estimated, Π_i is the industry fixed effect, and e_{it}^2 is the error term.

Equation (11) specifies an industry's exposure to imports simply as import share (or import penetration ratio). This specification does not distinguish between imports of final goods and imports of intermediate inputs. Final-goods imports have traditionally been called "import competition." The discussion in section 10.3 on measures of trade sensitivity focused on final-goods imports. A rise in the use of imported intermediate inputs has a more ambiguous effect on displacement. If the intermediate inputs were formerly produced domestically,[23] job loss may be associated with the increased use. At the same time, if imported intermediate inputs are less costly than domestically produced intermediates (perhaps due to a fall in

---

22. This decomposition of sales is explained in detail by Freeman and Katz (1991).

23. The decision to switch intermediate input production from domestic to foreign is often called outsourcing.

import prices), industry labor demand may increase, resulting in higher desired employment and fewer displacements.

As specifications of the effect of trade on job loss, equations (9) and (11) are clearly partial equilibrium at the industry level. They do not address indirect effects on job displacement that may result from local industry interactions that produce spillover effects on a given industry's employment and job loss.[24]

10.7   Multivariate Analysis of the Evidence on Trade and Job Loss

Before turning to the estimation results for job loss, it is useful to consider the "trade" version of equation (3), where the log change in employment is the dependent variable. Table 10.4 reports coefficient estimates for a specification using changes in import prices (panel A) and changes in import shares, exports, and domestic demand (panel B), with the log change in blue-collar employment as the dependent variable. The changes are annual, and the specification includes industry fixed effects. Consistent with expectations, industry employment is positively correlated with industry relative import prices. In panel B, employment falls as import share rises, and it rises as exports and domestic demand rise.

10.7.1   Cross-Industry Estimates

Turning to the regression framework, tables 10.5 and 10.6 report cross-sectional estimates of a very simple specification relating annual industry displacement rates to two industry trade indicators.[25] Table 10.5 reports estimates from a cross-sectional time-series version of equation (11), where the explanatory variables are changes in domestic demand, exports, and import share. Table 10.6 reports estimates of equation (9), where the main explanatory variable is the change in relative import prices. In both tables, the dependent variable is the difference between an industry's annual displacement rate and its mean displacement rate during the time period. Subtracting out the mean industry displacement rate eliminates some industry-specific differences in displacement. Turning first to table 10.5, increases in domestic demand and exports are associated with declining job loss. Rising import share is positively related to job loss, and the hypothesis that the export and import coefficients are the same in magnitude cannot be rejected. Over the time period, there was a significant downward trend in the rate of job loss.

Technological change is one of the important elements missing from the discussion so far. The literature points clearly in the direction of techno-

24. On this point, see Goldberg and Tracy (chap. 8 in this volume).
25. The reported standard errors are corrected for heteroskedasticity and the clustering of observations by industry.

366 Lori G. Kletzer

Table 10.4   Changes in Industry Blue-Collar Employment, Changes in Relative Import Prices, and Changes in Import Shares Panel, Fixed Effect Estimates

A	(1)
Time period	1983–92
Log change relative import price index	.1005
	(.0673)
Change in manufacturing industrial production index	.0039
	(.0011)
Industry fixed effects	Yes
Constant	−.0296
	(.0053)
R^2 (within)	.091
R^2 (between)	.071
R^2 (overall)	.073
N	214
Number of industries	27

B	(1)	(2)	(3)
Time period	1979–94	1975–94	1970–94
Weighted log change in domestic demand	.2851	.3202	.3402
	(.0298)	(.0249)	(.0275)
Weighted log change in exports	.7002	.5901	.4927
	(.1439)	(.1171)	(.1247)
Weighted change in import share	−.3221	−.3149	−.3919
	(.0929)	(.0863)	(.1014)
Industry fixed effects	Yes	Yes	Yes
Constant	−.0277	−.0293	−.0264
	(.0030)	(.0026)	(.0030)
R^2 (within)	.135	.159	.126
R^2 (between)	.396	.527	.462
R^2 (overall)	.147	.170	.134
N	1,100	1,372	1,612
Number of industries	70	70	70

Source: Author's calculations from data drawn from the NBER Trade Database, Bureau of Labor Statistics, U.S. Import and Export Price Indexes, and the Displaced Worker Surveys.
Notes: Standard errors are in parentheses. Panel A includes one lag in the import price index.

logical change as a key explanation to declining unskilled employment in manufacturing and increasing wage inequality (see Krugman and Lawrence 1994; Lawrence and Slaughter 1993; Berman, Bound, and Griliches 1994; Berman, Bound, and Machin 1997). The challenges of proxying technological change are clear, and in this case there is the additional issue of potential endogeneity. Industries facing increasing foreign competition may be driven toward technological change as a response.[26] As a first step,

26. See Lawrence (chap. 6 in this volume).

Table 10.5 Industry Displacement Rates and Changes in Import Share: Cross-sectional Estimation

	All Workers					Blue-Collar Workers			White-Collar Workers		
	(1)	(2)	(3)	(4)	(5)	(6)	(7)	(8)	(9)	(10)	(11)
Time period	1979–94	1979–94	1979–94	1979–94	1983–92	1979–94	1979–94	1983–92	1979–94	1979–94	1983–92
Weighted ln change domestic demand	−.0697 (.0247)	−.0719 (.0254)	−.0704 (.0240)	−.0714 (.0252)	−.0006 (.0541)	−.0875 (.0208)	−.0935 (.0232)	−.0011 (.0424)	.0628 (.0567)	.0564 (.0547)	.0868 (.0961)
Weighted ln change in exports	−.3060 (.0724)	−.3114 (.0716)	−.3068 (.0722)	−.3168 (.0713)	−.2803 (.1025)	−.3130 (.0676)	−.3134 (.0702)	−.3303 (.0901)	−.4801 (.1546)	−.4806 (.1529)	−.2803 (.1846)
Weighted change in import share	.1037 (.0587)	.0999 (.0636)	.0943 (.0631)		.1840 (.0910)	.0508 (.0850)	.0527 (.0866)	.1519 (.0500)	.0549 (.1040)	.0699 (.0992)	−.0940 (.1404)
Change in intermediate goods imports				.2916 (.3331)							
Change in manufacturing industrial production index	−.0005 (.0003)	−.0005 (.0003)	−.0005 (.0003)	−.0004 (.0003)	−.0003 (.0008)	−.0004 (.0003)	−.0005 (.0004)	−.0008 (.0007)	−.0006 (.0008)	−.00072 (.0009)	−.0002 (.0013)
Time trend	−.0010 (.0004)	−.0010 (.0004)	−.0009 (.0003)	−.0010 (.0004)	−.0010 (.0012)	−.0008 (.0004)	−.0009 (.0004)	−.0019 (.0009)	−.00012 (.0007)	−.0001 (.0008)	−.0020 (.0024)
Change in unionization (1983–95, annualized)		−.0041 (.0028)	−.0046 (.0029)	−.0041 (.0029)	.0012 (.0062)		.0006 (.0009)	.0022 (.0038)		−.0006 (.0013)	−.0041 (.0103)
Change in TFP		.0084 (.0274)		.0053 (.0276)	−.0091 (.0691)		.0231 (.0258)	−.0407 (.0745)		.0616 (.0742)	−.0812 (.1457)
Change in computer use (1984–93, annualized)			−.1172 (.1193)								
ln(Capital stock/Shipments)		−.0034 (.0026)	−.0033 (.0027)	−.0033 (.0024)	.0015 (.0016)		−.0015 (.0014)	−.00002 (.0022)	.0010 (.0070)	.0021 (.0017)	−.0006 (.0066)
Constant	.0198 (.0033)	.0136 (.0041)	.0155 (.0042)	.0132 (.0045)	.0120 (.0157)	.0134 (.0029)	.0131 (.0027)	.0226 (.0105)	.0026 (.0074)	.0026 (.0074)	.0167 (.0289)
R^2	.086	.090	.091	.088	.124	.083	.084	.154	.025	.026	.049
N	934	934	934	934	215	846	846	194	674	674	167
Number of industries	70	70	70	70	26	70	70	25	70	70	26

Source: Author's calculations from the Displaced Worker Surveys, 1984–96, U.S. Import and Export data, 1958–94, and the NBER Productivity Database.

Notes: Standard errors are in parentheses. Samples used in columns (5), (8), and (11) match the industries and time period used in table 10.6.

Table 10.6   Industry Displacement Rates and Changes in Import Prices, 1983–92: Cross-sectional Estimation

	All Workers			Blue-Collar Workers		White-Collar Workers	
	(1)	(2)	(3)	(4)	(5)	(6)	(7)
ln Change relative import price index	−.0403	−.0460	−.0406	−.0496	.0527	−.0702	−.0716
	(.0322)	(.0306)	(.0307)	(.0384)	(.0400)	(.0553)	(.0583)
Change in index of manufacturing industrial production	.0004	.0008	.0005	−.0005	−.0009	−.0006	−.0007
	(.0008)	(.0007)	(.0007)	(.0008)	(.0008)	(.0014)	(.0013)
Time trend	−.0017	−.0016	−.0016	−.0031	−.0032	−.0030	−.0030
	(.0011)	(.0011)	(.0012)	(.0012)	(.0012)	(.0022)	(.0023)
Change in unionization (1983–95, annualized)			.0013	.0043	.0063	−.0092	−.0094
			(.0074)	(.0027)	(.0029)	(.0096)	(.0097)
ln(Capital stock/Shipments)		.0002	.0005	−.0016	−.0024	−.0012	−.0019
		(.0027)	(.0032)	(.0018)	(.0021)	(.0075)	(.0075)
Change in TFP		−.1040		−.1308		−.0380	
		(.0545)		(.0662)		(.1454)	
Change in computer use (1984–93, annualized)			−.3028		.0459		.1861
			(.2351)		(.1171)		(.4532)
Constant	.0174	.0177	.0254	.0335	.0350	.0255	.0214
	(.0140)	(.0143)	(.0130)	(.0127)	(.0141)	(.0238)	(.0230)
R^2	.074	.089	.093	.132	.114	.046	.047
N	168	168	168	148	148	129	129
Number of industries	26	26	26	24	24	26	26

Source: Author's calculations from Displaced Worker Surveys, 1984–96, and U.S. Import and Export Data, 1958–94.

Notes: Standard errors are in parentheses. Specification includes one lag in the import price index.

columns (2) and (3) of table 10.5, use two distinct proxies for technological change, ignoring endogeneity, with insignificant results. Column (2) uses the year-to-year change in total factor productivity (TFP), calculated from the NBER Productivity Database. Changes in TFP appear to be positively correlated with job-loss rates, although the coefficient estimate is imprecise. In column (3), technological change is proxied by a variable that measures worker-reported changes in computer use within the three-digit CIC industry during the period 1984–93.[27] Increases in the use of computers are negatively correlated with industry displacement, but the coefficient is imprecisely estimated.

Controls for changes in industry union density and capital intensity are also included in columns (2)–(5). Because the trend in unionization in manufacturing was sharply downward during this time period (and therefore collinear with the time trend), changes in density are measured as the annualized long-period change in density during the period 1983–95. Although not measured precisely, industries with smaller declines in unionization had smaller job-loss rates. Through collective bargaining, workers may have been able to restrict displacement (through wage or other concessions). Lower job-loss rates are associated with the more capital-intensive industries, although the correlation is not statistically significant.

In practice, it is difficult to separate the effect of "import competition" on job loss from the effect of imported inputs on job loss, because industry import penetration is highly correlated with the use of imported inputs, or outsourcing. In an abbreviated fashion, column (4) considers the effect outsourcing. Does the use of imported intermediate goods reduce the demand for labor and contribute to job loss? In column (4), imports are measured as the annualized difference in imputed imports of intermediate goods between 1979 and 1990.[28] The estimated coefficient on the import measure is positive as expected, but not statistically significant.

Columns (6)–(11) present results separately for blue-collar and white-collar workers.[29] The results are basically the same across groups, with a few exceptions. Rising import share is associated with higher rates of job loss for both occupational groups, but the estimated coefficients are statistically insignificant for both. The significant downward time trend in job-loss rates is found only for blue-collar workers. Technological change, as

27. Computer use is available from CPS data for 1984 and 1993. The variable used here is the annualized change in computer use for workers in a three-digit industry between 1984 and 1993. The data are described in Autor, Katz, and Krueger (1997). I am grateful to David Autor for providing the computer use data.

28. The data are described in Feenstra and Hanson (1997). I am grateful to Gordon Hanson for providing the imported intermediate-goods data.

29. Service workers are combined with white-collar workers, so the divisions are approximately production and nonproduction.

proxied by changes in TFP, is associated with increasing job loss, although the estimates are imprecise.

For further comparison with the import-price regressions reported in table 10.6, columns (5), (8), and (11) of table 10.5 report estimates for the time period 1983–92 and for the subset of industries for which the import-price data are available. For this shorter time period, the coefficient on domestic demand falls appreciably in magnitude and is statistically insignificant. Job loss is positively related to import share and negatively related to exports. For the shorter time period, the proxies for technological change, changes in unionization, and capital intensity are all statistically insignificant.

Table 10.6 uses changes in relative import-price indices as the main explanatory variable. As expected, the correlation between changes in import price and job loss is negative. For all workers and for blue-collar workers, the estimates are imprecise, while for white-collar workers, the estimated coefficients are statistically significant. The sensitivity of displacement rates to the business cycle is captured by the change in the index of manufacturing industrial production, with the negative, but imprecisely estimated, coefficient showing the countercyclical nature of displacement. The main difference between the results in tables 10.5 and 10.6 is the sign of estimated correlation between technological change and job loss. Using import price during 1983–92, the correlation between changes in TFP and job-loss rates is negative, whereas the correlation is positive in the trade-quantity regression over the longer time period. The difference is not the specification of increasing foreign competition; it is the time period. Columns (5), (8), and (11) in table 10.5, using trade quantities, report a negative correlation between changes in TFP and job loss for the 1983–92 period. This estimated effect is consistent with the Rybczynski theorem, where factors flow into sectors experiencing technological advance. In an expanding sector, job-loss rates are expected to fall.

Overall, the estimates are consistent with some of the expectations about increasing foreign competition and job loss. Across industries, there is some evidence that the risk of job loss increases as imports rise and/or import prices fall. At the same time, this simple cross-industry specification explains little of the variation in job loss rates.

10.7.2   Within-Industry Estimates

Without more satisfactory proxies for technological change, and given the likely heterogeneity across industries in the use of layoffs, hiring, discharges, and quits to change employment levels, it may be desirable to estimate the relationships in an industry fixed effects framework. With industry fixed effects, the estimation focuses on changes over time in job loss and trade within an industry. That is, when a given industry faces increasing foreign competition, what happens to job loss?

Table 10.7 reports panel fixed effect estimates of a very simple specifica-

Table 10.7　　　　　**Industry Displacement Rates, Changes in Relative Import Prices, and Changes in Import Shares Panel, Fixed Effect Estimates**

A	(1)	(2)
Sample	Full	High import
Time period	1983–92	1983–92
ln Change	−.0868	.0831
relative import price index	(.0461)	(.1091)
Change in	.0011	−.00007
manufacturing industrial production index	(.0009)	(.0014)
ln(Capital stock/	−.0155	−.0236
Shipments)	(.0217)	(.0277)
Time trend	−.0017	−.0019
	(.0012)	(.0021)
Change in TFP	−.1364	−.1725
	(.0714)	(.0917)
Constant	.0514	.0581
	(.0181)	(.0257)
Industry fixed effects	Yes	Yes
R^2 (within)	.134	.113
R^2 (between)	.181	.351
R^2 (overall)	.096	.274
N	132	76
Number of industries	17	13

B	(1)	(2)	(3)	(4)	(5)
Sample	Full	Full	Full	Balanced	Panel A
Time period	1979–94	1979–85	1986–94	1979–94	1983–92
Weighted ln	−.0733	−.0571	−.0675	−.0576	−.0050
change in domestic demand	(.0191)	(.0256)	(.0298)	(.0344)	(.0475)
Weighted ln	−.3436	−.2364	−.2655	−.5614	−.4290
change in exports	(.0605)	(.0810)	(.0945)	(.0919)	(.1118)
Weighted change	.0703	.1266	.0126	.2037	−.0797
in import share	(.0627)	(.0883)	(.0855)	(.1399)	(.1022)
Change in	−.0005	−.0011	.0002	−.0010	.0008
manufacturing industrial production index	(.0003)	(.0004)	(.0006)	(.0005)	(.0009)
ln(Capital stock/	−.0041	.0091	.0131	−.0218	−.0576
Shipments)	(.0078)	(.0143)	(.0159)	(.0113)	(.0203)

(*continued*)

Table 10.7   (continued)

B	(1)	(2)	(3)	(4)	(5)
Change in TFP	.0329	−.0449	.0853	.0928	−.0477
	(.0341)	(.0482)	(.0473)	(.0604)	(.0818)
Time trend	−.0009	.0012	.0007	−.0014	−.0021
	(.0003)	(.0010)	(.0005)	(.0004)	(.0011)
Constant	.0600	.0644	.0491	.0535	.0215
	(.0061)	(.0121)	(.0128)	(.0009)	(.0174)
Industry fixed effects	Yes	Yes	Yes	Yes	Yes
R^2 (within)	.088	.137	.048	.141	.225
R^2 (between)	.025	.0009	.139	.017	.004
R^2 (overall)	.056	.0525	.0007	.046	.032
N	966	438	528	433	168
Number of industries	72	70	71	27	17

Source: Author's calculations from data drawn from the NBER Trade Database, Bureau of Labor Statistics, U.S. Import and Export Price Indexes, the Displaced Worker Surveys, and the NBER Productivity Database.

Notes: Full sample denotes the largest feasible data set with information on the relevant variables. Standard errors are in parentheses. Specification in panel A includes one lag in the import price index.

tion relating annual industry displacement rates to the two sets of industry trade indicators. Panel A reports estimates from a specification using changes in relative import-price indices. Column (1) uses the sample of 17 industries for which data are available during the period 1983–92. Column (2) is restricted to a group of high-import industries, those industries within the top quartile of mean import share during the period 1975–94. The estimated coefficients in columns (1) and (2) reveal that as relative import prices fall and imports become more competitive, displacement rises (the estimated effect of changes in relative import prices includes one lagged term). The effect of a change in relative import price is not different for the high-import-share industries. The business-cycle component of displacement is proxied by the index of manufacturing industrial production. Counterintuitively, the sign of the estimated correlation is positive (as it is in table 10.6), although the estimate is imprecise. Similar to table 10.6, technological change is associated with lower rates of job loss. Although generally consistent with expectations, this simple specification does not explain much of the within-industry variation in displacement.

Panel B of table 10.7 reports estimates from a specification of trade flows and domestic demand. Columns (2) and (3) break up the time period into subperiods 1979–85 and 1986–92. Displacement rates are lower with increases in domestic demand and exports. Increases in import share are positively correlated with industry job loss, with a considerably stronger effect found for the first half of the 1980s than for the second half. The fit

Table 10.8   **Changes in Industry In Displacement and Changes in Relative Import Prices Panel, Fixed Effect Estimates**

	(1)
Time period	1983–92
ln Change relative import	−1.5625
price index	(0.7457)
Change in manufacturing	−0.0105
industrial production index	(0.0107)
Industry fixed effects	Yes
Constant	8.9664
	(0.0510)
R^2 (within)	0.041
R^2 (between)	0.026
R^2 (overall)	0.011
N	209
Number of industries	28

Source: Author's calculations from data drawn from the NBER Trade Database, Bureau of Labor Statistics, U.S. Import and Export Price Indexes, and the Displaced Worker Surveys.
Notes: Standard errors are in parentheses. Specification includes one lag in the import price index.

of the regression is somewhat better for the first half of the decade. Column (4) uses a balanced panel of industries, with the results little changed.

As a check, table 10.8 reports coefficient estimates for a specification using the natural log of industry displacement as the dependent variable. This specification matches Haveman (1998), and it uses changes in relative import prices as the primary independent variable. The estimated coefficient is negative, as expected, and statistically significant. A 1 percent fall in import price raises industry displacement by 1.56 percent. This estimate is close to Haveman's elasticity estimate of 1.69.

The measured response of job loss to changes in import prices and import share is probably understated. Revenga (1992) notes that if the import price variable, in equation (3), is correlated with any of the components of the disturbance term, ordinary least squares (OLS) parameter estimates will be biased and inconsistent. She notes several factors that may induce correlation between the import-price measure and the error terms, such as unmeasured worldwide shocks to materials costs or unobserved and unmeasured taste or demand shifts in the United States that influence import prices due to the size of the U.S. market.[30] Similar arguments can be made for the endogeneity of the import-share variable. A comparison of Revenga's OLS and instrumental variables (IV) estimates suggests

---

30. Closer to the model discussed in Mann (1988), import prices may be set specifically for the U.S. market, and this price setting will produce a correlation between import price and the disturbance terms.

rather strongly the likelihood of omitted variables (or simultaneity) that influence industry employment, wages, and import price, as OLS estimates of import-price elasticities appear significantly downward biased.[31] The use of displacement here may weaken this correlation empirically, but conceptually it is still likely to exist.

10.8 Reemployment Following Job Loss: Where Do Displaced Workers Become Reemployed?

Does increasing foreign competition lead to a reallocation of labor? The linkages of changing trade patterns to changing employment patterns have been examined in a number of papers, including Borjas, Freeman, and Katz (1992, 1997), and Sachs and Shatz (1994, 1998). These studies confirm that the rise of net imports from developing countries is unskilled intensive relative to the rest of manufacturing and the rest of the economy. Sachs and Shatz (1998, 30) show "that a cutback in manufacturing employment (particularly import-competing manufacturing employment) will release relatively unskilled workers into the service sector, with the effect being larger should those employees come from the import-competing sector of manufacturing." These studies reveal a potentially important aspect of the link between trade and wages, that the reemployment of displaced import-competing manufacturing workers in the (lower-wage) service sector provides one avenue for downward pressure on wages with increasing trade. These papers consider the economywide aspects of labor reallocation, and the implications for increasing earnings inequality. The individual-level implications of labor reallocation are equally important, certainly for displaced workers, and for understanding the costs of trade-related displacement. In this section, I use the information available in the DWS to directly examine the pattern of reemployment following job loss and the possible link between reemployment sector and earnings losses.

The individual-level consequences of job displacement are well studied and well known. The state of knowledge in two areas will be briefly restated here (interested readers should consult Kletzer 1998a for more details). There is a sizable literature on the question of whether workers displaced from import-competing industries face different (or worse) post-displacement outcomes that workers displaced from (manufacturing) industries less influenced by trade.[32] In Kletzer (1998b), I reported that workers displaced from high-import-share industries have different char-

---

31. Revenga's primary instrument is a source-weighted industry exchange rate, defined as a geometric average of the nominal exchange rates of countries accounting for more than 2 percent of industry imports.

32. The Bureau of International Labor Affairs (ILAB) of the U.S. Department of Labor sponsored a number of empirical studies of trade-affected workers in the 1970s and early 1980s. See Aho and Orr (1981) and studies and citations in Dewald (1978).

acteristics than workers displaced from other manufacturing industries: they are younger, less educated, less tenured, and more likely to be female. Average predisplacement real weekly earnings are significantly lower in high-import-share industries. Workers displaced from high-import-share industries are significantly less likely to be reemployed following displacement and most of the difference is due to the fact that women are disproportionately employed in import-competing industries and women are less likely to be reemployed following displacement from any industry. Trade-displaced workers may have more difficult labor market adjustments, but the source of the difficulty is their otherwise disadvantaged characteristics, not the characteristics of their displacement industry.[33]

Second, displaced-worker studies have also revealed that industry (or more broadly sector) may be an important dimension across which skills are transferable. The postdisplacement earnings of individuals who change industry are lower than the earnings of otherwise comparable individuals who stay in the same industry (see citations in Kletzer 1998a). It is important to note that larger earnings losses for workers who change industry may not necessarily reflect lost specific human capital. Industry wage effects due to efficiency wages, union rents, incentive pay schemes, or internal labor markets may partially account for the earnings losses.

10.8.1 Where Are Displaced Workers Reemployed?

With these studies as a backdrop, table 10.9 reports a matrix of transitions, from predisplacement industrial sector to postdisplacement industrial sector, using a sample of reemployed displaced workers drawn from the DWS. The sample contains workers displaced during the years 1979–94, with each of the 16 years drawn from only one survey. The transitions are only available for those workers reemployed at their survey date. "Old Sector" refers to time of displacement and those sectors are listed in the first column; "New Sector" refers to reemployment and those sectors are listed across the top of the matrix. Each cell contains four entries: the first is the percentage of reemployed old-sector workers who are reemployed in the new sector, and the second is the mean difference in log weekly earnings, predisplacement to postdisplacement, for those workers. The third and fourth entries are cell counts. For example, the first cell reports that 5.3 percent of reemployed mining workers were reemployed in agriculture, and their mean weekly earnings loss was approximately 79 percent.

Focusing attention on manufacturing-nonmanufacturing comparisons, several points stand out. Sizable proportions of the sample stay within the same industrial sector. The highest return proportions are professional services (62.6 percent), construction (48.9 percent), and wholesale and retail trade (46.9 percent). Within manufacturing, 32 percent of reemployed

33. See Neumann (1978) and Kruse (1988, 1991) for more on this point.

Table 10.9   Postdisplacement Employment by Sector, 1979–94

Old sector	New Sector										
	Agriculture	Mining	Construction	Manufacturing, Nondurables	Manufacturing, Durables	Transportation	Trade	Professional Services	Other Services	Government	Total
Mining	5.3 -0.791 17.2 (9)	26.84 -0.027 124.9 (82)	10.44 -0.552 44.5 (34)	2.08 -0.885 9.6 (6)	10.71 -0.339 49.0 (26)	9.85 -0.349 30.5 (25)	12.19 -0.527 56.5 (34)	10.65 -0.586 38.0 (27)	9.16 -0.762 28.6 (21)	2.76 -0.558 6.9 (7)	2.2 -0.382 406.2 (271)
Construction	1.92 -0.088 30.7 (14)	0.44 -0.081 7.0 (4)	48.93 -0.037 878.2 (458)	3.25 0.77 52.9 (36)	7.91 -0.215 157.7 (82)	5.47 -0.097 104.6 (59)	12.48 -0.325 224.9 (128)	11.22 -0.238 229.0 (128)	6.32 -0.246 126.8 (69)	2.06 -0.064 41.5 (27)	10.1 -0.128 1,853.8 (1,005)
Manufacturing, nondurables	1.37 0.132 26.5 (16)	0.30 -0.098 5.6 (5)	3.81 0.020 84.0 (50)	32.0 -0.015 761.1 (424)	14.27 0.007 318.7 (159)	5.05 0.009 111.5 (61)	15.73 -0.190 359.1 (215)	15.48 -0.146 347.8 (203)	9.98 -0.279 215.4 (114)	2.00 -0.180 51.2 (30)	11.9 -0.087 2,281.3 (1,277)
Manufacturing, durables	1.15 -0.604 31.4 (16)	0.54 -0.002 27.6 (13)	6.44 -0.205 262.4 (147)	7.55 -0.048 341.3 (190)	39.16 -0.072 1,749.4 (929)	5.17 -0.124 210.3 (107)	14.08 -0.376 598.3 (348)	12.45 -0.289 530.2 (275)	11.28 -0.393 428.7 (218)	2.14 0.028 94.9 (56)	22.5 -0.183 4,275.0 (2,299)
Transportation	1.72 -0.498 16.8 (6)	0.57 0.106 9.0 (5)	5.73 -0.192 64.4 (43)	3.55 -0.248 42.9 (23)	6.36 -0.194 76.3 (42)	42.04 -0.083 538.9 (291)	14.92 -0.242 185.4 (100)	11.95 -0.248 150.2 (82)	10.68 -0.294 127.4 (62)	2.49 -0.203 35.6 (17)	6.89 -0.174 1,247.4 (671)
Trade	1.04 -0.066 26.4 (15)	0.17 0.154 7.0 (8)	4.52 -0.156 168.1 (87)	4.84 0.019 182.5 (97)	7.15 0.053 277.1 (144)	4.84 -0.047 178.8 (103)	46.93 -0.052 1,691.8 (940)	17.17 -0.022 673.3 (350)	11.40 -0.073 383.0 (202)	1.95 0.089 80.3 (47)	20.17 -0.038 3,668.7 (1,993)
Professional services	0.63 -0.559 6.2 (5)	0.42 -0.040 9.1 (8)	2.92 -0.335 78.9 (39)	3.61 0.009 105.3 (53)	4.37 0.085 121.7 (65)	3.14 -0.112 78.5 (44)	10.58 -0.191 289.0 (151)	62.63 -0.036 1,677.9 (876)	8.77 -0.355 236.9 (119)	2.91 0.188 88.6 (55)	14.55 -0.078 2,692.5 (1,415)

	(1)	(2)	(3)	(4)	(5)	(6)	(7)	(8)	(9)	(10)	(11)
Other services	1.39 -0.179 16.1 (7)	0.53 0.287 12.5 (7)	4.78 0.012 88.1 (47)	3.76 0.174 71.0 (41)	7.46 0.124 146.4 (75)	6.55 0.062 138.5 (71)	19.11 -0.120 363.2 (198)	19.87 -0.112 350.4 (195)	35.09 -0.068 594.6 (321)	1.45 0.147 30.4 (18)	10.45 -0.043 1,811.9 (980)
Government	1.42 -0.062 3.9 (3)	0.00 — 4.0 (4)	2.35 0.144 4.0 (4)	5.42 -0.020 14.0 (8)	2.93 -0.053 6.1 (6)	8.12 -0.162 21.5 (10)	11.09 -0.404 23.7 (14)	34.83 -0.101 85.8 (53)	7.73 -0.199 15.0 (10)	26.11 0.119 56.4 (37)	1.21 0.079 230.7 (145)
Total	1.32 -0.316 175.6 (91)	0.98 0.0036 203.0 (132)	9.32 -0.104 1,673.0 (909)	8.10 -0.017 1,581.2 (878)	14.88 -0.049 2,902.8 (1,528)	7.65 0.073 1,413.4 (771)	20.74 -0.168 3,792.3 (2,128)	21.92 -0.108 4,083.0 (2,189)	12.64 -0.220 2,156.8 (1,136)	2.45 0.030 486.3 (294)	100.0 -0.111 18,467.8 (10,056)
Top job loss	0.51 -0.156 2.1 (1)	0.22 0.134 2.1 (1)	5.28 -0.106 37.9 (23)	10.01 -0.148 85.5 (52)	37.74 -0.098 323.7 (172)	5.32 -0.198 35.8 (18)	15.69 -0.291 124.8 (74)	12.55 -0.385 95.7 (50)	10.11 -0.518 69.9 (33)	2.55 0.637 24.7 (14)	4.2 -0.186 802.6 (438)
Top job loss and top trade	0.0 — 0 (0)	0.47 0.134 2.1 (1)	3.03 -0.029 11.8 (8)	14.62 -0.138 58.4 (38)	35.26 -0.051 138.9 (83)	7.51 -0.054 20.3 (8)	17.33 -0.264 70.5 (44)	10.81 -0.215 44.1 (25)	8.06 -0.608 33.5 (18)	2.72 1.09 12.3 (8)	2.0 -0.131 392.4 (233)
Top trade	0.57 -3.52 2.1 (2)	0.34 -0.081 6.4 (3)	2.11 0.067 29.2 (20)	19.53 -0.038 327.1 (182)	31.38 -0.036 505.2 (265)	4.58 -0.238 61.0 (29)	14.62 -0.221 228.0 (126)	14.27 -0.111 232.2 (123)	10.82 -0.171 172.0 (92)	1.78 0.369 31.4 (20)	8.2 -0.091 1,595.1 (862)

Source: Author's calculations from Displaced Worker Surveys, 1984–96, and U.S. Import and Export data file, 1958–94.

Notes: First entry in cell is the percentage of reemployed old-sector workers who are employed in the new sector. Second entry in cell is the mean difference in log weekly earnings. Third entry in cell is weighted cell count in thousands. Fourth entry in cell is unweighted cell count (in parentheses).

Top job loss includes industries in the top quartile of industry mean job-loss-rate distribution; Top job loss and top trade includes industries in top job-loss-rate quartile and either top mean-import-share quartile or top mean-change-in-import-share quartile; top trade group includes industries in both top-import-share quartile and top-change-in-import-share quartile.

nondurable goods workers remain in the sector, and 39 percent of durable goods workers remain in the sector. Overall, there is movement out of manufacturing. Approximately 34 percent of reemployed workers were displaced from manufacturing; the percentage of workers reemployed in manufacturing was 23 percent. Trade and services represent approximately 54 percent of postdisplacement employment, up from 44 percent of predisplacement employment. Thus, many displaced workers are reemployed in the (growing) nontradable sector. The variation in earnings change is considerable. The average earnings change for the overall sample was −11.1 percent (a loss), and −8.7 percent for nondurable goods workers and −18.3 percent for durable goods workers. Among manufacturing workers, the largest earnings losses are experienced by workers reemployed in trade and services (ranging from 15 to 40 percent). It is interesting to note that workers displaced from the relatively lower-wage trade and services sector experience earnings gains if reemployed in manufacturing (and the reemployment percentages are small, ranging from 3 to 7 percent).

What happens to trade-displaced workers? It is difficult to isolate a set of workers displaced by trade. Instead of "trade-displaced," table 10.9 offers three definitions of import-competing. The first, listed in the table as "Top job loss," are workers displaced from the top quartile of mean job-loss-rate industries, those industries listed in table 10.2. For the most part, these industries are import-competing. How do these workers fare? Thirteen of the 17 top job-loss-rate industries are durable goods industries, so perhaps it is not surprising that the reemployment pattern of the top job-loss group looks like the durable goods group overall.[34] More than one-third of the group is reemployed in a durable goods industry, and these workers have the smaller earnings losses (9.8 percent). Very large earnings losses are experienced by workers who are reemployed in trade and services, ranging from 29 to 52 percent. The mean earnings change for this group is −18.6 percent, the median is −10.2 percent. For comparison, the mean earnings change for workers not in this group is −10.7 percent and the median is −4.7 percent.

The second group, called "Top job loss and top trade," includes workers displaced from industries that are in the top quartile of the mean job-loss-rate distribution and in either the top quartile of the mean import-share distribution or the top quartile of the mean change in import-share distribution. This tighter definition of import-competing job loss industry includes footwear; watches, clocks; leather products; toys; pottery and related products; radio and television; leather tanning; other primary metals; and cycles and miscellaneous transport. This group looks very similar

---

34. The nondurable goods industries are footwear, leather products (excluding footwear), leather tanning, and miscellaneous petroleum and coal products.

to the "Top job loss" group, with slightly smaller mean (13 percent) and median (7 percent) earnings losses. Again, large earnings losses are experienced by those workers reemployed in trade and services.

The last trade-displaced group is called "Top trade" and it includes workers from industries that are in the top quartile in both mean import share and mean change in import share, but without regard to job-loss rate. These industries (with their mean job-loss rates) are footwear (0.090); watches, clocks (0.091); leather products (0.142); miscellaneous manufacturing (0.053); apparel (0.052); office and accounting machines (0.0078); toys (0.067); photographic equipment (0.029); electronic computing equipment (0.045); pottery and related products (0.071); electrical machinery (0.039); radio and television (0.125); and leather tanning (0.074). Not all of the import-competing industries have high job-loss rates, in particular those industries with sustained strong demand such as office and accounting machines, computers, and photographic equipment. This group has the smallest average earnings losses of the three identified groups and losses that are slightly lower than the overall average (the mean change is −9.1 percent and the median change is −4.5 percent). Notably, this last group, while still predominantly durable goods industries, has smaller earnings losses across reemployment sectors. Those workers who return to manufacturing have smaller earnings losses than the average returning manufacturing worker and workers who become reemployed in services have smaller earnings losses than the average worker displaced from manufacturing and reemployed in services.

Table 10.9 confirms some priors: Workers displaced from manufacturing and reemployed in trade and services experience large earnings losses. Workers displaced from import-competing manufacturing, mostly durable goods, have the largest average earnings losses of any industrial group (with the exception of mining) and their losses are particularly large if reemployed in trade and services. An important qualifier to the last point is that earnings outcomes for workers displaced from import-competing and high-job-loss manufacturing industries appear to be different from (worse than) the outcomes of workers displaced from industries defined by import competition alone.

What cannot be learned from this kind of descriptive analysis is why earnings losses are large. The losses are partly due to lost firm- and industry-specific skills, but they are also due to losses of union rents, efficiency wages, and other industry-specific components of pay. These questions are beyond the scope of this paper.

10.8.2   Are Workers Reemployed in Exporting Industries?

Table 10.9 provides one straightforward answer to this question: no. The largest share of workers displaced from import-competing industries are reemployed in trade and services, largely nontradable sectors. The ques-

Table 10.10   **Top Reemployment Industries for Displaced Workers, with Export and Import Shares**

Industry	Number Reemployed ($\times 10^3$)	Manufacturing Reemployed (%)	Export Share	Import Share
Machinery (excl. electrical)	367.6	7.0	0.139	0.128
Electrical machinery	354.6	6.7	0.138	0.180
Motor vehicles	274.7	5.2	0.094	0.237
Furniture and fixtures	190.4	3.6	0.017	0.080
Fabricated structural metals	177.1	3.4	0.031	0.012
Manufacturing average			0.075	0.117

tion can be rephrased and narrowed as follows: Within manufacturing, are workers reemployed in exporting industries? Durable goods industries dominate the top quartile of export share industries (15 of the 18 are durable goods industries). As noted previously, durable goods industries also dominate the group of highly import competing industries. As larger (by employment) industries, durable goods industries account for larger shares of both displacement (22.9 percent) and reemployment (14.9 percent) than nondurable goods industries (12.6 percent and 8.1 percent). Within durable goods, the top reemployment industries are shown in table 10.10.

Large employers tend to dominate this list, rather than exporting industries, although electrical and nonelectrical machinery industries have both characteristics. If we consider the set of industries that are in the top quartile in both export share and changes in export share during the 1975–94 period, these industries accounted for 14.8 percent of manufacturing reemployment and 3.4 percent of all reemployment. The industries, with their mean import and export shares, are shown in table 10.11.

For workers and policymakers, an important characteristic of manufacturing exporting industries is that they tend to be high wage, in the sense of paying wages that are above average for manufacturing (and considerably above average for all industries). In table 10.11, high-wage industries are those with sizable positive wage differentials, in the range of 0.083 to 0.207, as measured by Katz and Summers (1989).[35] Workers reemployed in these industries experience smaller earnings losses than workers reemployed elsewhere. For nondurable goods–displaced workers, reemployment in these industries resulted in average earnings changes of +13.8 percent, compared to −9.4 percent for workers reemployed elsewhere. For

35. Katz and Summers (1989) control for the usual worker characteristics and estimate wage differentials for two-digit CIC industries, using the full year 1984 Current Population Survey (1989, 218–19, table 2). These numbers are the proportionate difference in wages between the average workers in a given two-digit industry and the average worker in all industries.

Table 10.11   **Industries with High Mean Export Share and High Mean Import Share, 1975–94**

Industry	Export Share	Import Share	High Wage
Ordnance	.131	.059	Yes
Scientific and controlling instruments	.209	.126	Yes
Aircraft and parts	.266	.091	Yes
Office and accounting machines	.180	.210	Yes
Leather tanning and finishing	.143	.208	
Electronic computing equipment	.246	.239	Yes
Electrical machinery	.138	.180	
Cycles and miscellaneous transport equipment	.163	.254	Yes
Engines and turbines	.217	.149	Yes

durable goods–displaced workers, average earnings losses were −4.8 percent if reemployed in these industries, compared to losses of −19.9 percent if reemployed elsewhere.

10.9 Conclusion

This paper has investigated the relationship between changes in foreign competition and job displacement for a sample of manufacturing industries during the period 1979–94. The results are broadly consistent with the perception that imports displace some domestic jobs. This broad consistency appears to be a result of a strong positive relationship between increasing foreign competition and job displacement for industries long identified as import competing; these are industries such as footwear, leather products, radio and television, watches and clocks, and toys. At the same time, there are a number of import-competing industries with below-average rates of job loss, such as office and accounting machines and photographic equipment. Over this time period, there was also considerable job loss from industries facing little or no change in import competition (e.g., guided missiles and space vehicles, wood buildings and mobile homes, and optical and health services supplies). With this variation, the overall relationship between increasing foreign competition and permanent job loss appears much less systematic. What is unknown is whether the trade/job loss relationship might be stronger within more narrowly defined industries. The displacement data do not allow further industry detail.[36]

Across industries, increasing foreign competition accounts for a small share of job displacement. There are high rates of job loss for industries

36. For related studies using establishment- and plant-level data, see Davis, Haltiwanger, and Schuh (1996) and Bernard and Jensen (1995).

with very little trade. This conclusion would be highlighted if the analysis sample included trade and service industries, where rates of job loss are high while the services produced are mostly nontradables. In the absence of satisfactory high-frequency proxies for technological change, the role of technological change remains in debate.

There is an important limitation to this analysis. Displacement is just one of the flows that contribute to net changes in employment. It is likely that firms use all the components of turnover (quits and new and replacement hiring, as well as displacement) to move actual employment toward its desired level as foreign competition changes. It may be difficult for the data to isolate one flow in the absence of the others.

Sizable earnings losses follow job displacement. Workers displaced from import-competing manufacturing, mostly durable goods, have the largest average earnings losses of any industrial group (with the exception of mining) and their losses are particularly large if reemployed in trade and services. Even if the causal model remains unclear, workers have good reason to worry about job and income insecurity in the face of increasing foreign competition.

Appendix

Table 10A.1   **Industries Ranked by Mean Import Share, 1975–94, with Mean Displacement Rate, 1979–94**

Industry	CIC	Mean Import Share	Mean Displacement Rate
Lowest Quartile, Mean Import Share < .043			
Newspaper publishing and printing	171	.0023761	.0250716
Paperboard containers	162	.0064723	.0244208
Paints, varnishes	190	.007349	.0445853
Bakery products	111	.0085282	.0270649
Grain mill products	110	.0099001	.0327966
Logging	230	.0117149	.0597909
Fabricated structural metal	282	.0117886	.0558123
Dairy products	101	.0149561	.0444522
Printing, publishing (excl. newspapers)	172	.0153291	.0379967
Cement, concrete, gypsum	251	.0167538	.034515
Soaps and cosmetics	182	.0182893	.0347624
Guided missles, space vehicles	362	.0256684	.0803838
Ship and boat building	360	.027272	.0746358
Iron and steel foundries	271	.0318033	.0514859
Metal forgings and stampings	291	.0363809	.0268301
Meat products	100	.0379604	.032494
Wood buildings and mobile homes	232	.0434898	.0972105
Second Quartile, Mean Import Share .044–.087			
Plastics, synthetics	180	.0473768	.0271835
Canned and preserved fruits and vegetables	102	.0476178	.0326721
Miscellaneous food	121	.0509952	.0395866
Miscellaneous fabricated metals	300	.0560881	.0316113
Floor coverings	141	.0570617	.0491985
Ordnance	292	.0586891	.0594666
Drugs	181	.0639753	.021542
Miscellaneous petroleum and coal products	201	.064999	.0720061
Yarn, thread, and fabric mills	142	.0666864	.0424119
Beverages	120	.0674657	.0215012
Miscellaneous wood products	241	.0753061	.0360452
Miscellaneous nonmetallic mineral and stone	262	.0789392	.0521278
Miscellaneous fabricated textiles	152	.0795402	.036756
Optical and health supplies	372	.0801311	.1262741
Furniture and fixtures	242	.0804759	.0242372
Glass and glass products	250	.0814068	.04817
Primary aluminum	272	.0828264	.0702517
Petroleum refining	200	.0879131	.0259471
Third Quartile, Mean Import Share .088–.1537			
Aircraft and parts	352	.0909808	.0292094
Railroad locomotives	361	.0925145	.1077487
Industrial and miscellaneous chemicals	192	.0961335	.0314104
Screw machine products	290	.1100422	.0292981

(*continued*)

Table 10A.1 (continued)

Industry	CIC	Mean Import Share	Mean Displacement Rate
Sugar and confectionery	112	.1104992	.0391602
Cutlery, handtools	281	.1158531	.0281042
Household appliances	340	.115925	.0471302
Structural clay products	252	.1209288	.083527
Miscellaneous textile mill	150	.1228917	.0424784
Sawmills and millwork	231	.1233245	.0387356
Other rubber products	211	.1257362	.0512525
Scientific and controlling instruments	371	.1265785	.0157536
Knitting mills	132	.128416	.0204538
Machinery (excl. electric)	331	.1285396	.0439213
Construction and material moving machines	312	.1327857	.0567377
Farm machinery	311	.1369748	.0614961
Engines and turbines	310	.1492626	.0393126
Metalworking machines	320	.1522968	.0356374
Blast furnaces	270	.1537628	.061097
Top Quartile, Mean Import Share >.154			
Pulp, paper, and paperboard	160	.1569003	.0227719
Tires and inner tubes	210	.1600136	.0439544
Photographic equipment	380	.1682403	.0294131
Electrical machinery	342	.1799477	.0388985
Other primary metals	280	.1853473	.0755787
Radio, television	341	.1957753	.1259439
Leather tanning	220	.2082242	.0739732
Office and accounting machines	321	.2099128	.0078594
Apparel	151	.2258708	.0523536
Motor vehicles	351	.2371851	.0507589
Electronic computing	322	.2396241	.0455519
Cycles and miscellaneous transport	370	.2542767	.093942
Miscellaneous manufacturing	391	.264089	.0536586
Toys	390	.3408123	.0677491
Pottery and related products	261	.3800826	.0717307
Leather products (excl. footwear)	222	.4079864	.142046
Footwear	221	.4954904	.0906134
Watches, clocks	381	.5229867	.0913399

Table 10A.2 **Industries Ranked by Mean Displacement Rate, 1979–94, with Mean Import Share, 1975–94**

Industry	CIC	Mean Displacement Rate	Mean Import Share
Lowest Quartile, Mean Displacement Rate, <.031			
Office and accounting machines	321	.0078594	.2099128
Scientific and controlling instruments	371	.0157536	.1265785
Knitting mills	132	.0204538	.128416
Beverages	120	.0215012	.0674657
Drugs	181	.021542	.0639753
Pulp, paper, and paperboard	160	.0227719	.1569003
Furniture and fixtures	242	.0242372	.0804759
Paperboard containers	162	.0244208	.0064723
Newspaper publishing and printing	171	.0250716	.0023761
Petroleum refining	200	.0259471	.0879131
Metal forgings and stampings	291	.0268301	.0363809
Bakery products	111	.0270649	.0085282
Plastics, synthetics	180	.0271835	.0473768
Cutlery, handtools	281	.0281042	.1158531
Aircraft and parts	352	.0292094	.0909808
Screw machine products	290	.0292981	.1100422
Photographic equipment	380	.0294131	.1682403
Industrial and miscellaneous chemicals	192	.0314104	.0961335
Miscellaneous fabricated metals	300	.0316113	.0560881
Second Quartile, Mean Displacement Rate, .031–.0439			
Meat products	100	.032494	.0379604
Canned and preserved fruits and vegetables	102	.0326721	.0476178
Grain mill products	110	.0327966	.0099001
Cement, concrete, gypsum	251	.034515	.0167538
Soaps and cosmetics	182	.0347624	.0182893
Metalworking machines	320	.0356374	.1522968
Miscellaneous wood products	241	.0360452	.0753061
Miscellaneous fabricated textiles	152	.036756	.0795402
Printing, publishing (excl. newspapers)	172	.0379967	.0153291
Sawmills and millwork	231	.0387356	.1233245
Electrical machinery	342	.0388985	.1799477
Sugar and confectionery	112	.0391602	.1104992
Engines and turbines	310	.0393126	.1492626
Miscellaneous food	121	.0395866	.0509952
Yarn, thread, and fabric mills	142	.0424119	.0666864
Miscellaneous textile mill	150	.0424784	.1228917
Machinery (excl. electric)	331	.0439213	.1285396
Third Quartile, Mean Displacement Rate, .045–.061			
Tires and inner tubes	210	.0439544	.1600136
Dairy products	101	.0444522	.0149561
Paints, varnishes	190	.0445853	.007349
Electronic computing	322	.0455519	.2396241
Household appliances	340	.0471302	.115925
Glass and glass products	250	.04817	.0814068

(*continued*)

Table 10A.2　　　(continued)

Industry	CIC	Mean Displacement Rate	Mean Import Share
Floor coverings	141	.0491985	.0570617
Motor vehicles	351	.0507589	.2371851
Other rubber products	211	.0512525	.1257362
Iron and steel foundries	271	.0514859	.0318033
Miscellaneous nonmetallic mineral and stone	262	.0521278	.0789392
Apparel	151	.0523536	.2258708
Miscellaneous manufacturing	391	.0536586	.264089
Fabricated structural metal	282	.0558123	.0117886
Construction and material moving machines	312	.0567377	.1327857
Ordnance	292	.0594666	.0586891
Logging	230	.0597909	.0117149
Blast furnaces	270	.061097	.1537628
Farm machinery	311	.0614961	.1369748
Top Quartile, Mean Displacement Rate, >.061			
Toys	390	.0677491	.3408123
Primary aluminum	272	.0702517	.0828264
Pottery and related products	261	.0717307	.3800826
Miscellaneous petroleum and coal products	201	.0720061	.064999
Leather tanning	220	.0739732	.2082242
Ship and boat building	360	.0746358	.027272
Other primary metals	280	.0755787	.1853473
Guided missles, space vehicles	362	.0803838	.0256684
Structural clay products	252	.083527	.1209288
Footwear	221	.0906134	.4954904
Watches, clocks	381	.0913399	.5229867
Cycles and miscellaneous transport	370	.093942	.2542767
Wood buildings and mobile homes	232	.0972105	.0434898
Railroad locomotives	361	.1077487	.0925145
Radio, television	341	.1259439	.1957753
Optical and health supplies	372	.1262741	.080131
Leather products (excl. footwear)	222	.142046	.4079864

Table 10A.3   Industries Ranked by Mean Change in Import Share, 1975–94, with Mean Displacement Rate, 1979–94

Industry	CIC	Mean Change in Import Share	Mean Displacement Rate
Lowest Quartile, Mean Change in Import Share <.0007			
Cycles and miscellaneous transport	370	−.0068314	.093412
Sugar and confectionery	112	−.0053447	.0391602
Petroleum refining	200	−.0033942	.0259471
Miscellaneous petroleum and coal products	201	−.0013748	.0720061
Miscellaneous textile mill	150	−.0012623	.0424784
Meat products	100	−.0002888	.032494
Dairy products	101	−.0000962	.0444522
Newspaper publishing and printing	171	−.0000713	.0250716
Cement, concrete, gypsum	251	−.0000165	.034515
Wood buildings and mobile homes	232	.0001035	.0972105
Logging	230	.0002047	.0597909
Bakery products	111	.0004583	.0270649
Printing, publishing (excl. newspapers)	172	.0004609	.0379967
Beverages	120	.0004957	.0215012
Fabricated structural metal	282	.0004979	.0558123
Paperboard containers	162	.0005126	.0244208
Grain mill products	110	.0006532	.0327966
Paints, varnishes	190	.0007758	.0445853
Second Quartile, Mean Change in Import Share .0007–.003			
Pulp, paper, and paperboard	160	.0008016	.0227719
Miscellaneous food	121	.0008925	.0395866
Ship and boat building	360	.0012961	.0746358
Metal forgings and stampings	291	.0013335	.0268301
Canned and preserved fruits and vegetables	102	.0013905	.0326721
Sawmills and millwork	231	.0014915	.0387356
Iron and steel foundries	271	.001629	.0514859
Soaps and cosmetics	182	.0016824	.0347624
Floor coverings	141	.001952	.0491985
Guided missiles, space vehicles	362	.0021725	.0803838
Screw machine products	290	.0025258	.0292981
Miscellaneous wood products	241	.0025542	.0360452
Drugs	181	.0025735	.021542
Miscellaneous fabricated metals	300	.0026224	.0316113
Farm machinery	311	.00266	.0614961
Industrial and miscellaneous chemicals	192	.0033692	.0314104
Miscellaneous nonmetallic mineral and stone	262	.003402	.0521278
Third Quartile, Mean Change in Import Share .003–.0075			
Optical and health supplies	372	.003507	.1262741
Blast furnaces	270	.0037119	.061097
Plastics, synthetics	180	.0037193	.0271835
Other primary metals	280	.0038447	.0755787
Glass and glass products	250	.003995	.04817
Furniture and fixtures	242	.0050339	.0242372
Household appliances	340	.0052597	.0471302

(*continued*)

Table 10A.3   (continued)

Industry	CIC	Mean Change in Import Share	Mean Displacement Rate
Motor vehicles	351	.0054276	.0507589
Ordnance	292	.0055606	.0594666
Cutlery, handtools	281	.0058958	.0281042
Yarn, thread, and fabric mills	142	.0059667	.0424119
Miscellaneous fabricated textiles	152	.006024	.036756
Structural clay products	252	.0060668	.083527
Primary aluminum	272	.0063072	.0702517
Machinery (excl. electric)	331	.0063173	.0439213
Aircraft and parts	352	.0065456	.0292094
Railroad locomotives	361	.0067265	.1077487
Engines and turbines	310	.0071777	.0393126
Tires and inner tubes	210	.0075621	.0439544
Top Quartile, Mean Change in Import Share >.0075			
Leather tanning	220	.00799	.0739732
Radio, television	341	.0081509	.1259439
Knitting mills	132	.0084907	.0204538
Scientific and controlling instruments	371	.0086181	.0157536
Metalworking machines	320	.0089322	.0356374
Other rubber products	211	.0092831	.0512525
Photographic equipment	380	.0095574	.0294131
Construction and material moving machines	312	.0096119	.0567377
Pottery and related products	261	.0105394	.0717307
Electrical machinery	342	.0118051	.0388985
Miscellaneous manufacturing	391	.0121933	.0536586
Apparel	151	.0152491	.0523536
Toys	390	.0177078	.0677491
Office and accounting machines	321	.0191396	.0078594
Electronic computing	322	.0192546	.0455519
Leather products (excl. footwear)	222	.0238756	.142046
Footwear	221	.0241364	.0906134
Watches, clocks	381	.0278894	.0913399

Table 10A.4   **Industries Ranked by Mean Change in Net Exports (as a share of output), 1975–94, with Mean Displacement Rate, 1979–94**

Industry	CIC	Mean Change in Net Export Share	Mean Displacement Rate
Lowest Quartile, Mean Change in Net Export Share, <.0029			
Footwear	221	−.0173007	.0906134
Watches, clocks	381	−.0160877	.0913399
Leather products (excl. footwear)	222	−.015963	.142046
Miscellaneous manufacturing	391	−.0111059	.0536586
Apparel	151	−.0107097	.0523536
Office and accounting machines	321	−.0104705	.0078594
Toys	390	−.0091293	.0677491
Photographic equipment	380	−.0085043	.0294131
Electronic computing	322	−.0079246	.0455519
Structural clay products	252	−.0063408	.083527
Knitting mills	132	−.0057957	.0204538
Miscellaneous fabricated textiles	152	−.0056321	.036756
Other rubber products	211	−.0056314	.0512525
Railroad locomotives	361	−.0055018	.1077487
Pottery and related products	261	−.0044469	.0717307
Metalworking machines	320	−.0038791	.0356374
Construction and material moving machines	312	−.0035712	.0567377
Blast furnaces	270	−.0034804	.061097
Furniture and fixtures	242	−.0029966	.0242372
Second Quartile, Mean Change in Net Export Share, −.003 to −.0008			
Yarn, thread, and fabric mills	142	−.0029837	.0424119
Metal forgings and stampings	291	−.0028382	.0268301
Machinery (excl. electric)	331	−.00264	.0439213
Tires and inner tubes	210	−.0025678	.0439544
Motor vehicles	351	−.002472	.0507589
Primary aluminum	272	−.0024263	.0702517
Drugs	181	−.0023017	.021542
Cutlery, handtools	281	−.0021052	.0281042
Electrical machinery	342	−.0019275	.0388985
Scientific and controlling instruments	371	−.0018343	.0157536
Iron and steel foundries	271	−.0018204	.0514859
Logging	230	−.0017241	.0597909
Household appliances	340	−.0016676	.0471302
Miscellaneous wood products	241	−.001543	.0360452
Glass and glass products	250	−.00122	.04817
Miscellaneous nonmetallic mineral and stone	262	−.000999	.0521278
Sawmills and millwork	231	−.0009384	.0387356
Guided missiles, space vehicles	362	−.0008502	.0803838
Third Quartile, Mean Change in Net Export Share, −.0008 to .00059			
Miscellaneous food	121	−.0007332	.0395866
Miscellaneous fabricated metals	300	−.0006225	.0316113
Fabricated structural metal	282	−.0005097	.0558123
Optical and health supplies	372	−.0003269	.1262741
Grain mill products	110	−.0002926	.0327966

(*continued*)

Table 10A.4 (continued)

Industry	CIC	Mean Change in Net Export Share	Mean Displacement Rate
Ship and boat building	360	−.0002632	.0746358
Floor coverings	141	−.0002121	.0491985
Canned and preserved fruits and vegetables	102	−.0001781	.0326721
Wood buildings and mobile homes	232	−.0000265	.0972105
Bakery products	111	8.26e-07	.0270649
Ordnance	292	.0000759	.0594666
Newspaper publishing and printing	171	.0001095	.0250716
Printing, publishing (excl. newspapers)	172	.000126	.0379967
Cement, concrete, gypsum	251	.0001543	.034515
Farm machinery	311	.0003342	.0614961
Paperboard containers	162	.0003597	.0244208
Pulp, paper, and paperboard	160	.0004148	.0227719
Radio, television	341	.0005997	.1259439
Top Quartile, Mean Change in Net Export Share, >.00059			
Aircraft and parts	352	.000614	.0292094
Dairy products	101	.0006212	.0444522
Industrial and miscellaneous chemicals	192	.0006395	.0314104
Paints, varnishes	190	.0006576	.0445853
Beverages	120	.0006595	.0215012
Screw machine products	290	.0006609	.0292981
Leather tanning	220	.000763	.0739732
Soaps and cosmetics	182	.0008036	.0347624
Plastics, synthetics	180	.0009911	.0271835
Miscellaneous petroleum and coal products	201	.0013933	.0720061
Meat products	100	.0028748	.032494
Engines and turbines	310	.0044416	.0393126
Petroleum refining	200	.0048386	.0259471
Other primary metals	280	.0052128	.0755787
Miscellaneous textile mill	150	.0058516	.0424784
Sugar and confectionery	112	.0089662	.0391602
Cycles and miscellaneous transport	370	.0155033	.093942

References

Abowd, John M. 1991. The NBER immigration, trade, and labor markets data files. In *Immigration, trade and the labor market,* ed. J. M. Abowd and R. B. Freeman, 407–22. Chicago: University of Chicago Press.

Addison, John, Douglas A. Fox, and Christopher J. Ruhm. 1995. Trade and displacement in manufacturing. *Monthly Labor Review* 118 (April): 58–67.

Aho, C. Michael, and James A. Orr. 1981. Trade-sensitive employment: Who are the affected workers? *Monthly Labor Review* 104 (2): 29–35.

Autor, David, Lawrence F. Katz, and Alan B. Krueger. 1997. Computing inequality: Have computers changed the labor market? NBER Working Paper no. 5956. Cambridge, Mass.: National Bureau of Economic Research.

Bednarzik, Robert W. 1993. Analysis of U.S. industries sensitive to international trade. *Monthly Labor Review* 116 (2): 15–31.

Belman, Dale, and Thea M. Lee. 1995. International trade and the performance of U.S. labor markets. In *U.S. trade policy and global growth,* ed. Robert Blecker, 61–107. Armonk, N.Y.: M. E. Sharpe.

Berman, Eli, John Bound, and Zvi Griliches. 1994. Changes in the demand for skilled labor within U.S. manufacturing industries: Evidence from the Annual Survey of Manufacturing. *Quarterly Journal of Economics* 109 (2): 367–97.

Berman, Eli, John Bound, and Stephen Machin. 1997. Implications of skill-biased technological change: International evidence. NBER Working Paper no. 6166. Cambridge, Mass.: National Bureau of Economic Research.

Bernard, Andrew B., and J. Bradford Jensen. 1995. Exporters, jobs and wages in U.S. manufacturing: 1976–1987. *Brookings Papers on Economic Activity, Microeconomics,* 67–119.

Borjas, George J., Richard B. Freeman, and Lawrence F. Katz. 1992. On the labor market effects of immigration and trade. In *Immigration and the work force: Economic consequences for the United States and source areas,* ed. George J. Borjas and Richard B. Freeman, 213–44. Chicago: University of Chicago Press.

———. 1997. How much do immigration and trade affect labor market outcomes? *Brookings Papers on Economic Activity,* no. 1: 1–90.

Brechling, Frank. 1978. A time series analysis of labor turnover. In *The impact of international trade and investment on employment,* ed. William G. Dewald, 67–86. Washington, D.C.: Bureau of International Labor Affairs, U.S. Department of Labor.

Cline, William R. 1997. *Trade and income distribution.* Washington, D.C.: Institute for International Economics.

Davis, Steven J., John C. Haltiwanger, and Scott Schuh. 1996. *Job creation and destruction.* Cambridge, Mass.: MIT Press.

Dewald, William G. 1978. *The impact of international trade and investment on employment.* Washington, D.C.: Bureau of International Labor Affairs, U.S. Department of Labor.

Dickens, William T. 1988. The effects of trade on employment: Techniques and evidence. In *The dynamics of trade and employment,* ed. Laura D'Andrea Tyson, William T. Dickens, and John Zysman, 41–85. Cambridge, Mass.: Ballinger Press.

Fallick, Bruce C. 1996. A review of the recent empirical literature on displaced workers. *Industrial and Labor Relations Review* 50 (1): 5–16.

Farber, Henry S. 1993. The incidence and costs of job loss: 1982–91. *Brookings Papers on Economic Activity, Microeconomics,* 73–119.

———. 1997. The changing face of job loss in the United States, 1981–1995. *Brookings Papers on Economic Activity, Microeconomics,* 55–142.

Feenstra, Robert C. 1996. U.S. imports, 1972–1994: Data and concordances. NBER Working Paper no. 5515. Cambridge, Mass.: National Bureau of Economic Research.

Feenstra, Robert C., and Gordon H. Hanson. 1997. Productivity measurement and the impact of trade and technology on wages: Estimates for the U.S., 1972–1990. NBER Working Paper no. 6052. Cambridge, Mass.: National Bureau of Economic Research.

Freeman, Richard B., and Lawrence F. Katz. 1991. Industrial wage and employment determination in an open economy. In *Immigration, trade, and the labor market,* ed. J. M. Abowd and R. B. Freeman, 235–60. Chicago: University of Chicago Press.

Grossman, Gene. 1986. Imports as a cause of injury: The case of the U.S. steel industry. *Journal of International Economics* 20 (3–4): 201–23.

———. 1987. The employment and wage effects of import competition. *Journal of International Economic Integration* 2 (1): 1–23.

Haveman, Jon D. 1998. The influence of changing trade patterns on displacements of labor. *International Trade Journal* 12 (2): 259–92.

Jacobson, Louis, Robert LaLonde, and Daniel Sullivan. 1993. *The costs of worker dislocation.* Kalamazoo, Mich.: W. E. Upjohn Institute for Employment Research.

Katz, Lawrence F., and Lawrence H. Summers. 1989. Industry rents: Evidence and implications. *Brookings Papers on Economic Activity, Microeconomics,* 209–90.

Kletzer, Lori G. 1998a. Job displacement. *Journal of Economic Perspectives* 21 (1): 115–36.

———. 1998b. International trade and job loss in U.S. manufacturing, 1979–91. In *Imports, exports, and the American worker,* ed. Susan M. Collins, 423–72. Washington, D.C.: Brookings Institution.

———. 1998c. Increasing foreign competition and job insecurity: Are they related? *Proceedings of the Fiftieth Annual Meeting,* ed. Paula B. Voos, 99–106. Madison, Wis.: Industrial Relations Research Association.

Krugman, Paul, and Robert Lawrence. 1994. Trade, jobs, and wages. *Scientific American* 270 (4): 22–27.

Kruse, Douglas L. 1988. International trade and the labor market experience of displaced workers. *Industrial and Labor Relations Review* 41 (3): 402–17.

———. 1991. Displaced versus disadvantaged workers. In *Job displacement: Consequences and implications for policy,* ed. John T. Addison, 279–96. Detroit, Mich.: Wayne State University Press.

Lawrence, Robert Z. 1994. Trade, multinationals, and labor. NBER Working Paper no. 4836. Cambridge, Mass.: National Bureau of Economic Research.

Lawrence, Robert Z., and Matthew J. Slaughter. 1993. International trade and American wages in the 1980s: Giant sucking sound or small hiccup? *Brookings Papers on Economic Activity, Microeconomics,* 161–210.

Leamer, Edward E. 1993. Wage effects of a U.S.-Mexican free trade agreement. In *The Mexico-U.S. Free Trade Agreement,* ed. P. M. Garber, 57–125. Cambridge, Mass.: MIT Press.

———. 1994. Trade, wages and revolving door ideas. NBER Working Paper no. 4716. Cambridge, Mass.: National Bureau of Economic Research.

Mann, Catherine L. 1988. The effect of foreign competition in prices and quantities on the employment in import-sensitive U.S. industries. *International Trade Journal* 2 (summer): 409–44.

Murphy, Kevin M., and Finis Welch. 1991. The role of international trade in wage differentials. In *Workers and their wages: Changing patterns in the United States,* ed. Marvin H. Kosters, 39–69. Washington, D.C.: AEI Press.

Neumann, George R. 1978. The labor market adjustments of trade displaced workers: The evidence from the Trade Adjustment Assistance Program. In *Research in labor economics,* ed. Ronald Ehrenberg, vol. 4, 353–81. Greenwich, Conn.: JAI Press.

Revenga, Ana L. 1992. Exporting jobs? The impact of import competition on employment and wages in U.S. manufacturing. *Quarterly Journal of Economics* 107 (1): 255–84.

Richardson, J. David. 1995. Income inequality and trade: How to think, what to conclude. *Journal of Economic Perspectives* 9 (3): 33–56.

Sachs, Jeffrey D., and Howard J. Shatz. 1994. Trade and jobs in U.S. manufacturing. *Brookings Papers on Economic Activity,* no. 1: 1–69.

———. 1998. International trade and wage inequality in the United States: Some new results. In *Imports, exports, and the American worker,* ed. Susan M. Collins, 215–54. Washington, D.C.: Brookings Institution.

Sachs, Jeffrey D., and Andrew Warner. 1995. Economic reform and the process of global integration. *Brookings Papers on Economic Activity,* no. 1: 1–118.

Schoepfle, Gregory K. 1982. Imports and domestic employment: Identifying affected industries. *Monthly Labor Review* 105 (8): 13–26.

Topel, Robert. 1990. Specific capital and unemployment: Measuring the costs and consequences of job loss. *Carnegie-Rochester Conference Series on Public Policy* 33 (autumn): 181–214.

U.S. Bureau of Labor Statistics. 1992. *BLS handbook of methods.* Bulletin 2414. Washington, D.C.: U.S. Government Printing Office.

Wood, Adrian. 1994. *North-South trade, employment and inequality.* Oxford: Clarendon Press.

Comment   Lisa M. Lynch

If one wants to understand some of the recent sources of resistance to further trade liberalization, then examining the gross flows data on employment rather than net employment numbers is critical. While the impact of trade on gross job loss is only part of the story of the overall impact of trade on employment, it is where much of the "emotion" that Ross Perot and Pat Buchanan tapped into lies. Lori Kletzer's paper does much to enhance our understanding of this issue.

There are several key findings in this paper. In Kletzer's descriptive analysis, she concludes that high rates of job loss are found for industries with high import shares and large positive changes in their import shares. However, increasing import competition from a lower level of import share is

Lisa M. Lynch is the William L. Clayton Professor of International Economic Affairs in the Fletcher School of Law and Diplomacy at Tufts University and a research associate of the National Bureau of Economic Research.

associated with below-average job loss. These are interesting facts that could benefit from future work to place these findings within an enhanced theoretical model of trade and employment.

In the multivariate analysis of job displacement rates in manufacturing presented in table 10.5, Kletzer finds that quantity measures of trade (especially log change in exports) seem to have a large effect on job displacement rates, while technology (as measured by total factor productivity or computer use) has no effect. But, as shown in table 10.6, when she uses price measures of trade (the change in relative import prices) she finds no effect of trade on displacement and a large effect of technology. In table 10.7, she examines within-industry displacement rates and finds that using import prices has no statistically significant effect on job loss. But when she uses quantity measures of trade, she finds that increases in exports lowers displacement rates significantly. So, depending on whether you look at trade quantities or prices you find different results and the reader is left to ponder what the "real" effects of trade and technology on job displacement rates actually are.

In perhaps the most interesting part of the paper, Kletzer looks at what happens to workers when they lose a job in terms of income loss. If there was not a big income loss, then we probably would not worry that much about the gross-flows analysis. Kletzer finds that displaced workers who come from import-competing and high-job-loss manufacturing jobs do much worse than those displaced workers from industries defined by import competition alone. In other words, it is not trade in your sector that hurts you, per se, just a lot of trade.

Leaders of organized labor might use these findings to conclude that this is a good reason to have quotas. But before they embrace all of the work presented in this paper, I have a few suggestions for the author and others doing research in this area. First, in the Displaced Workers Survey one of the interesting findings is that the reason for job loss has been changing over time. Examining reasons for job loss separately and how they are related to trade and technology would be valuable. Second, since much of the debate on trade's impact on the labor market has to do with changes in the relative demand for skilled labor, why not look at workers by educational attainment as well as blue-collar/white-collar occupational status? Third, the empirical analysis would probably be improved by using generalized method of movements (GMM) analysis to control for endogeneity bias. Fourth, it would be useful to distinguish between import competition from newly industrialized countries (NICs) versus industrialized nations, as some of the other papers in this volume have done.

More generally, I think that future work on the relative importance of technology and trade for job displacement rates would benefit from using data sets such as the U.S. Census Bureau's Longitudinal Record Database (LRD) on manufacturing establishments. By using the longitudinal dimension of the LRD, Kletzer's framework for measuring trade's impact

Table 10C.1   **Employees at Various Educational Levels by Changes in Male Inequality, 1979–90 (percent)**

	Math Level				
Country	Very High, 4/5	Medium, 3	Low, 2	Minimal, 1	Change in Inequality
United States	27.1	32.5	24.5	15.9	+0.28
Germany	27.6	45.2	22.9	4.3	−0.06
Canada	27.6	36.0	25.0	11.4	+0.13
Netherlands	24.8	48.0	21.2	6.0	0.00
Sweden	38.1	39.8	17.4	4.7	0.00

Source: OECD, *Literacy, Economy and Society: Results from the International Adult Literacy Survey, 1995* (revised data) and Freeman and Katz (1995).

on gross employment flows, and the periodic technology surveys done by the Census Bureau, we may improve our understanding of the relative importance of trade and technology for job loss in the United States.

In conclusion, let me raise a broader issue that has been addressed in part by other papers in this volume. I am left uneasy when I look at much of the literature on the relative effect of trade versus technology on the U.S. labor market and see that many European countries have experienced trade and technological changes similar to those in the United States without a corresponding increase in inequality. One explanation of the variance in the degree of inequality across countries in spite of similar technological and trade shocks is that the relative supply of skilled workers in some of these countries has been better able to keep up with the changes in the relative demand for skilled workers than in the United States. As Nickell and Bell (1996) discuss, countries that have an education and training system that produces a much more compressed distribution of human capital are also more likely to have experienced less increase in income inequality over the last 20 years. For example, as shown in table 10C.1, the variation in mathematics ability for workers is much smaller in countries like Germany, Sweden, and the Netherlands than in the United States or Canada. In particular, there are almost 4 times as many workers in the United States with minimal mathematics skills as compared with Sweden.

If we look in more detail at the ability levels of workers by age, there is even more disturbing data. As shown in figure 10C.1, there are almost 10 times as many young workers with zero or minimal math skills (i.e., unable to add two numbers together) in the United States as there are in Germany. Similar patterns hold for other European countries.

This suggests that there are other institutions or factors at play that ameliorate the effect trade and technology have on the distribution of wages. I would like to argue that education and training systems are an important part of these institutional differences. Europe seems to have

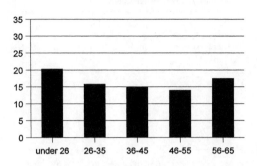

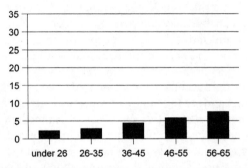

Fig. 10C.1   Percentage of employed workers with minimal math skills in the United States and Germany
Source: OECD Adult Literacy Survey.

done a better job in getting a higher percentage of the workforce skilled than the United States. In addition, while there has been a convergence in educational attainment among the major industrialized economies over the last 20 years, these data from the OECD adult literacy survey suggest that the "quality-adjusted output" of the educational and training systems of these countries seems to vary more than the years of completed schooling would suggest. Whatever one may think about the relative importance of trade and technology for labor market inequality, there seems to be much to be done in the United States to improve the skill levels of workers.

References

Freeman, R., and L. Katz, eds. 1995. *Differences and changes in wage structures.* Chicago: University of Chicago Press.
Nickell, S., and B. Bell. 1996. Changes in the distribution of wages and unemployment in OECD countries. *American Economic Review* 86:302–8.

Contributors

Robert E. Baldwin
Department of Economics
Social Science Building 7321
University of Wisconsin–Madison
1180 Observatory Drive
Madison, WI 53706

Andrew B. Bernard
Tuck School of Business
Dartmouth College
100 Tuck Hall
Hanover, NH 03755

George J. Borjas
Kennedy School of Government
Harvard University
79 JFK Street
Cambridge, MA 02138

Lee G. Branstetter
Department of Economics
University of California
Davis, CA 95616

Alan V. Deardorff
Department of Economics
240A Lorch Hall
University of Michigan
Ann Arbor, MI 48109

Jonathan Eaton
Department of Economics
270 Bay State Road, Room 501
Boston University
Boston, MA 02215

Robert C. Feenstra
Department of Economics
University of California
Davis, CA 95616

Linda Goldberg
Research Department, 3d Floor
Federal Reserve Bank of New York
33 Liberty Street
New York, NY 10045

Gordon H. Hanson
Department of Economics
University of Michigan
Ann Arbor, MI 48109

James Harrigan
International Research Function
Federal Reserve Bank of New York
33 Liberty Street
New York, NY 10045

J. Bradford Jensen
Director, Center for Economic Studies
U.S. Bureau of the Census
Washington, DC 20233

Lori G. Kletzer
Department of Economics
Social Sciences I
University of California, Santa Cruz
Santa Cruz, CA 95064

Alan B. Krueger
Woodrow Wilson School
Princeton University
Princeton, NJ 08544

Paul Krugman
Department of Economics, E52-383a
Massachusetts Institute of Technology
Cambridge, MA 02139

Robert Z. Lawrence
Council of Economic Advisers
17th and Pennsylvania Ave., NW
Room 314, OEOB
Washington, DC 20502

Edward E. Leamer
John E. Anderson Graduate School of
    Management
University of California, Los Angeles
Box 951481
Los Angeles, CA 90095

James A. Levinsohn
Department of Economics
University of Michigan
Ann Arbor, MI 48109

Magnus Lofstrom
Research Associate
Institute for the Study of Labor (IZA)
P.O. Box 7240
D-53072 Bonn, Germany

Mary E. Lovely
Department of Economics
Syracuse University
Syracuse, NY 13244

Lisa M. Lynch
Fletcher School of Law & Diplomacy
Tufts University
Medford, MA 02155

James E. Rauch
Department of Economics
University of California, San Diego
La Jolla, CA 92093

J. David Richardson
Department of Economics
347 Eggers Hall
Syracuse University
Syracuse, NY 13244

Andrew K. Rose
Haas School of Business
    Administration
University of California
Berkeley, CA 94720

Matthew J. Slaughter
Department of Economics
Dartmouth College
Hanover, NH 03755

Deborah L. Swenson
Department of Economics
University of California
Davis, CA 95616

Christopher F. Thornberg
Department of Economics
Clemson University
232 Sirrine Hall
Clemson, SC 29634

Joseph Tracy
Domestic Research Department,
    3d Floor
Federal Reserve Bank of New York
33 Liberty Street
New York, NY 10045

Author Index

Lang, Harald, 7n4
Lang, Kevin, 310, 325
Lawrence, Robert Z., 3, 15, 25, 130, 135, 155, 157, 195, 310n1, 311, 351n6, 366
Leamer, Edward, 15, 32, 37, 40, 64, 66, 71, 81, 85n1, 130, 135, 139–42, 146–47, 149, 156, 162, 166, 181, 185, 202n6, 351n7
Lee, David, 7n5, 251
Lee, Thea M., 351
Lemieux, Thomas, 230, 251
Lester, Richard K., 292
Levy, Frank, 228, 231
Lloyd, Peter J., 313n10
Love, J., 270
Lovely, Mary E., 317
Lundberg, Shelly, 49
Lundgren, Stefan, 7n4

MacDonald, James M., 202, 203, 209
Machin, Stephen, 2n1, 4n3, 229, 231, 352n8, 366
Macpherson, David A., 69, 252
Magee, Steven M., 129
Mann, Catherine L., 351n6, 354, 373n30
Markusen, James R., 86
Matsuyama, Kiminori, 86n2
Maynard Smith, J., 22
McKinnon, James G., 190
McKinsey Global Institute, 202
Mincer, Jacob, 212
Mishel, L., 25
Moffitt, Robert, 48, 49
Morrison, Catherine J., 213
Mortensen, Dale, 270n4
Murnane, Richard, 228, 231
Murphy, Kevin M., 2n1, 26, 30, 192, 221n1, 230–31, 233n8, 239, 242n15, 262, 351n6

Neumann, George R., 375n33
Neumark, David, 252
Nickell, S. J., 273, 395

Oi, Walter, 47, 66
Orr, James A., 374n32

Park, Jin-Heum, 193
Petersen, Bruce C., 202n7
Pierce, Brooks, 26, 233n8, 239
Pischke, Jorn-Steffen, 249

Ramey, Valerie, 230, 258n29, 262, 263, 310n2, 323n17

Rauch, James E., 33
Reich, Robert, 28, 31
Revenga, Ana L., 204n12, 270, 351, 362, 373
Richardson, J. David, 3n2, 310n2, 325, 332n29, 351, 352n10
Rivera-Batiz, Luis A., 199
Robertson, Raymond, 323
Rodrik, Dani, 200n3, 311n3, 320
Romer, Paul, 199
Rosen, Sherwin, 48
Rothgeb, Jennifer, 335n34
Rousslang, Donald J., 172
Ruhm, Christopher, 350n4
Rumbos, Beatriz, 40n1

Sachs, Jeffrey, 2n1, 34, 130, 135, 138–39, 149, 157, 198, 204, 310n1, 311, 349n2, 351, 374
Sandy, Carola, 316n11
Savin, Neil E., 190
Scheinkman, José, 186
Scherer, F. M., 202, 204
Schmidt, Christoph M., 328n25
Schoepfle, Gregory K., 352n9
Schuh, Scott, 351n6, 352n9, 381n36
Schumpeter, Joseph, 199
Shapiro, Carl, 49
Shatz, Howard J., 2n1, 34, 130, 135, 138–39, 149, 157, 204, 310n1, 311, 351, 374
Sheets, N., 269n2
Slaughter, Matthew J., 3, 15, 25, 130, 135, 151n6, 155, 157, 185, 195, 351n6, 366
Slichter, Sumner, 50
Smith, Adam, 199
Sockell, Donna, 67, 252
Solow, Robert, 202
Spence, A. M., 16
Stafford, Frank P., 40n1, 83
Staiger, Douglas, 217
Stern, Robert M., 129
Stiglitz, Joseph, 16, 49
Stock, James, 217
Sullivan, Daniel, 355n14
Summers, Lawrence H., 38, 50, 310, 325, 380
Swenson, Deborah L., 106

To, Theodore, 172
Topel, Robert, 230, 259n29, 262, 263, 265, 271, 272, 275, 281, 299, 300n21, 301, 310n2, 356
Trefler, Daniel, 85n1, 310, 325, 332

Subject Index

Wage premiums: correlation among skill premiums, trade flows, and, 325–38; model of trade flow relation to, 316–25

Wages: differentials in Stolper-Samuelson account, 23–24; of educated and uneducated workers, 20–24; effect of exchange rates on, 272; effect of international competition on, 3–4; effect on wage-effort offer curve, 38; efficiency-wage theory, 49–50; factors influencing levels of U.S., 3–4; impact of real exchange rates on, 8; link to industry prices, 6–7; outsourcing effect on skilled and unskilled workers, 85–86; production/nonproduction workers in U.S. manufacturing (1958–94), 2–3; regional variation in, 7–8; relationship among capital intensity, effort, and, 38–39; response to exchange rate changes, 269–300, 306–7; rise of real (1979–89), 25–26; of self-employed and wage-salary workers by education levels, 29–35; in Stolper-Samuelson theorem, 171–72; trade-off with effort, 52–54

Wages/hours: literature, 47–51; relation to capital intensity, 38–39

Workers: capital sharing, 41–42; changes in ratio of high school– to college-educated, 213–15, 220–21; good and bad in labor market model, 17–18, 29; relation of education to skills, 4; returns to experience and education, 238–41; wages and employment of production/nonproduction (1958–94), 2–3; wages of self-employed and wage-salary by education level, 29–35. *See also* Education; Labor markets; Outsourcing, foreign; Wage inequality

Workers, displaced: Displaced Worker Survey, 355, 356, 394; job displacement by industry, 358–62; job loss (1979–94), 356–57; reemployment after job loss, 374–81; relation of trade to, 9, 362–65

Workers, skilled: education as signal of skills, 4; intensity in outsourced goods, 92–100; pooling equilibrium in an economy, 4; separating equilibrium in an economy, 4; skill-biased technological change, 15–16, 211, 249–52; skill mix within sectors, 211–15; wages in United States, 201. *See also* Wage premiums

Workers, unskilled: in offshore assembly, 5–6; outsourcing effects on, 85–86